Games of the World

Two graceful figures play knucklebones. The terra-cotta statuette from Capua, Italy, dates from the third century B.C. (British Museum)

Games of the World

How to Make Them   How to Play Them   How They Came to Be

Edited by Frederic V. Grunfeld
Introduction by R. C. Bell
Design, Illustration & Game Models by
Pieter van Delft & Jack Botermans

Editorial Consultants R.C. Bell & Léon Vié

Texts by Gerald Williams, Kathleen Mathewson, Laura Smart,
Sally Foy, Mary Furness & Léon Vié

BALLANTINE BOOKS

NEW YORK

The French medieval ivory carving, above, once adorned the back of a noblewoman's mirror. It shows a young couple absorbed in a game of chess under a tent. Mythical beasts square off the corners.

The symbols appearing beside the title of each entry have these meanings:

 Indoor

 Outdoor

 Single

 Couple

 Group

 Mind Games

 Body Games

 Luck Games

 Short **Playing Time**

 Normal

 Long

 Short **Preparation Time**

 Normal

 Long

Created by:
Plenary Publications International,
Incorporated
300 East 40 Street, New York, N.Y. 10016

© 1975 Product Development International
Holding n.v.
© 1975 Léon Vié & J. F. Duwaer, Amsterdam
on the entries: Go, Backgammon, Shogi,
Chinese Chess, Jeu de Boules and Go-bang.

Published in the United States by Ballan-
tine Books, a division of Random House,
Inc., New York, and simultaneously in
Canada by Ballantine Books of Canada,
Ltd., Toronto, Canada.

Library of Congress Catalog Card
Number: 75-13812

ISBN 0-345-25531-3

This edition published by arrangement
with Holt, Rinehart and Winston

Manufactured in the United States of
America

First Ballantine Books Edition:
September 1977

Front Cover: Earthball in California
(Paul Fusco/Magnum); Tarot Cards
courtesy of the Deutsches Spielkarten
Museum, Leinfelden. Back Cover: The
Lotto Player, by Charles Chaplin (1825-
1891), photograph by Giraudon, courtesy
of the Musee des Beaux Arts, Rouen.

Contents

	Page	Indoor	Outdoor	Single	Couple	Group	Mind Games	Body Games	Luck Games	Playing Time Short	Playing Time Normal	Playing Time Long	Prep. Time Short	Prep. Time Normal	Prep. Time Long
Conkers	168	●		●		●		●			●				
Quoits	170	●			●	●		●						●	
Shuttlecock	173	●			●	●		●			●				
Spinning Tops	174	●	●	●		●		●					●		
Jump Rope	177	●	●	●		●		●			●				
Hoops	180	●		●		●		●			●				
Barrel Rolling	184	●		●		●		●			●				
Jeu de Boules	186	●		●		●		●		●	●				
Quilles	192	●	●	●		●		●						●	
Soap Box Racing	196	●		●		●		●						●	
Tlachtli	200	●		●		●			●		●				
Field & Forest Games	202														
Earthball	204	●				●		●			●				
Tug of War	206	●		●	●	●		●			●				
Pickaback Relay	208	●				●		●			●				
Water Jousting	209	●			●	●			●				●		
Follow the Leader	212	●		●		●			●		●				
Indian Kickball	214	●				●		●			●	●			
Prisoner's Base	217	●				●		●	●		●				
Kites	218	●				●					●			●	
Party & Festival Games	226														
Jackstraws	228	●			●	●		●			●				
London Bridge	229	●				●		●			●				
Pelele	230	●				●		●					●		
Pillow Fighting	233	●		●	●	●		●			●				
Piñata	234	●				●		●	●					●	
Ring the Bull	237	●				●		●						●	
Egg Jousting	238	●		●	●	●		●			●				
Camel Rush	240	●			●	●		●			●				
Stilts	242	●			●	●		●					●		
Potato-Sack Racing	244	●			●	●		●			●				
Hobble Racing	245	●			●	●		●			●				
Darts	246	●				●		●		●				●	
Puzzles, Tricks & Stunts	250														
Bilboquet	252	●		●				●	●		●				
Cat's Cradle	254	●		●	●			●	●		●				
Diabolo	260	●	●	●				●					●		
Yo-Yo	262	●	●					●			●				
Magic Squares	263	●		●	●	●		●					●		
Mathematical Puzzle	266	●		●		●		●			●				
African String Puzzle	267	●		●		●		●			●				
Match Games	268	●		●	●	●		●			●				

Between skirmishes in the Trojan War, Ajax and Achilles play an ancient board game – a detail from an Etruscan vase in the Vatican Museum, Rome.

Introduction

Nearly seven hundred years ago, in the year 1283, the king of Castile, Alfonso X, compiled the first book of games in European literature: the picture at left is one of the many miniatures that illuminate this magnificent *Libro de Juegos*. The king was a brilliant scholar himself – he was to go down in history as Alfonso *El Sabio* ('The Learned') – and he personally supervised a group of writers whose task it was to produce a series of books on all the most vital subjects of the day. These included history, law, religion, astronomy, and magic: the fact that gamesplay is included in this company testifies to its importance in the medieval scheme of things. 'God has intended men to enjoy themselves with many games,' the king declared in the introduction, pointing out that these entertainments would 'bring them comfort and dispel their boredom.'

Games of the World takes Alfonso's book as one of its points of departure, and indeed tries to arrive at very much the same result – a compendium of the most fascinating and remarkable pastimes designed 'to give pleasure,' and each in its own way 'appropriate to its time and place.' Alfonso's compilers, of course, were concerned only with the games of the Spanish and Moorish civilizations of the Middle Ages, while *Games of the World* deals with the subject on a global scale: the games of African tribesmen, Arctic Eskimos, Japanese intellectuals, Mexican Indians... Yet the scope of these two books, separated by 700 years, is not really so dissimilar. The principal board games discussed in Alfonso's manuscript had already traveled nearly halfway around the world, and some of them had histories going back a thousand years or more. Chess, the king's personal passion, had been developed in India centuries earlier, and in its travels westward its elephants, maharajas, and chariots had been replaced by castles, kings, and bishops. The morris games he describes date back to ancient Egypt, where they were popular among the common people. Backgammon, one of the great entertainments of the thirteenth-century nobility, had evolved from the

Solid stone game board and rudimentary 'checkers' from nineteenth- or twentieth-dynasty Egypt (1320–1085 B.C.) now repose in the ancient games collection of the British Museum, London.

Among the graffiti left by Roman soldiers during their occupation of the Holy Land is this nine men's morris diagram carved into the floor slabs of the ruined Fortress Antonio, in Jerusalem.

A goat and a lion, right, meet over a game of senet *– the most popular game of ancient Egypt – in a humorous scene from a papyrus dated 1200 B.C.*

The king and six nobles of his court play seven-sided backgammon, opposite, in an illustration from the thirteenth-century Spanish games book of Alfonso X. The sides represent the seven planets of the Ptolemaic astronomical system: Saturn (black), Jupiter (green), Mars (red), the sun (yellow), Venus (violet), Mercury (varicolored), and the moon (white).

Roman game *tabula,* though Alfonso's subjects probably learned the game from the Arabs, who called it *nard.* The games-impulse, in other words, is a universal one that has never known any cultural or linguistic boundaries.

Just as the ancient and primitive religions of the world show profound similarities in their fertility rites and their sun and moon worship, many games appear to be common property to human beings everywhere. Indeed, the comparison is not at all farfetched: many games now thought to be mere children's pastimes are, in fact, relics of religious rituals, often dating back to the dawn of mankind. Tug of war, for example, is a dramatized struggle between natural forces; knucklebones were once part of the fortune-teller's equipment; even hopscotch was related to ancient myths about labyrinths and mazes, later adapted to represent the Christian soul's journey from earth to heaven. In the palace of Medinet Haboo at Thebes in Upper Egypt there is a wall-painting showing Rameses III of the twentieth dynasty engaged in a board game with the goddess Isis, the wife of Osiris, Lord of the Dead. Herodotus, the Greek historian, reports that sometimes the pharaoh emerged the winner in these encounters; sometimes he was the loser. In the seventeenth chapter of the Egyptian *Book of the Dead* there is reference to a game played after death – the players are spirits of the departed living in the next world.

Casting lots, such as dice or knucklebones, gave human beings an opportunity to consult the gods in making difficult decisions, while the results of games played by champions were interpreted by priests and others skilled in reading the future. Even as late as 1895, when the French were storming the capital of Madagascar, the native queen and her people placed more faith for victory in the outcome of a divinatory game of *fanorona* played by the soothsayers than they did in their army. Who has not tossed a coin to make a decision?

Certain kinds of games undoubtedly originated as a training ground for the young, or as a means of maintaining acquired skills. Chess was an imaginative reconstruction of a battlefield, and the strategy and foresight demanded by the game are still thought to provide excellent intellectual training. More mundane but no less useful skills were involved in such games as darts, hoops, foot races, and virtually every other game demanding strength or dexterity. Japanese soldiers were once required to play shuttlecock for agility and speed; in a very different culture, American Indian youths developed their marksmanship by throwing darts through a rolling hoop.

Games of pure wit have intrigued men and women from earliest times. Guessing riddles must have been a campfire entertainment for the cavemen. Much later, at the ribald banquets of classical Greece, failure to guess correctly meant a forfeit – the loser had to drink a horn of mead or wine, sometimes adulterated with salt. Poor players fell asleep under the table, while the prize for solving the riddles consisted of sweetmeats, or a kiss from the lady of one's choice.

Games hold a mirror to civilization. In the Afghan game of *buzkashi,* groups of fierce horsemen contend in a no-holds-barred struggle for possession of a beheaded calf. The object is to carry off the slippery carcass, defending it against all challengers, and bring it around the field to the goal. As Jacob Bronowski explains in *The Ascent of Man,* 'The tactics are pure Mongol, a discipline of shock... what seems a wild scrimmage is in fact full of manoeuvre, and dissolves suddenly with the winner riding clear to score.' These players are,

The referee's whistle sounds over a playing field in Kabul, and buzkashi, *Afghanistan's national game, erupts into action. Whips clenched between their teeth, the riders, pictured opposite and below, engulf the calf's carcass. When Alexander the Great witnessed the ferocity and equestrian skill of the Afghan nomads, on his way to India, he believed he had encountered the mythical centaurs. Today, the National* Buzkashi *Cup is presented to the winning team at the end of the spring games held every March in Kabul.*

in essence, carrying on the tribal traditions of the mounted nomads who once struck terror into the Middle East and eastern Europe, 'the culture of conquest; the predator posing as hero because he rides the whirlwind.'

Just as the macabre plaything of *buzkashi* 'says something about the game, as if the riders were making sport of the farmer's livelihood,' the conflict between nomads and agriculturists is dramatized in the board game *dablot prejjesne*, which is played in Lapland. One player controls the fortunes of a Lapp king, Lapp prince, and 28 Lapp warriors; the other has a landlord, landlord's son, and 28 tenant farmers.

Though the modes of gamesplay tend to remain constant, their symbolism is often influenced by contemporary events, particularly by the politics of the day. During the Napoleonic Wars, for example, chess sets were made showing Napoleon as General, Napoleon as First Consul, Napoleon as Emperor – always, of course, with the Corsican assuming the position of the white king. The famous game of goose is one of those that has responded most spectacularly to the stimulus of historic events. Many of these spiral race games were produced during the eighteenth and nineteenth centuries as a means of teaching children history, geography, scripture, botany, and other subjects. The goose game might incorporate the rise and fall of nations or statesmen, the victories and defeats of military leaders, or the development of new inventions, especially in the field of

transportation. Shortly after the first airplanes had started to fly, people began playing the first 'aerial' game of goose, in which the players raced around a map of Europe with little model aircraft, mirroring in make-believe events the great technological achievements that were then taking place in the real world. Needless to say, rockets to the moon have long since been called into play.

Some of the most fascinating of primitive games are known in virtually every part of the globe, yet their local variations tell us a great deal about the nature of the particular culture to which they have been adapted. One of these universal games is cat's cradle, known in Africa, Asia, Europe, the western hemisphere, the Pacific... The Eskimos have several favorite games: one of them is cat's cradle. The player narrates a story at each stage, and in this fashion the legends of the Innuit (Eskimo) have been handed down unaltered from generation to generation: the individual string figures are a way of helping the storyteller remember his tales – a mnemonic device. The figures represent birds, kayaks, sledges, bears, foxes, and other features of Arctic life. Farther south, the Navaho Indians of the southwestern United States make string figures representing tents, coyotes, rabbits, and constellations of stars. In New Guinea they symbolize spears, drums, palm trees, fishes, and crabs. Each people has its own figures, taken from its own environment; each has its own set of values and traditions associated with the game. Some Eskimos believe in a 'spirit of cat's cradle,' and over-indulgence in the game may put a player in the spirit's power: hence, moderation in all things!

Children's games, above, are from a book of Games of the Four Seasons *published in Paris, 1816. Illustrated, from top to bottom, are marbles, spinning tops, prisoner's base, and diabolo.*

Greek athletes play a hockey-like ball game in this classic bas-relief, dated 475 B.C. Games held a vital place in Greek civilization: 'Our character,' declared the orator Demosthenes, 'depends on these … noble and honorable pursuits.'

The compulsive games-player, of course, is another universal phenomenon, particularly where gambling is a part of the game. The compulsive gambler is not made in a day: he descends an increasingly slippery path, eventually falling into a psychological trap from which escape is rare. The Chinese god of gambling, Tu Chieng Kui, represents a man who spent his life gambling until he died, deeply in debt. Traditionally, statuettes made of him – known as 'a devil gambling for cash' – show a figure in tattered clothes, his queue coiled carelessly around his head, with a lottery ticket stuck into his hair. Gamblers worshiped this image in their homes, burning incense and lighting joss sticks in his honor, and bowing their heads to the ground before him. All too often the devotee's fate was the same as his deity's!

Children's games of the Netherlands in the sixteenth century are shown in this composite painting by Martin van Cleef (1507 1537). With the exception of the seesaw and the stilts, these games require a minimum of equipment: wrestling, hand-clapping, and other improvised games predominate. For another, still more crowded version of the subject, see pages 226–7.

Fortunately, for most people the permanent fascination of games lies simply in the pure joy of playing. It is this intangible pleasure that distinguishes the true game from, say, the professional sport, where *winning* rather than *playing* is all-important. The turning of a game into a sport is exemplified by lawn tennis. In 1905 ladies played in full skirts, long sleeves, and with natty little straw hats perched on their heads. The game was a social event and fun. Seventy years later leading women players are highly trained athletes, on circuit for most of the year, and engaged in cut-throat competition. National prestige may depend upon the result of a tournament. The light-hearted joy of the game has disappeared; competitive sport has taken its place.

In compiling *Games of the World*, the editors have focused on traditional games
that have stood the test of time; games that reflect the accumulated wisdom
and ingenuity of mankind. 'Genuine, pure play is one of the main bases of
civilization,' wrote the historian Johan Huizinga in his famous treatise on 'man
the gamesplayer,' *Homo Ludens*. Here is the documentary and pictorial
evidence for Huizinga's thesis: some eighty entries covering just over a hundred
games of the most diverse kind, ranging from complex exercises in strategy like
shogi to the simplest 'games to start a game.' Spectator sports have not been
included, nor twentieth-century inventions readily available as packaged games.
But the choice is very broad, and reflects a cross-section both of exotic games,
and of the time-honored favorites that have played a role in European and
American history. There are games for every age, and those – not easy to find –
that can be shared by both adults and children. There are games for indoors
and out, which varying numbers can play on a multitude of occasions: on quiet
afternoons in the living room, at parties, in city playgrounds, or in the wide-open
spaces. A selection of traditional tricks and puzzles has also been included.
Equally important, whenever special equipment is required, step-by-step
directions and illustrations are given for its construction by the home craftsman.
This will enable every player to make his own authentic boards and devices
for many otherwise unobtainable games. And the photographs of the games in
action are intended as a grand tour of the world's game-playing activities: one
may notice surprising similarities and intriguing differences.

In selecting the actual games to be presented, the editors appear to have
followed much the same principles as the Leprecaun in James Stephens's classic,
The Crock of Gold: '"I'll teach you how to play Jackstones," said the Leprecaun,
and he picked up some pine-cones and taught the children that game. "Did you
ever play Ball in the Decker?... Did you ever play 'I can make a nail with my
ree-ro-raddy-O, I can make a nail with my ree-ro-ray'?... It's a nice game... and
so is Cap-on-the-back, and Twenty-four yards on the Billygoat's tail, and Towns,
and Relievo, and Leap-frog. I'll teach you all these games," said the Leprecaun,
"and I'll teach you how to play Knifey, and Hole-and-taw, and Horneys and
Robbers."' These, in other words, are the games that have not yet lost their
age-old magic, nor the ability to keep us playing as assiduously as in the days of
the Little People or the ancient kings of Castile.   R. C. Bell

On their island home of Nias, off the west coast of Sumatra, boys eagerly take turns to jump a stone piled with dry grass (opposite). The game is an early preparation for a ceremonial jump they will perform on reaching 16; to prove their manhood, they must clear a stone two yards high.

The 'middle man' easily dodges the ball as his Californian school friends try to tag him in this circle ball game (left). The player who tags him with the ball will take his place in the middle.

A mosque provides an impressive background for a young Afghan boy (below) from Mazar-i-Sharif, as he coaxes his hoop into play over stony ground.

Two boys from the western Pacific Truk Islands, opposite, steer their cleverly-made 'cars' on wobbly coconut wheels round the village streets.

On a rocky ledge, a Dogon boy, left, of Mali, West Africa, holds his friends spellbound as he recounts a tale while weaving a cat's cradle.

Trio Indian children, above, duck each other under the water in a friendly wrestling match near their village in Surinam, South America.

A glimpse of life among the nomadic Bushmen of the South African Kalahari desert (above): children squat in the scrub and entertain each other with hand-clapping games, while a meal simmers on the camp fire. They chant traditional rhymes, clapping their hands together, against their own knees or chest, or against each others' hands. Hand-clapping games, with their colorful accompaniment of songs and rhymes, are popular pastimes with children all over the world.

15

The first move in a game often gives a player or team a definite advantage over the opponents. There are many ways of deciding who has the privilege of the first move, all of them dependent on chance and luck, and therefore equally fair. They are simple games of amusement in themselves and are universally used whenever a quick decison is called for.

1. One of the most popular games to start a game is the flipping of a coin. One player makes a fist and places a good-sized coin (a quarter or a nickel) on his thumbnail, as shown above. With a sharp flick of his thumb, he spins the coin into the air and catches it as it falls, cupping it in his hand. He slaps the coin on the back of his free hand, and, keeping it covered, he asks, 'Heads or tails?' If his opponent guesses correctly, he may begin the game. If not, the first move passes to the coin-tosser.

3. A player holds a coin in one hand, then hides his hands behind his back. He can pass the coin to the other hand, if he wishes, or keep it in the same hand, the object being to confuse his opponent. He then brings his two clenched hands out in front of him and his opponent must guess which hand contains the coin. A correct guess will win him the first move.

2. One player holds as many matches in his hand as there are players in the game. One of the matches is shorter than the others but they are arranged in his hand so they appear to be of uniform length. Each player draws a match, as shown above; the winner is the one who picks the short match.

4. A simple and popular way to decide who makes the first move is to roll dice. This is common practice in many card and board games that incorporate dice in play. Each player rolls a die, as shown in the photograph above; the highest throw wins.

5. Each player has three matches, which he hides behind his back. He can keep all three in one hand, or transfer two, or one, or all three to his free hand, or back pocket. On a count of three, each player presents his fist, and guesses are made as to the total number of matches. The players then open their fists to reveal the true count. If no one is right, the process is repeated.

7. Players take a broomstick, baseball bat, or a walking stick. One by one, in rapid succession – and in no particular order – each player wraps a hand around the broomstick, starting at the bottom just above the broom. (The sides of the fists must touch.) Up and up they go until there is just enough room at the top of the stick for one full fist. The player who secures this position wins.

9. Each player extends forefinger and middle finger held together. One player holds his fingers in front of him, cushion side up, while his opponent, without warning, tries to slap his opponent's fingers with his own. His opponent tries to snatch his fingers away to avoid the blow. If the first player misses, the players change roles. The player who manages to strike his opponent begins the game. There is only one try per turn.

6. A box of matches is emptied on the table. Each player, in turn, picks up one match. The player to pick up the last match from the pile is the one to start the game. This is more fun if three or more players are involved.

8. This is a variation of the Japanese hand game, *jankenpon*. Two players face each other, each with one fist behind his back. On the count of three, they both throw out a number of fingers, calling 'Evens!' or 'Odds!' The player who guesses correctly wins.

10. Up to five players lay their right hands, palm up, on top of each other. They chant, 'One, two, three – hup!' raising and lowering their tiered hands with each count. With 'hup!' they free their hands and quickly lay them, palm up or down, on their knees. The player with an unmatched hand (palm up or down) wins. Repeat if necessary.

Eight Masai tribesmen of Kenya gather for a game of wari. In this photograph by John Moss, they play the local version called en dodoï, en geishei.

Wari

About the Game

Wari is one of many similar board games played in various parts of the world. They are generically known as *mancala* games and have been played for thousands of years in Egypt, where boards have been found carved into the stone of the pyramid of Cheops and the temples at Luxor and Karnak. The game spread to Asia and Africa, where the Arabs developed certain variations. It thus survived through all the epochs of Egyptian history. European travelers were introduced to it in the cafes of nineteenth-century Cairo, where it was customary for the loser to pay for the coffee drunk during the game.

African slaves brought *mancala* games to Surinam and the West Indies, where they survive unchanged. In some rural areas of Africa today, children play these age-old games on 'boards' scooped out of the ground.

Although generally considered a 'man's game' in Africa, *wari* is occasionally played by women and some of them are skilled at it. A man, however, will rarely challenge a woman who is known to be a good player. Any man who loses to a woman at *wari* is in for a ribbing from his fellow villagers.

Traditionally, *wari* is played for fun and prestige, not for money. In some regions, it also has a religious significance. In Surinam, mourners will sometimes play *awari,* a form of *wari,* at a funeral, on the day before the corpse is to be interred. This is done to amuse the spirit which has not yet departed, but at sundown the boards are put away. It is believed that if the game is played at night, ghosts will join the living players and fly off with their spirits.

Turkish harem girls play mancala *in this eighteenth-century engraving by a French artist fascinated by the then unfamiliar game.*

Molded in the oblong shape traditional in Africa for centuries, the handmade wari *board, above, is painted after the style of Nigerian folk art. In this case, dried peas are used for the playing pieces.*

How to Play the Game

The *wari* board has six cups or compartments on each player's side and a reservoir at either end to hold captured pieces. To begin, the twelve compartments must each hold four similar-sized objects, such as nuts, dry beans, ball bearings, etc. The first player removes all the pieces from one of the six holes on his side and sows the pieces, one by one, counter-clockwise (to the right) into the next four compartments.

Depending on which compartment he plays from, some or all of his pieces may be placed in cups on his opponent's side of the board. For example, if player B removes the pieces from the third compartment from his left and deposits them as previously described, the board will look like this:

A

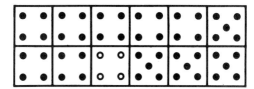

B

If his opponent, A, then takes the four pieces from the second compartment to his right, the board will look like this:

A

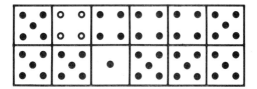

B

The pieces are no longer evenly distributed and, during a game, one compartment may eventually hold 20 or more pieces. So many pieces would go around the board more than once as they are sown into the cups. The emptied cup, however, is always skipped over, and left empty until the next turn.

The aim of each player is to capture pieces in his opponent's compartments. This is done when the last piece sown falls into a compartment on the opponent's side that already holds one or two pieces. With the deposited piece, the total is then two or three pieces, which are then 'captured.'

A capture can be made only with the last piece that is sown into a compartment. Two possible captures are shown in the diagrams below.

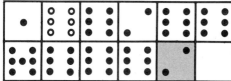

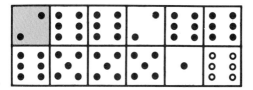

When the last piece falls into one of the opponent's compartments, making a total of either two or three pieces, the capturing player takes the pieces from that compartment and places them in the reservoir at his right. Once a player has captured, he is further allowed to take the pieces from the immediately preceeding cup, and likewise from the cups consecutively before that if (a) the cups are on the opponent's side of the board and (b) each cup contains the proper number of pieces to be captured – that is two or three pieces.

A game ends when all the compartments on one player's side of the board are empty, and it is his turn to play as shown in the diagram below.

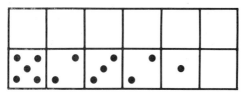

A player may not leave his opponent's compartments empty if he can still move pieces into them, as in the next diagram. Nor is a player allowed to make a move that would capture every one of his opponent's pieces, leaving him with nothing to play.

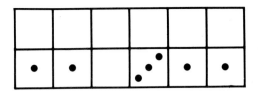

When there are no more possible moves, the player who still has pieces in his compartments removes them and adds them to those already collected in his reservoir. If only a very few pieces remain on the board, the players may agree to take those remaining on their own sides and end the game. The player who holds the most pieces at the end of the game is the winner.

Game Strategy

To play *wari* well, you will have to play careful attention to how many pieces are in each of your opponent's compartments, and which of your own cups are vulnerable, especially those holding one or two pieces. But even an empty compartment can be attacked if your opponent has more than eleven pieces in one of his cups, as shown in the diagram below.

A

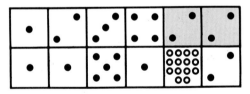

B

The compartment with the white pieces was played and B captures four pieces in two formerly vacant cups. (Don't forget that, if the pieces go around the board more than once, no pieces are sown in the cup just emptied.)

A compartment holding one or two pieces is threatened when your opponent's compartment contains the same number of pieces as the distance (in cups) from one compartment to the other. You can spot threats by counting backward from your compartment. At any time, you may openly count the number of pieces in your opponent's compartments.

Your strongest position is when you threaten the contents of several different enemy cups. In the next diagram, player B has the opportunity to attack three of the compartments on player A's side of the board.

A

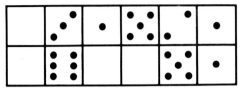

B

Player A can defend himself in several ways. He can move one of his single pieces to another cup or he can sow another piece into one of the threatening compartments on his opponent's side, so that the attack will overshoot the target. Or a player may choose not to defend his endangered pieces but rather plan a counterattack that would match or exceed his opponent's victory.

Two pieces in a vulnerable cup require the same strategy, or they can be safeguarded by sowing another piece into the cup, as player A does below:

A

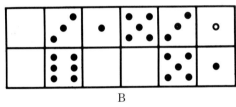

B

This move leaves player B with only one possibility of capture: the singleton on A's side.

A cup loaded with more than eleven pieces may threaten an empty cup, as in the first diagram in the game strategy section (above, left). It is almost impossible to defend an empty cup, and only overloading the attacking compartment will stop the threat. If a cup that holds one piece is threatened by a heavily loaded cup, you can sow another piece into the vulnerable cup to block the capture.

If the singleton is moved to the next space, the opponent will still capture at least two pieces when he plays into the empty cup. When you are playing a heavily loaded cup, watch carefully for the most favorable moment to sow the pieces. Study every compartment on the board before you play. There are many opportunities to capture a few pieces with a full cup, but a well-timed move can capture eight or more, as illustrated below:

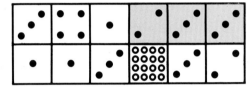

At the end of a game, players should attempt to hold as many pieces as possible on their own side of the board and as few on the opponent's side as can be managed. By distributing the pieces over many cups rather than a few, a player can move from lightly loaded compartments, and thereby control the progress of pieces into his opponent's side of the board.

The game often continues for some time when there are no more than six or eight pieces on the board. Although the players have the option of taking the pieces on their own sides and ending the game, the last pieces can often be crucial to the matter of who wins or loses the game. Since you are not allowed to capture all the pieces on your opponent's side, leaving him nothing to play, and since you must move pieces to your opponent's side if he has none left, the strategy is to get all the pieces on your side in such a way that nothing can be passed to your opponent, as shown below:

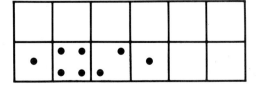

This cast bronze statuette is the work of the Ashanti tribe of Ghana. The woman, who is winning, is shown to be a person of high rank by the ceremonial stool on which she is seated.

Kenyan warriors in tribal dress park their spears while playing wari. *Known by names as varied as* aware, adi, ti *and* walu, *the game takes innumerable local forms in tribal regions throughout Africa.*

Materials

Plastic clay or modeling clay.
Poster paint.
Varnish.
Forty-eight small objects, such as coffee beans or dried peas.

Tools

A plywood panel or wooden board (on which the clay can be shaped and dried), rolling pin, knife, ruler, ping-pong ball, and a paintbrush.

How to Make the Game

A handsome *wari* board can be made of clay. Using a rolling pin, press the clay into a rectangle of 4 by 16 by 1½ inches, as shown in photograph 1. Cut away excess clay and score with the knife and the ruler to mark the positions of the holes (photograph 2). Press a ping-pong ball into the soft clay (photograph 3) to make compartments and reservoirs. (Before you begin, prick two holes in the ping-pong ball on opposite sides to prevent suction problems. Make certain that one pin-hole is pressed into the clay and the other is free to 'breathe.') Trim the corners of the tablet into a boat-shaped board, as in photograph 4. Let the clay dry and harden for at least a day. A glazed effect can be achieved by painting, then varnishing the hardened clay board.

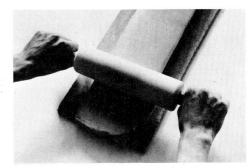

1: Flatten the clay with a rolling pin into a rectangular slab, 4 by 16 by 1½ inches.

2: At regular intervals, score the clay surface to indicate where each hole will be placed.

3: Press the perforated ping-pong ball into the clay to form the compartments and reservoirs.

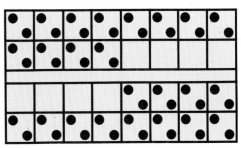

4: Trim off the square corners with a knife to make the board oblong, and smooth the edges.

Hus

Hus, played by the Hottentots of South Africa, is a distant relation of *wari.* The board is divided into four rows instead of two, and each player controls the two rows on his side of the board. Unlike *wari,* all pieces are in play during the game.

This type of four-row game is found among the different tribes in the south and east of Africa. The more sophisticated tribes play the game on handsomely worked wooden boards, but many others merely dig a series of shallow holes in the ground. Pieces of stone *hus* boards have been discovered in the excavations at Zimbabwe, Rhodesia, the remains of a civilization that flourished from 1450 to 1800 A.D.

Before playing *hus,* lots should be drawn for the first move of the game. Place two pieces in each of the eight holes of the back row on your side of the board. Two pieces should be placed in each of the four holes on the right half of the front rows. Moves are made in a clockwise (to the left) direction. You play only on your side of the board.

In the beginning of the game, remove the playing pieces from any hole on your side of the board and place them one by one into those holes consecutively neighboring the one just emptied. If your last piece should land in an empty hole, your turn is over and your opponent can begin. If, on the other hand, your last piece should land in a hole that is already occupied, you must pick up all the pieces in that hole,

The diagram above shows the arrangement of seeds for beginning a game of hus.

including the one you have just deposited, and continue to place these pieces into the neighboring holes.

If, at any time during your turn, your last piece falls into an occupied hole in the front row, and the opposite hole

on your opponent's front row is occupied too, you can remove the pieces from your opponent's hole and continue playing the stones you have captured, placing them now on your side of the board.

Several captures are possible in one turn. If the back-row hole behind the one you have just captured is occupied too, you can remove the pieces from that hole, as well as the pieces from another hole on that row of the board. You then place all of the pieces you have captured into the holes on your side of the board, starting from the hole that corresponds to the one on your opponent's side where you made your last capture. All moves must be made from holes containing two or more pieces. If you are left with only one

piece in each hole, you lose the game. If you capture all your opponent's pieces, it counts as a double win.

Hus is usually played in sets of seven games, and is noted for rapid changes of luck in the course of a game.

Hottentot women pass the afternoon hours with games of hus. *This type of four-row game is played through the south and east of Africa, but, according to some experts, it was probably an Arab invention. A similar game played in Zanzibar is called* kiarabu, *'the Arab game.'*

This typical hus *board is made of slender branches, cut to size and bound to produce the 32-pocketed table.*

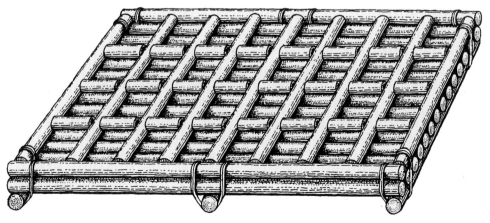

Pachisi

About the Game

Pachisi has been played in India for many centuries and is considered the country's national game. The name is derived from the Indian word for 'twenty-five,' the highest throw of the cowrie-shell dice. There are two other well-known versions of the game, *chausar* – the rules are given on page 29 – and *caupur,* which is played with ordinary dice. (The name *caupur* derives from the Sanskrit *catus pada,* meaning 'he who has four legs.') The game is also known as India, or Ludo, which was a patented modification introduced into England around the turn of the century.

Pachisi originated in India during the sixth century or perhaps even earlier. Traces of a cross-shaped *pachisi* board carved in stone can be seen today in one of the ancient cave temples of Ellora in the Deccan region of India.

In the sixteenth century, the great Moghul Emperor Akbar played the game on an enormous outdoor board of squares inlaid with marble, which included a raised central platform where he and his courtiers sat as they played. Instead of pieces, he used slave girls from his harem. Dressed in the appropriate colors, red, yellow, green, and black, they moved about the board as commanded with each throw of the cowrie-shell dice.

This antique Indian pachisi *board is made of velvet embroidered with silver cord. The beehive-shaped playing pieces are inlaid with ivory.*

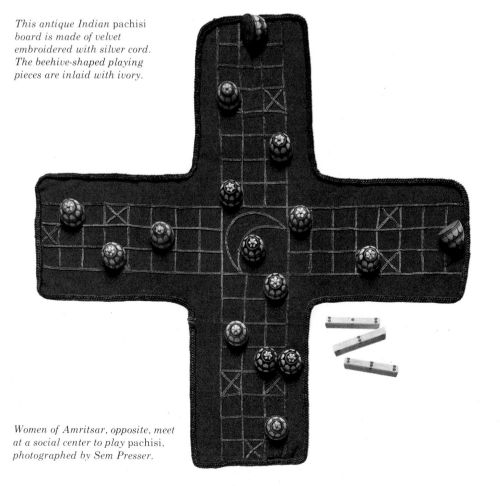

Women of Amritsar, opposite, meet at a social center to play pachisi, *photographed by Sem Presser.*

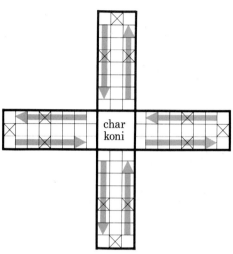

Figure A: Direction of movement – each piece first moves down the char (the center of its own arm), then makes a counterclockwise circuit of the board, traveling along the sides of the other arms.

How to Play the Game

Pachisi is played by two or three players, or by four playing as teams. The aim of each player is to move his four counters around the board and back into the center of the board (*char-koni*) before his opponents do.

Each player takes his place in front of an arm of the *pachisi* cross. Those sitting opposite each other are partners, red and black playing against yellow and green. *Pachisi* is played with cowrie shells used as dice. Scoring depends on how many shells land with their mouths up. The scores are:

2 cowries with mouths up... 2
3 cowries with mouths up... 3
4 cowries with mouths up... 4
5 cowries with mouths up... 5
6 cowries with mouths up... 6
1 cowrie with mouth up... 10 and another throw
0 cowries with mouths up... 25 and another throw
(If you use *chausar* dice, move the pieces in accordance with the *chausar* rules given on page 29.)

Like the traditional Indian gameboards, this modern pachisi *board is made of decorated cloth, which has the advantage that it can be rolled up and transported with the pieces in a light, compact package.*

During their travels round the board, the pieces are vulnerable to attack, except when they occupy one of the squares marked with an X, which are called 'castle' squares (see figure A). A player captures an opponent's piece by landing on the same square. The captured piece is lifted and placed back in *char-koni* to begin again, while the capturing player has another throw. Pieces on castle squares are free from attack and any number of pieces of any color may rest on them.

A player, or partners, can create a blockade by placing two pieces on any square. An opponent throwing a number that would take one of his pieces beyond the blockaded square cannot move the blocked piece, but the blockading pieces can be captured by an equal or larger number of men landing on them, unless they are on a castle square. Two or more of a player's pieces doubled up on any square may move together on a single throw of the cowries and travel round the circuit in fewer throws.

A player may refuse to play his turn (without, or after, having thrown the shells) in order to help his partner in some strategic way, or to avoid capture by one of his opponent's men. Also, a player may send any of his pieces around the board for a second circuit, if it is helpful to his partner.

Each throw allows a player to move one piece the indicated number of squares. If there is more than one throw in a turn, each throw can be used to move a different piece.

Beehive-shaped playing pieces for pachisi *or* chausar, *below, were made by a master craftsman for a Bengali maharajah in the eighteenth century. The pieces are inlaid with ivory in double tiers whose arcaded pattern reflects the architecture of the Moghuls, rulers of northern India for 300 years.*

To begin the game, each player throws the six cowries. The highest scorer throws again and then moves one of his pieces from *char-koni* down the center strip of squares (the *char* or home path) of his limb of the cross. All pieces move counterclockwise around the board until they arrive back at the player's home arm, as shown in figure A. On reaching the *char*, they are laid on their side as proof that they have completed the circuit. They are then moved up the center strip to *char-koni*, which they must reach on an exact throw of the cowries.

In team play, if your partner is lagging behind, you can assist him by keeping one or more pieces back to form blockades or capture enemy counters. If one partner goes out long before the other, the opposing team has two throws of the shells to the remaining partner's one. In this situation, they can easily attack his pieces and send them back to *char-koni* to begin again. In *pachisi*, teamwork should be a major consideration. Both partners win or lose the game together.

Chausar

Chausar, a variant of *pachisi,* is not played with cowries but with three oblong, four-sided dice. These dice are marked with 1 and 6, 2 and 5 on opposing sides. There are no castles in *chausar,* though it is frequently played on *pachisi* boards with the same markings. Black and yellow traditionally play against red and green. All the black pieces must return to *char-koni* before the yellow can return. Likewise, the red must go out before the green. When two dice come up showing the same number, pieces that are doubled on a square may be moved twice the number shown. If the player has no doubled pieces, the pieces move the number shown. Blockades may be formed only by pieces that have completed half their journey around the board. If four are playing, a player continues throwing the dice after all his pieces are back in *char-koni,* giving the partner still on the board the benefit of the throws.

Three modern Indian princesses play pachisi *in the courtyard of the maharaja's palace in Udaipur, Rajasthan.*

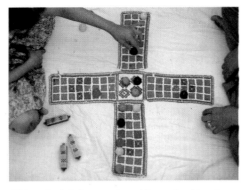

This colorful chausar board is made of bead embroidery and comes from Bikaner, one of the cities of Rajasthan famed for its beadwork, tapestries, and decorations. The players are seated on the roof terrace of a Bikaner town house. The dots shown on these hollow bone dice belong to their lattice-work ornamentation and do not figure in the scoring; the actual number dots are too small to be seen in the photograph.

Materials
Orange felt: one strip 30 by 6 inches, two strips 12 by 6 inches.
Red felt: four strips 12 by 4½ inches.
Blue felt: one square 4½ by 4½ inches.
Purple felt: 48 squares 1½ by 1½ inches.
All-purpose glue, thread, and decorative cord.

Three wooden blocks, 2½ by ½ by ½ inches, for *chausar* or six cowrie shells for *pachisi*.
Sandpaper and paint.
Clay or heavy paper.
Paint or felt-tip pens in yellow, green, black, and red.

Alternate materials (for a cardboard or wooden board)
Cardboard or wood 30 inches square.
Three wooden blocks, 2½ by ½ by ½ inches, for *chausar* or six cowrie shells for *pachisi*.
Clay or heavy paper.
Paint and all-purpose glue.
Marking pens in yellow, green, red, and black (if paper counters are made).

Tools
Sewing needle, straight pins, ruler, pencil, tailor's chalk, paintbrush, and a pair of scissors.

Alternate Tools
Ruler, pencil, fine paintbrushes, saw, knife or scissors.

How to Make the Game
In India, *pachisi* or *chausar* boards are usually made of embroidered cloth. Follow these instructions to make the colorful felt gameboard shown on page 28. Lay out the large orange section first. Then sew the two smaller orange strips on either side of this section. Center them exactly on each side of the longer strip so that they seem to be running in a continuous line to form the basic cross pattern of the board.

Figure B: Sew the orange strips together to form the basic cross, then attach the blue square to the center of the board. First glue, then sew the red strips of cloth to make the arms of the cross.

Place the blue square exactly in the center of the cross, so that all four arms seem to stem from it. Pin, then sew it down. Apply glue to the four corners of each red section and fasten these sections onto the four orange arms of the board, making sure that one end of each red arm is flush against the blue central square. (See figure B.) Center the red pieces on the orange arms so that the orange border now surrounding the outer edges of the red arms is the same width on all sides. After the glued corners have taken hold, sew the red pieces down fast.

3: With tailor's chalk trace the outline of the paper pattern onto the blue square in the center. Use this outline as a guide when you sew the cloth star on the center square.

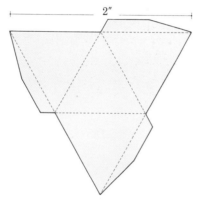

Figure D: Use this pattern to cut out heavy paper to make the playing pieces for pachisi or chausar. Fold on the dotted lines and glue the overlaps to make a pyramid shape. Then, with felt marking pens, decorate them in the proper colors.

Figure C: Use this pattern to cut out the appliqué for the center square of the pachisi board.

1: First glue, then sew the purple squares in a checkered pattern on the arms of the board.

Arrange the 48 purple squares in a checkered pattern on the four red arms (photograph 1). Fasten these squares with a little glue and let it dry. This will secure them while you sew them on. Embroider the X's on the castle squares or sew them on with decorative cord.

You can make the 16 playing pieces or counters from clay, then paint them, four of each in the traditional colors of red, green, yellow, and black. You can also make the pieces from heavy paper, using figure D as a pattern. Wooden counters may be a little more difficult to make, but obviously they will last longer.

2: The board can be decorated with colored cord sewn around the borders of the four arms.

If you desire, you can decorate your *pachisi* board by sewing black or colored cord trimming around its borders (photograph 2), and by sewing a cloth star on the blue square in the center. To cut out the cloth star, make a stencil from heavy paper in the shape of figure C. Use this as the pattern for the star. Then, with tailor's chalk, trace the outline of the star stencil onto the blue square (photograph 3) to be used as a guide when the appliqué is sewn onto the board. If you prefer, you may purchase an attractive appliqué for the center of the cross.

These colorful cardboard playing pieces are simple-to-make versions of the dome-shaped counters used in the standard Indian game.

To follow the traditional method of playing pachisi, *use cowrie shells, if available. Otherwise, the handmade oblong* chausar *dice may be used.*

Make the three dice for *chausar* from blocks of wood $2\frac{1}{2}$ by $\frac{1}{2}$ by $\frac{1}{2}$ inches. Sand them down smooth. Then, paint them black or white and let dry. On the four sides of each die, the dots, one, two, five, and six, can be applied with ink or paint, or paste on paper circles made with a hole punch.

Chinesenspiel

About the Game

Chinesenspiel, German for the 'game of the Chinese,' is a simplified children's version of *pachisi*. The game set shown below was made in Germany in the nineteenth century, a rustic remnant of the *chinoiserie* vogue that inundated western Europe with lacquer work, painted silk, and bamboo bird cages. Though they had little direct contact with either culture, the Germans were particularly fascinated by tales of the opulent Moghul empire in India, and by stories of mandarin China. In *Chinesenspiel*, they enjoyed a mélange of the two Eastern influences – an Indian game with little wooden Chinese for playing pieces.

Exotic tales of mandarin China inspired this German children's game of the nineteenth century.

How to Play the Game

Chinesenspiel is a game for two, three, or four players. Each player has one man, either red, yellow, green, or blue. The game is played with one large die which is white on two sides and marked with red, yellow, green, or blue on the four remaining sides. The object of the game is to take each man on a complete circuit of the board, and then up the diagonal arm from his home square to the center of the board.

To begin the game, each player places his man on the corner of the board which shows a corresponding color. One player throws the die until a colored side comes up; the player with the matching piece takes the first turn. He throws the die. If the die shows the same color as his piece, he may move his man one space in a counter-clockwise direction and throw again. If a white side shows on the die, the piece is not moved but the player may throw again. If any other color appears on the die, the turn passes to the next player on the right.

The game proceeds in this fashion and the first player to bring his man around the board and into the center wins.

Materials

A plywood board, 12¾ inches square, ⅜ inch thick.
Four plywood boards, 1⅞ by 12¾ inches, ⅜ inch thick.
Four strips ornamental molding, ⅜ inch wide, 12¾ inches long.
Four contoured wooden handles, about 1 inch in diameter, 3 inches long (cut to the proper length, if necessary).
Four wooden balls, 1 inch in diameter.
A wooden ball, 2 inches in diameter.
Four nails, 1 inch long.
Wire nails, about ¾ inch long.

Four flat-headed plastic cabinet knobs (screw-on type), 1¼ inches in diameter.
Wood glue. Wood putty. Wood primer.
Gloss paint: red, yellow, light blue, dark blue, green, black, and white.
Black plastic adhesive tape.
Yellow plastic adhesive tape.

Tools

A ruler, pencil, scroll saw, hammer, primer brush, sandpaper, putty knife, artist's camel-hair brush, paintbrush, scissors, vise, backsaw, wire cutters, wood rasp, and drawing compass.

How to Make the Game

To prepare the plywood boards for finger joints, place one 1⅞-by-12¾-inch board horizontally before you. On the long edges, mark points ⅜ inch from both corners. Draw straight lines to join the opposite points. On each of these lines and on the 1⅞-inch edges beside them, mark points at ⅜-inch intervals. Connect points on the edges with the corresponding points on the lines beside them. Repeat these steps on the remaining three 1⅞-by-12¾-inch boards.

With the scroll saw, cut out three alternating ⅜-inch-square sections at one end of each board, starting with the first section at the corner. At the other end of each board, cut out two alternating sections, starting with the second section from the corner of the board.

Spread a light coat of glue along all the finger joints. Join the boards so that the fingers of one dovetail with the fingers of another. Hammer a few wire nails part way into each corner. Spread glue over the top edges of the frame and position the square plywood board so that the edges of the square match the sides of the frame. Hammer a few nails partly into the corners. When the glue has dried, remove the nails.

Fill the gaps around the finger joints with putty; allow to dry. Paint the frame and surface of the board with wood primer; allow to dry. Lightly sand the primed surfaces.

On each of the four edges of the top surface of the board, measure and mark points at $\frac{3}{8}$ inch and $1\frac{7}{8}$ inches from each corner. Draw lines connecting points on opposite sides of the square. You will now have a $1\frac{1}{2}$-inch-wide path running around the inside of the square. Divide this path into $1\frac{1}{2}$-inch squares as shown in the figure at right.

Draw two diagonal lines across the board from corner to corner of the unmarked square in the center of the square path. On both sides of each diagonal, at a distance of $\frac{3}{4}$ inch, draw lines parallel to the diagonals. Erase the central diagonals and divide these $1\frac{1}{2}$-inch-wide diagonal paths into $1\frac{1}{2}$-inch squares, as in figure A. (The ends of the diagonal paths will not be complete squares.)

With an artist's camel-hair brush, carefully paint the board as shown on the model at right. First paint the triangles between the diagonals and the sides of the board with light blue paint. Allow to dry thoroughly. Then, working with one color at a time – and allowing each color to dry before going on to the next – paint the squares on the board as shown in the model. Paint a star in the central square.

Cut strips of black plastic tape to $\frac{1}{16}$-inch widths and tape over all dividing lines on the board.

Cut a strip of yellow plastic tape and decorate the sides of the frame, as shown in the model.

Clamp the middle of one of the ornamental molding strips in the vise so that its flat side is facing up. Line up the perpendicular of your protractor with the edge of the left end of the molding strip, the base of the protractor in line with the bottom edge. Mark a point on the top edge that is 45 degrees from the bottom corner. Repeat this at the right end of the strip, measuring and marking a 45-degree angle to the left. Cut along these lines with a backsaw. Repeat these steps on the remaining three molding strips.

Paint the strips dark blue and allow to dry. Glue the flat side of the molding strips to the edges of the top of the board. Hammer wire nails to hold the strips in place while the glue dries, then remove the nails.

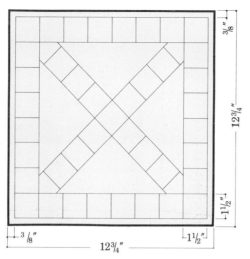

This simple-to-follow Chinesenspiel *diagram will help you in laying out your game board.*

To make the wooden men, mark the center point on the broader base of one of the wooden handles. Screw a cabinet knob in the handle at this point. Screw knobs onto the other handles.

With a wood rasp, file a flat section $\frac{1}{4}$ inch in diameter on each wooden ball. Hammer a 1-inch nail halfway into each flat section. Cut off the heads of the nails with wire cutters. Hammer the rest of each nail into the center point of the narrow end of the wooden handles by hammering on the wooden ball, until the ball is flush with the end of the handle. Using the photographed model as a guide, paint the playing pieces.

To make the die, clamp the 2-inch wooden ball in the vise. Set the drawing compass at a radius of $\frac{1}{2}$ inch, place the needle on the ball, and draw a circle. With a backsaw or wood rasp, cut this section off, making a flat area on the ball.

Turn the ball over so that the flat area is facing exactly downward. Repeat these steps, making another flat surface on the ball. Clamp the two flat surfaces of the ball in the vise and repeat the same steps, making flat areas exactly opposite each other on the surface of the ball, until you have made six flat sides.

Sandpaper all rough and splintered areas on this six-sided die until smooth. Apply a coat of primer, let dry completely, then sand lightly.

Paint each flat surface of the die white. Allow to dry. Paint the surrounding areas black. Allow to dry. Draw a diagonal cross on each flat surface of the die. On two opposite sides, paint over the lines of the cross in black paint as shown in the photographed model. When the paint is dry, paint two sections on each side of the die in a color which matches one of the playing pieces. (Use the model as a guide.) There should be one side marked with red, one with blue, one with yellow, and one with green.

Clean lines and bright colors modernize the traditional design of a Chinesenspiel *board.*

Shove Ha'penny

About the Game

In Shakespeare's England this was an immensely popular game, known variously as shovel-board, shove-groat, slide-groat, and slip-groat. The groat was an old English coin worth four pence, ideal in size and weight for this form of 'finger billiards.' Later it was to be replaced by a ha'penny, which was an equally convenient sliding coin so long as it retained its Victorian size and weight. In Britain's current decimal coinage, however, the ha'penny is far too small to serve this purpose, and modern players continue to use (and carefully hoard) the old pre-decimal ha'pennies.

Though now known primarily as a tavern game, in its heyday shove-groat alias shove ha'penny was played by kings and courtiers. The household accounts of Henry VII, in 1532, mention a gambling debt 'paid to my lord Wylliam for that he won of the king's grace at shovillaborde.' Shove-groat is frequently named in the anti-gambling laws of the sixteenth century. At Oxford, for example, it was included among the 'unlawfull games' prohibited to both students and townspeople. By then the fifteenth-century groats that had given the game its name had been replaced in popular favor by the Edward VI shilling, called the 'shove-groat shilling.' Shakespeare playfully alludes to two Elizabethan games at once when he has Falstaff, in *Henry IV,* Part II, telling Bardolf to toss Pistol downstairs: 'Quoit him down, Bardolf, like a shove-groat shilling!' (For quoits and the proper method of throwing them, see page 170.)

Shove-groat was a great favorite of the British landed gentry, who had boards of exquisite workmanship made for their country houses: the famous shovel-board at Chartley Hall, in Staffordshire, was 'ten yards, one foot and one inch long,' and its marquetry inlay consisted of 260 pieces. But when billiards became the fashionable gentleman's game, shove ha'penny slid down the social ladder. In 1708, one status-conscious observer noted that it had been abandoned by the aristocracy and was now played only by 'citizens and peasants.'

One version of the game emigrated overseas, where it was vastly enlarged and transformed into a shipboard pastime called shuffleboard. In this form it has also attracted a sizable following on dry land, notably in Florida.

In Britain, shove ha'penny fell on hard times for a while, but has made a comeback in the more tradition-minded pubs. Hundreds of fine old boards are said to be in use throughout the country. In Oxford alone, 28 teams with some 270 players regularly gather at local pubs to play in organized matches.

A shove ha'penny player in a British pub stands in typical playing stance, his pint of beer at one side. With the ball of his thumb he taps the ha'penny at the edge of the board, just sharply enough to propel it the required distance.

How to Play the Game

The target area of the shove ha'penny board is divided into nine horizontal zones or 'beds.' Each bed has a scoring square on either end. The object of this game is to shove a coin or disc so that it falls within the borders of one of the nine beds. Shove ha'penny is a game for two people, each player using five coins or discs per turn. The player who first scores three coins in each of the nine beds is the winner of the game.

The manner of shoving or propelling the coins is simple. Each coin or disc is positioned on the bottom end of the board so that a portion of it sticks out over the edge. The coin is then tapped

The ha'penny at right has landed in a bed and scores the third point, which is chalked across the first two in the scoring square at left.

or struck with the palm of the hand or ball of the thumb so that it sails up the board and lands in one of the beds. A coin that comes to rest beyond the bed area is considered 'dead' and immediately removed from the board, as is a coin that lands more than half over the line into the scoring squares. Any coin that lies on a line between two beds or less than half over the line into the scoring squares may remain on the board, but does not score unless it is nudged into a bed by another coin. A poorly propelled coin that lands short of the first line may be reshot.

The board has a slat underneath its bottom end so that it can be steadied against the edge of the table while the game is played. There is also an arc-shaped ridge at the upper end of the board so that coins can ricochet into a bed. One coin may strike another as a means of moving a badly positioned coin into a bed. If a coin lands on top of another, neither scores. The beds may be filled in any order; experienced players, however, often begin by filling the more distant beds first.

To score, a coin must be completely within a bed, not touching any line. At the end of each turn, the player places his scoring coins in the square at his end of the appropriate bed. All other coins are retrieved to be played again in another turn. If a player shoots more than the three required coins into one bed, the excess points are added to his opponent's score if the opponent lacks points in that bed. The final or winning point must be scored by the player and not his opponent.

A variation of shove ha'penny called 'progressive' allows the player an additional shot for each point scored.

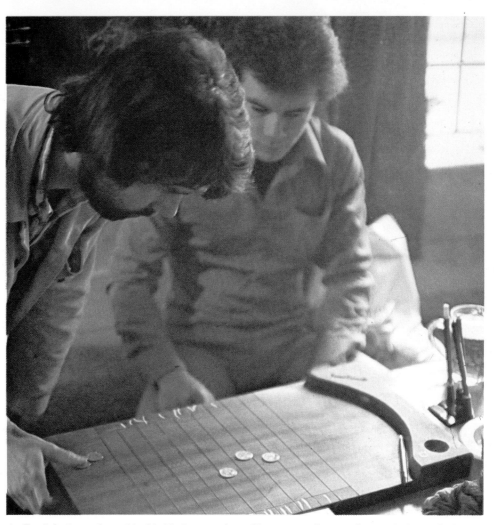

An English player shoves his third ha'penny, above. If opponents disagree that a coin is in a bed, another coin is rolled along the groove. If it moves the disputed coin, no point is scored.

Sixteenth-century English shillings, above, were popular coins for playing shove-groat. They depict the heads of Henry VIII's three children, all of them in succession heirs to the English throne: Edward VI (top), Mary Tudor, with her husband Philip of Spain (left), and Elizabeth I (right).

Materials

A plywood board, 16 by 24 inches, $\frac{1}{2}$ inch thick.
A plywood slat, 16 by $1\frac{1}{4}$ inches, $\frac{3}{4}$ inch thick
A plywood plank, 16 by 4 inches, $\frac{1}{2}$ inch thick.
Three screws, $\frac{3}{4}$ inch long.
Three screws, 1 inch long.
18 green felt squares, $1\frac{1}{4}$ by $1\frac{1}{4}$ inches.
60 plastic or metal discs, approximately the size of a half-dollar.
Neutral wood stain (optional) and paste wax for floors or furniture.

Tools

A screwdriver, ruler, pencil, felt-tip pen, drawing compass, all-purpose glue, scroll saw, hand or electrical drill, wood file, and sandpaper.

How to Make the Game

To make the curved backboard of the shove ha'penny board, take the plank, 16 by 4 inches, and mark a line down its length, 1 inch from one of the long edges. Then, draw lines $1\frac{1}{2}$ inches from each short edge. Using a compass, draw an arc that rounds off the inside corner. Cut along these lines with a scroll saw to make the curved ridge of the backboard.

With a wood rasp, file the inside corner at the bottom of the ridge into a slight curve, and sand down all sharp edges until smooth. Bore three holes into the ridge, one in the middle of its length and the others $1\frac{1}{2}$ inches from the end of each arm. Use $\frac{3}{4}$-inch screws to attach the ridge to the face of the board, making sure the outer edges are flush with the outer edges of the board.

Bore three holes in the plywood slat, 16 by $1\frac{1}{2}$ inches, and use the 1-inch screws to attach it to the underside of the board at the opposite end. The edges should be flush.

1: Measure and mark the nine 'beds' and the scoring squares on either side of the board.

2: After drilling holes in the backboard, glue it to the board, then secure it with screws.

3: Secure the plywood slat to the bottom of the shove ha'penny board in the same manner.

4: Dig a slight groove in all the lines in the scoring area with the blade of a screwdriver.

To make the target area on the face of the board, draw a horizontal line across the board, 5 inches from the bottom edge, and another line, 4½ inches from the inner rim of the ridge at the top of the board. Divide the area between these lines into the nine 'beds' by drawing eight lines, 1½ inches from each other and the two boundary lines.

Draw two vertical lines, perpendicular to the 'bed' lines, 1½ inches from each side of the board. This makes the two rows of scoring squares.

Using the ruler as a guide, go over all the lines with a screwdriver, digging in a slight groove. Accentuate the lines with a felt-tip pen and stain the board, if you wish.

Glue a green felt square in the center of each score square, and the shove ha'penny board is complete. To guarantee a good sliding surface, wax the face of the board with paste wax.

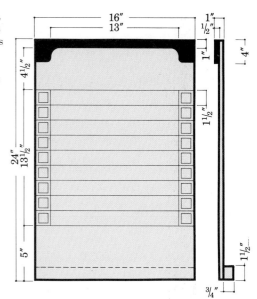

Follow these dimensions when measuring the scoring area of the shove ha'penny board.

Based on a classic British pub model that has stood the test of time, this shove ha'penny board is a simple crafts project. Players soon learn to shoot with greater accuracy than was shown by the novice who shoved the two line-riding coins that are shown in the photograph above.

Alquerque

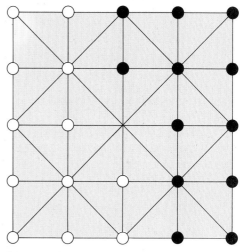

About the Game

Alquerque is the Spanish name for a board game introduced into Spain by the Moors, who ruled most of the country for five hundred years. Called *el-quirkat* in Arabic, the game is mentioned in the Moorish book, *Kitab al-Aghani,* written in the tenth century, but it is known to have been played for several thousands of years in Egypt and the Middle East. There is an unfinished *alquerque* diagram engraved in one of the roofing slabs of the temple at Kurna, Egypt, which was built around 1400 B.C.

Several versions of *alquerque* are described and illustrated in the great *Libro de Juegos* (Book of Games) of King Alfonso the Learned. One of them, the *alquerque de doce,* or twelve-man *alquerque,* closely resembles the game still played in the cafes and bodegas of Spain.

It is essentially an early form of checkers: Alfonso's book says that it resembles chess, 'in that it is played with the mind.' The book also notes that the initial advantage lies with the person who has the second move, rather than the first, and that 'if the game is played by two equally knowledgeable players, the game will end in a draw.'

How to Play the Game

Alquerque is a game for two players, each equipped with a set of twelve playing pieces, either black or white. To begin the game, the pieces are arranged on the 25 stations of the board as shown in figure A. Turns alternate between the two players.

Figure A: Set up the playing pieces in the pattern shown here to begin a game of alquerque.

According to the traditional Spanish rules, the game is played as follows: a piece may move from its position to any adjacent empty point. If a player's piece is confronted by one belonging to his opponent and the space behind that is empty, the player's piece may jump over the opponent's piece, occupy the vacant station, and remove the opponent's piece from the board. (This piece is considered captured as in checkers and does not return to play.) When possible, a series of jumps is permitted, and change of direction is allowed. If a piece has the opportunity to jump an opponent's piece and does not jump in its turn, it is removed from the board and considered captured.

The winner is the first player to capture all of his opponent's pieces.

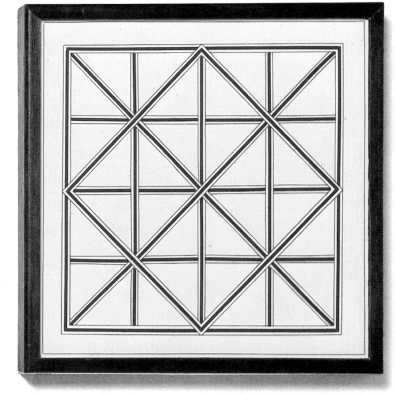

Alquerque, *the ancient forerunner of checkers, is played on this handsome homemade board.*

Two bearded gentlemen, accompanied by advisors who are also archers, play alquerque *in this illustration from the royal games book of Alfonso X, produced in 1283 by artists working at the court of Seville. As in the other illustrations of Alfonso's huge tome, the artist views the players from the side but shows the board from above – a brilliant solution to the 'how to play' and 'how to make' problems posed by the book. Equally ingenious is the way the artist has 'attached' the board to the frame of his picture with a cord whose tassel hangs down into the surrounding white space on the page.*

Materials

Composition board faced with white plastic, 16 inches square, $\frac{3}{8}$ inch thick.
A roll of brown plastic tape, cut into $\frac{1}{8}$-inch strips.
Four strips of picture-frame molding, $\frac{1}{2}$ inch wide on one side, 1 inch wide on the other, $\frac{1}{4}$ inch thick, and $16\frac{1}{2}$ inches long.

Wood glue.
Playing pieces for checkers, twelve black and twelve white.

Tools

A ruler, pencil, scissors, vise, protractor, and backsaw.

How to Make the Game

Lay the board on the table with the plastic surface facing up. Placing the ruler at one edge of the square, measure from the corner and make light pencil marks at the following points: 2, 5, 8, 11, and 14 inches.

Repeat this step on each edge of the square, then draw ruled lines connecting corresponding points on the opposite sides of the board. Using the photograph on page 38 as a guide, draw the diagonal lines on the board.

Cover the lines of the game diagram with the slender strips of brown tape, as shown in the photograph, and wash off any extra pencil marks with a barely damp sponge.

To prepare the picture-frame molding for the miter joints, take one piece and clamp the middle of the 1-inch side in a vise. The $\frac{1}{2}$-inch side is now flat before you, the cornered edge of the molding lying toward you. At the left end of the molding, line up the perpendicular of the protractor with the sawed edge of the $\frac{1}{2}$-inch side, lining up the base of the protractor with the cornered ridge of the molding.

Mark a point on the top edge of the ½-inch side that is 45 degrees from the cornered ridge. Draw a line from the corner edge to that point. Do the same on the right end of the molding, marking a 45-degree angle to the left.

Using a backsaw, miter both sides of the left end of the molding simultaneously while sawing along the line drawn. Do the same at the right end of the molding. Prepare the remaining three molding strips for miter joints, following the steps just given.

Spread glue on the inner sides of these strips, then fasten them to the sides of the board so that the ends of the ½-inch sides join correctly. Place the board face down on a table and allow the glue to dry thoroughly.

1: After measuring and marking the game board pattern on the white plastic surface, cover the lines with narrow strips of colored plastic tape.

2: With a protractor or try-and-miter square, measure a 45-degree angle from the cornered edge of the molding to the edge of the ½-inch side.

Peralikatuma

A version of *alquerque* played in Ceylon is called *peralikatuma*. Each player has 23 men which are arranged on the board as shown in figure B. The players take alternate turns, and each piece may move in any direction on the board to the next point of intersection. The rules are the same as in *alquerque,* and the player capturing all his opponent's pieces is the winner.

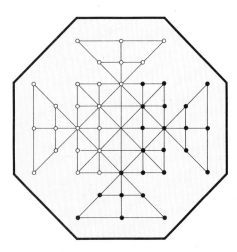

Figure B: This diagram shows the arrangement of pieces for the Asian game of peralikatuma.

Peralikatuma, *a Ceylonese version of* alquerque, *is played on this do-it-yourself game board.*

*In Tananarive, Madagascar, a handful of
kibitzers watch over a game of* fanorona, *another
member of the* alquerque *family. In the past, the
progress of certain ritual games was even more
closely observed – as the results were considered a
prophesy of things to come.*

Awithlaknannai

Awithlaknannai is an *alquerque*-type
game played by the Zuni Indians of
New Mexico. The board is a series of
bisected diamonds, as shown in figure
C. At the beginning of play, all the
intersections, except the central one,
are covered with black or white pieces.
Players take turns moving one piece at
a time to an adjacent empty square.
Pieces are captured in the same manner
as in *alquerque*. The game is ended
when one player has lost all his pieces.

*Figure C: Arrange the playing pieces in the
manner shown above to play* awithlaknannai.

This easy-to-make board is for awithlaknannai –
alquerque *as played by the uni Indians.*

About the Game

Often called the oldest of games, *Go* is still a newcomer to the West. It came to Europe at the end of the last century, and until about 1920 only a few enthusaistic pioneers knew of it. Among them was the chess master Emanuel Lasker, who thought it had cosmic significance: 'Chess is confined to the inhabitants of this earth, but *Go* somehow passes beyond our world. If on any planet there are rational beings, then they know *Go*.'

Go has an impressive history. It figures in Chinese literature of 2,000 years ago, but its origins are much earlier. Masters were highly esteemed in ancient China and given titles such as *sei* (holy man) or *shing* (sage).

For centuries after its introduction to Japan in 735 A.D., only the nobility played it. In due course the game spread to all levels of society and gifted players could attend *Go* academies. Masters merited special positions at the courts of Japanese feudal barons, or wandered the country giving lessons in the innumerable variations of play. Until 1600, *Go* was a compulsory course at the military academy of Japan.

The game of *Go* has a more severe simplicity and a more rigorous logic than chess. Both games are depictions of battle. Chess mirrors the battles of the age of chivalry: *Go*, despite its antiquity, is more comparable to modern warfare.

Excellence in games is esteemed by the Chinese. An audience gathers as two wei-ch'i *(Go) masters consolidate their territory, below, in this print from the Chinese K'ang-hsi period (1662–1723).*

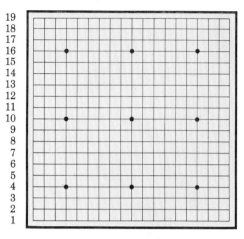

a b c d e f g h i k l m n o p q r s t

Figure A: The Go board is a grid of 19 by 19 lines. (The grid is annotated here with letters and numbers to clarify this demonstration of the rules.)

How to Play the Game

Go is a board game for two players. One player uses the white stones, the other player uses the black stones. The *Go*-board is a grid of 19 horizontal and 19 vertical lines. The stones are played on the intersections of the lines, not on the squares. There are 361 intersections or 'points.' The nine marked points on the board only have special meaning when a player is given a handicap. (Handicaps are explained on page 47.)

In theory each player has an unlimited number of stones. In reality, there are 181 black stones and 180 white, enough to occupy every point on the board. This many stones are never used in the game, and players may use a set for years before noticing that a few stones have been lost.

The game

The game of *Go* starts out with an empty board. The players alternately place a stone on any unoccupied point; black takes the first turn. A stone, once played, is not moved again. Instead of placing a stone, a player

In the classic nineteenth-century Japanese print, above, a Go player pauses to think, his black stone unplaced, as a tricky moment arises in the opening stages of the game.

may decide to 'pass' or miss his turn – but this only makes sense toward the end of the game.

A stone or group of stones is captured by 'enclosure': by being completely encircled by enemy pieces. Stones that are captured are immediately removed from the board, put aside, and counted when the game is over. A stone or group of stones is captured or 'killed' when it loses its last 'freedom.'

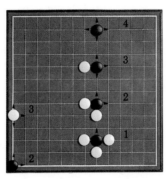

1: The black stone at the top has four 'freedoms' – it is connected by lines to four unoccupied points. Each time a white stone is placed on one of the points, the black stone loses a freedom.

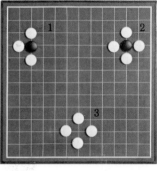

2: A stone is 'killed' when its last freedom is lost. Here the black stone has only one freedom; white moves a stone onto that point: the black stone is killed and removed from the game board.

Freedom

If a black stone is placed on an empty board, it has four freedoms – that is, the stone is surrounded by four unoccupied points, which are all connected by lines to the point on which the stone rests. A stone on a border line has three freedoms; a stone on a corner only two.

If three white stones are placed successively on the points adjacent to the black stone, as shown in photograph 1, the black stone has three, two, and finally only one freedom left. The black stone is now *atari* or in a threatened position: if it is white's move, the black stone could be captured.

Capture

A stone is captured as shown in photograph 2. A white stone is placed on the black stone's last freedom, enclosing it completely. The captured black stone is removed from the board. If it is black's turn to move in photograph 1, he can avoid capture by 'fleeing,' i.e. by placing a stone, as in photograph 3. The two black stones, connected by a line, form a 'chain.'

If two or more stones of the same color are connected by lines, they are all part of a chain. A chain 'lives or dies in unity, as a unit,' meaning that a single stone out of the chain cannot

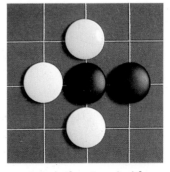

3: When a stone is threatened with capture, it can flee, as shown above. The two black stones, connected by a line, form a 'chain' which must be captured as a unit.

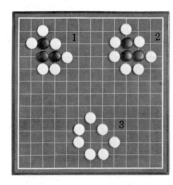

4: A chain is captured in the same way as a single stone – by losing all its freedoms. Here white places a stone on the black chain's last freedom: the chain is killed and taken from the board.

be captured. A chain is captured in the same way as a single stone. In photograph 4, white moves to the black chain's last freedom (there are no diagonal connections in *Go)* and the captured stones are removed.

When a chain is captured, both players may occupy the points which have become vacant. The captured stones are put aside until the end of the game and counted in the final settlement. In photograph 5, white has four chains – one of four, one of three, and two of two stones – and a single stone. Black has a chain of ten stones. The black chain has seven freedoms. If a black stone were placed on any of these points, it would be included as part of the chain – in one case, (e5) the added black stone would increase the freedoms of the chain to eight. A stone on c5 or d2 would not influence the freedom. Occupation of any other point would decrease it to six.

Two Japanese workmen, photographed by Elliot Erwitt, play a game of Go in the traditional fashion, seated on the ground. They are playing on a typical board with short detachable legs, and a hollow depression cut under it to increase the resonance of the stones being placed on it. Cheap stones are often made of glass; the best sets have white stones of shell, black stones of slate.

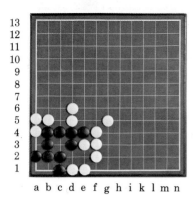

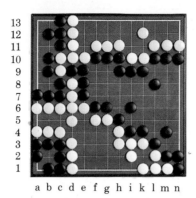

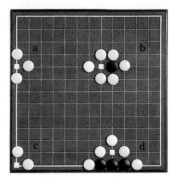

a b c d e f g h i k l m n   a b c d e f g h i k l m n

5: A chain is not necessarily made stronger by adding more stones. Of seven possible additions, there is only one point (e5) on which black can place a stone to give his chain more freedoms.

6: At the end of the game, each player counts the number of points in the territory he has surrounded. Here, black encircles 45 points: white's stones surround an area of 41 points.

7: If a black stone were placed on any of the surrounded points, marked by white squares on the board, it would be committing 'suicide' and be immediately captured and removed from the board.

Prisoners

It is not always necessary to totally 'kill' a chain. It often happens that a threatened chain or stone is not robbed of its last freedom, but remains on the board as a 'prisoner.' (The player who has defeated the chain may not want to waste a move to complete its capture when other moves on the board may be more important.)

At times, the encirclement of the chain may itself be defeated, and the chain subsequently liberated once again. Normally, however, a chain does not recover and remains a prisoner. It is counted as captured at the end of the game and removed from the board.

Scoring

The object of *Go* is to collect more points than the opponent. Points are scored in two ways: by occupying territory, and by capturing hostile stones. Controlling the greater territory on the board is the most important factor in play. To explain the term 'territory,' photograph 6 illustrates the final layout of an imaginary game.

At top left, black surrounds a territory of nine vacant points. At lower left is a corner of two points and, in the center, a large territory of 34 points. Therefore, black has a territory of 45 encircled points.

White has encircled an area of 41 points. If white captured one stone during the game and black captured none, black wins with 45 points to white's 42. Other facets of the end of the game will be discussed on page 47.

A reduced board is photographed here to simplify the explanation. A game of *Go* played on a standard board usually takes about an hour and a half. The 13-by-13 line board, shown here, can be used for a shorter game.

Live groups

As more stones are placed on the board, it might appear that all groups would eventually threaten each other, but it is possible to construct a group so that it cannot be captured. The black group at the top left of photograph 6, for instance, is totally encircled by white stones, but this black fortification is in no danger whatsoever. White can never take away the inside freedoms. Any white stones placed behind the black lines would soon be killed. Danger exists only when: (1) the group is too small, or too compact, or (2) when the space inside the group is so large that the enemy stones can create 'a state within a state.'

The construction of a secure or 'live' group is based on the formation of 'eyes.' But before eyes can be described, the concept of 'suicide' in the game must be defined.

Suicide

When a stone is placed on a point that has no freedoms at all, this stone may be committing suicide. In photograph 7, when a black stone is placed on any of the encircled points (marked by small squares), it is automatically killed, possibly together with several other black stones.

But when a stone in placed on an enclosed point, thereby robbing a hostile group of its last freedom, as illustrated in photograph 8, this is not a suicide. Instead the entire hostile group is killed and removed.

If black moves into the middle of the white territory shown in photograph 9, black loses his stone. But if, as in photograph 10, one black stone can rob the white group of its last freedom, black captures the entire chain of white stones.

Eyes

The white group in photograph 11 has two freedoms, two enclosed vacant points. If black attempts to occupy either of these vacant points, he commits suicide. Thus, it is impossible to capture the white group: a group with two 'eyes' is live, in other words, completely secure from capture.

In photograph 12, white achieves the same result with five less stones. It is easier to make eyes on the border of the playing board. The danger of the

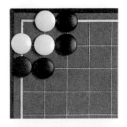

8: *It is not suicide when a stone is placed on an enclosed point and, by occupying that point, robs an enemy chain of its last freedom.*

9: *Black cannot kill the white group above in a single move, because the group has two freedoms.*

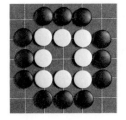

10: *Here, white has one freedom, and the entire chain is killed by one stone placed in the center.*

one-eye configuration is shown again in photograph 13.

White is helpless; black can place a stone on either of the inner points. If white captures the black stone, as in photograph 14, black can occupy the last vacant point on his next turn and kill the group. If white does not act, black still occupies the remaining space and captures the whole group.

In photograph 15, white must move to the center vacant point to secure the safety of two eyes. If it is black's turn to move, however, his best move is to

the same point – and the white chain is lost in the next few moves, no matter what white may attempt.

In photograph 16, white can make two eyes by placing stones on either f1 or e1; but the move is not urgently required. If black placed a stone at e1, white could move to f1, and vice versa. In this configuration, it would be a wasted move for white to make two eyes. There are probably more useful moves to be made, and white can always intervene if black attacks.

The basis of most *Go* problems is making the eyes or preventing them from being made, but for each game, the circumstances are different. It is only through practice that the player can learn how to deal with the various problems that arise in play.

Ko

To the inexperienced player, the so-called *ko* situation may be tricky but the rule is not really difficult.

In photograph 17, black can capture and create the second configuration. If white captures in return, the first configuration is formed again. The *ko* rule prevents indefinite repetition of these moves. The rule states that, in a configuration in which capturing for the second time would result in the same configuration that existed before the first capture, a different move must be made.

In the case of photograph 17, once black has captured, white cannot capture in return, but must make a move somewhere else on the board. In the next move, black can fill the *ko*, thereby ending the situation. If, for some reason, black does not fill in the *ko*, white can, if he wishes, capture 'in *ko*,' since he waited a turn. As it is still a *ko* situation, now black would not be allowed to capture in return, but must wait a turn, allowing white the opportunity to fill in the space.

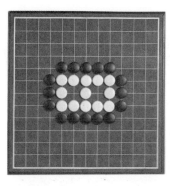

11: *The white group above has two 'eyes' – that is, two enclosed vacant points. If white attempts to occupy either of these points, it is suicide.*

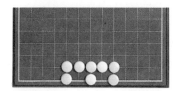

12: *Another 'live' group shows that it is easier, and takes less stones, to construct a group with two eyes on the points at the edge of the board.*

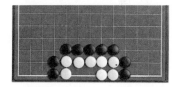

13: *Though the white group above has two inner freedoms, it has only one eye, and therefore is extremely vulnerable to attack by black stones.*

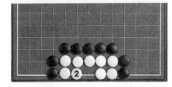

14: *Black attacks the vulnerable group, and is immediately captured. But white has only one freedom left, and black captures on the next move.*

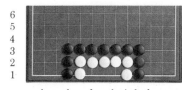

15: *A white stone must be placed on g1, making two eyes for the white group, before black plays a stone on that point   a move which ruins white's chances to save his surrounded chain of stones.*

47

This rule applies only to genuine *ko* configurations. Photograph 18 does not show such a configuration. Though white may capture two black stones, and black immediately capture a white stone, the original configuration is not repeated after the two moves.

Seki

Seki happens when the players are in a deadlock on some part of the board. In photograph 19, neither player can attack without seriously endangering his own group. Such situations remain on the board untouched. The battle in this territory is a draw, and the area (in this case, two points) cannot be claimed by anyone.

In photograph 20, the first of the configurations is a clear *seki* situation. By making another move, both white and black would bring their group into *atari*. The second configuration, however, is no *seki*, as black can attack and capture white's whole group.

Playing with a handicap

The result of a game between two beginners is largely decided by chance, but with experienced players, even a slightly better player will repeatedly beat his opponent. With a handicap, the difference in game experience can be accurately resolved, with the result that both players must really exert themselves to win.

In any game, black has the first move and has, in fact, a handicap of one stone. With a greater handicap, the stones are positioned as follows: two stones d4, q16; three stones d4, q4, q16; four stones d4, d16, q4, q16; five stones d4, d16, k10, q4, q16; six stones d4, d10, d16, q4, q10, q16; seven stones d4, d10, d16, k10, q4, q10, q16; eight stones d4, d10, d16, k4, k16, q4, q10, q16; nine stones d4, d10, d16, k4, k10, k16, q4, q10, q16. The player who receives a one-stone handicap is not obliged to place the stone on any particular point. Otherwise the placing

6
5
4
3
2
1

a b c d e f g h i k l m n

16: White should not waste a move to make eyes here: no matter where black places a stone, he could not successfully attack this white group.

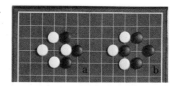

17: This is a ko *situation: black kills the white stone, turning position 'a' into 'b.' Then white kills the black stone, recreating position 'a.'*

18: This is not a genuine ko *situation – though both black and white can capture, the original configuration is not repeated after two moves.*

19: A seki or deadlock situation occurs in an area of the board when neither player can attack without seriously endangering his own pieces.

20: Position 'b' is a seki: *neither player can safely move a stone into the configuration's inner freedoms, but in position 'a', black can capture the inner white chain—therefore it is not* seki.

of the handicap stones is considered to be black's first move, and white then proceeds to play.

End of the game

In every game, there arrives a moment when it is no longer possible to capture more territory or protect against hostile attacks. Photograph 21 shows such a game on a small board. There is now no advantage to further moves in one's own territory (that would simply reduce the territory), while a move in hostile territory would give the opponent another prisoner. The fight, therefore, is over. At this stage, players begin to occupy those points which cannot be claimed by either side. When these *dameh* points are filled, the hostile chains are joined without interruption.

When the last *dameh* point is occupied the game is finished. Prisoners are then taken from the board. (In this photograph the prisoners are marked with a circle drawn on the stone.)

If there is a difference of opinion on whether a certain group can be killed – a question which frequently arises between beginners – the game is continued. It will soon be resolved, without affecting the final result. (In resolving questions of this kind, players may not pass and must match moves, stone for stone.) For example, the four white stones at lower left of photograph 21 could be captured, but the spaces in his own territory that black would occupy in making the capture (thereby losing that much enclosed area) would be matched by the same loss on white's side: since the players in this case must make alternate moves, white would also have to place a stone in his own territory each time.

Photograph 22 shows the situation after the *dameh* points (marked 1, 2, 3, and 4) are occupied and the imprisoned stones are removed from the board. At

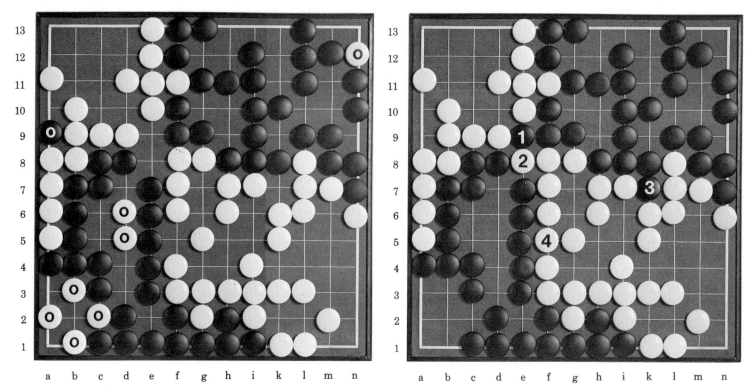

21: The end of a game – the territory is claimed and there is no longer any point in attacking. The marked stones above are 'prisoners' which are taken away after the dameh points are filled.

22: The neutral points, called dameh points, are filled in. These points, marked with numbers on the board above, connect the hostile chains into unbroken walls around the claimed territory.

Enthusiasts in Tokyo meet at a public Go-playing house, below, for intensive game practice.

this point, the players begin to count their score. The stones which were captured during the game and set aside are now counted; white has captured twelve of black's stones and black has killed 13 of the white stones. The score for white is: these twelve captured stones, one prisoner, and a territory of 36 points, making a total of 49 points. Black's score is 13 stones, seven prisoners, and a territory of 33 points, totaling 53 points. Black wins by a margin of 4 points.

Counting can be simplified by placing all captured stones in the other player's territory. This makes no difference to the final count, as the player loses a prisoner with each stone so placed, and his opponent loses a point of territory.

Materials

A plywood board, $19\frac{1}{4}$ inches square, $\frac{3}{8}$ inch thick.

Four plywood boards, 9 by 20 inches, $\frac{3}{8}$ inch thick.

Four lengths of pine, $\frac{3}{8}$ inch square: two $19\frac{1}{4}$ inches long, two $18\frac{1}{2}$ inches long.

Four half-round molding strips, $\frac{3}{8}$ by 20 inches.

Six wooden balls, $2\frac{1}{2}$ inches in diameter.

Two plywood boards, 4 inches square, $\frac{3}{8}$ inch thick.

White plastic adhesive tape, $\frac{1}{16}$ inch wide.

Four wooden dowels, $1\frac{1}{2}$ inches long, $\frac{3}{8}$ inch in diameter.

Wood glue.

Two dozen wire nails, $\frac{3}{4}$ inch long.

Wood stain: 'walnut' and 'teak.'

White gloss paint.

Clear varnish.

Tools

A ruler, pencil, scroll saw, backsaw, hammer, paintbrush, scissors, artist's camel-hair brush, vise, protractor, and electric drill or brace with $\frac{3}{8}$-inch bit.

How to Make the Game

Place one of the 9-by-20-inch boards horizontally before you on the work table. On each long edge, measure and mark points $\frac{3}{8}$ inch from each corner. Draw vertical lines connecting those points opposite each other. On each of these lines and on the 9-inch edges beside them, measuring from the bottom edge, mark points at $\frac{3}{4}$-inch intervals. Draw ruled lines connecting the points on the lines with the corresponding points on the edges beside them. Repeat these steps on the remaining three 9-by-20-inch boards.

With the scroll saw, cut out six alternating sections on one side of each board, starting with the bottom section. On the other side of each board, cut out six alternating sections, starting with the top section, as in photograph 23. Spread a light coat of glue along all the finger joints of the four boards. Join the boards together in a frame, so that the fingers of one dovetail with the fingers of the other.

On each of the 4-inch-square boards, draw one ruled diagonal line, connecting opposite corners of the square. With the backsaw, cut each of the boards in two pieces along the diagonal line. You now have four triangles, 4 by 4 by $5\frac{1}{2}$ inches. Apply glue to the 4-inch edges of each triangle, and set the triangles in the corners of the frame, flush with the edges of the frame, as in photograph 24. Nail the triangles to the frame with two nails, driven through each end of the free edge of the triangle into the frame. Allow the glue to dry thoroughly.

23: Hold the plywood sideboard steady with one hand, while you use a scroll saw to carefully cut out the 'fingers' for the corner joints.

24: After sawing the plywood squares in half to make four triangles, nail a triangle into each corner of one end of the game-table frame.

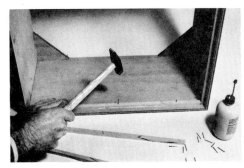

25: Measure and draw lines $\frac{3}{8}$ inch from the edge of the other end of the frame, then nail the pine slats inside the frame at these lines.

26: After measuring the 19-by-19-line grid on the board's surface, mark the lines with narrow tape and paint tiny dots on the handicap points.

This Go board is a rewarding crafts project. The stones are sold in their classical wooden bowls.

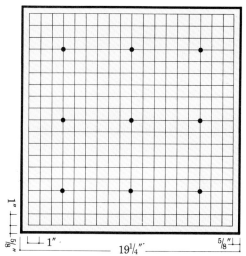

Figure B: Mark the 19¹⁄₄-inch-square board as shown above. Be sure to paint each of the nine 'handicap points' marked on the illustration.

Turn the frame so that the triangles are at the bottom. Inside the frame, ³⁄₈ inch from the top edge, mark points at opposite ends of each of the four sides. Draw ruled lines connecting the points on each board. Nail one of the 19¹⁄₄-inch-long pieces of pine to the inner surface of one side of the frame, ³⁄₈ inch from the edge, using the line as a border guide (see photograph 24). Nail the other 19¹⁄₄-inch length of wood to the opposite side of the frame. Use three nails, spaced at equal distances, for each piece of wood. Fasten the remaining two lengths of pine to the other sides of the frame in the same way.

Stain the outside surfaces of the frame 'walnut' and the 19¹⁄₄-inch-square board 'teak.' Allow both to dry thoroughly.

Place the square board on the work table, stained side up. Lightly mark points on each side that are ⁵⁄₈ inch from each corner. Connect points on opposite sides of the board with straight lines, making an inner 18-inch square. Mark points at 1-inch intervals on each side of the inner square, measuring from the corners.

Connect corresponding points on opposite sides of the square with straight lines, dividing the square into 324 cells.
Go over the lines drawn with ¹⁄₁₆-inch strips of white plastic tape, as shown in photograph 26. With the tip of the camel-hair brush, paint white dots at the following cross-points on the board: on the fourth, tenth, and sixteenth horizontal lines (counting from the bottom) where each of them intersects the fourth, tenth, and sixteenth verticals (counting from the left).

Apply glue to the top edges of the lengths of pine inside the frame, as well as the ³⁄₈-inch space above them. Position the game board on the frame so that it rests on the pine strips. Allow the glue to dry thoroughly.

Clamp one of the molding strips in a vise, so that its flat side is facing up. Line up the perpendicular of the protractor with the left edge of the strip, the base of the protractor in line with the bottom edge of the surface. Mark a point on the top edge that is 45 degrees from the bottom corner. Draw a line from the corner to that point. Do the same thing at the right end of the board, marking a 45-degree angle to the left. Cut through these lines with a backsaw. Repeat these steps on the remaining three molding strips.

Stain the strips 'walnut' and allow them to dry thoroughly. Apply glue to the bottom sides and mitered ends of the four molding strips. Join the strips to make a square frame on the top of the game board. The outer edges of the molding frame should exactly match the outer edges of the top of the platform. Allow the glue to dry.

Clamp one of the wooden balls in a vise. Mark a point on the top of the ball and, from this point, draw a circumference line bisecting the ball. With the backsaw, saw the ball in half along this line. Repeat these steps on another wooden ball. Clamp a half-ball in the vise so that its flat side faces downward. Mark a point in the center of its round side and, placing the point of the bit there, drill a hole ³⁄₄ inch deep. Repeat these steps on the remaining half-balls.

Clamp one of the whole balls in the vise. Mark a point on the ball and drill a hole in the ball, ³⁄₄ inch deep. Repeat these steps on the other three balls. Apply glue to one of the 1¹⁄₂-inch dowels and insert half of it into the hole drilled in one of the half-balls. Place glue on the other half of the dowel and insert it into the hole in a whole ball, connecting the two so that they are flush together. Repeat these steps to join the other balls and half-balls. Allow the glue to dry.

Turn the game box over so that the playing board is underneath. Apply glue to the flat sides of the half-balls and position them on each of the four triangles at the corners of the frame. Allow the glue to dry thoroughly. Stain the four ball sections 'walnut' and allow them to dry.

Varnish all the outer surfaces of the game box and allow to dry.

Figure C: It is relatively simple to assemble the components of the Go game table, as illustrated above. Once the finger-jointed sideboards are fastened together, it is no problem to fit the finished playing board into the square wooden frame, and then attach the handsome ball feet.

Go-bang

About the Game

A game of *Go* has been played. No one wants another game just yet, but the board and pieces are still on the table; that's the time to play *Go-bang*. The kibitzers, the children, everyone can play, for *Go-bang* is quite simply tic-tac-toe on a grand scale: the first player to get five stones in a straight line wins. That is not to say that *Go-bang* has no strategy – playing this simple game can be developed into a fine art.

How to Play the Game

This is a game for two players, each having either black stones or white. Most players use the board and stones of *Go*, but any surface ruled off into a minimum of 13 by 13 squares will do. Players take turns at placing a single stone at a time. The game can be played in either of two ways: by placing the stones within the squares or, as in *Go*, on the intersections of the lines. Once played, a stone is not moved. There is no capture. The winner is the first player who forms a row of five adjacent stones, horizontally, vertically, or diagonally.

When the Japanese play *Go-bang*, they have one peculiarity: they put the fifth stone in a row not with a shout of triumph, but very quietly, hoping the opponent will not notice that he has just been beaten. Then, sighing and shaking their heads in apparent distress, but quietly complicating things all the time, they try for another winning row of five.

There is an optional rule of play for masters of the game. Two (and only two) stones of the same color may be captured and removed from the board if they are caught between two enemy stones. Thus, if there is a row in any direction consisting of, for example, a white stone followed by two black stones, and it is white's turn to move, he may place a white stone on the other side of the two black ones and remove them. There is no 'suicide,' however; stones placed inside an enemy 'bracket' are quite safe and remain on the board.

From the salon to the steam bath, Go-bang *is enjoyed anywhere, anytime in Japan. In the photograph above, taken at the turn of the century, two Japanese women finish a game of* Go-bang *before taking tea. Left, a modern game of* Go-bang *is played in the considerably less formal surroundings of a communal steam bath.*

Senet

About the Game

Senet, written 〰〰〰 ⊔⊔⊔⊔ in hieroglyphics, was by far the most popular and important of the many board games of ancient Egypt. The archeological evidence points to the fact that it was played by people at all levels of Egyptian society. *Senet* diagrams scratched into tombs and temples indicate that watchmen, priests, and building workers whiled away their time with it. Peasants played it in the sand, with stones or improvised ceramic pieces – as games like *yoté* are to this day (see page 90). But the pharaohs played it on magnificent boards made of rare woods, ivory, and faience. Some of these superb examples of Egyptian craftsmanship, such as the one found in the tomb of Tutankhamon (c. 1347–1339 B.C.), have come down to us in a state of perfect preservation.

The wall paintings of many tombs show the deceased at a festive dinner party, attended by dancers and musicians, playing *senet* with his wife or some other member of his family. Rameses III (c. 1182–1151 B.C.) had himself portrayed on the high gate of the temple of Medinet Haboo playing *senet* with two ladies of his harem. Egyptian religious writings mention games of *senet* that are played by the spirits of the departed in the underworld.

How to Play the Game

None of the surviving Egyptian documents tell us exactly how the game is played, but the following rules, based on the available evidence, have been devised by the Swiss archeologist, Gustave Jéquier. The main points of his system have been corroborated by exhaustive research into *senet* recently undertaken by the German Egyptologist, Edgar B. Pusch.

An Egyptian gentleman plays senet *against an invisible opponent while his wife peers over his shoulder in this illustration from a 3,000-year-old papyrus. The picture refers to the religious and mystical meaning of the game: played with the help of the gods, the moves of the pieces on the board represented the wanderings of the human soul in the underworld.*

Senet is a race game for two players. Each player has five counters, black or white. The playing pieces move over a boustrophedon track – that is, with lines alternating the way the ox plows (see figure, opposite). To begin, the pieces are placed on squares 1 through 10. The white pieces occupy the odd-numbered squares, the black pieces those that are even-numbered.

Movement of pieces is determined by throws of four two-sided dice. The dice score as follows:
One white side up… 1
Two white sides up… 2
Three white sides up… 3
Four white sides up… 4
Four black sides up… 6

Players alternate throwing the dice, until one throws a 1. This player has the black playing pieces and moves the piece on square 10 to square 11. After the first move, the player continues to throw the dice. If he throws 1, 4, or 6, he moves any of his pieces the indicated number of squares along the game track, and throws again. If he throws a 2 or 3, he moves a piece the indicated number of

squares, and the turn passes to his opponent. The second player must make his first move from square 9, but with subsequent throws of the dice, may move any of his playing pieces. Each turn ends with a throw of 2 or 3.

If a piece lands on a square occupied by an opposing piece, the opposing piece is 'attacked' and moved back to the square just vacated by the piece in play. Two pieces of the same color may not occupy one square, but two pieces which occupy consecutive squares (such as 18 and 19) protect each other from attack by opposing pieces. Three pieces of the same color which are placed in a row form a protected blockade: they can neither be attacked nor be passed by enemy pieces, though they do not block the progress of pieces of the same color.

Any dice throw which cannot be used to make a forward move must be used to move a piece in the reverse direction on the game track. (A piece may not move backward onto a square occupied by another piece of either color.) If no move can be made in either direction, the turn ceases.

Square 27, marked by an 'X,' is the 'trap.' Any piece landing on this square must return to square 1 (or if that is occupied, the first vacant square on the track) and begin the journey again. Squares 26, 28, 29, and 30 are 'havens' where pieces are not vulnerable to attack by enemy playing pieces.

When a player has moved all his pieces into the last (exit) row of the board, he may begin to take them off by landing them exactly on square 30. If any of the pieces on the exit row are attacked and thrown back to the first or second row, the pieces of the same color which remain on the board may not be moved off until the lagging piece returns to the third row.

The player who first moves all his pieces off the board is the winner. In a series of games, score may be kept by awarding the winning player of each game 1 point for any enemy pieces still on the last row (unless they are in haven squares), 2 points for pieces in the second row, and 3 points for those in the first row.

This senet *board is an attractive project for the home carpenter. It includes a convenient drawer for storing the five spherical and five cubic playing pieces, and the long black-and-white dice. The symbols on the bottom row are burned into the wood with the tip of a soldering iron.*

1: To make the cupboard drawer, glue the three mitered pine sections to the 6-by-$4\frac{3}{8}$-inch board. Secure with wire nails while the glue dries.

2: Glue the wooden tiles into the frames on the board, positioning them so that the run of their grain contrasts from one square to another.

Materials

Two plywood boards, $4\frac{3}{8}$ by 16 inches, $\frac{3}{8}$ inch thick.
Two white pine boards, 2 by $16\frac{3}{8}$ inches, $\frac{1}{4}$ inch thick.
Two white pine boards, 2 by $4\frac{3}{4}$ inches, $\frac{1}{4}$ inch thick.
One white pine board, $\frac{7}{8}$ inch by $4\frac{3}{8}$ inches, $\frac{3}{16}$ inch thick.
Two pieces of wood, 16 inches long, $\frac{1}{4}$ inch square.
Twenty-seven pieces of wood, $1\frac{3}{8}$ inches long, $\frac{1}{4}$ inch square.
One white pine board, 6 by $4\frac{3}{8}$ inches, $\frac{3}{16}$ inch thick.
Two white pine boards, $\frac{7}{8}$ inch by 6 inches, $\frac{3}{16}$ inch thick.
Thirty three-ply squares, $1\frac{3}{8}$ inches square, $\frac{3}{16}$ inch thick.
Ten white pine cubes, $\frac{3}{4}$ inch on each edge.
Ten wooden balls, $\frac{3}{4}$ inch in diameter.
Ten wire nails, $\frac{3}{4}$ inch long.
Two wooden dowels, 4 inches long, $\frac{1}{2}$ inch in diameter.
Flat black paint. Wood glue.

Tools

A vise, protractor, pencil, ruler, backsaw, wood rasp, hammer, soldering iron, sandpaper, and paintbrush.

How to Make the Game

Clamp a white pine board, 2 by $16\frac{3}{8}$ inches, in a vise so that the narrow $\frac{3}{16}$-inch edge is upward. Line up the perpendicular of the protractor with the left edge of this surface; the base of the protractor should be in line with the bottom edge of the board. Mark a point on the top edge that is 45 degrees from the corner. Draw a line from the corner to that point. Do the same at the right end of the board, measuring and marking a 45-degree angle toward the left.

If your protractor is too wide for this, make a 45-degree angle by marking a point on the top edge, the same distance from the left corner as the width of the narrow face of the board – i.e. $\frac{1}{4}$ inch. Join this mark to the bottom left corner with a straight line.

Using a backsaw or wood rasp, miter both ends, cutting along the lines drawn. Repeat all these steps with the remaining 2-by-$16\frac{3}{8}$-inch board, both 2-by-$4\frac{3}{4}$-inch boards, the $\frac{7}{8}$-by-$4\frac{3}{8}$-inch board, and at only one end of both the 6-by-$\frac{7}{8}$-inch boards.

Apply glue to one mitered end of each of the two 2-by-$16\frac{3}{8}$-inch boards. Join these ends to the mitered ends of the 2-by-$4\frac{3}{4}$-inch boards. Apply glue to three edges of one of the $4\frac{3}{8}$-by-16-inch plywood boards, and position the frame around it so that the mitered ends of the frame extend beyond the length of the board. To further secure the board, hammer several wire nails, evenly spaced, along the sides and at the end. Allow the glue to dry, then remove the nails.

Place the remaining plywood board horizontally in front of you. Place the ruler along the top edge and mark off, from the left corner, a series of alternate measurements: $1\frac{3}{8}$ inches, $\frac{1}{4}$ inch, $1\frac{3}{8}$ inches, $\frac{1}{4}$ inch, $1\frac{3}{8}$ inches, and so on to the other end of the board. Repeat these steps at the bottom edge and along both sides. Connect all opposite points with straight lines so that the board is divided into thirty $1\frac{3}{8}$-inch squares, $\frac{1}{4}$ inch apart.

On the inside surfaces of the three-sided frame, mark several points $\frac{3}{16}$ inch from the top (open) edge. Apply glue to three edges of the remaining plywood board. Position it in the frame so that its top marked side is flush with the three $\frac{1}{4}$-inch points marked on the inside of the frame. To secure this piece while the glue is drying, hammer three wire nails into the sides of the frame. After the glue has dried completely, remove the nails.
Apply glue to the mitered ends of the two 6-by-$\frac{7}{8}$-inch boards and join these to the mitered ends of the $\frac{7}{8}$-by-$4\frac{3}{8}$-inch board.

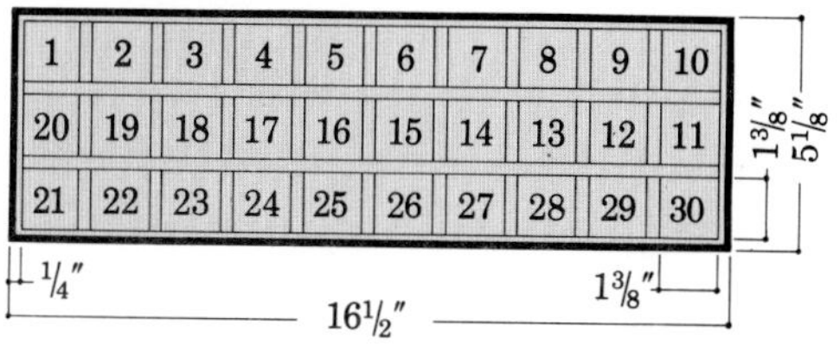

1 2 3 4 5 6 7 8 9 10
20 19 18 17 16 15 14 13 12 11
21 22 23 24 25 26 27 28 29 30
1¼″
1⅜″
16½″
1⅜″
5⅛″

After the top board of the game box is measured and marked, it will resemble the drawing above: thirty $1\frac{3}{8}$-inch squares, $\frac{1}{4}$ inch apart. The squares in the drawing are numbered only to clarify the game rules, which begin on page 53.

At the same time, glue the bottom of the three-sided frame to the 6-by-$4\frac{3}{4}$-inch board, as in photograph 1, so their dimensions match exactly. To secure the board while the glue dries, hammer several wire nails, evenly spaced, along the sides and end of this top surface. Allow the glue to dry thoroughly and remove the nails.

Slide this drawer, back end first, partly into the game board box. Apply glue to the three exposed ends of this drawer. Position the remaining 2-by-$4\frac{3}{4}$-inch board, its mitered ends facing inward, against these three ends of the drawer so that when the drawer is shut, the mitered board is flush with the mitered ends of the game board box. Hammer wire nails through the glued surfaces to hold them while they dry, and remove the nails later.

Apply glue to one side of the two 16-inch-long wood strips. Apply these glued surfaces on the two long horizontal paths of the same size, marked on the top of the plywood board.

Apply glue to one side of each of the $1\frac{3}{8}$-inch wood strips and place them on the paths of corresponding dimensions marked on the plywood board. Allow the glue to dry.

Apply glue to one flat side of each of the three-ply squares and position them on the 30 squares on the board, between the lengths of wood (see photograph 2).

On the bottom row of squares, in the sixth, seventh, eighth, and ninth squares from the left, burn in these symbols with a soldering iron: ♁, X, III, II. Use the photographed model as a guide. Varnish the finished board if you wish.

To make the dice, clamp one of the dowels vertically in a vise. With a backsaw, cut down the center of the dowel to make two lengths, each with one flat and one semicircular surface. Repeat these steps with the other dowel. Sand down any rough surfaces, and paint the rounded side of each die black.

To make the playing pieces, sandpaper each of the $\frac{3}{4}$-inch-square blocks until all edges are smooth. Paint the cubes black and allow to dry. With a wood rasp, file down one side of each of the ten wooden balls until it has a flat edge of about $\frac{1}{2}$ inch in diameter.

Royal Game of Ur

About the Game

The remarkable work of art shown on the opposite page is one of the oldest game boards in the world. It was last used some 4,500 years ago in the Sumerian city of Ur – the biblical Ur of the Chaldees. Now it belongs among the major treasures of the British Museum, London.

During the intervening centuries, while the very existence of Sumerian civilization was forgotten, the board lay undisturbed under a mound of ruins and rubble overlooking the lower reaches of the Euphrates. It was brought to light, finally, by the British archeologist Sir Leonard Woolley, when he unearthed the greatest hoard of ancient art ever discovered in Mesopotamia (the land that lies between the Tigris and the Euphrates). As leader of a joint British Museum-University of Pennsylvania expedition to Ur in the 1920's, Sir Leonard excavated a series of mysterious mass graves – the tombs either of royal personages, or of priests sacrificed to propitiate the gods.

A number of elaborately inlaid game boards were among the treasures of Ur. The one pictured here, according to Sir Leonard, is 'the most striking example found.' The game seems to have been a favorite with the Sumerian upper classes, since the boards only turn up in rich or royal graves. Presumably they were placed in the tombs so that the souls of the dead would also have a pastime with which to while away eternity in the next world.

The archeological evidence indicates that the 'royal game' of Ur was played with two sets of seven counters, black and white. The men found with this board were either of shell with lapis lazuli dots or black shale with shell dots. Six pyramid-shaped dice were found, each die having two marked and two plain corners. Although no written rules for the game have been preserved, the method of play can be deduced from the shape of the board and other evidence. The game of Ur, in fact, is probably the original ancestor of the backgammon group of games: in this, as in other areas, the Sumerians made vital beginnings that have had significant consequences. It was they who invented cuneiform writing, and their method of keeping time – 24 hours, 60 minutes – is with us yet. Dividing a circle into 360 degrees was alsó a Sumerian invention.

Now on display in the Sumerian section of the British Museum, this game board was discovered by Sir Leonard Woolley in the tombs of Ur.

The wooden game board at right, a handsome replica of the ancient Sumerian race game, is an enjoyable crafts project.

How to Play the Game

The royal game of Ur is a race game. The winner is the first player to move all seven of his men on and off the board, along a route of 20 squares, shown in the accompanying diagram.

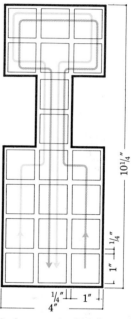

Though no rules have survived for the game of Ur, a possible method of play is described here. Each player's counters follow one of the paths (red or blue) shown on the game diagram above.

In addition to seven black or white men, each player is equipped with three pyramid-shaped dice. Each die is marked on two of its four corners and, when the dice are thrown, the score is as follows:
Three marked tips... 5 points
Three unmarked tips... 4 points
Two unmarked tips... 0 points
One unmarked tip... 1 point

To begin the game, the two players throw the dice for the privilege of the first turn. A counter may be moved onto the board with a dice score of 1 or 5, which will bring the counter to the first or fifth square on the track. These squares and two others on the board are decorated with 'rosette' designs. A counter may also be entered on the first square if another counter of the same color lands on any rosette square on the board. Once on the board, the men move along the course according to the dice scores. When a piece has completed the first 14 squares of its journey, it is turned over, marked side down, to differentiate it from the counters going 'up' the center row of squares on the board.

There is no limit to the number of counters which may be stacked on any square, but once the counters are in the center track and the circuit at the top of the board, they may be attacked. If a counter lands on a square occupied by one or more opposing counters, those counters are taken off the board and must begin all over again. The rosette squares and the exit square on the track are safety squares where counters of both colors may rest without danger of attack. 'Rising' counters may only attack other rising counters, and counters that have been turned over may only be attacked by other reversed counters.

In order to go off the board, a piece must land exactly on the exit square. Once there, a throw of 4 will take it off. If a player has more than one counter piled on the exit square, all his men may be moved off in one throw.

Each player has three pyramid-shaped dice. The dice scores are counted by the number of marked tips that come up each time they are thrown.

Materials

A pine block, $10\frac{1}{4}$ by 4 by $1\frac{1}{4}$ inches.
A wooden dowel, $\frac{3}{4}$ inch in diameter, 4 inches long.
Flat paint: red, blue, black, and white.
Heavy white paper.
Modeling clay.
All-purpose glue.

Tools

A pencil, ruler, backsaw, chisel, sandpaper, soldering or woodburning iron, artist's camel-hair brush, vise, and scissors.

How to Make the Game

On one $10\frac{1}{4}$-by-4-inch side of the wood block, draw a line $\frac{1}{4}$ inch from each edge, making an inner rectangle of $9\frac{3}{4}$ by $3\frac{1}{2}$ inches. Beginning at the corners of this new rectangle, mark each line with 1-inch measurements at $\frac{1}{4}$-inch intervals: 1 inch, $\frac{1}{4}$ inch, 1 inch, $\frac{1}{4}$ inch, etc. Connect opposite points horizontally and vertically, dividing the surface into 1-inch squares with $\frac{1}{4}$-inch borders.

Mark off an area $2\frac{1}{4}$ by $1\frac{1}{4}$ inches on each long side of the board by darkening the lines around the third and fourth squares from the bottom. Include the space between them and the border that extends to the edge of the block. These two areas should be opposite each other, leaving the $1\frac{1}{2}$-inch-wide neck of the finished board between them. Extend these markings down the sides of the block. These lines will then serve as cutting guides.

With a backsaw, cut into the lines on the sides of the block to a depth of $1\frac{1}{4}$ inches. To remove the sawed sections, place a chisel on the uncut $2\frac{1}{4}$-inch line on each side of the marked surface of the board. Hammer on the handle with the heel of your hand as you move the chisel blade along the line. Smooth down all rough edges and splintered areas with sandpaper.

Decorate each square freehand with a pencil, following the patterns on the Sumerian board on page 56 and the model on the previous page. Burn in the designs and border lines with a wood-burning tool or the tip of a soldering iron. Paint the top and sides of the board in colors that correspond to the original. Coat with varnish and allow to dry thoroughly.

Lay the dowel on its side and clamp it in a vise. Using a backsaw cut it into 14 coin-like sections about $\frac{1}{8}$ inch thick. (The length specified is more than you will actually use, to allow for mistakes and a bit for the vise to hold.) Sandpaper each piece down smooth. With the Sumerian pieces as a guide, mark five points on one side of each piece and burn in the points with the tip of a soldering iron. Paint seven of the pieces white and seven black. Paint the

1: On each square of the board, draw a freehand design in pencil, following the design of the inlay on the original Sumerian board on page 56.

2: With a wood-burning tool or the tip of a soldering iron, carefully burn the markings into the top surface and sides of the block of wood.

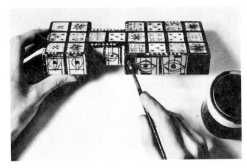

3: Following the colors of the original game board, paint in the designs on the top and sides with an artist's fine camel-hair brush.

burned-in pips on the white pieces black and the pips of the black pieces white.

To make the pyramid-shaped dice, cut six paper copies of the pattern at right. Bend the paper at all the dotted lines, but glue only two of the overlaps on each of the six dice. When the glue is dry, fill each of the cones with modeling wax. Pack the wax in tightly, taking care not to rip the paper, then fold over the top flap and glue the last overlap.

Paint each die in white gloss paint. When the paint is dry, mark two corners of each die with red gloss paint. Allow to dry.

Nine Men's Morris

This nine men's morris board was made in Germany about 1600. The board, with a diamond-shaped playing field, is intricately worked in birch wood and black-stained oak, with pewter inlay.

About the Game

Nine men's morris is one of the oldest board games in the world. At the temple of Kurna in Egypt, a morris board is incised on a roofing slab, probably carved by the workmen who built the temple around 1400 B.C. A morris diagram was found in the excavations of the first city of Troy. Another board, carved into a stone at a Bronze Age burial site in County Wicklow, Ireland, suggests that early traders from Greece or Phoenicia brought the game to northern Europe. Centuries later, it was important among the Vikings: a board was placed in the funeral ship of a king buried about 900 A.D. at Gokstad, Norway.

The first morris boards were like the ones used today, consisting of concentric squares with lines intersecting their sides. In the fourteenth century, when the game was immensely popular in the courts of Europe, a variant was devised in which diagonal lines were added to the corners of the squares. A twelve-man version of morris, using this new board, was brought to America by early British settlers. The game in the United States is still played on this board, and includes a rule that allows a 'mill,' or row of three counters, to be made on the diagonal corner lines.

Morris players from the game book of Alfonso X sit cross-legged in the traditional Moorish fashion.

Morris is mentioned not only in King Alfonso's thirteenth-century *Book of Games*, but in such diverse sources as the Talmud and Shakespeare's *A Midsummer Night's Dream*. Indeed, morris players appear frequently in the medieval writings of France, Germany, and Britain.

In Germany the game has always been called *Mühle* (mill). In France, it was originally called *mérelles*, but in modern French, it is also known as *jeu de moulin* (game of mill). The English 'morris' is probably adapted from the medieval French, for early versions of the game were called 'merills' or 'morell.' In addition to nine men's morris, several other versions of the game have been widely played: they are known as five-penny morris and three men's morris, according to the number of men used. The nine men's morris presented here uses the diagram prevalent in Europe today, without the diagonal lines.

How to Play the Game

Nine men's morris is a game for two players, each having nine black or white men. The game is played on the 24 'points' on the board. These points are the corners of the three squares and the intersections of the squares with the lines crossing their sides. Before beginning the game, players draw lots for the first turn.

There are two parts to a game of morris. First the players take turns placing a man on any empty point of the board. In the second part, when all the pieces are on the board, a turn is taken by moving a piece to an adjacent vacant point. In both the placement and movement of the men, the object is to form a 'mill' or row of three pieces on a line. Every time a player makes a mill, he may remove one of his opponent's men. Unless there are no other pieces to take, a player may not take a piece from a mill made by his opponent. Once a piece is removed from the board, it does not return into play.

A mill may be 'opened' by moving one of the three pieces off the line, 'closed' by returning the piece to its former position. Thus a new mill is formed, and the player is entitled to remove another opposing piece from the board.

The game is won when a player either reduces his opponent's forces to two men, or blocks all his opponent's men from making further moves. (Some players agree to let the last three pieces move 'wild,' that is, from any point to any other point.)

Two young Spanish noblemen – with friends to hold their lances and lend advice – play nine men's morris at the thirteenth-century court of Alfonso 'The Learned' in Seville. They are using dice, a method of play that was eliminated from later versions of this ancient board game.

Materials

A plywood board, 16 inches square, $\frac{1}{2}$ inch thick.
Walnut stain.
A roll of yellow plastic adhesive tape, cut into $\frac{1}{8}$-inch strips.
Clear varnish.
Four strips of picture-frame molding, $16\frac{1}{2}$ inches long, 1 inch wide on one side, $\frac{1}{2}$ inch wide on the other side, and $\frac{1}{4}$ inch thick.
Wood glue.

Tools

A pencil, ruler, paintbrush, scissors, vise, protractor, and backsaw.

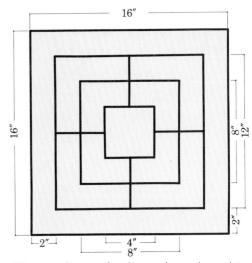

The game diagram for nine men's morris consists of three concentric squares, connected by straight lines that intersect each side of the squares.

How to Make the Game

Place the ruler on one edge of the plywood board and, measuring from the corner, make pencil marks at 2-inch intervals. Repeat this step on the remaining three edges of the board.

Place the ruler vertically on the board and draw light pencil lines connecting the points opposite each other on the top and bottom edges. Place the ruler horizontally and connect the corresponding points on the right and left edges.

Following the pattern, opposite, darken lines which are the boundaries of the three concentric squares and the four lines that intersect their sides. Then paint a light coat of walnut stain on the board surface and allow to dry thoroughly.

Cover the lines you have darkened on the board with the strips of yellow plastic tape, cut to the proper measurements. You may further decorate the board with thinner strips of tape placed on either side of these lines, as shown in the example below. Varnish the face of the board to secure the tape; allow to dry.

Clamp the middle of the 1-inch side of the picture-frame molding in a vise. The ½-inch side is now flat before you, the cornered edge of the molding lying toward you. At the left end of the molding, line up the perpendicular of the protractor with the edge of the upright ½-inch side, so that the base of the protractor is in line with the cornered ridge of the molding. Mark a point on the top edge of the ½-inch side that is 45 degrees from the cornered edge. Draw a line from the corner edge to that point. Do the same on the right end of the molding, measuring and marking a 45-degree angle toward the left. Using a backsaw, miter both sides of the left end of the molding simultaneously while sawing along the line drawn. Do the same at the right end of the molding. Prepare the remaining molding strips for miter joints, following the steps just given.

Spread glue on the inner sides of these strips, then fasten them to the sides of the board so that the ends of the ½-inch sides join correctly. Place the board face down on a table and allow the glue to dry thoroughly.

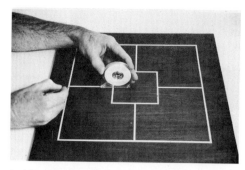

1: After painting the board with a light coat of walnut stain, cover the board markings with narrow strips of yellow plastic adhesive tape.

2: Varnish the board to secure the tape permanently and allow to dry before gluing on the mitered strips of picture-frame molding.

Both black and white have formed mills in a nine men's morris game. The attractive board is an easy-to-make project for home craftsmen.

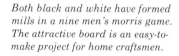

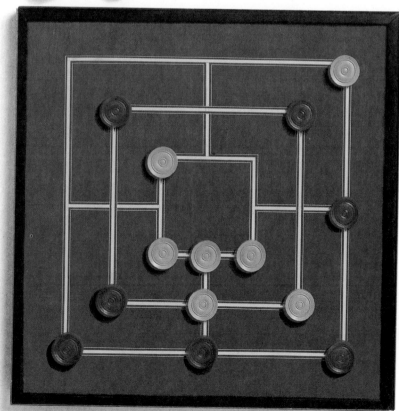

Chess

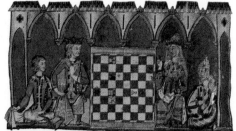

About the Game

Chess is considered 'the royal game' not only because it holds undisputed first place among the intellectual pastimes of western civilization, but because it was once played by the kings and nobles of feudal Europe. It is, by its very nature, a game for strategists and men of decision: imagination, concentration, and the ability to anticipate events are all needed to make a great chess player. As Benjamin Franklin wrote in 1779, chess can teach 'foresight, which looks a little into futurity… circumspection, which surveys the whole chessboard… caution, not to make our moves too hastily… and, lastly… the habit of not being discouraged by present bad appearance in the state of our affairs, the habit of hoping for a favorable change, and that of persevering in the search of resources.'

Although the evidence is scanty, scholars are generally agreed that chess in a recognizable form originated as a war game in India during the seventh century. It was first known as *chaturanga*, a Sanskrit word referring to the four elements of an army – elephants, horses, chariots, and foot soldiers. From India, chess made its way to Persia and was thence taken to Europe by the Arab conquerors of medieval Spain. The Vikings of Scandinavia, meanwhile, may have learned their chess directly from the Persians: they had trade routes through Russia linking Sweden with Baghdad and Constantinople. In Europe, the name and character of the pieces gradually adapted to new cultural circumstances. The shah in the Persian version became the king (but we still remember his antecedents in the phrase 'checkmate,' derived from *shah-mat* – the shah is helpless). The vizir, *firz* or *firzan* (wise man, counsellor) who sat

In the games book of Alfonso X, a Moorish sheik plays against a Christian opponent (opposite): 'Black plays and mates white in eleven moves.'

Seated on carpets in the traditional Eastern fashion, below, two Afghan players meet over a chess game in a tea shop at Mazar-i-Sharif.

The chess 'diagrams' of Alfonso's book, above, also depict a cross section of players at his Seville court, including the king himself (top).

The bishop above dates from about 1170 A.D., and belongs to a collection of walrus ivory chessmen discovered on the island of Lewis, Scotland.

next to the shah was replaced by a more western figure – the queen – who for a long time continued to be known as *ferzia* or *fierge* (which suggested *vierge* to the French poets, who often compared her, symbolically, to the Virgin Mary). The original Indian elephant, *alfil,* was variously transformed into a sage, a count, or a fool (*fil* had suggested *fol* to the French), but more often into a bishop. Obviously, Europeans knew very little about elephants and still less about their employment as instruments of war. The Arabic *faras* (horse) was identified with the European knight who fought on horseback. The *baidaq* (foot soldier) remained substantially unchanged as the expendable *pedes (pedona, paon, pion,* or pawn). The modern rook or castle bears the least relation to its original ancestor, and there has been much learned dispute as to its real meaning. The great paleographer Sir Frederick Madden came to the conclusion that the piece is descended from the Persian *rokh* – a hero or military adventurer – and

The fifteenth-century bishop above carries his crozier on horseback and is surrounded by 14 smaller figures – six priests and eight archers carrying crossbows. The piece is of walrus ivory.

Lucas van Leyden's painting, 'The Chess Players,' left, dates from about 1510. It shows a variant of chess known as the 'courier's game,' played on an unconventional board with 24 pieces to a side, including a 'courier,' a 'counsellor,' and a 'sneak.'

indeed, many of the early medieval rook pieces are carved in the form of a warrior biting his shield in the traditional manner of the frenzied 'berserk-runners' who struck terror into the hearts of the foot soldiers. How such a mobile piece came to be represented by the static symbol of a castle remains a mystery – except that towers at the end of the line fulfilled the medieval idea of how a defense should be conducted.

The first great chess treatise of Europe is the beautifully produced games book of Alfonso *El Sabio* (1221–1284), king of Castile and León. As his kingdom was the meeting place of Arab and European cultures, his book reflects that conjunction in the game of chess, and is based on Arabic and Persian models. The chess portion of his treatise consists of 103 problems – 'black mates white in five moves,' and so on – all presented in the form of diagrams that not only show the position of the pieces on the board, but also portray the players. A black Moorish king may play against a white Christian king; ladies are pitted against gentlemen of the court (one of the first recorded instances in medieval Europe of true sexual equality, at least with respect to gamesplay); Arabian lords are shown in their resplendent costumes, and Alfonso himself is depicted playing against one of the women of his court. Sometimes musicians are in attendance, playing soft background music on lutes or harps while the players ponder their next move.

Chess became one of the great passions of the Middle Ages. Many of the old romances describe killings that take place when the players quarrel over a game of chess. But chess is also the occasion for the beginning of great love affairs. Tristan and Yseult fall in love over a game of chess; Lancelot visits Guinevere on a chess pretext. Huon of Bordeaux, another medieval hero, boasts of his prowess on the board: 'I can play at chess or tables as well as any other can do, nor have I ever found a man who could win of me if I lyst!' Hearing this, his host, King Yvorin, proposes that Huon should play a game against his daughter,

Fourteenth-century Danish chess king, above, rides a lion as a symbol of his royal authority. The diminutive footman (known as a Nebenmann *or* Nebish) *carries the king's lance and buckler.*

Danish thirteenth-century chess queen, above, is seated on her walrus-ivory throne and wears a crown (now worn with use) over her head-scarf.

'Lady Howe Checkmating Benjamin Franklin,' right, recreates a chastening moment in Franklin's career as envoy to Great Britain. The painting is the work of the English-born American artist Edward Harrison May (1824–1887).

also a chess expert, with the wager that 'if she win thou shalt loose thy head, and if thou canst mate her thou shalt have her one night in thy bed to do with her at thy pleasure.' Huon wins, but only because the lady has fallen in love with him in the course of the game…

Toward the end of the Middle Ages chess became a much faster game. Important changes were made in the rules governing the moves of the queen and bishop, and these completely altered the method and style of play: opening moves became much more important since they now had a more decisive effect on the game. The modern form of chess had, in effect, been fully formulated by the end of the fifteenth century. The new game displaced the old very rapidly – in Italy and Spain the old version was obsolete by 1510. It was now played in a more analytic fashion, and the struggle itself was shortened and intensified. Gradually, the game produced celebrated masters whose exploits were widely admired and written about. Sixteenth-century Italy led the field with a number of chess players who went from court to court giving public exhibitions of their skill. Paolo Boi, for example, nicknamed 'il Siracusano,' demonstrated his ability to play three games simultaneously while wearing a blindfold.

But it was only from the eighteenth century onwards that chess became an international activity dominated by masters who traveled throughout the world in order to play against each other. The Age of Reason was also the age of the first chess clubs, which provided the meeting-places, and also the funds necessary to underwrite matches and exhibition games by famous players. In Paris, after a beginning in the Café Procope (where Voltaire and Rousseau played chess), the serious players moved to the Café de la Régence, in the Place du Palais-Royale, which became the acknowledged chess center of the city. It was here that André Philidor, the first internationally known chess master, and the strongest for nearly half a century, made his debut and discovered his talent for blindfold chess exhibitions. He was also one of the most gifted composers of the day, and divided his time between composing operas and playing chess, touring Germany and England, where he was hailed as 'a phenomenon in the history of man.'

Exhibitions by important players became increasingly popular during the nineteenth century (they had already been a feature of Persian chess play in the eleventh century). During the 1890's, H. N. Pillsbury, an American with a freak memory, played 22 simultaneous blindfold games at the same time as a hand of whist. He also operated Ajeeb, the mechanical chess player. Several chess automatons had already astonished the European chess world, the best-known being a life-size figure dressed as a Turk and seated behind a table, on which he played all comers and nearly always won. Even Napoleon played against this mechanical marvel, and lost. For a long time no one guessed the secret of the automaton, for there was apparently no space to conceal a human being. But in fact a chess expert supplementing his income was crouched inside the machinery, and saw the moves of the game from the underside of the board. The Turk ultimately emigrated to America; or rather, he was bought from his European owners and shipped to Philadelphia, where he remained on display at the Chinese Museum until its destruction by fire in 1854.

In London, which became the world capital of chess after Paris, the chess clubs were Parsloe's, in St. James's Street, and the Chess Divan, started by the headwaiter Simpson in what is now the famous Simpson's Restaurant in the Strand. An Englishman, Howard Staunton, was the world's leading player in

the 1840's. A notoriously quarrelsome and difficult man, who always wrote favorably about himself in *The Chess Player's Chronicle,* he lost to Adolf Anderssen of Germany in 1851, the year of the first international chess tournament. Anderssen, in turn, lost to Paul Morphy of the United States, who, in many ways, constitutes the supreme legend of chess history. A tiny man, always nattily dressed, he beat opponent after opponent, and went in pursuit of the great champion Staunton in order to meet him over the chess board. But Staunton just as consistently managed to evade a showdown, always finding new excuses and obviously frightened of the very real possibility of defeat. When Morphy attended the Opéra in Paris, he was spotted by the Duke of Brunswick and Count Isouard, two chess enthusiasts who promptly invited him into their box for a game. He beat both of them easily during *The Barber of Seville.* When Morphy returned to America, a hero's welcome awaited him: there were Morphy hats, Morphy cigars, even a Morphy basketball team. But Morphy went mad in the closing years of his life, and died aged fifty, in 1887.

The most spectacular player at the beginning of the twentieth century was José Raoul Capablanca (1888–1947), a Cuban prodigy who held the world's chess championship from 1921 to 1927. Capablanca lost only 35 of approximately 700 tournament games he played during his lifetime. He learned to play at the age of four, and at twelve had already defeated the reigning Cuban champion. Unlike most of the grand masters, he never studied the game, and claimed that he had read only one chess book during the whole of his career. He, Morphy, and Fischer are generally considered the greatest natural chess players of all time.

International chess has become increasingly formal over the years. Timed games were introduced in 1861, and the mechanical chess clock in 1883. In 1924 a worldwide organization, FIDE (Fédération Internationale des Échecs), was formed in order to standardize and regulate the game. It controls all of the world's chess events, and determines tournament rules and procedures. Every two years there is an international team tournament in which each member country is represented by a team of four players, with two in reserve.

In recent years there has been a crescendo of public interest in chess, caused by the emergence of a series of formidable grand masters in the Soviet Union (where chess is considered the national game, and widely subsidized), and by the dazzling career of the American prodigy, Bobby Fischer. Many chess experts regard Fischer as the greatest player in chess history, for the game is continually evolving, and its champions tend to grow more sophisticated with each generation. Chess literature has multiplied, and indeed the number of books on chess exceeds that on all other games put together. Clearly chess excites as much passion as it ever did in the Middle Ages, and it is still, as in Franklin's day, the ideal way to develop certain mental qualities – notably foresight, circumspection, and courage under stress.

Duke Albrecht V of Bavaria and his duchess, Anna of Austria, play a game of chess in this title page illustration, by Hans Müehlich, from a German manuscript dated 1552. Behind them are some of the family retainers; beside them, two puppies. Their silver and gold chessmen were probably made by the court goldsmith.

How to Play the Game

The newcomer to chess may well be intimidated by its reputation as a game for men of towering – and possibly eccentric – intellect. But while chess does inspire geniuses, it can also provide plenty of fascination and entertainment for anybody – man, woman, or child.

All the novice player needs to know is the basic rules. With practice he will soon become fluent in the game, but if he wants to master the fine points and become a serious player he should study some of the many excellent chess books that have been published for both masters and novices. Joining a chess club is also very helpful. The rules given here are an authorized translation of Part One of the official FIDE (Fédération Internationale des Échecs) Laws of Chess. This extract is reproduced by kind permission of the British Chess Federation.

Fourteenth-century German bishop on horseback is flanked by two monks and attended by a retinue of crossbowmen. The figure is 5 inches high.

Article 1

Introduction

The game of chess is played between two opponents by moving pieces on a square board called 'a chessboard.'

Article 2

The Chessboard and its Arrangement

1. The chessboard is made up of 64 equal squares in color alternately light (the 'white' squares) and dark (the 'black' squares).
2. The chessboard is placed between the players so that the square in the corner to the right of each player is white.
3. The eight rows of squares running from the edge of the chessboard nearest one of the players to that nearest the other player are called 'files.'
4. The eight rows of squares running from one edge of the chessboard to the other at right angles to the files are called 'ranks.'
5. The rows of squares of the same color touching corner to corner are called 'diagonals.'

Article 3

The Pieces and their Positions

At the beginning of the game one player has 16 light colored pieces (the 'white' pieces). The other has 16 dark colored pieces (the 'black' pieces).

These pieces are as follows:

A white King	indicated by ♔ symbol
A white Queen	,, ,, ♕ ,,
Two white Rooks	,, ,, ♖ ,,
Two white Bishops	,, ,, ♗ ,,
Two white Knights	,, ,, ♘ ,,
Eight white Pawns	,, ,, ♙ ,,

A black King	indicated by ♚ symbol
A black Queen	,, ,, ♛ ,,
Two black Rooks	,, ,, ♜ ,,
Two black Bishops	,, ,, ♝ ,,
Two black Knights	,, ,, ♞ ,,
Eight black Pawns	,, ,, ♟ ,,

The initial position of the pieces on the chessboard is as follows:

Article 4

The Method of Play

1. The two players must play alternately and make one move at a time. The player who has the white pieces commences the game.
2. A player is said 'to have the move' when it is his turn to play.

Elaborately inlaid German chessboard of 1600 is made of ebony squares alternating with ivory plates engraved with a whole menagerie of animals.

Article 5

The Move in General

1. With the exception of Castling (Article 6), a move is the transfer of one piece from one square to another square which is either vacant or occupied by an opponent's piece.
2. No piece, except the Rook when Castling or the Knight (Article 6), can cross a square occupied by another piece.
3. A piece played to a square occupied by an opponent's piece takes it as part of the same move. The captured piece must be immediately removed from the chessboard by the player who has made the capture. See Article 6 (b) for taking 'en passant.'

Article 6

The Moves of the Individual Pieces

The King. Except when Castling, the King moves to an adjacent square that is not attacked by an opponent's piece. Castling is a move of the King and a Rook, reckoned as a single move (of the King), which must be carried out in the following manner – the King is transferred from its original square to either one of the nearest squares of the same color in the same rank; then that Rook towards which the King has been moved is transferred over the King to the square which the King has just crossed.

Castling is permanently impossible (a) if the King has already been moved, or (b) with a Rook that has already been moved.

Castling is prevented for the time being – (a) if the original square of the King or the square which the King must cross or that which it is to occupy is attacked by an opponent's piece, or (b) if there is any piece between the Rook involved in the move and the King.

The Queen. The Queen moves to any square on the file, rank, or either of the diagonals on which it is placed.

The Rook. The Rook moves to any square on the file or rank on which it is placed.

The Bishop. The Bishop moves to any square on either of the diagonals on which it is placed.

The Knight. The Knight's move is made up of two different steps. It takes one step of one single square along the file or rank, and then, still moving away from the square it left, takes one step along the diagonal.

The Pawn. The Pawn can only move forward.

(a) Except when making a capture it advances from its original square either one or two vacant squares along the file on which it is placed, and on subsequent moves it advances one vacant square along the file. When making a capture it advances one vacant square along either of the diagonals on which it is placed.
(b) A Pawn attacking a square crossed by an opponent's Pawn which has been advanced two squares on the previous move can capture the opponent's Pawn as though the latter had only been moved one square. This capture can only be made on the move immediately following such advance and is known as taking 'en passant.'
(c) On reaching the end of a file a Pawn must be immediately exchanged, as part of the same move, for a Queen, a Rook, a Bishop, or a Knight at the player's choice and without taking into account the other pieces still remaining on the chessboard. This exchanging of a Pawn is called 'promotion.' The promoted piece must be of the same color as the Pawn and its action is immediate.

Article 7
The Completion of a Move
A move is completed:
(a) In the case of the transfer of a piece to a vacant square, when the player's hand has quitted the piece; or
(b) In the case of a capture, when the captured piece has been removed from the chessboard and when the player, having placed the piece on its new square, has quitted the piece with his hand; or
(c) In the case of Castling, when the player's hand has quitted the Rook on the square crossed by the King; when the player's hand has quitted the King the move is still not yet completed, but the player no longer has the right to make any other move except Castling; or
(d) In the case of the promotion of a Pawn, when the Pawn has been removed from the chessboard and the player's hand has quitted the new piece after placing it on the promotion square; if the player's hand has quitted the Pawn that has reached the promotion square the move is still not yet completed, but the player no longer has the right to move the Pawn to another square.

Article 8
Touched Piece
Provided that he first warns his opponent, the player whose turn it is to move can adjust one or more pieces on their squares.
Apart from the above case, if the player whose turn it is to move touches one or more pieces, he must make his move by moving or taking the first piece touched which can be moved or

taken; and if he touches pieces of opposite colors, he must take the enemy piece with his own touched piece, or if this is not possible, with another piece. If none of the touched pieces can be moved or taken, the player is free to make any legal move he chooses.
If a player wishes to claim a violation of this rule, he must do so before he touches a piece himself.

Article 9
Illegal Positions
1. If during the game it is ascertained that an illegal move has been made, then the position shall be set up again as it was immediately before the making of the illegal move. The game shall then continue in accordance with the rules given in Article 8 as regards the move replacing the illegal move.
If it proves impossible to set up the position again then the game must be annulled and a fresh game played.
2. If, in the course of a game, one or more pieces have been accidentally displaced and are not correctly replaced, the position must be set up as it was immediately before the mistake and the game continued.
If it proves impossible to set up the position again then the game must be annulled and a fresh game played.
3. If, after an adjournment, the position is incorrectly put up, then the position as it was on adjournment must be set up again and the game continued.
4. If during the game it is ascertained that the initial position of the pieces was incorrect, then the game must be annulled and a fresh game played.
5. If, during the game, it is ascertained that the position of the chessboard is incorrect, then the position that has been reached must be transferred to a chessboard that has been correctly placed and the game continued.

Article 10
Check
1. The King is in check when the square which it occupies is attacked by an opponent's piece; in this case the latter is said to be 'checking the King.'
2. The check must be met on the move immediately following. If the check cannot be met then it is called 'mate' (see Article 11, 1).
3. A piece that intercepts a check to the King of its own color can itself give check to the opponent's King.

Article 11
Won Game
1. The game is won for the player who has mated the opponent's King.
2. The game is considered won for the player whose opponent declares he resigns.

Article 12
Drawn Game
The game is drawn:
1. When the King of the player whose turn it is to move is not in check, and such player cannot make a move. This is called 'stalemate.'

2. By agreement between the two players.
3. At the request of one of the players when the same position appears three times, and each time the same player has had the move. The position is considered the same if pieces of the same kind and color occupy the same squares.
This right of claiming the draw belongs to the player:
(a) who is in a position to play a move leading to such repetition of the position, if he declares his intention of making this move; or
(b) who is about to reply to a move by which such repeated position has been produced.
If a player makes a move without having claimed a draw in the manner prescribed in (a) or (b) he then loses his right to claim a draw; this right is however restored to him if the same position appears again with the same player having the move.

Interpretation of S. 3
(i) A game cannot be declared drawn on the basis of Article 12, clause 3, unless the same player has the move after each of the three appearances of the same position on the chessboard.
(ii) The right of claiming the draw belongs exclusively to the player who:
(a) has the possibility of playing a move leading to the repetition of the position, provided that he indicates the move and claims the draw before making the move;
(b) must reply to a move by which the repeated position has been produced, provided that he claims the draw before executing his move.
(iii) If the claim proves to be incorrect and the game continues, then the player who has indicated a move according to para. 2a is obliged to execute this move on the chessboard.
4. When the player whose turn it is to move proves that at least fifty moves have been played by each side without a capture of a piece and without a Pawn move having been made. This number of fifty moves can be increased for certain positions providing that this increase in number and these positions have been clearly laid down before the commencement of the game.

Young chess players from the village of Tjeluk, on Bali, have to restrain a baby sister who wants to take a hand in their game. Chess is immensely popular in even the remotest villages on the island.

Chinese Chess

About the Game

Chess, Chinese chess *(choo-hong-ki)* and Japanese chess *(shogi)* all evolved from the seventh-century Indian game *chaturanga;* but among the modern versions of chess, it is the Chinese game that still displays most of the characteristics of their common ancestor. The emperor is supported by two mandarins, which have the same limited movement as the original *chaturanga* vizirs (which in chess developed into the powerful queens). The elephants amble two squares at a time, as they did centuries ago, before they became the wider-ranging bishops. The rook, or castle, is often known in Chinese chess as the chariot – a name more appropriate to its sweeping powers of attack.

Chinese chess has its own unique personality. The emperors, confined to cramped fortresses, are forbidden to 'see' each other; their domains are separated by a 'river' representing the *Hwang-ho,* the great Yellow River of China. Having invented gunpowder, the Chinese added their formidable cannon to the conventional game pieces. The surprising way these cannon move into action is typical of Chinese chess, and one of its greatest charms.

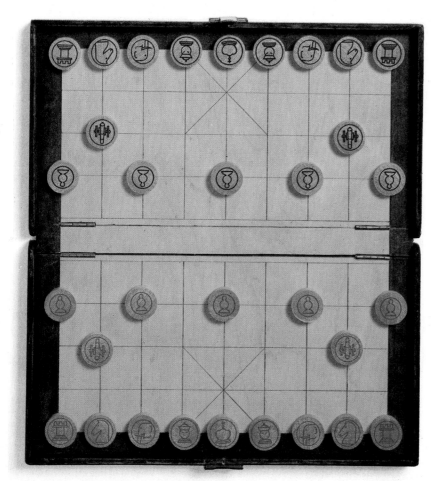

Chinese children, photographed by Brian Brake, play Chinese chess. The game gained popularity when mah-jong *fell under a ban against gambling.*

A simple but attractive homemade board for Chinese chess (above) can be folded up as a carrying container for the playing pieces.

How to Play the Game

The aim of the game, as in chess, is to capture the leading enemy piece – i.e. the emperor. The language of the game is also similar to that of chess. If the enemy emperor is threatened, it is said to be 'in check'; if it cannot be defended against capture, it is 'checkmated,' and the game is over. If it cannot move without entering into check, it is 'stalemated' – which in Chinese chess is considered a defeat, and the end of a game.

Chinese chess is played on a board of 8 by 9 squares, but it is more accurate to speak of 9 by 10 lines, since the pieces are played on the intersections of the lines.

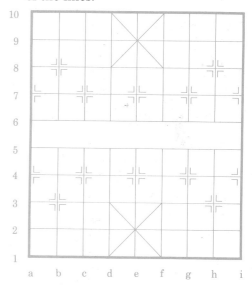

Figure A: The board for Chinese chess is marked with lines along which the pieces move. The fortresses, the river, and the starting points of pawns and cannon are also indicated.

The middle of the board is occupied by an empty horizontal strip, known as the river, where the vertical lines are interrupted. Pieces may move across the river as if the vertical lines were continuous; except in the case of the elephant, which is not allowed to cross the river at all.

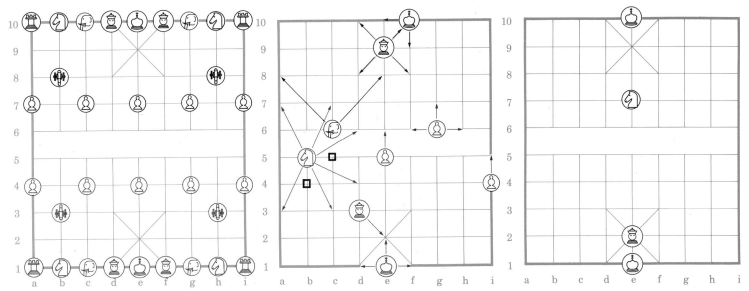

Figure B: The pieces are arranged as shown here before the start of the game. Each player's pieces include an emperor; two each of mandarins, elephants, knights, rooks, and cannon; and five pawns. The elephants are not allowed to cross the 'river' to the opponent's side of the board.

Figure C: Some examples of the movement of knight, mandarin, and king are illustrated here. If any piece occupies b4, the knight may not move to a3 or to c3. If a piece occupies c5 the knight may not go to d4 or d6. The mandarin may only go to f10 after the emperor has moved.

Figure D: Emperors may not 'see' each other in Chinese chess. In the example above, if red moved his mandarin, black could not move his knight, and vice versa. Alternatively, one player could move another piece to block the line of 'sight' between the opposing emperors.

Two squares, each three points by three, are marked with diagonal lines. These are the 'fortresses.' The emperors and the mandarins are confined to the fortresses formed, for red, by the points d1, d2, d3; e1, e2, e3; f1, f2, f3; and, for black, by the points d8, d9, d10; e8, e9, e10; f8, f9, and f10 (see figure A).

The points marked b3 and h3 (for red) and b8 and h8 (for black) indicate the position of the cannon at the beginning of the game. The other marks show the positions of the starting ten pawns, five on each side.

The pieces and how they move
At the beginning of the game, each player has 16 pieces of either red or black, listed and named as follows (their equivalent initial letters – used in diagrams and notation of moves – are given in parentheses):
one emperor (EM)
two mandarins (M)
two elephants (E)
two knights (K)

two rooks or castles (R)
two cannon (C)
five pawns (P).
The pieces are positioned as shown in figure B. Red plays first.

Certain basic rules govern all moves. No more than one piece may occupy a point; except for the knight and the cannon, no piece may jump over a hostile or friendly piece, and a draw due to a position of 'perpetual check' is not allowed – if the same position, with the same player to move, arises in two consecutive moves, then that player must make another move.

The emperor (red, e1; black, e10) may move one point in a vertical or horizontal direction only, not diagonally, and must remain within the nine points of the fortress. (See figure C.)

Although the emperors are never able to approach each other, they still have a significant influence on each other.

They may not stand on the same vertical line unless at least one other piece stands between them, i.e. they are not allowed to 'see' each other. This long-range power is only exerted by the emperors on each other, but a piece may get 'pinned' between them.

If a player removes his last intervening piece from between the two emperors, he places his own emperor in check, which is forbidden. (See figure D.)

The mandarins, like the emperor, are confined within the fortress at all times, and may only move one point per turn, in a diagonal direction; there are thus only five points in the fortress open to them. (See figure C.)

An elephant moves two points per turn, no more and no less, in a diagonal direction only; the point in between must be unoccupied. Because the elephant cannot cross the river, there are only seven points on which it can stand, on its own side of the board.

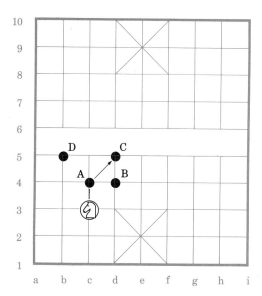

Figure E: A knight may not always jump over other pieces. For example, if point B is occupied by another piece, the knight may move unimpeded to point C, via a straight step to point A. If a piece stands on point A, however, the knight may not move to either point C or point D.

Photographed in imperial China, before the revolution of 1911, two villagers (above) of Hopei province in northern China smoke opium pipes as they begin a game of Chinese chess.

A knight moves like a knight in chess, but the ability to jump over other pieces is restricted. A knight's move is along a straight, one-point line, followed by one point diagonally. (See figures C and E for examples.)

A pawn may only move one space forward at one turn. After it has crossed the river, it may also move one space sideways. It may never move backward or diagonally. A pawn may move again and again in the same sideways direction, and take as it moves (see Capturing). If a pawn reaches the enemy's back row, it can only move sideways. There is no 'pawn promotion' as in chess; its capacities only change as it crosses the river.

The Chinese rook, or castle, behaves just like its equivalent in chess. It may move any number of points in a straight line, forward, backward, or sideways; it may not move diagonally, or jump over other pieces.

The cannon moves like the rook, with one important difference – it must always jump over another piece, be it ally or enemy, landing as many points beyond it as desired. The cannon may not jump over two pieces, but it may jump over one and capture the second. If there is no piece that a cannon may jump over for its move (i.e. no piece to serve as its 'shield') it may not be moved. (See figure F.)

Capturing

Every piece 'captures as it moves'; that is, if it can move according to the rules to a point occupied by an enemy piece, then it can capture the piece and occupy its place. Capturing is not obligatory. The captured pieces are removed from the board for the duration of the game.

Check and counter-check

The emperor is placed in check when it is either threatened by an enemy piece, or when both emperors stand on the same vertical line without another piece between them.

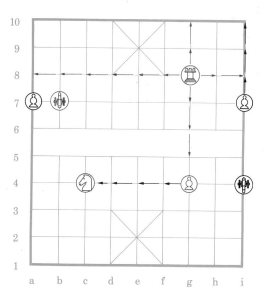

Figure F: A cannon may not be moved without a piece to act as its 'shield.' In this example, the red cannon has no shield and therefore may not be moved. The black cannon may not move to i5 or i6, but may proceed to i8, i9 or i10. It may not go to i3, i2, i1, or h4; but may move to f4, e4, d4. or capture the knight. The rook needs no shield.

73

There are three possible responses to a check. The attacking piece may be captured, the emperor may move out of check, or the emperor may be protected by interposing a piece between it and its attacker.

If the attacking piece is a rook, another piece may be placed between it and the emperor. If the attacking piece is a knight, a piece may be placed on the corner point of its path (see figure C). If the attacking piece is a cannon, a second piece may be placed in its path, or the piece in between it and the emperor (the cannon shield) may be removed. Capturing the shield does not help, as the capturing piece then becomes a new shield.

If the threat cannot be repelled, then the emperor can be taken and the game is lost (checkmate).

Nobody is safe in the fortress
In Chinese chess the emperor is extremely vulnerable. All offensive plans are influenced by the question of whether a safe place can be found for the emperor.

There is no closed rank of pawns it may hide behind; in fact the pawns are out of reach and far apart. The elephant is willing to help – if only it knew how – and the other pieces are primarily designed for attack.

So the emperor remains locked in its fortress, surrounded by clumsy mandarins; it is constantly in danger, but becomes very adept at concealment and last-minute escapes. Such a Houdini-like escape artist can often, in a position of apparent weakness, give a false sense of superiority to the opponent, tempting him into an ill-advised and costly attack.

A sample game
More a comedy of errors than a master's game, this is a demonstration of the powers of the cannon.

Red, as always, makes the first move (1); therefore odd-numbered moves are red, even-numbered moves are black. Refer to figure A for the board positions. A dash (–) means 'moves to'; × means 'captures'; + means 'check.'

(1) C:b3–i3. (2) C:b8–i8.
(3) C:i3–c3. (4) C:i8–g8.
(5) C:c3 × c7. (6) C:h8–e8; three moves were necessary to get the black cannon to the center line, from where it could attack the red fortress. By passing a knight, the cannon can reach the e-line in two moves, but if the cannon start so aggressively it is better to keep the knight for defense. (7) C:c7 × g7; now red threatens to capture black's rook with C:g7 × g10 + . (8) K:h10–i8; this defends the elephant which is now protected by the rook, and attacks the cannon. (9) C:g7–c7; the threatened red cannon has to move. On g9 or g10 it would be captured – and an exchange with the elephant is of course extremely advantageous to black. Red chose c7 in order to retain the

possibility of returning via the c-pawn, but g3 would have been a better move. (10) C:e8 × e4; black surprisingly neglects C:g8 × g1 + . (11) K:b1–c3; attacks the cannon but it would have been better to move E:g1–i3, because black C:g8 × g1 still threatens. (12) C:e4–e9 + . (13) M:d1–e2. (14) C:e9–e6 + . (15) K:c3–e4. (16) C:g8 × g1 checkmate.

In an old people's home on a Chinese commune, below, players with a lifetime's experience of Chinese chess pass an afternoon playing the game.

The staff of a restaurant on a Chinese junk – part of the Floating Village complex in Aberdeen Harbor, Hong Kong – snatch a moment between serving meals to play Chinese chess (below).

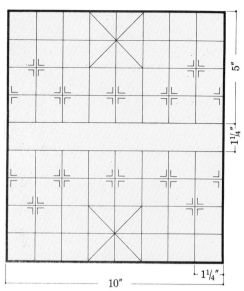

Figure G: The Chinese chess board is made up of sixty-four $1\frac{1}{4}$-inch squares, broken up into two equal, opposing marked fields.

Chinese workers attract spectators to their impromptu Chinese chess game in an open square, left. Portable game boards often consist of paper squares, thrown away when they become tattered.

Materials

A three-ply board, $11\frac{1}{4}$ by $12\frac{1}{4}$ inches, $\frac{3}{8}$ inch thick.

Six plywood strips, $\frac{3}{16}$ inch thick: four, $\frac{5}{8}$ by $5\frac{13}{16}$ inches; two, $\frac{5}{8}$ by $11\frac{5}{8}$ inches.

Four brass hinges, 1 inch wide, each leaf $\frac{3}{8}$ inch deep, roughly $\frac{1}{16}$ inch thick.

Eight brass hinge screws.

A dozen wire nails, roughly $\frac{3}{8}$ inch long.

A brass hook-and-eye lock, or suitcase-type clasp.

A metal carrying handle (optional).

A wooden dowel, 12 inches long, 1 inch in diameter.

Neutral walnut stain.

India ink.

Wood glue.

Tools

A vise, protractor, pencil, ruler, wood rasp, technical drawing pen, masking tape, paintbrush, coping saw, chisel, awl, screwdriver, hammer, sandpaper, and backsaw.

How To Make The Game

Clamp the middle of one of the $\frac{5}{8}$-by-$11\frac{5}{8}$-inch strips in a vise so that the $\frac{3}{16}$-inch edge is facing upward. Place the protractor so that the perpendicular is lined up with the left end of this side and the base of the protractor is in line with the bottom edge. Mark a point on the top edge of the side that is 45 degrees from the bottom corner. Draw a line connecting this point to the corner. Repeat these steps at the right side of the strip, drawing a 45-degree angle to the left. Miter these ends by filing along the lines drawn with a wood rasp. Repeat these steps with the other $\frac{5}{8}$-by-$11\frac{5}{8}$-inch strip.

With the wood rasp, round off one corner on each of the four $\frac{5}{8}$-by-$5\frac{13}{16}$-inch strips. Miter the corners on the opposite ends of the strips: two with 45-degree angles to the right, and two with 45-degree angles to the left.

Place the three-ply board on the work table so that its long edge lies horizontally before you. Measure and draw lines that are $\frac{1}{2}$ inch from each of the $11\frac{1}{4}$-inch sides of the board. (Draw lightly with the pencil as some lines will later be erased.) Measure and draw lines that are $\frac{5}{8}$ inch from each of the $12\frac{1}{4}$-inch edges.

There is now a rectangle, 10 by $11\frac{1}{4}$ inches, centered in the board. Divide this rectangle into a grid of squares, $1\frac{1}{4}$ inch on each side. There will be eight rows of nine squares. Using figure G as a guide, draw in the necessary markings on the field of squares and erase the lines that

cross the 'river,' in other words, the central vertical row of eight squares.

Trace over the penciled lines and markings with india ink, using a technical drawing pen. Allow the ink to dry thoroughly.

On the front side of the board, measure and mark points on the $12\frac{1}{2}$-inch edges, $5\frac{3}{4}$ inches from the corners. Draw ruled lines to connect the corresponding points on opposite sides of the board. With the coping saw, cut along the board on the these two lines.

With masking tape, carefully tape off the the game board area on each of the three sections of the board. Apply the walnut stain to the border of the gameboard and allow to dry thoroughly. Remove the tape. Turn the board sections over and stain. Allow to dry.

Place one $5\frac{3}{4}$-by-$11\frac{1}{2}$-inch section on the work table so that the sawed edge is facing you. Mark points 1 inch and 2 inches from the left corner of this sawed edge. At each of these points, make another mark on the board, $\frac{1}{16}$ inch from the sawed edge. Draw a line connecting the two points you have just marked. Repeat these steps at the right end of the sawed edge, then at the sawed edge of the other $5\frac{3}{4}$-by-$11\frac{1}{2}$-inch section, and the two sawed edges of the $\frac{3}{4}$-by-$11\frac{1}{2}$-inch section.

With the coping saw, cut through each of the marks on the sawed edges to the corresponding marks $\frac{1}{16}$ inch into the board. Place the chisel blade on the 1-inch lines on each of the pieces and, with a hammering blow of the heel of your hand, chop out the eight 1-by-$\frac{1}{16}$ inch sections.

Place a hinge leaf in each indentation in the sawed edges of the board. (When attached, the knuckled backs of the hinges will be on the same side as the playing field.) With the awl, press a hole in the middle of each of the screw holes in the hinge leaf. Screw the four hinges into place, connecting the three pieces so that the narrow strip is in the middle and all hinge knuckles are on the same side as the marked side of the board.

Apply glue to the side edges of the game board sections (not the middle strip). Apply glue to the mitered ends of the six plywood strips and fasten them together against the edges of the game board, using figure H as a guide for positioning the components. Hammer a few wire nails partly into the sides of these strips and edges of the game board to hold all the pieces in place. When the glue has dried, remove the nails.

Sandpaper any rough and splintered areas of these strips if necessary. Apply walnut stain to all sides of the plywood strips and allow to dry.

Close the box and rest it on its spine. Measure and mark the middle point ($5\frac{13}{16}$ inches from either edge) on both top strips. At these points, attach the clasp for the box. When fastening the clasp, make sure that it is positioned to lock properly when the box is closed.

For added security and to prevent the sections of the box from shifting when the box is closed and locked, open the box and hammer a wire nail a short way into the edge of the left and right sides, directly behind each half of the clasp. Remove one of the nails and, with wirecutters, cut off the head of the nail still in place. The nail will now fit into the hole on the opposite side when the box is closed.

A carrying handle may also be fitted to one side of the lid, if you wish.

Clamp the dowel lengthwise in the vise and from one end mark off points at $\frac{1}{4}$-inch intervals.

Make 32 points. Place the ruler across the dowel and extend these points into partial lines. With the backsaw, cut through the dowel along these lines to make 32 disc-shaped playing pieces. Sand them down lightly. With the technical pen, mark the pieces with the designs shown in the photograph at right.

Figure H: After the three parts of the playing board are connected with hinges, glue on the sideboards; then attach the lock and handles.

The ideograms on the Chinese chess pieces can easily be 'translated' into more familiar symbols, as shown in the right-hand column above.

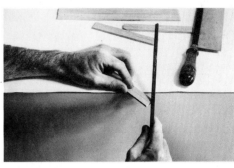

1: To shape the ends of the sideboards for mitered corners, first mark the 45-degree angle, then file down the measured ends of the wood with a rasp.

2: With a technical drawing pen and india ink, draw the game diagram, including the 'fortresses' and the 'river,' onto the surface of the board.

3: Before you paint the borders of the playing board with wood stain, lay a protective band of tape around the edges of the game diagram.

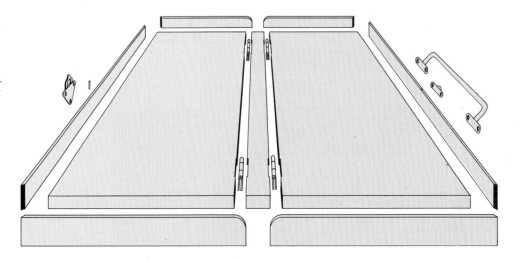

Shogi

About the Game

The Japanese have been familiar with the present form of *shogi*, or Japanese chess, since the early sixteenth century. At that time Ohashi-Sokei established his reputation as the greatest *shogi* master of all time, and wrote books on the game which are still standard reference works. He was appointed chief chess player by the emperor, an honor which passed to his descendants. Later Japanese governments instituted *shogi* schools, employed state teachers around the country, and sponsored annual tournaments.

Such tournaments still take place in modern Japan, when the best of the ten million *shogi* players compete for the supreme master's title, *meijin*.

Although *shogi* is believed to have developed from Chinese chess, it is quite distinct from that or any other existing version of chess. The most obvious difference is that *shogi* pieces are all of the same color, as they may be called upon to fight on behalf of either player during a game.

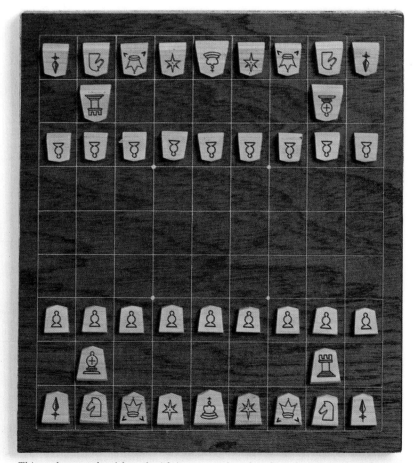

This mahogany shogi *board with its unusual wedge-shaped playing pieces is a replica of a traditional Japanese chess set – a handsome crafts project.*

How to Play the Game

Shogi is rightly called Japanese chess, since the point of the game is to checkmate the king; and the three most important pieces – king, castle, and bishop – move just as they do in chess. But there are several important differences between *shogi* and chess. The following is a brief outline of the basic rules; descriptions of strategy and examples of play are fascinating, but too complex to be entered into here. The *shogi* enthusiast will find many books to further his understanding of the game.

First impressions of the game

The chess player who sits at the *shogi* board for the first time might think that he has very little material. The queen is missing, the number of castles and bishops is halved, and the knight has lost most of his power. There are two spears that are not even allowed to move backward, and a group of 'lame ducks,' the generals.

But after a while, he will notice that all those knights, spears, and pawns, which can be promoted to gold generals, and which can cover each other so easily, can put a lethal web around the enemy king. Moreover, as soon as some pieces from both sides have been captured, an apparently dull game becomes surprisingly dynamic. The possibility of 'parachuting' a piece at random on the board, even into the enemy camp, means that dangerous attacks can occur at any time. The loss of a piece is a double penalty in *shogi*, for 'prisoners of war' may have to fight for their captor...

Some see this as a disadvantage of the game; a player loses a bishop... and suddenly the opponent has two. This is an unpleasant experience and, for

beginners, often bewildering. But against this is the fact that *shogi* is also a game of last-minute reprieves. Just as the attacker thinks he has clinched it, and drops his last paratrooper, the defender may still find an opportunity to escape and even launch a nimble counterattack. Thus *shogi* is a game which involves sudden and dramatic changes of fortune.

The board and pieces
The *shogi* board is a rectangle of nine by nine spaces (these are rectangular, to accommodate the long playing pieces). The squares are all of one color. Pieces are placed within the squares, not on the lines as in Chinese chess.

Two intersections on the fourth line and two on the seventh are marked with a dot, dividing the board into three strips of three by nine squares.

The pieces of the two players are not differentiated by color. The ownership of a piece in *shogi* is shown by the direction in which the pointed end of the piece is facing. All pieces face the enemy back row during play. If a captured piece is brought into play on behalf of its captor, it faces in the same direction as the other pieces of its new owner – i.e. the direction opposite to the way it first faced.

The opening formation of pieces for the game is shown in figure A.

In the first row (a1 to i1 and a9 to i9) for both players, reading from left to right, are: spear, knight, silver general, gold general, king, gold general, silver general, knight, and spear. (The gold general and the silver general are usually referred to as gold and silver.)

In a garden at Kyoto, the capital of ancient Japan, John Launois photographed an old man and his son absorbed in a game of shogi. *The old man holds a captured piece, deciding where to place it 'out of the blue' on the board – a method of play unique to this form of chess.*

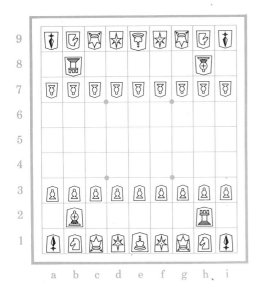

Figure A: Each player arranges his pieces as shown, in the three rows at his side of the board, behind the two dots on the third row of squares. The pieces point in the direction of play.

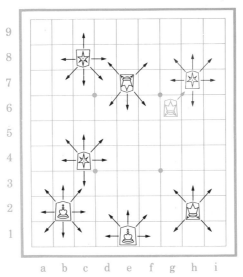

Figure B: The king, and the gold and silver generals, may move one square at a time in the directions shown by the arrows. After promotion, a silver general becomes a 'gold' (top right).

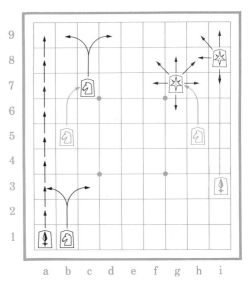

Figure C: The spear and knight (at left) have limited powers of movement: but after promotion (at right) they move as gold generals, straight and diagonally forward, sideways, and backward.

In the second row, the bishop is placed on b2 and the castle on h2 (b8 and h8 for the other side). The nine pawns are arranged along the third and seventh rows.

The movement of the pieces
King: one square in any direction, as in conventional chess.
Gold: one square, in six directions; straight forward, diagonally forward, sideways, or straight backward; but not diagonally backward.
Silver: one square, in five directions; straight forward, diagonally forward, or diagonally backward; but neither sideways, nor straight backward.
Knight: the classical knight's move, one square straight and one square diagonally, but only to left or right in a forward direction. (Thus, out of the eight possible squares which a knight can reach in chess, only two remain.) The knight is the only piece which can jump over other pieces, allied or enemy.
Spear: forward only, for an optional number of squares.
Castle: any number of squares in a straight forward, backward, or sideways direction, just like the rook in conventional chess.

Bishop: any number of squares on any of the diagonals, just like the bishop in conventional chess.
Pawn: one square, straight forward only. There is no option to move two squares on the first turn, as the chess pawn has; the *shogi* pawn also captures as it moves, in a straight line, not diagonally as in chess.

Promotion of pieces
As soon as one of the pieces from row 1, 2, or 3 reaches row 7, 8, or 9 (see figure A) – or vice versa – it may be promoted; either immediately on its arrival, or later in the game, as the player wishes. Promotion is shown by turning the red underside of the piece upward. It remains pointing in the same direction as before.

King and gold cannot be promoted. Silver, knight, spear, and pawn all promote to gold. The castle becomes a 'crowned castle,' which means that apart from its usual movement, it may also move as a king. The promoted bishop, called a 'crowned bishop,' may also move as a king.

It is clear that pawn, bishop, and castle can only gain by promotion, so these pieces will always be promoted as soon as possible. With silver, the original position of the piece may be momentarily preferred. A player may also wish to retain the course of a knight or a spear; but if these pieces arrive at the enemy's back row, they must be promoted, or remain 'dead' on the board with no ability to move at all.

To promote a piece, it is turned upside down as soon as it arrives in the promotion area. At the end of the move the piece has thus already been promoted, and the opponent has to deal with it accordingly.

Promotion is not compulsory, and it may be postponed. A piece may be promoted at any time when it is being moved within, into, or out of the promotion area. Once a piece has been promoted, it retains its new rank as long as it stays on the board; 'demotion' is not possible.

As soon as a piece is captured it loses its promotion. When a player takes a piece from his opponent and replaces

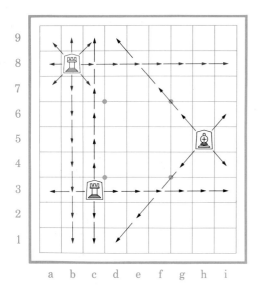

Figure D: A promoted or 'crowned' castle may also move one space diagonally, like a king. A bishop, before promotion, moves for any number of squares along the diagonals, as in chess.

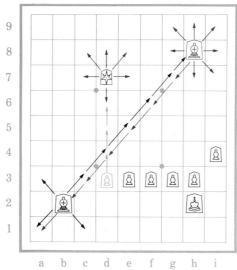

Figure E: A promoted or 'crowned' bishop may move one space forward or sideways, as well as along the diagonals. A promoted pawn (center) becomes a gold general, with wide powers.

it on the board, it always appears in its original capacity.

When setting a piece on the board directly within the promotion area, no promotion may take place. Promotion may occur in a later move, however, according to the above rules.

To be promoted, a piece has to be moved from its square. It may not be promoted and stay in the same place.

Bringing pieces out of the blue
On any turn a player is allowed, instead of making a move, to bring into play, 'out of the blue,' a piece which has been previously captured from the opponent, and place it on any unoccupied square on the board. When a captured piece is brought back into the game, it appears facing contrary to its original direction. As already mentioned, when a promoted piece is captured, it can only be brought back into play in its original capacity, though it may be re-promoted at a later stage.

A player may not set a piece on a square from which it would not be able to move. Thus a pawn or spear may not be set on the opponent's back row, and a knight may not be placed on the opponent's back two rows.

Extra restrictions apply to pawns. A player may not place a pawn on a vertical row already occupied by an allied pawn; 'double pawns' are not allowed in *shogi*. Promoted pawns on the same line are permissible. Also, a player may not bring a pawn into play in such a position that it checkmates the opponent's king.

Function and value of the pieces
Castle and bishop are by far the strongest pieces in *shogi* and it is obvious that players should try to develop them, and to open lines and diagonals for them. A bishop 'out of the blue' can present a dangerous bilateral threat, and in exchanging bishops, e.g. along the b2–h8 diagonal, the player who first loses his bishop to the enemy may see it brought quickly back into play against him.

The gold generals are not usually advanced since their retreat can easily be cut off, and they can render excellent service in defense of the king. A captured gold, on the other hand, which can be dropped behind the enemy lines, is a popular offensive weapon. Silver generals may be advanced, usually supported by some pawns.

Knight and spear are undoubtedly the weaker pieces. They frequently become active only later in the game. A knight, advanced too soon and arriving at the fifth row after two jumps, can easily be attacked by a pawn and often appears unable to escape. Spear and knight often fall victim to a predatory promoted bishop or castle, and can then be used to great effect by the enemy.

Three or four pawns are usually kept on the third row for the protection of the king. The taking of pawns is not always advisable, especially when one or two have already been captured. If a player has, for example, eight pawns on the board, not more than one can 'come out of the blue,' because double pawns are not allowed. By taking too many pawns, moreover, new lines may be opened up for the enemy, and more places provided for the dropping of captured pawns.

The castle is the strongest piece. Some estimate its value at three generals, others at two generals plus a knight or spear. The bishop is at least equal to two generals; it is most effective during the opening phase of the game.

There is little difference between gold and silver; in most positions gold is a little stronger, especially in defense. A gold general is about as strong as two knights or two spears.

All this is of course a theoretical evaluation; the value of a piece in play is determined primarily by its position on the board.

Materials

A board of Philippine mahogany, $11^{11}/_{16}$ by $12^{1}/_{4}$ inches wide, $^{3}/_{4}$ inch thick. Three molding strips (preferably slanted molding), one $1^{1}/_{4}$ by $4^{1}/_{2}$ inches, the second 1 by 10 inches, and the third $^{3}/_{4}$ by $9^{1}/_{2}$ inches, all $^{1}/_{4}$ inch thick.
Yellow gloss paint.
Yellow plastic adhesive tape, $^{1}/_{16}$ inch wide.
Varnish.
Oil-based ink: red and black.

Tools

A ruler, pencil, awl, backsaw, artist's fine camel-hair brush, scissors, paintbrush, technical drawing pen, and sandpaper.

How to Make the Game

Place the $11^{11}/_{16}$-by-$12^{1}/_{4}$-inch board horizontally on the work table. Using the ruler, measure and mark points $^{1}/_{2}$ inch from the corners of each side. Connect all opposite points to make an inner rectangle of $10^{11}/_{16}$ by $11^{1}/_{4}$ inches. Place the ruler at one of the $10^{11}/_{16}$-inch edges and, measuring from the corner, mark off points at $1^{3}/_{16}$-inch intervals. Do the same at the other $10^{11}/_{16}$-inch edge and connect the points opposite each other. On both $11^{1}/_{4}$-inch sides, mark off points at $1^{1}/_{4}$-inch intervals and connect the points opposite each other.

The inner rectangle is now divided into 81 rectangular cells measuring $1^{1}/_{4}$ by $1^{3}/_{16}$ inches each. Using the awl and the ruler, dig a slight groove into the lines drawn. Paint the grooves yellow (or decorate them with strips of yellow adhesive tape) and leave to dry. Paint yellow dots on the crosspoints of the fourth lines, as shown on the model at right. The board now has a central area of nine cells. Varnish the board and allow to dry thoroughly.

To make the 36 counters, place the $1^{1}/_{4}$-by-$4^{1}/_{2}$-inch molding strip horizontally on the work table. (If you are using a slanted strip, turn the broad side to face you.) Measuring from the left, mark off points at $^{3}/_{4}$-inch intervals on the bottom edge of the side of the molding strip. On the top edge, mark a point $^{1}/_{8}$ inch from the left corner. From that point, mark points at $^{1}/_{2}$- and $^{1}/_{4}$-inch intervals, i.e. $^{1}/_{2}$ inch, $^{3}/_{4}$ inch, $1^{1}/_{4}$ inches, $1^{1}/_{2}$ inches, 2 inches, etc.

The playing pieces for shogi (left) shown in the right-hand column alongside their Japanese equivalents, are drawn in black in their original value, red in their promoted value. From the top downward: king; castle and crowned castle; bishop and crowned bishop; gold general (no promotion); silver general, knight, spear, and pawn, all of which promote to gold general.

1: Mark the lines on the playing surface of the board, then go over each line with the point of an awl, making light indentations in the wood.

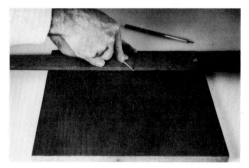

2: When the lines have been scored, paint them with a fine camel-hair brush or cover them with narrow strips of yellow plastic adhesive tape.

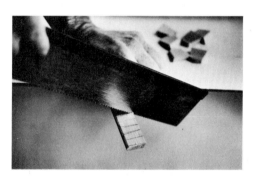

3: Measure and mark the molding strips, then cut out the tapering playing pieces. Sand down the narrow end of each piece to a slight point.

Draw a line connecting the bottom corner with the first point on the top edge. Connect the first point on the bottom edge with the second and third points on the top edge. Connect the second point on the bottom with the fourth and fifth points on the top, etc. Using the backsaw, cut through the strip along the lines drawn.

Place the 1-by-10-inch molding strip horizontally on the work table. Measuring from the left corner, mark off points at $\frac{5}{8}$-inch intervals. On the top edge, mark a point $\frac{1}{8}$ inch from the left corner. From that point, mark at $\frac{3}{8}$- and $\frac{1}{4}$-inch intervals, i.e. $\frac{3}{8}$ inch, $\frac{5}{8}$ inch, 1 inch, $1\frac{1}{4}$ inches, etc. Connect the points as on the previous molding strip and saw along the lines.

Place the $\frac{3}{4}$-by-$9\frac{1}{2}$-inch molding strip horizontally on the work table. On the bottom edge, measuring from the left corner, mark points at $\frac{1}{2}$-inch intervals. On the top edge, mark a point $\frac{1}{8}$ inch from the left corner and, from that point, mark at $\frac{1}{4}$-inch intervals as illustrated before. Connect these lines and cut along them with the backsaw.

Glue a square of sandpaper to a small block of wood and sand each half of the narrow top edge of each counter at a slight angle, so that the middle point is peaked, as shown in the model at right. The largest playing pieces comprise two bishops, two castles, and two kings, with the middle-sized pieces consisting of four spears, four horses, four silver and four gold generals. The 18 small pieces act as pawns. Draw in the black markings on the counters as shown in the photograph opposite. On pieces with a different promoted value (see How to Play the Game, and the color photograph opposite) draw the appropriate symbols in red.

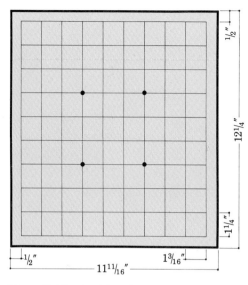

Figure F: The shogi board is a grid of ten by ten lines, marked at four intersections.

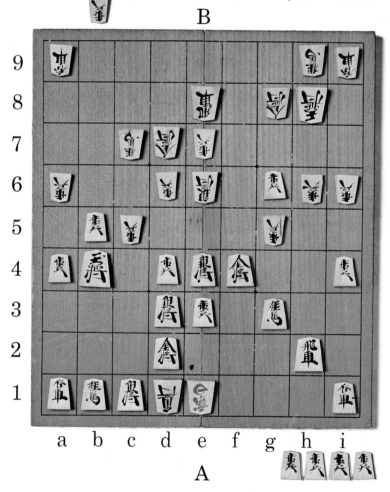

A game of shogi with Japanese pieces, above, draws toward final checkmate. The European equivalents of the playing pieces may be seen on the opposite page. Player A has captured four pawns to B's one; all of them may be reentered 'out of the blue' to play on behalf of their captor, and may subsequently be 'promoted' to become gold generals. Player B has brought two pieces alongside the king on A's back row: a bishop on 1d and a promoted bishop on 1e. Only A's gold general at 2d can protect his endangered king against a successful move to checkmate.

Checkers

About the Game

The modern game of checkers originated in Europe about the beginning of the twelfth century, using the playing pieces of medieval backgammon, the board of chess, and the number and movement of pieces in *alquerque*. The pieces took the name of the queen in French medieval chess, the *fers,* and the game was known as *fierges*. Later the chess queen was called *dame* and French checkers became the *jeu de dames* as it is still known today.

Originally the capture of pieces in a checkers game was optional, as in chess, but early in the sixteenth century compulsory capture of pieces was introduced. Any piece which neglected to make a possible capture was 'huffed,' or removed from the board. This enlivened the game and increased its appeal. The new game, which included the huffing maneuver, was called the *jeu forcé,* the old game being referred to as the *jeu plaisant.* Modern English draughts is this same *jeu forcé,* and was taken by British settlers to North America, where it became known as checkers.

There are still many variations in modern checkers games as played in different countries. Perhaps the most important is Polish checkers. This appears to have been invented in Paris, about 1730, by a French officer of the royal household, and his opponent, a Polish gentleman. Polish checkers is played on a board of 100 squares and each player has 20 pieces; rules of play are different, especially as regards the powers of movement of a king. Polish checkers is played in several European countries, notably France. Other countries use either the English or Polish type of board, with minor variations in the rules of play.

How to Play the Game

Each player has twelve pieces or 'men,' arranged on a board of 64 squares, as shown below:

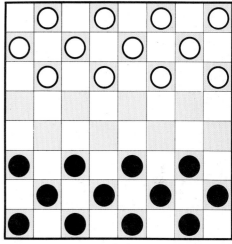

This checkers board shows the arrangement of pieces at the start of play. Black moves first, and the pieces are played only on the colored squares.

Two Moroccan Arabs, below, enjoy an outdoor game of checkers on a terrace overlooking the coast of the Mediterranean: it is early spring, and the landscape is dotted with almond blossoms.

Craftsmen bestowed great artistry on these early European checkers, above. The largest was carved of morse (walrus) ivory around 1250. Next to it, a bone piece, c. 1300. Top row: two men of 1530.

Checkers players at the Café Lamblin, Paris, (opposite) were painted by Louis-Léopold Boilly around 1820. The old gentleman wearing the cross and ribbon of the Legion of Honor is evidently a veteran of the Napoleonic Wars. (Musée Condé)

The game may be played using either the black or the white squares; if black is used, the black corner square should be on the player's left; if white is used, the board should be turned so that the white corner square is on his left.

Black moves first. The men are moved diagonally forward one square onto a vacant square of the same color. When a man reaches the opponent's back row it is 'crowned' by placing another checker of the same color on top, and becomes a 'king.'

A man may capture an opposing man by jumping over it diagonally to an empty square; the captured piece is removed from the board. If the same man is now in a position to capture one or more enemy men by continuing to make diagonal forward jumps, it must do so.

If a man reaches the back row of the opposing side and becomes a king, the turn ends, even if other captures are possible. A king may move one square at a time, or capture, both forward and backward. A king may be captured by a man or another king.

If a man can make a capture it must do so. If it fails to make a possible capture, or fails to complete a series of possible captures, the opponent may choose between three alternatives: he may insist on the correct move being made, and the piece wrongly moved being replaced in its previous position; he may allow the incorrect move to stand if it is in his favor; or he may 'huff' (remove from the board) the man which should correctly have made a possible capture. A huff does not count as a turn of play, so the player then continues immediately to make his next move.

If two or more alternative captures or series of captures are possible in any move, the player may choose which capture(s) to make. He does not have to make the move which involves the greatest possible number of captures; but if he chooses to do so, he must take them all, or he may be huffed by his opponent.

When several men are captured in one move they are left in place until the move is completed; but each man may be jumped over only once.

A player wins when he has captured all his opponent's men, or blocked them so that they are unable to move. If neither player has sufficient advantage to win, a draw is declared. At the end of a game, players change the color of their men.

Checkers players around the world frequently improvise both boards and men as the need arises. The Chinese children at the bottom of the page use bottle-tops and a homemade cloth board to play a game in the waterfront market in Singapore. The Senegalese youths in the other pictures move square-cut wooden men on a board that has seen so much use that its checkerboard pattern has faded and worn away with time; they play on a mere memory of the original board.

One man draws his sword, the other a pistol in Gaspare Traversi's painting (left) of a quarrel over an Italian checkers board, dated about 1750.

Materials

Five sheets of transparent, polished acrylic plastic, each 12 inches square, $\frac{3}{16}$ inch thick, with $\frac{3}{8}$-inch diameter holes drilled in each corner, $\frac{1}{4}$ inch from adjacent edges.
Four transparent acrylic plastic rods, 2 inches long, $\frac{3}{8}$ inch in diameter.
Two acrylic plastic rods, one transparent and one black, 6 inches long, $1\frac{1}{4}$ inches in diameter; each cut into twelve discs $\frac{1}{2}$ inch deep, and polished.
A sheet of gray adhesive film, 6 by 12 inches.
A sheet of paper, 12 inches square.
Chloroform glue.

Tools

A ruler, pencil, utility knife, steel straightedge, and pipette or syringe.

How to Make the Game

When you order five sheets of acrylic plastic from the factory or craft shop, have $\frac{3}{8}$-inch holes drilled through each corner, and have the flat surfaces of each sheet polished. Also have each of the two 6-inch rods cut into twelve rounds, and polished. This requires special equipment not normally found in a home workshop.

With a ruler, mark points at $1\frac{1}{2}$-inch intervals along the sides of the 12-inch square piece of paper. Connect opposite points with straight lines, so that the paper is divided into 64 exact squares. Shade alternate squares in pencil to make a checkerboard pattern.

Mark points at $1\frac{1}{2}$-inch intervals along each side of the sheet of adhesive paper. Connect the opposite points with ruled pencil lines. Lay the straightedge along these lines, and with the utility knife, cut very neatly through the film to make 32 gray squares.
Position the paper pattern directly under a sheet of acrylic plastic, and stick eight of the gray film squares at random over any eight of the shaded squares on the pattern underneath. Make sure that the gray film squares are exactly aligned with the pattern lines underneath.

Place the paper pattern under another of the square sheets and stick down eight more of the gray film squares, on any positions except those filled on the first sheet. Repeat these steps on two of the remaining three sheets. When all 32 gray squares are in place, lay the four sheets of acrylic plastic directly on top of each other; when the board is looked at from above, the full checkerboard pattern should be visible.
Place the fifth, blank, sheet of plastic on top of the four sheets with gray squares. Remove

the paper pattern. Keeping the five layers of plastic together, place them on a book or similar object, about $1\frac{1}{16}$ inches thick. The corner holes should line up.

Insert a 2-inch long rod through each of the four corner holes. The rods will extend $1\frac{1}{16}$ inches below the holes. With the top of the rods flush with the top surface of the board, squirt chloroform glue through a pipette or syringe around each of the corner rods. When the glue is dry, the board will stand on its legs. Arrange the 24 pieces on the board.

Young men from St. Louis, Senegal (above), are engrossed in a game of checkers on a board of ten by ten squares. This version of the game is known in Europe as 'Polish' checkers. Sliding-panel compartments on either side of the board hold the playing pieces when they are not in use.

A three-dimensional effect is achieved by the checkers board below, which is simple to make but employs acrylic plastic cut on equipment available only in factories or crafts shops. This up-to-date version of a traditional game is the work of the Dutch designer Jack Botermans.

Chinese Checkers

About the Game

Chinese checkers has had a checkered career. It is basically a variation of the game of halma (from the Greek for 'jump'), which was developed about 1880, and first became popular in Sweden. But some sources claim that, as the name implies, Chinese checkers was originally introduced to Europe from China. There is no question that Chinese checkers is played in modern China – but it may have been brought there from Europe, via Japan!

Wherever it is played, the Chinese checkers board is made in the form of a six-pointed star. On many boards, the corners of the star are colored to correspond to the six colors of the playing pieces.

How to Play the Game

If there are two players, each takes 15 pieces or pegs of one color, and places them in the 15 holes of his home base – one of the points of the star. Two players take opposite home bases.

If there are three or more players, each player takes ten pieces of one color and places them in the ten holes at the back of his home base. Three players take alternate home bases, each facing an empty corner. Four or more players may choose which points to use as base.

The object of the game is for a player to be the first to transfer all his pieces to the corner opposite his home base. Order of play (for three or more players) is clockwise.

Each player takes a turn, in which he may move a piece into an adjoining empty hole; or he may jump over a single peg of any color, to an empty space beyond. If he is then able to jump one or more further pegs, he may do so. Pieces may jump along the lines in any direction. Only one piece may be moved in one turn, but it may be taken as far as the jumping possibilities allow.

A popular strategy is to place some pieces so that they form a 'ladder' along which the other pegs can jump toward their goal; such a ladder may be equally useful, however, to an opponent who is moving his pieces in the opposite direction.

At a day-care center in Peking, two little girls, left, move their playing pieces in a game of Chinese checkers. They play on a board with ten holes in each home base instead of the usual 15 holes.

Materials

A plywood board, 16 inches square, $\frac{3}{8}$ inch thick.

Four strips picture-frame molding, $16\frac{3}{8}$ inches long, $\frac{3}{8}$ inch wide on one side, 1 inch wide on the other, $\frac{3}{16}$ inch thick.

Six wooden dowels, $\frac{1}{8}$ inch in diameter, 15 inches long.

Ninety wooden beads, about $\frac{3}{8}$ inch in diameter; the hole should be $\frac{1}{8}$ inch in diameter.

Wood glue.

Wood primer.

Gloss paint in six colors.

White plastic adhesive tape: $\frac{1}{32}$ inch wide, and $\frac{1}{16}$ inch wide.

Black stain.

Tools

A vise, protractor, pencil, ruler, backsaw, drawing compass, pencil eraser, electric drill or brace with $\frac{1}{8}$-inch bit, paintbrush, and scissors.

A bright design, borrowed from modern 'optical illusion' art, gives new dash to an old favorite, Chinese checkers. Home craftsmen can experiment with different designs around the six-pointed star.

How to Make the Game

Clamp the middle of the 1-inch side of one of the strips of picture-frame molding in a vise; the $\frac{3}{8}$-inch side should be facing up, the cornered edge of the molding lying toward you. On the left end of the strip, measure with the protractor a 45-degree angle from the corner on the edge to the long edge at the top of the $\frac{3}{8}$-inch side. (Or, more simply if the edge is cut straight, measure a point $\frac{3}{8}$ inch from the end on the top edge and draw a line connecting that point with the corner on the left edge.) Measure a 45-degree angle to the left at the right edge of the strip, then repeat these steps on the other three molding strips. With a backsaw, cut along the lines drawn, mitering both sides of the molding simultaneously. Stain the strips black.

Mark a middle point on each side of the square plywood board (8 inches from each corner). Draw straight lines connecting the middle points on opposite sides of the board. These lines intersect at the center of the board; placing the needle of the drawing compass at that point, draw a circle with a radius of 6 inches. Then, being careful not to change the setting of the compass, place the needle where the top of the circle is intersected by the vertical line and draw an arc which crosses the circumference of the circle in two places. Place the needle of the compass at the lower intersection of the circle and the vertical line, and draw another arc which crosses the circle in two places.

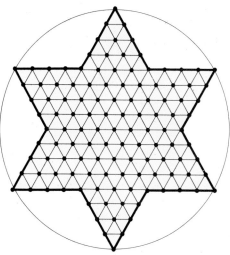

To illustrate the movement of the playing pieces, each point on the board is connected by lines to the points surrounding it, as shown above.

Erase the horizontal line on the board. The circle is now crossed at six points by the vertical line and the two arcs. With ruler and pencil, draw straight lines connecting alternate points. Erase the vertical line and the circle; you now have a six-pointed star.

Each point of the star is also an equilateral triangle. With ruler and pencil divide each side of each triangle into four equal parts. On each triangle, connect corresponding points on adjacent sides with ruled lines. Draw straight lines to connect points on opposite sides of the central hexagon. When all the lines are filled in, the diagram will look like the pattern above.

Drill $\frac{1}{8}$-inch holes at all the points and cross-points. Sand down all rough and splintered areas until smooth. Coat the board with wood primer and let dry. Sand lightly.

Redraw the outline of the star; then elaborate on the design by repeating the basic lines of the star, as in the model at left. Paint the board in bright colors and allow to dry thoroughly. Join the holes on the board with strips of tape, following the same pattern as the lines originally drawn on the board. Cover the main lines of the star with $\frac{1}{16}$-inch plastic tape and the inner lines with $\frac{1}{32}$-inch plastic tape.

Spread glue on the inner sides of the four molding strips, then fasten them in a frame on the four sides of the game board. Place the board face down on the table, and allow the glue to dry.

Use the backsaw to cut the dowels into 1-inch sections. Apply glue to one end of each section and insert it into the hole in a bead. Allow the glue to dry thoroughly. Paint each group of 15 pegs a different color.

Yoté

About the Game

The game of *yoté* is played throughout West Africa. Its great popularity is probably due to the simplicity of setting up a game: the 'board,' five rows of six holes, is scooped out of the ground, and the playing counters are pebbles and bits of stick, which are available anywhere.

Finding the equipment is probably the only easy part of *yoté*. The rules allow for a variety of movements, and the game demands strategy and quick thinking. Because every piece captured allows the capturing player to take another of his opponent's pieces, a disadvantage can rapidly become a rout. Even for the best players, changes of fortune are speedy and surprising, which makes *yoté* a perfect gambling game. In Senegal, particularly, it is usually played for stakes.

Eyes peeled for a quick capture, two boys of East Senegal, photographed by Pamela Johnson Meyer, place their pieces in an unconventional yoté game (opposite) where both players use sticks.

How to Play the Game

Two players are each equipped with twelve pieces, either pebbles or short bits of stick. Each player attempts to capture all his opponent's pieces.

The player with pebbles starts the game by putting a pebble in any hole. The other player places one of his pieces in another hole. Only one piece may be played in each turn. A player does not have to place all his pieces on the board before he starts to move those he has already put down; he may hold some in reserve until later in the game. Pieces may be moved one space in a straight line (but not diagonally) and only to a vacant hole.

A player may capture one of his opponent's pieces by jumping over it and removing it from the board. He is then allowed a bonus capture, the choice of removing any one of his opponent's pieces still on the board.

Though most *yoté* games come to a quick and decisive conclusion, it is possible for a game to end in a tie, when each player has three pieces or less left on the board.

How to Make the Game

Scoop a *yoté* board, like the one in the photograph on the left, out of the sand in a children's sandbox, on the beach, or in the soil of your own backyard. The playing surface is five rows of six holes. The traditional playing pieces are simply twelve pebbles for one player and twelve bits of stick for the other.

Unable to capture at this point in the game, a native of the Upper Volta, left, contemplates his next move. Played in West African villages and cities, many variations of yoté *have developed through the influence of European checkers.*

Fox & Geese

About the Game

Fox and geese is typical of a group of 'hunt' board games for two players, which are played throughout Europe and Asia. One player has very few pieces; but they have the power to capture or 'kill' the opponent's pieces, which are greater in number but more restricted in movement.

The earliest reference to the game in European literature appears in the Icelandic *Grettis Saga* of about 1300, but gameboards dating from the same period have been found in England and Italy. An entry in the household accounts of Edward IV, king of England from 1461 to 1483, lists 'two foxis and 26 hounds of silver overgilt,' i.e. two complete game sets. A later royal enthusiast of the game was the young Queen Victoria, who enjoyed playing fox and geese with Prince Albert during their courtship.

Originally the game consisted of 13 geese and one fox; the fox could 'kill' the geese, but both had the power to move in any direction. After 1600, the game began to change – the geese were no longer allowed to move diagonally or backward, but their number was increased to 17.

How to Play the Game

Arrange the 'fox' and the 'geese' on the board as shown in the photograph below. Players draw lots for control of the geese or the fox. The fox takes the first turn in the game.

Able to move in any direction – forward, backward, diagonally, or to the side – the fox attempts to 'kill' the geese by jumping over each victim into a vacant hole. Multiple jumps are allowed, but the fox is not obliged to jump at every opportunity. A goose, once killed, is removed from the board. The geese may move forward or to the side, never backward or diagonally, one move in each turn. Though unable to jump the fox, they try to corner him so that he cannot move. The fox wins the game if he kills twelve geese.

Wildebeest

Wildebeest, named after the African antelope, is a game for two players created for the fox and geese board by games expert Léon Vié. Players have 11 marbles each in contrasting colors and take turns to place a man in any hole: they must not, however, place two men next to each other in the same line. (This rule may prevent players from bringing all their men into play.) In the second stage, when placement has been completed, each player moves a man horizontally or vertically, the aim being to get three men in a line – a 'wildebeest.' When a player forms a wildebeest, he 'eats' one of his opponent's men (removes it from the board). The player who eats all his opponent's men wins the game.

This fox and geese board is laid out correctly for the start of the game. The mobile fox moves first, then attempts to jump and 'kill' the geese, whose only defence is to crowd around the fox so closely that it can no longer make a move.

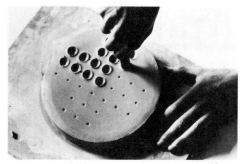

1: With a rolling pin, roll out the clay until it forms a smooth slab, roughly 1 foot in diameter.

2: After placing a dinner plate on the clay, cut around the edges of the plate with a table knife.

3: After marking the game diagram in the surface of the clay, make a hole at each of the 33 points.

Materials

Two pounds of clay.
Eighteen marbles, all of one color except for one contrasting marble.
Poster paints in two bright colors.
Clear varnish.

Tools

A rolling pin, large dinner plate, knife, ruler, pencil, screwdriver or other tool with a round handle about $1/2$ inch in diameter, and paintbrush.

How to Make the Game

Roll out the clay with the rolling pin until it is approximately an inch thick and has a smooth surface slightly larger than the dinner plate. Place the plate over the clay and carefully cut around it, removing all excess clay.

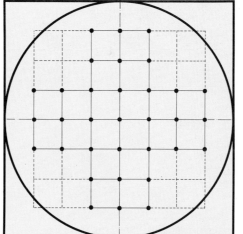

Draw a grid of six by six squares, as shown in the illustration above, to mark the 33 points of the cross shaped fox and geese game board.

With ruler and pencil, divide the surface of the clay into six rows of six squares, 1 inch on each side. Mark the clay very lightly so that all lines can be smoothed away. Following the pattern at left, press the point of a pencil into the 33 intersections that will form the cross-shaped diagram of holes.

Press the end of a screwdriver handle into the clay at each cross point. Wipe with a damp cloth after each pressing to insure a clean and definite indentation in the surface of the board. With the flat edge of the knife or your fingertip, round off the top edges of the board and smooth any surface roughness.

Allow the clay board to dry in a warm airy place. When it is hard, paint it a bright color, with a contrasting color in the holes. A coat of clear varnish will give the board a glossy surface which can be easily cleaned with a damp cloth.

Moving Problem

Here is a game for two players using the fox and geese board, with eight marbles in contrasting colors for each player. Arrange the marbles as shown in the photograph at right. The aim of each player is to move all his marbles into the positions occupied by his opponent's marbles. There are two ways to play this game. One is to set a time limit of 15 minutes. At the end of this period, the player with the most marbles in his opponent's territory is the winner. An alternative way to play is to see which player can occupy all points of his opponent's territory first.

The marbles on the fox and geese board are laid out for the moving problem detailed on the left.

 # Asalto

About the Game

Asalto, a variant of fox and geese, is based on the idea of a numerous but poorly armed force attacking a small but powerful stronghold. The game is played in many European countries, including Germany, France, and England. Though it is usually called asalto or the 'assault game,' it acquired a new name – 'officers and sepoys' – during the Indian mutiny, 1857–58, when Indian troops (the sepoys) revolted against their British officers.

Superbly made of nutwood, pine heart, and oak, the German asalto board below dates from the second half of the eighteenth century. A small drawer inside the board, containing some of the 'foot soldier' playing pieces, is released by a secret catch on one of the playing positions. A marquetry inlay at the top of the game board suggests the walls of a military fortress, and the knotted grain of the base wood resembles the scarred earth of a genuine battlefield.

How to Play the Game

One player has two playing pieces, the officers, which he places on any points in the marked square representing the fortress. The other player has 24 pieces, the foot soldiers, which occupy all the surrounding stations.

An officer may advance one hole at a time in any direction, but the foot soldiers may only move toward the fortress, in a straight line or diagonally. The officers may capture the foot soldiers by jumping over them to a vacant space beyond; the captured foot soldier is then removed from the board. But if an officer misses a possible capture, it is itself removed.

The foot soldiers win the game if they trap two of the officers, making it impossible for them to move, or if they occupy every point within the fortress. If the foot soldiers become so reduced in numbers that this is impossible, the officers win the game.

Shiny 'cat's-eye' marbles, above, are ideal playing pieces to complement a colorful asalto board.

How to Make the Game

The gameboard for asalto can be made from the same materials as the board for fox and geese. Roll the clay 1 inch thick, and cut out a 12-inch square.

Make a grid of 36 squares, 1 inch on each side, as shown on the pattern on page 93, but do not make indentations with the marble until the 'fortress' has been applied to the board.

Roll out a piece of the remaining clay until it is $\frac{1}{4}$ inch thick. Cut out a square, 4 by 4 inches; then trim the square to the shape of the green fortress on the board below. Moisten one side of the form and press it into place on the board.

When the fortress has been correctly positioned, it will cover part of the grid of squares. Redraw the grid on the surface of the fortress; mark the 33 points of the cross and indent holes in the clay with the round base of a screwdriver or other tool, as for the fox and geese board.

With the rounded tip of a kitchen knife, cut two gutters alongside the opposite edges, to hold captured pieces. Allow the board to dry, then paint as shown in the photograph below. Finally varnish the board for a more durable and washable surface.

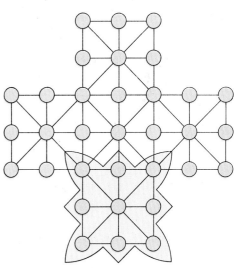

This pattern illustrates the placement of the holes in the asalto board. Make no indentations in the clay until after the fortress has been attached.

The playing pieces are set in place for the beginning of a game on a home craftsman's asalto board (left) – a simple project made of clay, painted with gloss paint, and varnished for durability. The two marbles representing the officers should be different in color from the marbles representing the 'foot soldiers.'

Solitaire

About the Game

The invention of solitaire has been attributed to an unfortunate French nobleman of the eighteenth century. Sentenced to solitary confinement in the Bastille, he whiled away his lonely hours on an improvised fox and geese board, and developed this ingenious game for one person.

The game spread to England, where it developed into a craze during the Victorian era. The solitaire board, whether a simple wooden set or an elaborate creation of carved ivory, was a feature in every parlor.

Almost forgotten by the beginning of this century, solitaire is enjoying a revival today. Handsomely worked sets have become popular 'executive toys,' as commonly seen in the well-appointed office as they once were in the sitting room. For those who become hopelessly intrigued by the mathematics of the problem, several books on the game have been published in recent years.

The crafts-project solitaire board, below, is a simple wooden square with 33 holes. This is the traditional English version; French solitaire players normally use a board with 37 holes.

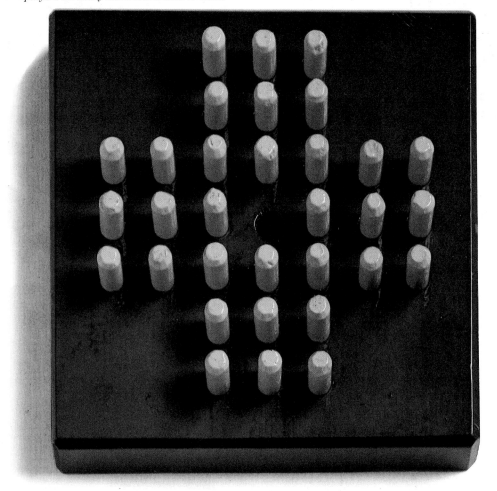

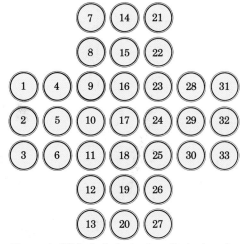

Figure A: With the holes in the solitaire board numbered in this sequence, you can unravel the center-hole problem with the solution given below.

How to Play the Game

The most popular way to play solitaire is the center-hole game, which begins with the pegs arranged as in the photograph at left.

A peg moves by jumping backward, forward, or sideways, but not diagonally, over another peg, which is then removed from the board. The game should end with the last peg in the center hole.

Careful thought and concentration are required to solve the problem but it is possible. If you get stumped too many times, this system is one possible solution. Number the holes as shown above and move in this sequence:

15→17, 28→16, 21→23, 24→22, 7→21,
21→23, 26→24, 33→25, 18→30, 31→33,
33→25, 6→18, 13→11, 10→12, 27→13,
13→11, 8→10, 1→9, 16→4, 3→1, 1→9,
18→16, 16→4, 4→6, 6→18, 18→30,
29→17, 10→24, 23→25, 30→18, 19→17.

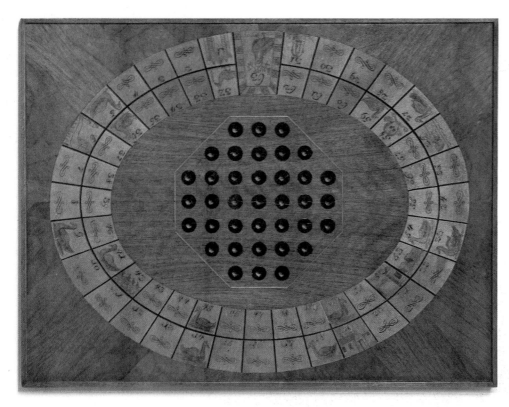

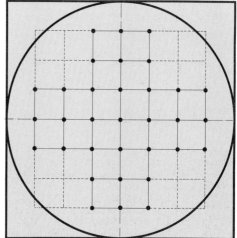

A master cabinet maker created this solitaire board (left) in eighteenth-century Germany, where it was known as the 'hermit's game.' The nutwood board is circled by an ivory-inlaid goose game.

Figure B: To find the 33 points of a solitaire or fox and geese board, first make a grid of six by six squares, then mark the points for the holes.

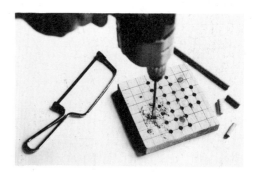

Materials

A block of wood, 6 inches square, 1 inch thick.
One yard of wooden dowel, $\frac{1}{4}$ inch in diameter.
Gloss paint in two contrasting colors.

Tools

A pencil, ruler, electric drill or brace with a $\frac{1}{4}$-inch bit, coping saw, pocketknife, sandpaper, and paintbrush.

1: Measure and mark the grid of six by six squares on the wooden block; saw the dowel into 32 pegs.

How to Make the Game

Though solitaire can be played on any fox and geese board, a smaller, more portable set can be constructed of wood. (For a pocket-sized game, reduce the measurements of the wooden panel.)

Divide the 6-by-6-inch surface of the wood into 36 squares, six horizontal rows and six vertical, 1 inch on each side. Mark the 33 intersections as shown in the pattern in figure B. Drill holes $\frac{1}{2}$ inch deep in each marked crosspoint.

Saw the dowel into 32 1-inch lengths and round the ends slightly by whittling at the cut edges with the knife. Sand down all rough edges on the board and pegs.

Paint the board and pegs in contrasting colors, as shown in the photograph opposite, and allow to dry thoroughly.

2: Mark the 33 cross-points on the surface of the game board, and drill a $\frac{1}{4}$-inch hole at each point.

A novel way to package the game: carried in an oakwood box, the pocket-sized solitaire board above uses spent brass shell cases as pegs.

Caroms

About the Game

When they have finished helping their parents in the market place, Yemeni children like to join their friends for a game of *caroms*. If no one thought to bring a board along, the children scratch a game diagram in the dirt. The game has been a favorite in India, Burma, and the Yemen for the past hundred years: it is probable that this simple type of pocket billiards was first played by the Egyptians or the Ethiopians.

In Sa'dah, northern Yemen, a group of boys play caroms – *or, as they call it,* kairam – *on a local variant of the game board. The player on the right proudly holds aloft the discs he has captured.*

How to Play the Game

Each player has nine discs, black or white. A red 'queen' and a 'striker' complete the equipment. The pieces are arranged as shown opposite, the stem of the Y formed by the white discs facing the opening player.

White shoots first by placing the striker anywhere within the rectangular box on his side of the board and flicking it toward the cluster of discs. His aim is to knock one of his own discs into a pocket. Only the fingers may cross the foul line, and only the fingers and hand are allowed over the base line. If a player infringes on these rules, he must return one of his pocketed discs to the inner circle. If he cannot meet the penalty, he must pay as soon as he can.

The first player's turn continues as long as he pockets a white disc with each shot; the player returns his striker to the player's box after each shot. The striker may ricochet from the walls to strike a disc, or it may hit an opposing disc to pocket one of the player's discs. If a player pockets one of his opponent's discs, it remains in the pocket and his turn ceases. If the striker lands in a pocket, the player owes a penalty and his turn is over.

If a disc flies off the board, the turn ceases and the opponent replaces it as close as possible to the center circle. If the striker falls onto a disc, it is removed without disturbing the disc. If a disc falls on the striker, the striker is removed and the disc left in place.

The red queen may be pocketed any time after a player has scored his first disc; she scores five points for the player (unless he has 24 points, in which case she counts for one point).

A 'board' is over once a player has pocketed all his discs. He scores the number of his opponent's discs still on the board, plus five points if, during the round, he pocketed the queen (the queen scores only for the winner of the board). There are several boards to a 29-point game. A match consists of three games.

Materials

A plywood board, $23\frac{1}{2}$ inches square, $\frac{3}{8}$ inch thick.
Four wooden slats, 1 by $\frac{3}{4}$ inch, 25 inches long.
Wood glue.
Wood primer.
Yellow gloss paint.
Black wood stain.
India ink (oil base).
Four furniture-leg studs.
Nineteen rubber-cushioned furniture-leg studs, 1 inch in diameter.
Adhesive paper dots: red, black, and white.

Tools

A drawing compass, scroll saw, primer brush, sandpaper, ruler, soft pencil, paintbrush, technical drawing pen, vise, protractor, backsaw, and wire cutters.

How to Make the Game

Set your drawing compass to 2 inches. Place the point of it at the tip of one of the corners of the board and draw a 90-degree arc from edge to edge of the board. Repeat this at the other three corners. Using the scroll saw, cut out these four corner wedges. Sand down all rough surfaces until smooth. Apply a coat of wood primer to one side of this board and allow it to dry thoroughly. Sand down this surface lightly. Paint this side of the board with yellow gloss paint, and allow it to dry.

Using the ruler and a soft pencil, lightly draw two diagonal lines on the painted surface, crossing at the center of the board and bisecting the four corner arcs. Place the point of the drawing compass at the central crosspoint, and draw three concentric circles: one $1\frac{1}{4}$ inches in diameter, one 6 inches in diameter, and the third 7 inches in diameter.

Using the figure as a guide, measure and mark two concentric squares: one 15 inches on each side, the other 18 inches. Connect the inner square to the outer by drawing two perpendicular

lines from each corner – one to each edge of the outer square. Erase the corners of the outer square between these perpendicular lines. Also erase the diagonal lines within the three circles.

Trace over the remaining lines on the board with the technical drawing pen. The line of the second circle and those of the outer square frame should be twice as thick as the others. Allow the india ink to dry thoroughly.

Clamp the middle of one of the slats in the vise so that its $\frac{3}{4}$-inch side is facing upward. Line up the perpendicular of the protractor with the edge of the left end of this side; the base of the protractor is in line with the bottom edge of the slat. Mark a point on the top edge that is 45 degrees from the bottom corner edge. Draw a line from the corner edge to that point. Do the same at the right edge of the slat, measuring and marking a 45-degree angle toward the left.

Using a backsaw, miter both ends of the slat, cutting along the lines drawn. Prepare the remaining three slats for miter joints, following the same steps. Sandpaper all rough edges of the four wooden slats. Apply glue generously to the mitered ends of the slats and stick them together to make a frame. Wipe off excess glue, and allow to dry. Apply stain to the frame; leave it to dry completely.

Apply glue to the straight side edges of the playing board, but not to the arc corners. Place the black frame over the board so that the glue-covered edges are flush with the lower part of its inner sides. Allow the glue to dry. Turn the board over and fix the four furniture-leg studs to the bottom of the frame.

Make the playing pieces for the game by cutting the nails or screws off the furniture-leg studs. Fasten black dots to both sides of nine studs, white dots to another nine, and red dots to both sides of the remaining stud.

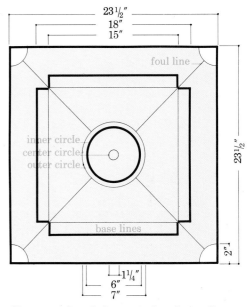

Measure and mark the caroms *board according to the dimensions shown on the diagram above.*

The arrangement of discs to start a game is shown on the caroms *board, below, which can be made by a home craftsman in only a few hours.*

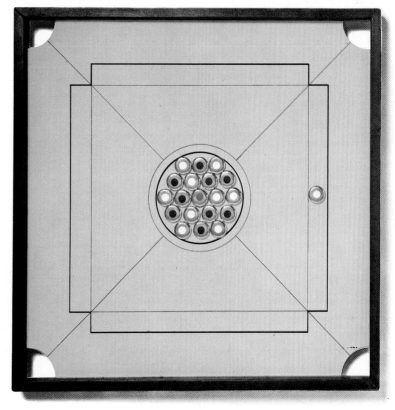

Table Hockey

About the Game

Table hockey is a fast and rowdy indoor version of the equally exciting outdoor sport, field hockey. Originating in Persia, hockey was one of the sports that featured in the Olympic and Isthmian games of ancient Greece, and was later introduced into much of Europe by the Romans. Schoolboys in medieval England played a similar game with sticks and a ball, called 'the London Balle Playe,' which was really an excuse for a free-for-all, while ancient games of the hockey type were known as 'hurley' in Ireland, and 'shinty' in Scotland.

Modern hockey was standardized by the Wimbledon Club in England in 1886, and is played today by children and adults in schools and clubs around the world. Table hockey obviously does not afford the players as much exercise as the field version, but it does not require so much space – and can be enjoyed whatever the weather.

How to Play the Game

The Soviet version of table hockey presented here can be played by two, four, or six players. If two are playing, each one stations himself at one end of the game table so that he can easily move the three hockey players on his side of the field by shifting the handles underneath the board. (If more players are participating, they form two teams and decide among themselves which handles to control.)

At a Young Pioneer Center in Leningrad, four Russian boys man the controls of their wooden players in a fast game of nastolny hockey.

A referee places the ball in the center of the board between two hockey players from opposing sides. When he gives the signal, the hockey players are manipulated so as to strike the ball into the goal at the opponent's end of the board. The winner can be the first to score five goals, or the highest goal scorer in 15 minutes of play; the time-limit is flexible.

Materials

A plywood board, 16 by 32 inches, ³⁄₈ inch thick.
Twelve plywood boards, 2³⁄₄ inches wide, ³⁄₈ inch thick: four 5¹⁄₂ inches long, two 5³⁄₄ inches long, four 3¹⁄₂ inches long, two 32³⁄₄ inches long.
Two white pine strips, ³⁄₈ inch square, 32 inches long.
Twelve strips half-round molding, ³⁄₈ inch wide: four 5¹⁄₂ inches long, two 5³⁄₄ inches long, four 3¹⁄₂ inches long, two 32³⁄₄ inches long.
Four wooden dowels, 8 inches long, 1 inch in diameter.
A plywood board, 6 by 24 inches, ³⁄₈ inch thick.
Six screw-on wooden handles, 4 inches long, 1 inch in diameter.
Six lengths of wire, 8¹⁄₄ inches long, ¹⁄₁₆ inch in diameter.
Two dozen wire nails, ³⁄₄ inch long.
Four screws, 1¹⁄₄ inches long, ¹⁄₈ inch thick.
Four rubber grips for table legs.
Wood glue.
Wood primer.
Gloss paint: red, white, blue, black, yellow, and green.
A wooden ball, 1 inch in diameter.

Tools

A ruler, pencil, electric drill or brace with ¹⁄₁₆-inch and ¹⁄₈-inch bits, scroll saw, hammer, vise, protractor, backsaw, primer brush, sandpaper, paintbrush, tracing paper, carbon paper, pliers, artist's camel-hair brush, and screwdriver.

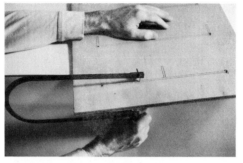

Figure A: Each of the 'players' moves in one of the slots cut out of the board. After drawing the grid, mark the six columns for the slots.

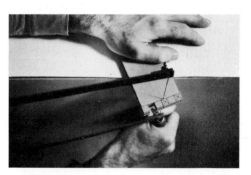

1: Drill a small hole into the ends of the columns and fit the blade of the scroll saw into these holes. Refasten the blade to its frame; cut out each slot.

2: Measure and mark the row of squares at the ends of the sideboards, then cut out alternating 'fingers' for the corner joints of the frame.

3: Glue the joints so that the fingers of one board dovetail with the fingers of another, then secure with nails until the glue dries completely.

How to Make the Game

Place the 16-by-32-inch board horizontally on the work table. Measuring from the left edge, mark the following points at the top and bottom 32-inch edges: 3, 3¹⁄₄, 8, 8¹⁄₄, 13, 13¹⁄₄, 18³⁄₄, 19, 23³⁄₄, 24, 28³⁄₄, and 29 inches. Connect the corresponding points on opposite sides of the board with ruled lines.

Measuring from the bottom, mark the following points at the left and right 16-inch edges: 2, 2¹⁄₄, 7⁷⁄₈, 8¹⁄₈, 13³⁄₄, and 14 inches. Connect corresponding points on opposite sides of the board with rules lines.

Place the ruler on the top horizontal line and, measuring from the left edge of the board, mark the following points: 9¹⁄₂ and 22¹⁄₂ inches. Mark the same points on the second horizontal line from the top, and the two horizontals at the bottom of the board. On the two horizontals at the center of the board, measuring from the left edge, mark points at 4¹⁄₂, 14¹⁄₂, 17¹⁄₂, and 27¹⁄₂ inches. Connect the corresponding points on each pair of horizontal lines. With figure A as a guide, draw heavier lines over the six columns and their extensions. Erase all other lines.

Using the electric drill or brace with the ¹⁄₁₆-inch bit, drill a hole at one corner of each of the six columns. Unfasten the blade of the scroll saw and insert the blade in one of the holes. Refasten the blade to the frame of the saw and saw along the lines drawn to cut out that section (see photograph 1). Cut out the other five columns in the same manner.

On each edge of the board, mark points 1 inch from each corner. Connect corresponding points on opposite sides of the board. At the four points where the lines intersect, drill holes with the ¹⁄₈-inch bit. Sand down all rough areas.

Measure and mark all of the 2³⁄₄-inch wide boards for finger joints. To do this, place each board horizontally before you. On each of the long edges, mark points that are ³⁄₈ inch from each of the 2³⁄₄-inch edges. Draw vertical lines to connect corresponding points on opposite sides of the twelve plywood boards. Measuring from the bottom edge, mark points at ³⁄₈-inch intervals on the 2³⁄₄-inch edges and the lines beside them. Draw straight lines to connect corresponding points on the edges and the lines beside them. Each ³⁄₈-inch wide section on the ends of each board is now divided into six ³⁄₈-inch squares.

With the scroll saw, cut out alternate squares on each side of the 32³⁄₄-inch boards. (The first square cut should be on the same edge at both ends of the board.) Cut out alternate squares in the same manner on the two 5³⁄₄-inch-long boards. Cut out alternate squares at one end only of the 5¹⁄₂-inch-long boards and 3¹⁄₂-inch-long boards.

On the uncut end of each of the 5¹⁄₂-inch and 3¹⁄₂-inch boards mark the three consecutive squares that begin at the same edge as the first cut-out space on the other end of the board.

Cut these three squares out in a block, leaving a block of three squares on the other side of the edge. Apply glue to the finger joints and join all the 2¾-inch boards together, as shown in photograph 3. The fingers of one joint should dovetail with the fingers of another, each corner forming a right angle. To hold the boards in place while the glue is drying, hammer a nail through one of the fingers and its corresponding slot at each joint. Remove the nails after the glue has dried.

Clamp one of the molding strips in the vise so that the flat side is facing up. Line up the perpendicular of the protractor with the left edge of the strip; the base of the protractor is in line with the bottom edge of the surface. Mark a point on the top edge that is 45 degrees from the bottom corner. Draw a line from that corner to the point. Repeat these steps at the right end of the strip, measuring and marking a 45-degree angle to the left. Repeat these steps on the remaining eleven molding strips.

With a backsaw, cut through the wood along these lines. Apply glue to the flat sides of the strips and arrange them on the top edge of the hockey board frame so that their mitered corners form right angles. Nail them partially to the frame until the glue is dry.

Place the frame on one of its long sides. On the inner side of the frame, along the bottom edge, fasten a pine strip with glue, then with several evenly spaced nails. Attach the other pine strip to the inside of the other long side of the frame.

Apply a coat of wood primer to all the components of the hockey board and allow it to dry thoroughly. Sand it down lightly. Paint the 16-by-32-inch board and the 8-inch dowels green. Paint both sides of the frame blue, and the molding strips on the frame red. Allow the paint to dry thoroughly.

Place the frame on the work table so that its molding strips face upward. Apply glue along the top sides of the slats inside the frame. Insert the 16-by-32-inch board, painted side up, into the frame, so that it rests on these slats. Allow the glue to dry thoroughly.

Mark a center point on one end of each of the four dowels. Using the ⅛-inch bit, drill a hole ½ inch deep in each of the dowels at that point. Match the holes in the dowels with the holes drilled in the four corners of the game board; screw the dowels fast to the board.

Place the 6-by-24-inch plywood board horizontally on the work table. On the long top and bottom edges, mark points 3¾ inches from the left edge. Draw lines connecting the points. There is now a rectangle at one end of the board.

On each side of this rectangle, measure and mark with the pencil at ³⁄₁₆-inch intervals. Connect corresponding points at opposite sides of the rectangle. Using the enlarged grid you have just drawn, transfer the outline of the hockey player in figure C to the plywood board.

Saw the player out with the scroll saw, then

4: After mitering the ends of the half-round molding strips, glue them to the top edge of the sideboard and nail them securely in place.

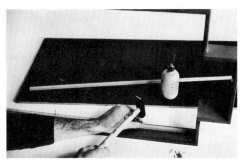

5: Tack the wooden strips to the inner edges of the long sides of the sideboard frame; these strips will support the table hockey 'playing field.'

The team is in position, the ball is on the field – everything is ready for a fast game of table hockey. More compact but no less exciting than the outdoor version, this table hockey game is inexpensive crafts project and fun to make.

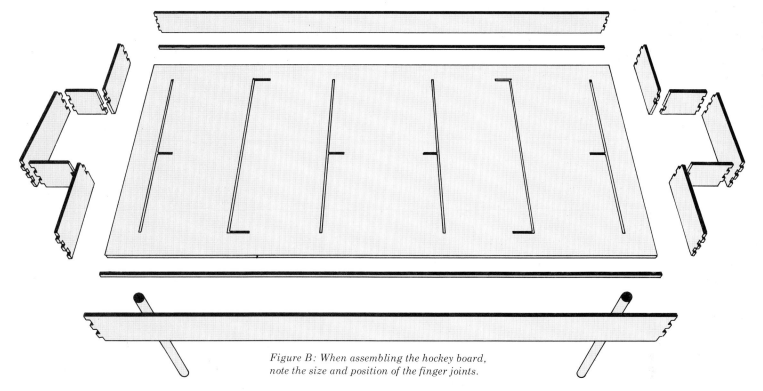

Figure B: When assembling the hockey board, note the size and position of the finger joints.

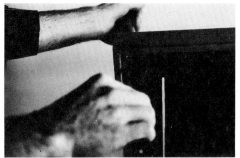

6: *Glue the playing field into the sideboard frame. Drill holes in each corner of the field and screw the dowels to the board to make the table legs.*

7: *Transfer the enlarged outline of the hockey player onto the board; cut it out with the scroll saw and trace its outline five times onto the board.*

8: *Paint the players, drill holes in the extended hands and position the wire hockey sticks. Screw the wooden handles into the players' feet.*

place this cut-out piece on the plywood board to draw the outlines of the other five players. Cut them out, and sand down any rough areas. With the ¹⁄₁₆-inch bit, drill a hole, ¹⁄₂ inch deep, in the hand sections of each player. Drill a similar hole in the front foot of each player.

With the pliers, bend each piece of wire to resemble the hockey stick in figure C; the shaft should be roughly 4¹⁄₄ inches long. Apply glue to the end of each shaft and insert into the hand hole of a player. Allow the glue to dry thoroughly. Apply wood primer to each of the players; allow

it to dry, then sand lightly. Paint each player with a red cap and shirt, white hands and face, yellow trousers, and black shoes. (Paint one side, allow to dry, then paint the other side.) Place each man upright on one of the six slots in the board. Attach the handles to the players' feet by fastening the screw into the drilled hole. The players should move easily in their slots when the handles are manipulated under the board.

Attach a rubber grip to each of the four legs of the table hockey board.

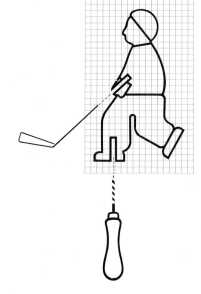

Figure C: To enlarge the hockey player, draw a grid of ³⁄₁₆-inch squares, and redraw the figure, square by square, in the grid you have drawn.

Dominoes

About the Game

Dominoes were invented by the Chinese at least three centuries ago. Once used in divination, they are now essential to games and gambling throughout China and Korea. There are 21 pieces which represent the permutations of throwing two dice (each half of the domino stands for one die). The 'one' and 'four' spots are red, as on Chinese dice. Eleven pieces are duplicated, making a set of 32. The duplicated pieces are called 'civil' and the others 'military,' an important distinction in some games. Old sets were carved of dark woods, ivory, or bone.

Dominoes were introduced into Europe through Italy in the mid-eighteenth century, and there is some speculation – but no proof – that they were brought there from China. By the end of that century they had arrived in England, where they were criticized as 'a very childish sport,' by Joseph Strutt in his classic *Sports and Pastimes* of 1801. Dominoes, he wrote, 'could have nothing but the novelty to recommend it to the notice of grown persons in this country.' His patronizing judgement was blithely ignored by the public, who took to the game with enthusiasm and have played it ever since.

Early European dominoes were made of thin pieces of bone. By 1840 the bone strip was glued to an ebony backing, and fastened with sprigs of brass to make small tiles that would stand on edge. The availability of cheap sets, made of wood stained black (and recently, of plastic) brought the game a popular following, and it is still widely enjoyed in cafes in Europe and Latin America.

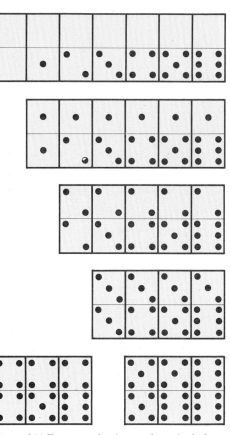

A set of 28 European dominoes, above, includes blanks, which do not appear in Chinese dominoes.

How to Play the Game

At the beginning of a game of European dominoes, the 28 'bones' are placed face down on the table and shuffled by the players.

Four players can play the 'block' game. Each player draws seven dominoes from the central pile or 'boneyard,' and sets them on their edges so that their faces are hidden from the other players. The player who draws the double 6 starts by placing it on the table face up, vertical to him. Turns are taken clockwise round the table.

Russian domino players disregard the winter cold in Gorky Park, Moscow (opposite), during a game of European dominoes. The doubles are set at right angles to the line; since one end of the layout has reached the end of the table, the last player has placed his 'bone' to turn a corner.

Eskimo walrus-ivory dominoes are marked with higher values but played like European dominoes.

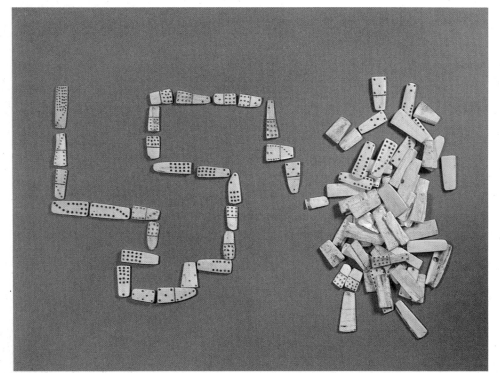

The next player must put down a domino with one end valued 6, for example a 6:3. The third player must then match either the other side of the double 6, or the 3 at the opposite end of the layout; and so on.

Double bones are always placed crosswise, vertical to the first player; other bones are placed end to end in a line. (If the layout becomes too long for the table space, a bone may be set sideways so that a corner is formed.)

If a player cannot match either end of the layout, he calls 'pass' and the next player takes his turn. The game ends when one player has put down all his dominoes. The value of the dominoes held by the other players is added up and becomes the score of the winner.

If none of the players can place any of their remaining dominoes, they reveal them and the player with the lowest number of points is declared the winner. The points of the other players are added up and the winner deducts his own remaining points to arrive at his scoring total. The first player to reach 200 points is the outright winner.

Domino games do not depend on mere chance; accurate calculation and rapid deduction are essential to good play. A long suit consisting of several dominoes bearing the same number – such as 4:5, 4:4, 4:2, 4:0 – can be very helpful and should be played as soon as possible, to block the opponents.

The 'draw' game is played by two or three players. The bones are shuffled,

each player turns up one, and the highest score designates the first player. The dominoes are replaced and reshuffled. Each player draws seven; the remaining seven (or 14) dominoes are left in the boneyard.

The first player places any domino he chooses on the table, and the next player must match one end of it. Players take turns clockwise. If a player cannot match either end of the layout, he draws a bone from the boneyard; if he can play it he does so straight away. If not, he keeps it and continues to draw until he can play a bone, or until there are only two left in the boneyard, in which case he passes. As in the block game, the first player to place all his bones is the winner, and takes the score of the other players' dominoes.

Chinese Dominoes

Chinese dominoes can be used for many games – the following are simple to play and require only one set.

Tjak-ma-tcho-ki is a Korean game for two to four players. The dominoes are shuffled face down, and each player draws one; the highest scorer is the leader. The dominoes are reshuffled; the leader draws six and the other players five each. Players put down a stake before they examine their draw.

To start the game, the leader tries to make a matching pair (i.e. two identical dominoes from the eleven pairs in the 'civil' series) from those in his hand. If he can do so he places them face up on one side and discards any domino in his hand. If he cannot make a pair, he simply discards one domino.

The second player may pick up the discarded domino if he can match it with one in his hand to make a pair. If not, he picks up one from the stock pile, makes a pair if he can, and

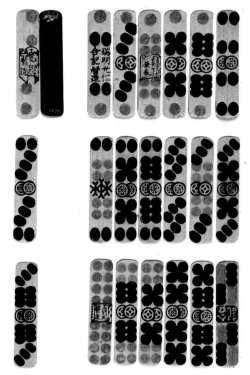

Chinese domino cards, called t'ien chiu p'ai, *(above) were printed from woodcuts about 1850. Their values are the same as Chinese dominoes except that there is no paired 'civil series.' The characters drawn in the middle of the cards represent coins. Others are shown opposite.*

discards one. This process is repeated, in a clockwise direction, until one player has three pairs.

When two or three people play, the double 6 cannot be used to make the third (winning) pair.

If the third pair is completed by a domino drawn from the stock pile, all the players pay their stake to the winner; but if it was completed by using a discarded piece, only the player who made the discard pays.

Tsung shap, 'to dispute for tens,' is a game for two players with Chinese dominoes. The bones are shuffled and piled face down in a stack four high, and each player takes half the stack (16 dominoes). The first player draws the top right domino from his stack and lays it face up on the table. The second player draws one from his stack and lays it alongside the one already played. The players continue to take turns to lay down one domino, at either end of the layout.

If a player plays a domino which matches one at either end of the row, he takes both, scoring ten points for each spot on them.

If a player plays a domino on which the spots – if added either to the spots on the two dominoes at one end of the row, or to the spots on the single dominoes at both ends of the row – add up to ten or a multiple of ten, he takes the three bones and counts one point for each spot on the dominoes.

If there are only two dominoes on the table and a player can take them, he scores 40 points and places them on top of each other: this is called *táp ti,* 'a sweep.' He then lays another domino on the table.

Should a player place a domino without noticing that it makes a winning combination – a pair or a scoring trio – his opponent may take the dominoes and continue with his turn.

A set of Chinese dominoes consists of 32 pieces or 'bones.' The 'civil series' are the matched pairs in the center and right columns above.

Materials

A pine board, $\frac{1}{4}$ inch thick, 32 inches long, 4 inches wide.

Tools

A ruler, pencil, coping saw, sandpaper, soldering iron, and red felt-tip pen.

How to Make the Game

Place the board horizontal to you on a work table. With the ruler and pencil, mark off points at 1-inch intervals from the left to the right end of the board, along the top edge. Repeat at the bottom edge. Draw vertical lines connecting these points, to make 32 rectangles.

Using the coping saw, cut through the board along the penciled lines, making 32 domino pieces. Sand down all rough surfaces.

To make the spots on the dominoes, remove the head from the soldering iron and use the circle that held the head to burn open spots into the wood surface. Follow the arrangement of spots shown in the illustration at left.

Refasten the head onto the soldering iron and fill in the centers of the spots on all the domino face numbers except the 'one' and 'four' spots. With a red felt-tip pen, fill in the centers of the 'one', 'four', and 'six' spots, as shown in the photograph below.

Simple wooden Chinese dominoes, above, when played on a table, make sharp clicking sounds that turn into the barrage of percussion often heard in crowded Chinese casinos.

Lotto

About the Game

Lotto, or loto, was developed from *il Gioco del Lotto in Italia*, the Italian national lottery, which has been held, almost uninterruptedly, at weekly intervals since 1530. Players pay a stake and are given a card. In the classic version of the game, the card is divided into three horizontal and nine vertical rows. Five numbers between 1 and 90 appear in each horizontal row, the other spaces being blank. In the Victorian era, pictures and letters replaced the numbers, in educational games such as 'botanical lotto,' 'spelling lotto,' and 'historical lotto.'

Bingo, one of the most important gambling games of our times, grew out of keno, a nineteenth-century American version of lotto. In bingo houses round the world hundreds of people play simultaneously, as much for the fun of the game as for the huge cash prizes that are offered to the winners.

How to Play the Game

The version of lotto presented here is for four players, and is intended for young children. Each player chooses one of the lotto frames, and places it in front of him on the table.

A fifth person acts as game organizer. He takes the 32 postcard sections and shuffles them face down on the table. At random, he selects one of the sections, turns it over and calls out the number on it. The player who has this number on his frame board calls out, and the organizer hands him the piece, which he places face up over the corresponding section on his frame. Then the organizer picks and calls out another number. The game continues until one player covers all the sections of his board, and calls 'Lotto!'

'Le Loto' (opposite) by the Anglo-French painter Charles Chaplin (1825–1891) captures the sheltered atmosphere of a French bourgeois childhood in the 1860's. The standing girl uses two cards to keep a tally of the wooden numbers that she picks up from the table and reads out to her companions. The two seated girls cover the numbers on their own cards with red chips.

The thinking man's lotto (below): although the basic arrangement is similar, the Japanese game karuta, *or 'hundred poems,' depends not on chance, but on the players' intimate knowledge of certain masterpieces of Japanese poetry. Here a family is engrossed in* karuta: *as the father reads out the first line of a poem, the others vie in picking out a card containing the last lines.*

Materials

Four pieces of plywood, 6 by 8 inches, $\frac{1}{8}$ inch thick.

A sheet of poster board, 12 by 16 inches.

Two sets of press-on numbers, 1 through 32: one set about $\frac{1}{2}$ inch high, the other set about 1 inch high.

Gloss paint: red, yellow, green, blue.

India ink.

Wood primer. Wood glue.

White plastic adhesive tape (optional).

Four picture postcards, 4 by 6 inches. (The pictures should have vertical, rather than horizontal designs.)

Tools

A ruler, pencil, drill or brace with $\frac{1}{16}$-inch bit, scroll saw, sandpaper, primer brush, paintbrush, utility knife, steel straightedge, and technical drawing pen.

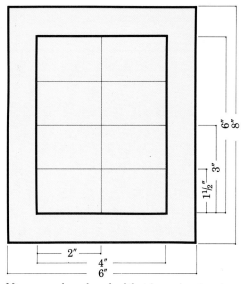

Measure and mark each of the plywood rectangles as shown above. Then cut out the large inner rectangle, and saw it into eight smaller sections.

How to Make the Game

Take one of the 6-by-8-inch boards, and with ruler and pencil, measure and mark lines 1 inch from each of the four edges, making an inner rectangle of 4 by 6 inches.

Mark this inner rectangle with three points $1\frac{1}{2}$ inches apart on the 6-inch sides, and two single points 2 inches along the 4-inch sides. Connect opposite points with ruled pencil lines, so that the inner rectangle on the board is divided into eight smaller rectangles of $1\frac{1}{2}$ by 2 inches. Drill a $\frac{1}{16}$-inch hole at one corner of the inner rectangle.

Unfasten one end of the blade of the scroll saw. Insert this blade into the hole in the board, and refasten it to the scroll saw frame. Cut out the inner rectangle along the lines drawn. Then cut the rectangle into its eight marked sections. Repeat these steps on the remaining three 6-by-8-inch boards. Sand down all rough and splintered surfaces.

Apply wood primer to the frames and allow to dry. Sand the frames down lightly. Paint one frame red, one yellow, one green, and one blue. Allow the paint to dry thoroughly. Decorate the frames if you wish with thin strips of white plastic adhesive tape, as in the models photographed at left.

Place one of the frames on the corner of the poster board, and trace round the outer and inner sides. Repeat on the other three corners of the poster board. Using a utility knife and steel straightedge, cut out the four 6-by-8-inch rectangles, but not their inner rectangles.

With pencil and ruler, divide each of the inner rectangles on the poster boards into eight 2-by-$1\frac{1}{2}$-inch rectangles, as you did on the plywood. With the technical drawing pen and India ink, rule heavy black lines over these pencil lines. If you wish, draw smaller inner rectangles, as on the photographed models.

Place the cards vertically in front of you, and apply stick-on numbers in the middle of the small rectangles on each board. Arrange the numbers at random, so that no two consecutive numbers appear on one board.

When all the cards are numbered, apply glue to the undersides of the plywood frames, and place the frames on top of the poster board frames so that they match exactly.

Picture postcards of 1920's belles add an air of nostalgia to a children's lotto set that is easily assembled by a home craftsman. As the game progresses, the pictures build up like a jigsaw puzzle. The cards are framed in gay colors.

A German lotto game of 1850, above, was designed to teach children multiplication; each number on the card is given with its two factors. The colored etchings portray various characters of everyday life, such as a bank clerk, scholar, grocer, and housewife. The playing boards and card sections are stored in a compartmented box.

Reassemble each group of eight plywood pieces to form rectangles of 4 by 6 inches. Apply glue to the back of a colored picture postcard and glue it on top of one of these 4-by-6-inch rectangles. Allow the glue to dry. Turn the postcard over, and with the utility knife, cut down between the plywood sections to divide the postcard into eight pieces. Repeat these steps with the other three groups of plywood pieces, and postcards.

Place a postcard group, assembled to its full rectangular size, next to one of the lotto frames. With press-on numbers, repeat the numbers shown on the lotto board, so that the same numbers appear in the same sections on both board and postcard.

The little girl at left upsets a chair in her haste to call 'Lotto!' In this Italian nineteenth-century print a group of Neapolitan neighbors gather to play an informal version of the game that has also been played as the national lottery since 1530.

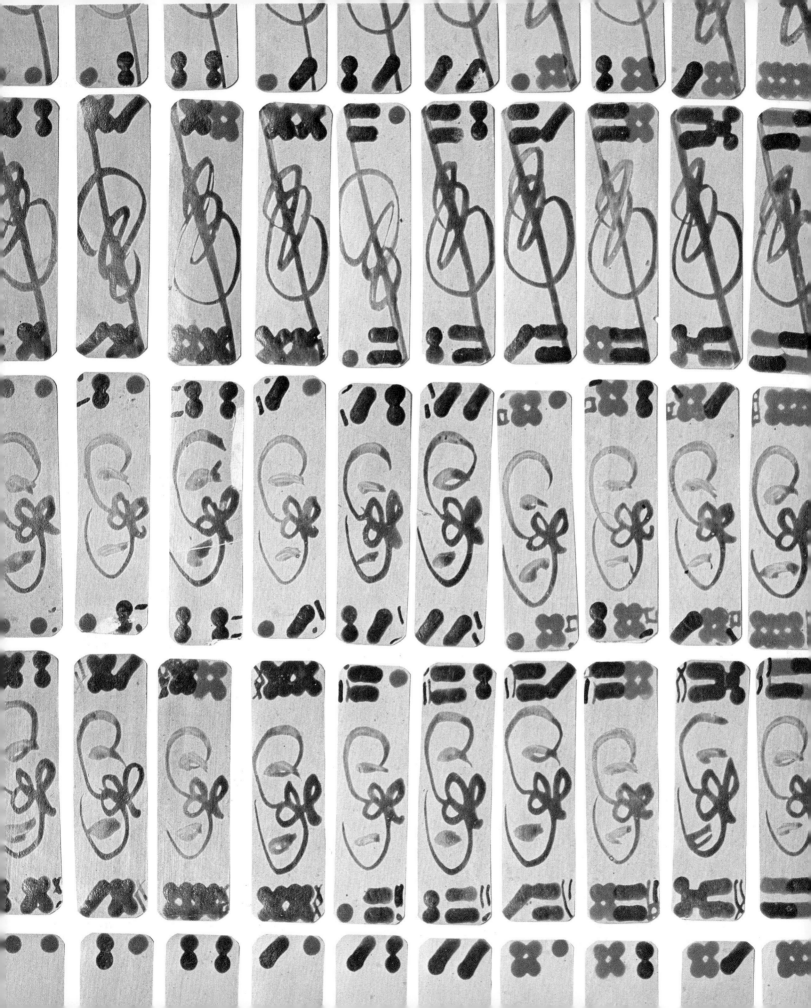

Cards

About the Game

Cards are the most versatile and popular of all 'game implements': a vast variety of them have gradually evolved, both in Asia and the West, and innumerable games have been devised for them. The conventional deck of 52 cards constitutes an ingenious and flexible system of symbols, readily adapted to games combining luck and skill in varying degrees. In bridge and poker, for example, the skill and experience of the player are of paramount importance, while in many others, winning or losing is wholly a matter of luck.

At least part of the continuing fascination of cards is that they appeal to the player's tactile sense: they feel exciting to the touch, and many people delight in displaying virtuoso ways of shuffling and dealing that add immeasurably to the 'theatre' of card playing. At the same time, cards also appeal to the visual sense, and are often decorated with designs of great beauty. Of all the minor objects of everyday life, none has received more loving and careful attention from painters and graphic artists than the deck of cards. Finally there is an air of mystery and magic about cards which science and logic have been unable to dissipate: it is an ancient tradition of the occult, kept alive by gypsy fortune-tellers and amateur *tarot*-readers (as well as one of the scenes of Bizet's *Carmen*).

The history of playing cards begins, in fact, with the sticks and arrows that were used in an earlier form of divination. The games scholar Stewart Culin has shown that the arrow shafts once used for fortune-telling in Korea bore painted emblems denoting their rank; in time these symbols were copied, first onto gambling sticks, then onto long, narrow strips of paper, and the result was a stylized pack of playing cards, divided into suits known as man, fish, crow, pheasant, antelope, star, rabbit, and horse. In ancient Chinese literature, cards are mentioned as early as the Tang dynasty (618–907 A.D.), and subsequent centuries witnessed a great proliferation of card games throughout the Orient.

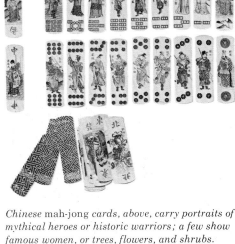

Chinese mah-jong *cards, above, carry portraits of mythical heroes or historic warriors; a few show famous women, or trees, flowers, and shrubs.*

Chinese domino playing cards, known as t'ien chiu p'ai (opposite), come from a handmade deck of 126 cards divided into six stylized suits.

Playing cards below, representing only a few varieties in the vast range of Chinese cards, are (left to right) two elaborate domino cards, a mah-jong *card, and two so-called 'money' cards,* shih-hu p'ai, *the pictorial equivalent of coins, which anticipated the invention of paper money.*

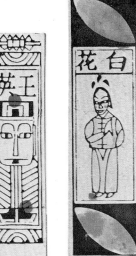

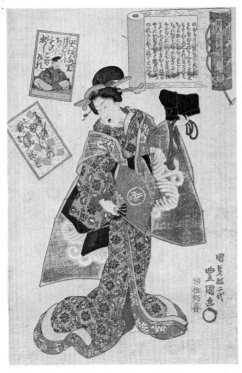

The lady in the kimono, above, belongs to a set of cards used in the Japanese 'hundred poems' or karuta *game, shown in a photograph on page 109.*

113

There were literary and theatrical cards, number cards, 'money cards' symbolizing coins (and scarcely distinguishable from the earliest forms of paper money), *mah-jong* and domino cards, picture cards, alphabet cards, flower cards, teaching cards – even chess-playing cards. Not only paper and cardboard but also bone 'sticks' and thin leaves of ivory were employed in their manufacture.

Traditional Asian cards are very different from European cards, however, and there is very little evidence to indicate how the idea of playing cards ultimately found its way to the West. It has been pointed out that the Hindu deity Ardhanari (half Siva, half Devi) is often depicted holding a cup, a scepter, a sword, and a ring – a combination that suggests a possible Indian ancestry for the four suits of the old European *tarot* pack: cups, batons, swords, and coins. The gypsies (an Indian nomad caste which wandered into Europe) are sometimes credited with having brought cards with them, but they did not arrive in appreciable numbers until the middle of the fifteenth century, a hundred years after cards had come into general use throughout Europe.

It seems more probable that playing cards, like chess, were introduced by the Arab conquerors of Spain and Sicily: significantly, cards are called *naipes* in Spain and *naibi* in Italy, terms derived from the Arabic *nabi* (prophet), referring to their use in fortune-telling. At any rate, cards are mentioned in various European documents of the 1370's and '80's; some of these are government decrees condemning the use of cards in games of chance. By 1423 they had

A rich, gorgeously attired young man is about to be fleeced by an experienced cardsharp and his courtesan confederate in the painting at left by Georges de La Tour (1593–1652). Known as Le Tricheur à l'as de carreau – 'The Cheater with the Ace of Diamonds' – this long-forgotten canvas is now one of the best-known French Baroque masterpieces in the Musée du Louvre, Paris.

The nine hand-painted cards, above, are known as the 'goldsmith' cards on account of their gold-leaf backgrounds. Probably produced in Provence, France, during the fifteenth century, most of them, apart from the five of 'clubs,' depict cryptic versions of the classic tarot trumps. The man with the dog may represent the tarot 'magician'; the crowned sea-monster, the devil.

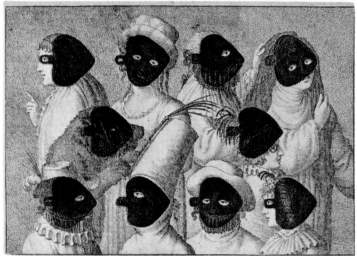

Four of the 'transformation cards' issued by the German publisher, Cotta, around 1810, together with a series of 'card almanacs.' Romantic ladies and gentlemen would give each other one card a week for a year, till the recipient owned a whole deck of these intriguing hide-and-seek designs.

'All Four' – H. W. Bunbury's satiric view of the great card-playing craze that swept through the clubman's London during the eighteenth century.

become sufficiently notorious that St. Bernardino of Siena preached a sermon against them in which (like many later churchmen) he attributed their invention to the devil. Yet the earliest European cards were often educational in purpose: they covered such subjects as heraldry, geography, grammar, and logic. Hand-painted by master artists, some of them mirrored the courtly ideal of the age of chivalry, showing knights and ladies in formal or hunting dress, with the suits divided into falcons, stags, hounds, and ducks. Magnificent sets of *tarot* (or *tarocchi)* cards were produced in Italy. Venice favored a 78-card deck, while in Florence the deck usually had 97 cards, and in Bologna, 62. It is the *tarot,* with its 22 *atouts,* or major trumps, which has supplied fortune-tellers with their traditional arsenal of mysterious symbols, for the deck includes such enigmatic and ambiguous figures as *le pendu* (the hanged man), *la roue de fortune* (the wheel of fortune), *la papesse* (the woman pope), death, and the devil.

The conventional deck of 52 cards now common in the games world (called numeral cards to distinguish them from *tarots)* were to undergo a separate evolution. The four suits of early German cards were hearts, bells, leaves, and acorns. Spain and Italy retained (and continue to use) the old division into cups, batons, swords, and coins. French cards of the sixteenth century, however, introduced the marks still current in France and the English-speaking world: *coeur* (hearts), *trèfle* (clubs), *pique* (spades), and *carreau* (diamonds).

On a stormy day, a Copper Eskimo woman from Bathurst Inlet, Canada, lays a game of solitaire. Early whalers introduced cards to the Arctic.

Turkish men play cards in an old Istanbul cafe: here, as elsewhere along the Mediterranean, the local cafe serves as social club and card center.

Though cards originated in China and Korea, these Young Pioneers in modern Peking play with a deck based on traditional European design.

During the fifteenth century, cards began to be printed from woodblocks rather than painted by hand, and this thriving industry gave rise to a breathtaking variety of card designs. During the early nineteenth century, German artists vied with each other to produce ingenious 'transformation cards,' in which the hearts, diamonds, etc., are cleverly incorporated into some overall picture: a boating party, a group of monks, or a flight of birds, for example. In the twentieth century, too, modern artists like A. M. Cassandre and André François have tried their hand at designing decks of cards. For the most part, however, cards continue to embody the stylized traditions of another age: the familiar court cards of the standard English or American pack are still attired in the costumes of Henry VII's reign.

The annals of gamesplay contain an almost limitless selection of card games. For most of them, a deck or two of cards is all the equipment needed. But cards do not lend themselves to crafts projects; it is very difficult, if not impossible, for an artist without elaborate printing equipment to produce a usable deck of cards. On the other hand, the home craftsman can easily make the special boards required for the two card games presented in the following pages: English cribbage and German *Poch*, each of them with an ancient and honorable history. They are included here as representatives of the whole genus of card games that take advantage of the tremendous flexibility of this medium, 'with spots quadrangular of diamond form, ensanguined hearts, clubs typical of strife, and spades, the emblem of untimely graves' (as the poet William Cowper describes them in *The Task*).

Millions of francs changed hands in gaming rooms like the one shown below, in an engraving of the Directoire period (1795–9). Here Parisians played such card games as ombre, piquet, and reversi.

La Bouillotte?

Cribbage

About the Game

Cribbage is a card game in which a pegged board is used to keep track of the scores that accumulate rapidly during play. The game first came into prominence early in the seventeenth century, when it ranked as a favorite of gentlemen gamblers in many parts of Europe. The cribbage board was evidently adapted from earlier dice-game scoreboards; the rules of play seem to be descended from an English card game called noddy.

'Sir John Suckling invented the game of Cribbige,' states the seventeenth-century author of *Brief Lives,* John Aubrey, but it may be that Sir John was merely the man who codified the game. In the absence of further evidence, it is impossible to say with certainty how a game as old as this came to be invented. Sir John, in any event, is further described as 'the greatest gallant of his time, and the greatest Gamester, both for Bowling and Cards.'

During his lifetime (1609–42) he became famous as a poet and courtier: 'He played at Cards rarely well, and did use to practise by himselfe a-bed, and there studied how the best way of managing the cards could be.' But he also liked to cheat. He manufactured his own cards, and sent his decks 'to all Gameing places in the countrey,' having taken the trouble to mark the cards 'with private markes of his,' so that whenever he showed up for a game he could read his opponents' hands like a book. 'He gott twenty thousand pounds by this way.'

Early English settlers brought cribbage to America, where its popularity still endures, especially in New England. Played either with or without stakes, cribbage is a fast, absorbing two-handed game, which makes it ideal for sailors and fishermen: hence the cribbage boards that Eskimos used to manufacture for sale to the crews of ships that visited their coasts. Originally brought home as souvenirs, some of these walrus-ivory boards are now valuable museum pieces. In Europe, too, there are some superb examples of marquetry cribbage boards and elaborately inlaid cribbage-tables: on one of them, in 1809, King Gustavus IV of Sweden signed his abdication.

The four-handed version of the game is no longer as popular as in Victorian times, when Charles Dickens wrote about four-handed cribbage in *The Old Curiosity Shop.* Dickens's Mr. Quilp, like Sir John Suckling, is a dishonest player: 'Among his various eccentric habits he had a humorous one of always cheating at cards, which rendered necessary on his part, not only close observance of the game, and a sleight-of-hand in counting and scoring, but also involved the constant correction, by looks, and frowns, and kicks under the table, of Richard Swiveller, who being bewildered by the rapidity with which his cards were told, and the rate at which the pegs travelled down the board, could not be prevented from sometimes expressing his surprise and incredulity.'

How to Play the Game

Modern six-card cribbage has become the standard game in most areas, replacing the older, and slower, five-card hand. The game is played by two people, using a 52-card deck. In cribbage, the ace is always the lowest card, counting as one point. The others retain their face value except the court cards (jack, queen, king) which count as ten points each.

For thousands of years, game players have kept score on cribbage-type boards: the hounds and jackals game, above, of ebony and ivory, was found in the Egyptian tomb of Renseneb (1800 B.C.).

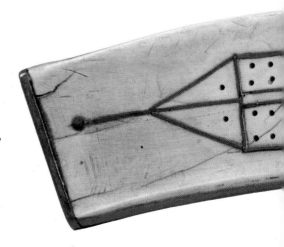

Score is kept on a board with two scoring pegs for each player. There are 30 holes in each long row and each player moves his pegs up the outer row and down the inner row on his side of the board. When a player has scored through all the holes and back onto the foot of the board, a game of 61 points is finished. A 121-point game can be played by moving the pegs twice around the course. When the game begins, one peg is moved up the board the number of the player's first score. When he scores again, the player moves the rear peg the correct number of points beyond the first peg. In this way, the total score is always visible, as well as the last score made.

To begin the game, each player cuts the deck. Whoever turns up the lower card becomes the first dealer of the game. The non-dealer is called the 'pone.' The dealer shuffles the deck and the pone cuts it in two, face down on the table. The dealer picks up the lower part of the deck and deals six cards to his opponent, then six to himself. The remaining cards are placed on top of the rest of the deck.

Each player examines the cards in his hand, then discards two to form the 'crib,' an extra hand that belongs to the dealer but is not used while the hand is played. At the end of the hand, when all the dealt cards have been played, the crib is added to the dealer's score. As compensation for the dealer's crib, the pone is given three points at the start of the game and may advance his peg three holes on the outer row of his side of the board.

The pone cuts the deck again. The dealer turns over the top card of the lower part of the deck and places it, face up, on top of the crib. This is the 'starter' and will be used at the end of the hand, when both players tally their scores. If the starter is a jack, however, the dealer announces 'two for his heels' and advances his peg two holes.

The pone begins the actual game by throwing down a card, face up, on his side of the table. He calls out its value. On all subsequent plays, the total value of the cards played is called out. (For instance, the pone may lay down a jack and call 'ten,' and the dealer, going next, lays down a 3 and calls 'thirteen.') Each player keeps the cards he plays face up in front of him.

After the pone has laid down a card, the dealer discards one of his cards and calls out the totaled value of his card plus his opponent's. On this play, he tries either to match his opponent's card and make a 'pair' or to add to it so that the total is 15. If he makes a pair or 15, he gains two points and advances his rear peg two holes beyond the forward peg.

The pone, in his turn, attempts to build on the cards already played. Besides trying for a 15 or a pair, each player can try for a 'pair royal,' three of a kind which scores six points; or a 'double pair royal,' four of a kind which scores twelve points. In pairs, triplets, and fours, the cards must be consecutively played with no other cards intervening. (Though all court cards count ten points, the rank must match to make a pair.)

The players continue to lay down cards in turn as long as the totaled value of the cards does not exceed 31. A 'run' of three cards in numerical sequence gains three points. The cards do not have to be played in order; for example, the play might be 4, 5, 3. The player who put down the last card would score three points. Four-, five-, six-, and seven-card runs count as many points as there are cards. Again, there may be no interrupting cards, and the ace always counts as the low card. It may not be used together with a king and queen in a run.

When the total value of the cards played comes to 31, the 'stop' or round is over. If a player cannot lay down a card and stay below 31, he calls 'go.' If the opponent is in a similar position, he does the same and a point is given to the player who first said 'go.' If, however, the second player can discard and stay under 31, no 'go' is

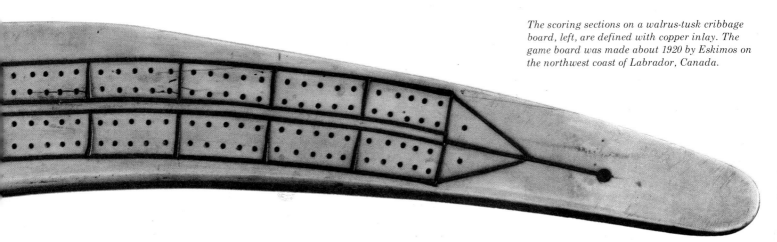

The scoring sections on a walrus-tusk cribbage board, left, are defined with copper inlay. The game board was made about 1920 by Eskimos on the northwest coast of Labrador, Canada.

scored and the second player begins to lay down his cards. He scores one point for every card he can play without going over 31. If he scores 31 exactly, he wins two more points. If the player has been able to lay down any cards and stay within the confines of 31, but cannot score it exactly, he calls 'go' after his last card and scores one point for the 'go.'

As soon as one stop of 31 points is completed, or a 'go' has been scored, the cards played are turned face down to prevent confusion in the next stop. The remaining cards in hand are played, the called score starting with the value of the next card. The player discarding the last card wins a point, or two points if he is able to score 31 with the last card.

In cribbage, 'melding' is done after all the dealt cards have been played. That is, all the cards in a player's hand are tallied for the scoring combinations possible, and this score is added to whatever is already pegged on the board. In tallying the points, the starter is considered the fifth card in each hand. The scoring combinations are the same as those used in play, plus the combinations included below.

Double runs are made up of a pair plus a run. The run is counted twice because it can be constructed with two different cards. For example, 10, 10, 9, 8 scores

eight points. Likewise, in counting 15's, each combination scores two points. A hand of 7, 7, 8, 8 would score for four different combinations of 15, and for its two pairs. If, in this case, the starter was a nine, there would be an additional score of 16 points for a quadruple run.

Scored points when melding:
15... 2 points
Pair... 2 points
Royal pair... 6 points
Double royal pair... 12 points
Run... 1 point for each card
Double three-card run... 8 points
Double four-card run... 10 points
Triple three-card run... 15 points
Quadruple run... 16 points
Four-card flush (all in hand of the same suit)... 4 points
Five-card flush (with starter)... 5 points
(The crib cannot score for a four-card flush.)
'His nobs' (jack of the starter's suit)... 1 point

The pone is always the first to meld after each hand. At the end of the game, this can be an important privilege because if the pone makes game score he wins. The dealer may be able to make a winning score too, but it is not counted if the game has already been won by the pone. In tallying the value of a hand, the 15's are counted first, then the pairs, then the runs and, finally, the flush.

If the pone has not made game score, the dealer tallies first his hand and then the crib. Each score should be announced by name and points so that the opponent can verify it. Experienced players sometimes agree to use the 'muggins' rule, which allows a player to call 'muggins' and score for himself any points his opponent missed in melding. Of course, this rule is never used between a skilled player and an inexperienced player.

The deal alternates between the players from hand to hand. After each hand the cards are shuffled as at the beginning of the game. The loser of a game deals first in the next game.

Variations
Cribbage can be played with more than two people. When three play, each is dealt five cards and one card is dealt into the crib. Then a card from each hand goes into the crib. The player to the left of the dealer plays first and deals in the next round. The game score is 121. A triangular scoreboard is used in the three-handed game.

In four-handed cribbage, those sitting opposite each other are partners. Each player is dealt five cards, one of which goes to the crib. The deal shifts to the left, as in three-handed cribbage. The standard scoring board is used and the partners score for each other.

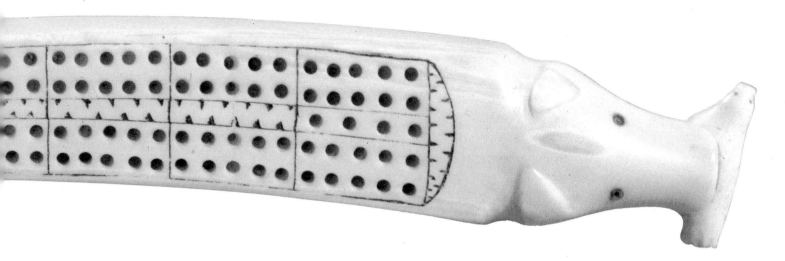

Materials

A plywood board, 16 by 18 inches, ³/₁₆ inch thick.
Sixteen ¹/₄-inch nails.
Wood glue.
Four wooden balls, 1 inch in diameter.
A fireplace-sized match, 10 inches long.
Four wooden beads, ¹/₄ inch in diameter.
Gloss paint or enamel.

Tools

A pencil, ruler, coping saw, scroll saw, awl, brace or electric drill with ¹/₈-inch bit, hammer, vise, sandpaper, woodcarver's gouge with ³/₈-inch blade, wood rasp, and paintbrush.

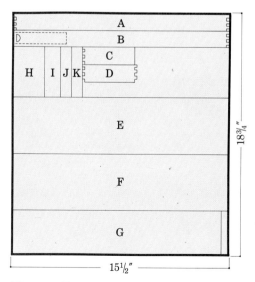

Figure A: To save time and wood in cutting out the eleven pieces for the cribbage board, map them out on the plywood board as shown here.

How to Make the Game

With ruler and pencil, divide the plywood board into eleven rectangles of the following dimensions: two rectangles (A, B) 1¹/₂ by 15¹/₂ inches; one rectangle (C) 3¹⁵/₁₆ by 1¹/₂ inches; one rectangle (D) 4¹/₈ by 1¹/₂ inches; two rectangles (E, F) 4¹/₈ by 15¹/₂ inches; one rectangle (G) 3³/₄ by 15¹/₈ inches; one rectangle (H) 2¹/₂ by 3³/₄ inches; one rectangle (I) 1 by 3³/₄ inches; two rectangles (J, K) 1¹/₁₆ by 3³/₄ inches.

You can save time and material if you lay out the rectangles as shown in figure A. Several of the sections (A, B, C, D) will be joined by finger joints. When drawing these 'fingers,' mark a line ³/₁₆ inch from the 1¹/₂-inch ends of the proper sections (that is, both ends of A and D, and one end only of sections B and C). Measure and mark at ¹/₄-inch intervals along the drawn line and the plywood edge next to it. Connect the points that are opposite each other with straight lines. Cut out the rectangles with a scroll saw. With the same saw, cut out three alternating ¹/₄-inch sections on the marked ends of A, B, C, and D. When this is done, each end should have three 'fingers' separated by spaces of the same size.

Place a 4¹/₈-by-15¹/₂-inch section (F) on the work table and draw a line ³/₈ inch from each of the 4¹/₈-inch edges. Then, measuring from the top edge of the board, mark the two lines with points at ³/₈ inch, 1¹¹/₁₆ inches, 2⁷/₁₆ inches, and 3³/₄ inches. Place the ruler horizontally on the board and connect corresponding points.

On the top horizontal line, from left to right, mark off a series of 2¹/₄-inch measurements at ¹/₄-inch intervals: 2¹/₄ inches, ¹/₄ inch, 2¹/₄ inches, ¹/₄ inch, etc. Repeat at the bottom horizontal line. Place the ruler vertically on the board and connect all points directly opposite each other. The board is now divided into twelve 1⁵/₁₆-by-2¹/₄-inch rectangles, as shown in figure B.

Placing the ruler along the 2¹/₄-inch edges of each rectangle, measure from the corner and mark the following points: ¹/₈ inch, ⁵/₈ inch, 1¹/₈ inches, 1⁵/₈ inches, and 2¹/₈ inches. Connect opposite points on each rectangle with straight lines.

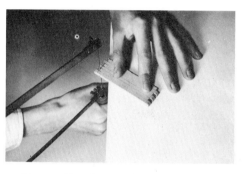

1: After marking the row of ³/₈-by-³/₈-inch squares, on each end of the sideboards, cut out alternate squares to make the finger joints of the cabinet.

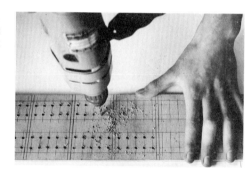

2: With an electric drill or brace, drill holes in the 122 points that have already been marked on the top section of the cribbage board.

3: Apply wood glue to one side of section G, then place it over the drilled top section, leaving a ³/₈-inch border overlapping on all sides.

121

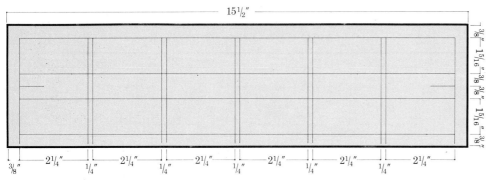

Figure B: Divide the surface of section F into twelve 1⁵/₁₆-by-2¹/₄-inch rectangles, as shown here.

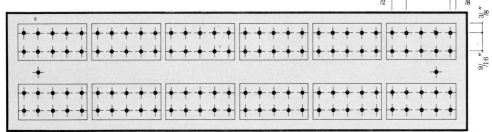

Figure C: Mark each rectangle with the ten points that will be the holes for the scoring pegs.

4: Glue the divider sections onto the bottom board to separate the cupboard sections that will hold the cards and the four scoring pegs.

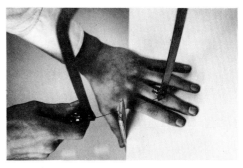

5: Holding the saw at a slant to match the markings at the edge of section B, carefully cut out the sliding door for the inner cupboard.

6: Fit the finger joints together at the corners, as you glue the sideboards to make a frame around the top section of the cribbage board.

7: Apply glue to the edges of the bottom board, and fit it over the frame, positioning it so that the sliding door opens onto the cupboard.

Place the ruler on the 1⁵/₁₆-inch edges of each rectangle and, measuring from the corner of the rectangle, mark these points: ³/₈ inch and ¹⁵/₁₆ inch. Connect the points opposite each other with ruled lines. Each of the twelve rectangles now contains ten points of intersection, as shown in figure C. With the awl, press a hole into each of these 120 points.

With the board lying horizontally before you, line up the ruler vertically with the second row of crosspoints in the first rectangle on the right. Make a mark in the center of the board (2¹/₈ inches from the top edge) and press a hole with the point of the awl. Repeat these steps on the left side of the board's surface.

Using a brace or electric drill with a ¹/₈-inch bit, drill holes through the board at the 122 points you have marked with the awl. Sand the board, smoothing down any rough or splintered areas.

Spread glue evenly on section G (3³/₄ by 15¹/₈ inches). Place this on the unmarked side of the board containing the 122 holes. Center it so that the rim of the larger board is exactly ³/₁₆ inch on all sides. Hammer a nail at each corner of the smaller board.

On the remaining 4¹/₈-by-16¹/₂-inch board (E), draw a line ³/₁₆ inch from each of the four edges, making an inner rectangle of 3³/₄ by 15¹/₈ inches. Spread glue on one side of section H (2¹/₂ by 3³/₄ inches) and place this on the left side of section E, so that its three edges exactly fit the inner rectangle you have just drawn. Press down for a few minutes; then hammer nails at the four corners of section H.

Spread glue evenly on one 3³/₄-inch edge of section J. Spread a thin strip of glue, too, on either side of this edge, then place it upright,

flush to the right side of section H (see photograph 4). To the right of this partition, glue section I (1 by 3³/₄ inches). Hammer nails at the four corners of section I. Spread glue on one 3³/₄-inch edge of section K and place it upright, flush to the piece just fastened. Carefully place the whole construction aside and allow the glue to dry thoroughly.

Place section B (1¹/₂ by 15¹/₂ inches) horizontally on the table so that the notched 1¹/₂-inch edge is at the right. Draw a vertical line 3³/₄ inches from the plain edge at the left. On this line and on the left edge of the board, measure and mark points ¹/₄ inch from the top and bottom of the section. Connect the points on the line with the opposite points on the edge of the board. Turn the section over and draw a line 3³/₄ inches from the left edge that corresponds exactly with the line on the reverse side. Measure and mark points ¹/₈ inch from the top and bottom edges on the line and the left edge. Draw lines connecting those points directly opposite each other.

Place this section lengthwise in a vise with the marked area well above the mouth of the vise. Using the ruler, measure and mark a line on the 1¹/₂-by-³/₁₆-inch edge that connects each ¹/₄-inch mark on one side with the adjacent ¹/₈-inch mark on the other side.

With the scroll saw, cut along these slanted lines, as in photograph 5, until you reach the horizontal line 3³/₄ inches from the edge. First saw one slanted line, then the other. When you reach the end point on the second line, turn the saw blade and saw along the horizontal line until you exactly meet the slanting edge of the first line sawed. You should now be able to slide this section out from the rest of the board.

With fine sandpaper, smooth down the edges of this door and the grooves in the board. The door should now slide easily against its slot.

To make a door-grip, draw a vertical line ½ inch from the left edge of the door and another line ¾ inch from the edge. With a woodcarver's gouge, dig a shallow path from the middle of the line at the right to the middle of the line at the left, deepening it slightly as the latter line is approached. Using a pocketknife blade, cut straight down on the line at the left, severing the gouged strip from the wood. Sandpaper the door-grip until smooth.

Lay the top of the cribbage board so that section G is facing up. Apply glue to the ³⁄₁₆-inch rim where section F overlaps section G. Spread a light coat of glue on the finger joints of sections B and D. Place these sections on adjoining sides of the rim of section F, dovetailing the 'fingers' at the corner. Apply glue to the fingers of section A and join it with section D, as shown in photograph 6. Make sure all three sections are snugly fitted against section G before you glue the finger joint at the corner of sections A and C.

Remove the sliding panel and apply glue to the inner surface of section B, above and below the doorway. Join this inner side with the edge of section C and press the two pieces together for a few moments. Allow the glue to dry thoroughly.

Spread glue carefully on the exposed edge of the rectangular frame. Do the same to the top edges of the partitions glued to the bottom board of the cribbage cupboard (section E). Pick this

section up, turn it over and place it on top of the rectangular frame so that the sliding door will open onto the double cupboard formed by partitions J and K (see photograph 7). Allow the glue to dry completely and hammer nails into the four corners of the bottom board.

File down each of the wooden balls on one side until you have a flat section about ½ inch in diameter. Apply glue to these flat surfaces on the four balls and fasten them to the corners of the upturned bottom board. When the glue is completely dry, sand down all rough surfaces on the cribbage board.

Paint the board in bright colors, using gloss paint or lacquer. If you like, use a contrasting color for the peg squares, as shown in the model below. You may also want to decorate the board with narrow strips of colored plastic adhesive tape.

To make the cribbage pegs, cut the fireplace match into four 2-inch lengths. Whittle one end of each section to fit in the peg holes. Whittle the other end to fit in the bead. Apply glue to the end of each stick and insert it into the hole of a bead. Allow the glue to dry thoroughly and paint with bright gloss paint.

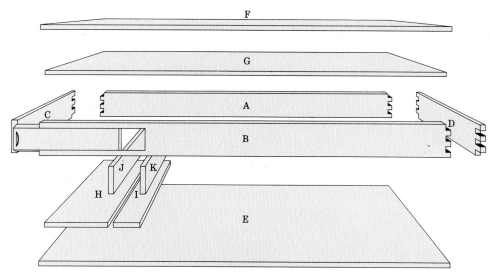

Figure D: The lettered components of the cribbage board are assembled as shown here. Note that the corner of sections B and C has no finger joint, leaving room to open the sliding panel of the cupboard.

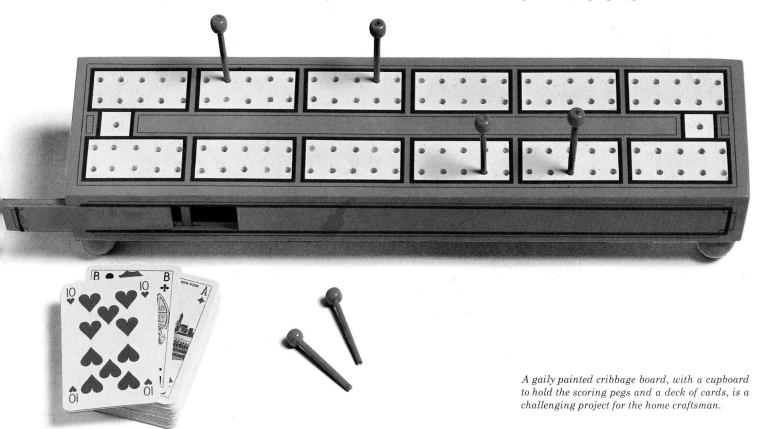

A gaily painted cribbage board, with a cupboard to hold the scoring pegs and a deck of cards, is a challenging project for the home craftsman.

123

Poch

About the Game

The name of the game comes from the word *pochen*, which in turn derives from the medieval high German *bochen*, meaning 'to knock' – with a hammer, or on a door. In card games, knocking with the fingers on the table signifies 'I defy you' or 'I'll stay in the game,' and in this sense the name *Poch* probably refers to the bidding procedure in the second stage of the game. *Poch* is an amalgam of at least three old card games, which are reflected in its three stages of play.

Poch originated in sixteenth-century Europe; one of the earliest (1558) references to the game appears in the works of the famous Nuremberg *Meistersinger,* Hans Sachs. The oldest *Poch* board in the Bavarian National Museum, Munich, is dated 1527. *Poch* boards may have eight or nine holes; old ceramic or wooden boards were often decorated with exquisite paintings.

Poch boards resemble those used for an old English card game, Pope Joan (named after a legendary woman pontiff of the ninth century).

A Poch-type game board from southern Germany, below, was made of painted linden wood in 1713. The eight egg-shaped depressions have verses written round them, referring to moves of the game.

How to Play the Game

Poch is played by four people, with a pack of 32 cards comprising the ace, king, queen, jack, 10, 9, 8, and 7 of all four suits.

The dealer shuffles the pack and deals eight cards face down to each player. Before looking at the cards, each player puts a chip into each of the eight pockets on the board. The dealer looks at the last card he dealt himself, and names its suit as trumps.

Players examine their hands. If a player has the value in trumps of any of the cards or card combinations shown on the board – i.e. the 7-8-9, the 10, the jack, the queen, the king, the ace, or both king and queen, he collects the chips in the appropriate pocket. A player who has both king and queen of trumps collects both from the individual king and queen pockets, and the joint king/queen pocket. If no player has both king and queen, or 7-8-9, the chips remain in those pockets until the next game.

The second stage of the game involves play from the pocket marked *Poch*. The player on the dealer's left 'bids' one or more chips into the *Poch* compartment. Any player who wishes to stay in the game must match the bid. A player with a poor hand may 'pass' at this stage, losing the opportunity to gain the *Poch* stakes, though still having a chance to win the third stage. After the other players have bid or passed, the first bidder may raise the stake.

When bidding stops, each player lays out his best combination of cards, and the highest score wins the stakes in the *Poch* pocket. Combinations score on pairs, threes, or fours of a kind, as follows. The greatest number of the same face value scores highest: i.e. four 8's score higher than three queens. If two players have the same number of cards in their combinations, i.e. three kings against three 10's, the higher rank wins; the kings score over the 10's. Aces beat kings. In the case of two players each having a pair of the same face value – i.e. two pairs of jacks – the pair that includes a trump (named at the start) scores higher.

All players take back their cards, and the third stage of the game is started by the winner of the *Poch* stakes, who lays a card face up on the table. Any player (there is no order of play) follows with the next card up in the same suit, and another player follows with the next, until the ace of that suit is played. This is a 'stop' and the player of the ace may then lead with any card he wishes, in the same suit or a different one; the process continues up to the next 'stop' card, and so on. The first player to lay down all his cards wins this final 'race' stage, and the other players pay him one chip for each card left in their hands.

The cards are reshuffled and dealt by the player on the left of the last dealer. Each player 'dresses' the board by placing a chip in each pocket, and the game begins again.

Because the game is of German origin, the clay board, above, incorporates models of German playing cards. With its three stages of play, Poch *offers an interesting alternative to the usual card games.*

Materials
Two pounds of clay.
Gloss paint: yellow, green, blue, red, white, and black.
At least 40 playing chips for each player: use real gambling chips, buttons, tiddledywinks, or beads.

Tools
A rolling pin, awl, utility knife, piece of string about a foot long, ruler, protractor, wooden ball 3 inches in diameter, paintbrush, and artist's camel-hair brush.

How to Make the Game
Roll out the clay with the rolling pin into a roughly circular shape, about 18 inches in diameter and 1 to 1½ inches thick. Tie one end of the string to the awl and the other end to the utility knife, about 1½ inches from the end of the blade. The length of string between the awl and the knife should be 8 inches.

Place the point of the awl in the center of the clay tablet, pull the string taut, and run the knife evenly round in a complete circle, cutting through the clay. Remove excess clay. Adjust the string between the awl and the knife so that it is now 6 inches long. With the awl still in the center of the clay, run the knife tip very lightly round the clay circle so that it scores a shallow line concentric with the edge of the board. Detach the knife; remove the awl from the clay. Lay a ruler across the center of the clay tablet and run the tip of the knife lightly along it, to score a line dividing the circle in two. With a

protractor, mark four 45-degree angles on each side of this bisecting line; then line them up with the ruler and score lightly with the knife, so that the board is divided into eight wedge-shaped sections.

At each point where a straight diameter line crosses the circular scored line, press the wooden ball into the clay, making an indentation about ¾ inch deep.

Roll out long coils of clay, about ½ inch in diameter, to make lips for the cups. Join the lips smoothly to the edge of the clay holes by wetting your fingers and smoothing the clay into place. Smooth the joints where the two ends of the lip coils meet in a circle.

With the rolling pin, roll out a sheet of clay about ⅜ inch thick. Using the card designs below as a guide, cut out seven corresponding card shapes, about 2 inches by 1½ inches. Wet the backs of these card forms and position them in the right order inside the cup holes on the board, aligned on the diameter lines, as shown in the pattern at right. With a wet fingertip, smooth over the scored lines between the cups and across the center of the board; fill in and smooth over the hole made by the awl. Allow the clay to dry completely in a warm, airy place.

Paint the main surface of the board with yellow gloss paint, and paint the cup holes green. Using the model as a guide, paint the designs on the cards with a fine camel-hair brush; they should represent an ace, a king, a queen, a jack, a 10, a king and queen together, and a 7, 8, and 9 together. Paint a banner in front of the eighth cup hole, and paint the letters POCH on it. Allow the paint to dry.

The German playing cards below can be used as models for the cards on the crafts-project Poch board. They were printed by one of the first companies to use color lithography for cards.

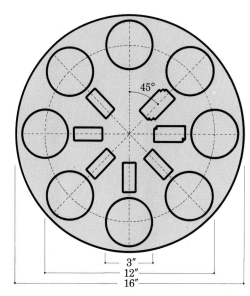

To place the cup holes and 'cards' on the board, first divide the circle into 45-degree segments.

1: Knead the clay to make sure that there are no air bubbles in it, before you roll it to form a disc shape about 18 inches in diameter, 1 inch thick.

2: With one hand holding the awl in place, draw the utility knife steadily round the clay disc, keeping the string taut and the knife blade vertical.

3: Press the wooden ball evenly into the clay to make the cup holes. Use excess clay to roll out long coils to form the raised lip round each cup.

4: Following the pattern at the top of the page, cut out the card shapes from a thin sheet of clay. Use the cards at left as a guide for painting them.

Game of Goose

About the Game

The game of goose owes its celebrity to Francesco de' Medici of Florence. During his reign, 1574–87, he despatched a goose game to Philip II of Spain, as a gift. The king and his court were undoubtedly delighted by the sudden changes of fortune they encountered on the board's spiral course, and the game spread rapidly to other parts of Europe. On June 16th, 1597, the game was acknowledged in England and entered in the Register of the Stationer's Hall in London, as 'the newe and most pleasant game of the Goose.'

The earliest goose boards were little more than a cardboard base, on which an elaborate spiral course of 63 squares was drawn. The squares were ornamented with such emblems as a pair of dice, a death's head, an inn, a bridge, a maze, and, at regular intervals, a goose. These emblems symbolized rules of play which would either hinder the player or speed his way to the final victory square.

The first printed goose game boards were introduced into England early in the seventeenth century and inspired a host of similar games. The game-track became a reflection of life itself, and boards appeared illustrating such issues as the French Revolution, the Dreyfus Affair, political intrigues, celebrated romantic entanglements, and even World War I. On a more innocent theme, one could journey round the world, learn one of Aesop's fables, or follow the adventures of Don Quixote and Sancho Panza on their journey through La Mancha.

The original goose games were simple journeys and adventures, helped or hindered by the roll of the dice. Goose squares occurred at regular intervals, allowing a second throw. By the eighteenth century, however, the games had acquired a far more moral bias. In the French engraving above, the parents are using the game to give their child a 'picture of life.' Their game must have been very similar to the two English boards below, printed some 30 years later. Overleaf: a goose board printed in 1790 shows the trials and rewards of life in Georgian England. ▶

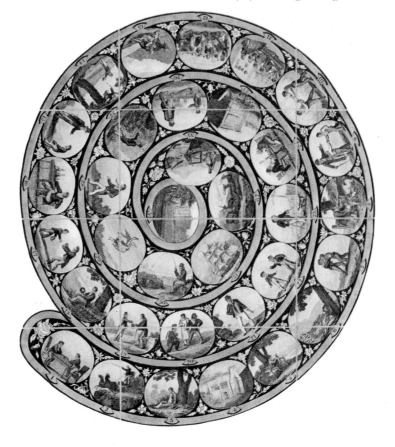

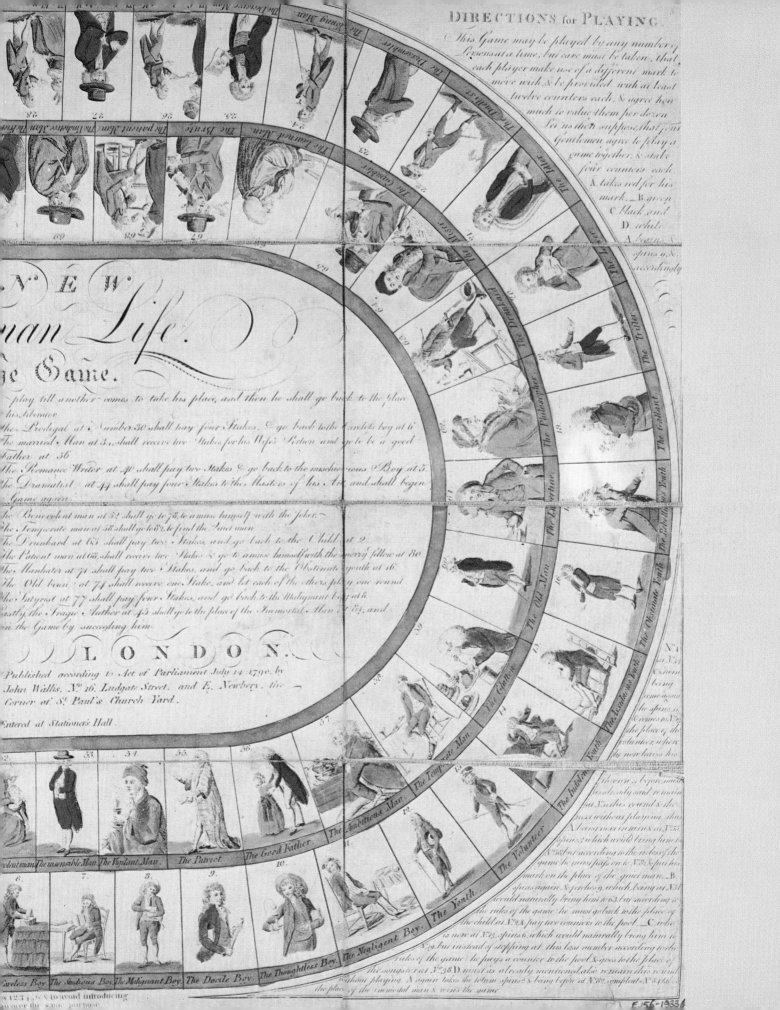

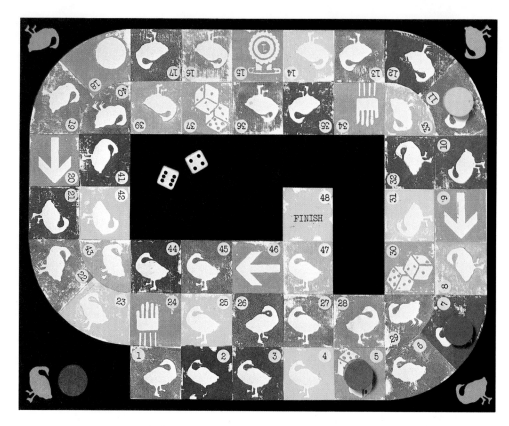

Tools

A ruler, pencil, compass with pencil point, lino-cut knife, ruler with steel straightedge, lino-cut tool with several V-shaped and semi-circular blades, hand roller, sheet of picture glass about 9 by 12 inches, and scissors.

How to Make the Game

With a ruler and pencil, mark points at 2-inch intervals along each side of the board, and connect opposite points with straight lines to divide the board into 2-inch squares.

Where the spiral track turns a corner – for example, the rounded squares 29, 6, and 7 on the model in the photograph at left – set a pencil compass at a radius of 2 inches. Place the compass point at the inner corner of square 29, and draw an arc connecting the two opposite outer points of the square. Then set the compass radius at 4 inches and draw an arc connecting the outer corners of the 6 and 7 squares. Repeat these steps on the corresponding squares at the other three corners of the game track. Divide the 6 and 7 squares along a diagonal line ruled across the corner section.

Using a steel straightedge and lino-cutting knife, cut several 2-inch square pieces of linoleum. Trace the shapes of the corner segments and cut out pieces of lino to fit.

On the lino pieces, sketch and, using the lino-cut tool, cut out symbols like those shown here: a goose facing forward, a goose facing backward, an arrow (which can be turned to face in either direction), a pair of dice, a hand, a first-prize button, and a disc.

To print the lino-cuts, squeeze some printing ink from the tube onto the glass sheet, and spread it with the roller, until the roller is evenly coated with color. Roll a layer of ink on the face of the lino-cut, pick up the lino carefully by its edges, and place it face down on the penciled square it is to occupy. Press firmly on the back of the lino, then lift it straight up without sliding it sideways. Allow the ink to dry. Repeat with the other symbol designs, using a variety of colors.

When all the squares of the board are filled in with lino-cut symbols, and the ink is dry, carefully cut round the game track. Apply glue to the back, and center it on a sheet of black poster board. Decorate the corners with cut-out goose motifs.

With a fine felt-tip pen, neatly write the numbers of the squares, from 1 to 48 (or more if your game track is longer) on white adhesive paper tabs, and stick them on the squares in the correct order. Write FINISH in the last square.

How to Play the Game

Part of the fun of making your own goose game board is inventing symbols and the moves that they represent. The simplified children's board shown in the photograph above is an example. To play this goose game, each player has a counter of a different color. Players take turns to throw two dice and advance their counters the corresponding number of squares.

If a counter lands on a square marked with two dice, the player may throw and move again on the same turn. If a counter lands on an arrow pointing backward, it must return to the square from which it started on that turn. If the square shows an arrow pointing forward, the player moves his counter onward for the same number of squares again. If the square shows an upheld hand, the counter is 'imprisoned' and must stay there until each other player has had two turns, or until another player's counter lands on the same square and itself becomes 'imprisoned.'

If a counter lands on square 15, the player wins a 'first prize button' and immediately advances to square 18, which shows a disc representing the 'prize money.'

The first player to land his counter directly on the finish square is the winner, but if on his last throw he scores a higher number than needed, he must take his counter backward from the finish square for the excess number of squares, hoping to throw the exact number on his next turn.

Materials

White poster board, 14 by 18 inches.
Black poster board, 15 by 19 inches.
Artist's linoleum for lino-cuts.
Lino-cut printing ink in various colors..
At least 48 round adhesive paper tabs, ¹⁄₂ inch in diameter.
All-purpose glue.
Fine black felt-tip pen.
Two dice.
A different-colored playing piece for each player, such as a tiddledywink.

Snakes & Ladders

━━

About the Game

Symbolically, a game of snakes and ladders is a moral journey through life to heaven. The path is shortened by virtue and good deeds, lengthened by evil and vice. The fortunes of the road are decided by the throwing of dice… This is the original meaning of snakes and ladders, one of the best known of children's board games. It is based on the game called *moksha-patamu,* often used in India for religious instruction. According to some Hindu sages, good and evil *(pap* and *punya)* exist side by side in man; but only virtuous acts – represented by the ladders – will shorten the soul's journey through a series of incarnations to the state of ultimate perfection. Thus human wrongdoing (symbolized by the head of a snake) leads inevitably to reincarnation in a lower, animal, form.

Most western versions of snakes and ladders have lost this religious symbolism, and the game is enjoyed simply as an obstacle race.

How to Play the Game

Any number of players, each having a different-colored counter, can take part in snakes and ladders. The moves are controlled by throws of one die, or a pair of dice. In order to start, each player must throw a 6 (with one die) or a pair (with two dice). He then throws again and moves his counter along the board from the first square according to the score of the dice.

If a player throws a 6 or a pair on any turn he advances his counter accordingly taking it up a ladder or down a snake if he lands on such a square – and then has a second throw.

If a counter lands on a square with the head of a snake, it must follow the snake down to the square occupied by its tail. If the counter lands on a square showing the bottom of a ladder, it moves straight up to the square at the top of the ladder.

The first player to land on the hundredth square wins, and the others continue for places. The last throw, however, must land a counter directly on the last square; if the number thrown is more than needed, the counter is moved backward one square for each excess point, and the player tries again on his next throw.

A snakes and ladders board, left, based on a classic Indian design, can be made in a few hours. Serpents of painted clay coils may be added around the board, to make this game of good versus evil appear even more dramatic.

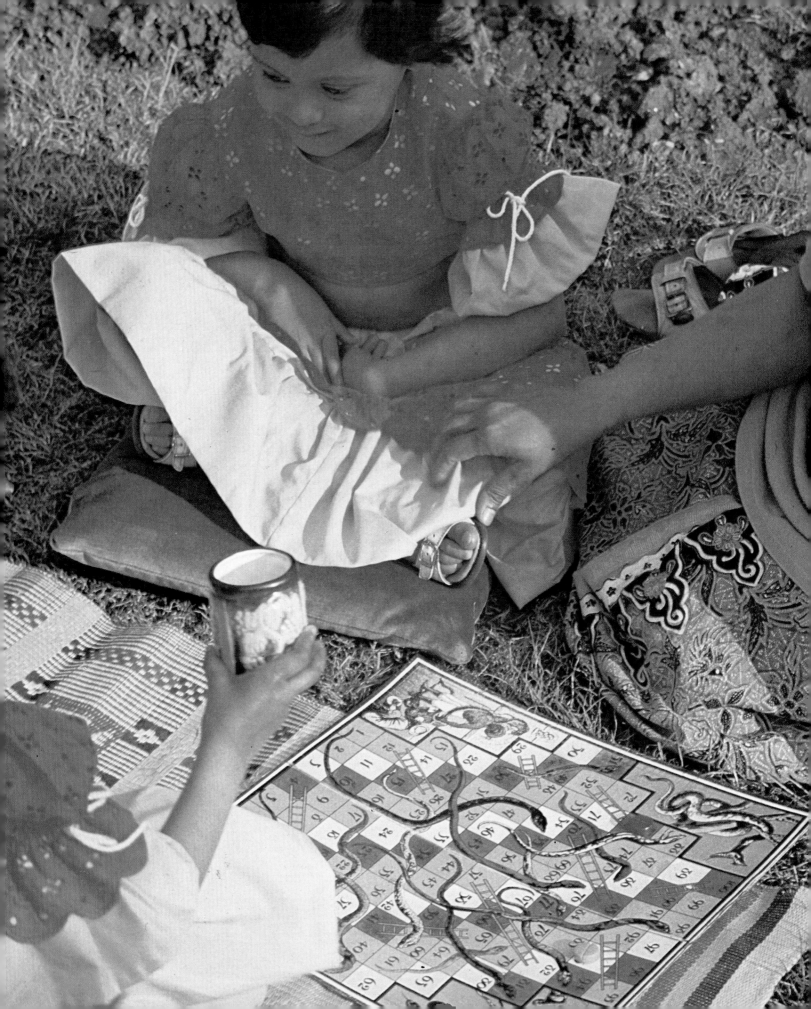

Materials

A plywood board, about $\frac{1}{4}$ inch thick, 15 inches square.
White poster board, at least 15 inches square.
Poster paint in various colors.
Water-based black felt-tip pen.
All-purpose glue.
Spray varnish.
Two dice.
One playing counter per player, such as buttons in various colors.

Tools

A pencil, ruler, sandpaper, and artist's camel-hair brush.

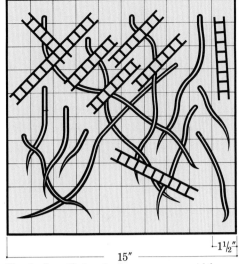

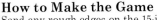

Use the board's hundred squares as a grid for drawing the snakes, ladders, and animals.

How to Make the Game

Sand any rough edges on the 15-inch square of plywood. Place it on top of the poster board and, holding it steady with one hand, trace closely around it with the pencil. Remove the plywood and straighten any unevenness of the pencil lines by re-drawing them with a pencil and ruler. Cut out the poster board square.

Lay the ruler along the edge of the poster board square and make pencil marks at $1\frac{1}{2}$-inch intervals. Repeat on the other three sides. Laying the ruler across the board, join the marks opposite each other, dividing the board into 100 squares.

Using these squares as a grid, and the model photographed at left as a pattern, draw in the snakes, the ladders (use a ruler), and silhouettes of animals. When everything is correctly drawn in pencil, paint the board, using poster paint of different colors for the background of the squares, the snakes, ladders, and animal shapes.

When the paint is completely dry, draw in the board-square numbers, using a water-based black felt-tip pen. Follow the numbering of the squares shown in the model at left.

In the original Indian version of the game board, each snake's-head square signifies a human vice, and each square from which a ladder rises represents a virtue. If you wish, you can write in these vices and virtues as follows. The snake's head squares are: 41, Disobedience; 44, Vanity; 49, Impurity; 52, Stealing; 58, Lying; 62, Drinking; 69, Debt; 73, Murder; 84, Anger; 92, Greed; 95, Pride; and 99, Desire.

The squares at the foot of the ladders are: 12, Faith; 51, Steadfastness; 57, Almsgiving; 60, Devotion; 63, Good Conduct; 66, Compassion; 76, Knowledge; 78, Asceticism.

When the game board is completed and quite dry, spread all-purpose glue over the back of it and on one side of the plywood square, and stick the two carefully together so that all edges are flush. Allow to dry. Apply a coat of spray varnish, and allow to dry.

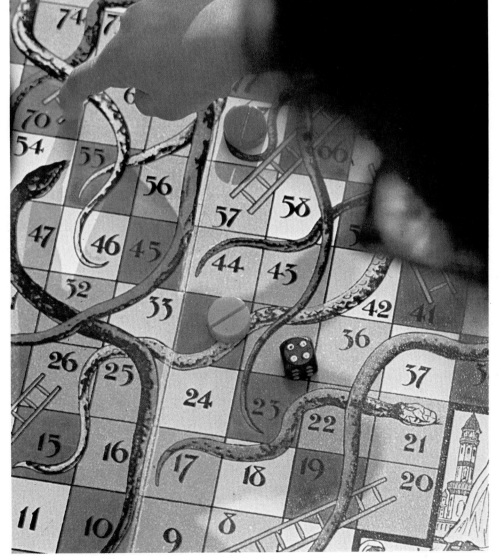

Ceylonese girls (opposite page) throw dice to determine their fortunes in a garden game of snakes and ladders. The board on which they are playing (left) was made in England in the nineteenth century, adapting ancient Hindu principles for both English and Indian players.

Dice

About the Game

'Iacta alea est!' (the die is cast) said Julius Caesar, as he ordered his troops to cross the Rubicon and wage civil war. The *alea* of which he spoke was exactly the same as the die (plural, dice) that we know today. This is a cube engraved or painted on each side with dots from one to six, arranged so that the opposite sides always total seven.

The use of dice for gambling and games of chance goes back at least 5,000 years. The earliest known dice were found in the Sumerian royal tombs of Ur, dating from the third millenium B.C. They are pyramid-shaped, with two of the four corners inlaid; three made of ivory and three of lapis lazuli. (See page 56.)

Egyptian tombs have yielded both four-sided long dice of ivory and bone, and cubic dice. Dice were played at banquets in classical Greece, and in special dicing rooms in the palaces of imperial Rome. In northern Europe, dice and dice boxes have been found on Iron Age sites. Dice may have developed from knucklebones (the ankle bones from sheep's legs) which were used for divining the future, and for gambling games.

Dice may be thrown from the hand, or from special dice boxes, which in the past were often made of valuable materials and lavishly ornamented. Cheating at dice is perhaps as old as the dice themselves: references to loaded dice, i.e. with one side weighted so that the required face falls uppermost, have been found in ancient Greek literature.

In modern times, dice are used for determining the moves in many board games; they are also employed in gambling games such as craps, which is especially popular in the United States. Craps was invented by black Americans in New Orleans after 1800, based on the complex French game of hazard. The name derives from 'crabs' which designated the lowest scoring throw in hazard. (George Gershwin set a craps game to music in his opera *Porgy and Bess*.)

Other types of dice include crown and anchor dice, in which the six sides are marked with a crown, an anchor, a spade, a diamond, a club, and a heart; players bet on the outcome of throwing three dice. Poker dice or liar dice are marked like cards – nine, ten, jack, queen, king, and ace. Players throw five dice, and score on combinations similar to those used in the card game of poker.

Lords of the Spanish royal court, opposite, shake dice from a cup in this Gothic illustration from the games book of Alfonso X. The artist, more concerned with the score than the appearance of the dice, has given them various odd shapes. In actual fact, medieval dice were carefully made cubes. The two dice at right – one in the shape of a human figure, carved in ivory, the other of hollow bone – are both of German origin. They date from the fifteenth and sixteenth centuries.

Illustrations from royal manuscripts of Alfonso X depict scenes from the uncertain life of gamblers in thirteenth-century Spain. At top there is a punch-up between two players while the rest roll dice. Those in the frame below are calmer, but one keeps a knife on the table before him. In the third frame, one persistent loser has gambled away his clothes. Other victims, similarly denuded by their gambling mania, appear in the lowest picture.

How to Play the Game

There are many games that can be played with dice; those described here are simple and fast-moving.

Craps

The enduring popularity of craps is probably due to the fast and exciting pace of the game, and the variety of betting combinations offered to the players. Even children can enjoy this basic version of craps, using candies, matchsticks, or buttons, as tokens.

Two dice are used. One player, by general consent, becomes the first 'shooter.' The next shooter is the player on his left, and turns are taken clockwise round the circle of players. Players may join or leave the circle at any time during the game.

Players place their bets on the table, and the shooter may cover (place an equal amount on) any or all of them. He then 'shoots' or throws the dice. If on his first throw he lands a total of 7 or 11, this is called a 'natural' and the shooter wins all the stakes. If he throws 2, 3, or 12, it is a 'crap' and he loses anything he had wagered.

If any other number is thrown, it is called a 'point.' The shooter then continues to throw the dice until he comes up with the same point, in which case he wins the bets; but if he throws a 7 first, he loses, and the other players win their covered bets. The next player becomes the shooter; but any player may refuse his turn, and pass the dice to the player on his left.

'Soldiers Playing Dice' by Jean Valentin de Boullogne (1594–1632) illustrates the perils of gambling in the turbulent Europe of the Thirty Years' War (below). The youngest soldier, who seems to be having a streak of luck, prepares to roll his dice, adding to those already on the table. His bearded companion, meanwhile, has to be forcibly restrained from drawing his sword to protest his bad luck; indeed, the whole group looks ready to fight at the slightest pretext.

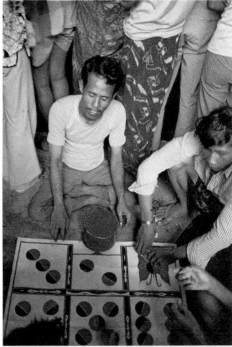

A sidewalk gambling operator in Bali, above, runs a popular but illegal dice game. Players place bets on any number and double their money if it is rolled once, triple if it comes up twice.

The game board at left dates from about the same period as Valentin's painting. The dice scores painted on the pine board are used for gambling on a version of Glückshaus *(see page 140).*

Buck Dice

This game can be played by any number of people, often to decide who pays for an evening's entertainment.

To determine the order of play, each player throws one die; the highest score denotes the first player, and so on. The lowest scorer throws one die again, and its value becomes the 'point number' for the game.

The game starts with the first player throwing three dice. He scores one point for each 'point number' that comes up. He continues to throw until he fails to score any point numbers on a throw, and the turn passes to the next player. Each player drops out of the game when he scores 15 points; the last one in the game is the loser, and pays the check.

If a player throws three of a kind, not point numbers, he scores a 'little buck' worth 5 points. If he throws three point numbers, known as a 'big buck,' he scores 15 points and is immediately out of the game. When a player has 13 or 14 points, he must achieve the final 15 exactly; if he throws too many point numbers the throw does not count.

Chicago

Any number of players can join in this game. On the first round, each player in turn throws two dice, and tries to turn up 2; if he does so, he scores 2 points, but if he fails he scores nothing. On the second round, the players try to throw 3; anyone who succeeds scores 3 points.

The game continues in the same way for eleven rounds, each round having a target throw one point higher than the last, and scoring the equivalent number. The player with the highest score after the eleven rounds wins.

Thirty-six

This game with one die, for any number of players, is similar to the card game of *vingt-et-un* or pontoon. Before the game starts, each player places a stake in the center of the table. Players then throw the die to determine order of play, the lowest score denoting the first player of the game.

Each player, in turn, throws the die and adds up the value thrown each time, aiming for a total of 36 – or as close to it as possible. If he exceeds 36, he is 'bust' and out of the game. At the end of the round, the player with the score nearest to 36 wins the stakes.

Bell & Hammer

About the Game

This amusing game of chance originated in Germany, where it is known as *Schimmel*. It was first played in England in the early nineteenth century, taking its name from the bell and hammer depicted on one of the playing cards. Five picture cards are used, showing a white horse, an inn, a hammer, a bell, and a bell and hammer, together with eight cubic dice with five plain surfaces. Six of the dice are numbered one to six on one side, the remaining two dice with a bell and a hammer. A small wooden mallet, a dicing cup, and 36 counters for each player complete the set. The finest bell and hammer sets were made of ivory, but those fashioned in wood or bone also display a high level of craftsmanship.

This ornate set of five bell and hammer cards was made in Germany in 1840. At top right is their cedarwood box, gaily bordered with acanthus leaves.

How to Play the Game

Any number of players may join in the game, which is divided into three phases. Armed with 36 counters, each player enters phase one by throwing the eight dice. The player with the highest throw becomes the auctioneer and calls for four counters from each player to form a pool. He then auctions off the five cards one at a time, in exchange for counters that are added to the pool. A player without a card cannot participate in the round, and if he is unlucky enough to be out for two successive rounds, his remaining counters are added to the pool.

The auctioneer bangs his wooden hammer on the table and begins the second phase. Each player throws the dice in turn. If the dice are blanks, the players pay one counter to the owner of the white horse. If the bell, or hammer, or both bell and hammer appear, the other dice being blank, the owners of these cards pay one counter to the owner of the white horse. If the bell, or hammer, or both bell and hammer appear with one or more numbers, the auctioneer pays the sum of the numbers in counters from the pool to the owner of the corresponding card or cards. If only blanks and

numbers are thrown, the auctioneer pays the sum of numbers thrown to that player. If a player throws a sum of numbers equal to the counters in the pool the game ends; but if a larger number is thrown, the player pays the difference to the holder of the inn, known as 'mine host.' Mine host opens the inn and phase three begins.

If a player throws all blank dice, the owner of the white horse pays one counter to mine host. If the bell, or hammer, or both bell and hammer are thrown, the other dice being blank, the owners of these cards pay one counter

138

to mine host. If a number is thrown with the bell, or hammer, or the bell and hammer, the owners of these cards pay mine host the difference between the number thrown and the counters remaining in the pool. The corresponding number of counters are won from the pool if a player throws a number less than the counters in the pool. He wins the round by throwing the same number as there are counters in the pool, adding them to his store. The winner in one round is the auctioneer in the next. The game ends when one player holds all the counters.

Hammer and dice are sanded and painted.

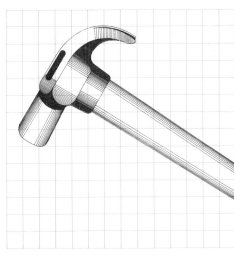

Following the blue grid, draw the hammer card.

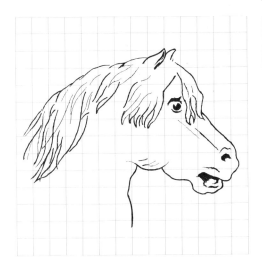

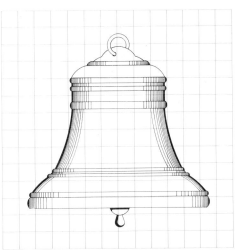

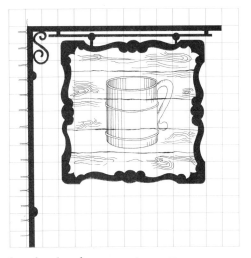

Lightly pencil a grid of 14 by 14 squares on 3½-inch squares of poster board. Carefully follow the lines in these drawings from square to square.

Materials

A ½-inch square piece of wood, 4 inches long.

A wooden dowel, 3½ inches long, 1¼ inches in diameter (or an old chair leg or post, cut to size).

A wooden dowel, 8 inches long, ½ inch in diameter.

Flat paint: white and black.

India ink (oil-based).

Wood glue.

Wood primer.

White poster board.

Felt-tip pens of various colors.

Tools

A ruler, pencil, backsaw, sandpaper, primer brush, paintbrush, technical drawing pen, scissors, and pencil eraser.

How to Make the Game

Place the 4-inch length of wood horizontally on the work table. Measure and mark points at ½-inch intervals on three of the 4-inch edges of the piece. Connect corresponding points with ruled lines. With the backsaw, cut through the wood on these lines. Sandpaper all rough surfaces on the eight cubes. Apply a coat of wood primer to the cubes and allow to dry. Sand lightly, then paint the cubes white and allow to dry completely.

Using a technical drawing pen, neatly draw a single spot on one face of one of the dice; two spots on one face of another; three spots on one face of a third, and so on, to the sixth. On the seventh die, draw a picture of a bell, using the design in the model photographed above as a guide. On the eighth die, draw a hammer.

To make the hammer, clamp the 3½-inch dowel lengthwise in the vise. Measure and mark a middle point (1¾ inches from the end), and drill a hole about ¾ inch deep. (If you prefer, you may use part of an ornamental chair leg, as was done in the model photographed above, instead

of a dowel.) Apply glue in the drilled hole, and insert one end of the 8-inch dowel. Allow the glue to dry; paint with a coat of primer, and when that is dry, sand lightly, and paint the hammer black.

To make the cards for the game, draw five squares, 3½ inches on each side, on the poster board. For the designs on the cards: bell, hammer, horse, inn, and bell and hammer, copy the patterns on the grid above. To enlarge the pattern to full size, draw lightly in pencil on each square card, a grid with the same number of squares as the pattern (i.e. 14 by 14 squares) but in which each square measures ¼ inch on each side. Then following the pattern very closely, draw the design in pencil, square by square, until it is complete. Color the designs with felt-tip pens, allow to dry, and lightly rub out the pencil grid.

Fantasy flowers decorate a sixteenth-century German Glückshaus board, made of beech wood painted with tempera. Below the king, a wedding scene is flanked by a well-dressed couple and a trio of cherubs. In the center is the knave of hearts. Below him are a dice player, a servant with a horse whip, and a pair of crossed lances (called Saufedern, *'sow's feathers'). In the square above the wild boar sits a woman with a flag.*

Glückshaus

★★★

About the Game

Das Glückshaus – 'the house of fortune' – is the German version of a dice game that was played throughout Europe during the Middle Ages, and can still be found in some of the mountain inns of Austria and Switzerland. It was the forerunner of such gambling games as roulette and *Poch* (see page 124). *Glückshaus* boards were usually laid out in the form of a cross and divided into eight to eleven squares bearing numbers, symbolic figures, or both. The one shown opposite, dated 1583, is a splendid example of South-German folk art. Its most important squares are that of the *König,* or king, who rules the board and is equivalent to a 12; the *Schwein,* or 'lucky pig,' which stands for a throw of 2, and the couple being married by a priest, representing the 7 on this board, and marked with an H for *Hochzeit* (wedding). A wedding, of course, is an expensive event to which it was customary to bring a gift; hence the player always loses when rolling a 7.

Materials

A plywood board, ³⁄₈ inch thick, 12 inches square.
White artist's primer.
Paint: oil or poster, in a wide range of colors.
Spray varnish.

Tools

Sandpaper, primer brush, tracing paper, pencil, ruler, and artist's fine camel-hair paintbrush.

Numbers should be added to the board squares, as shown above, to indicate the scoring system.

How to Make the Game

Sand down any rough surfaces or edges on the board, and apply white artist's primer to one side and the edges. Allow to dry, and sand lightly.

To transfer the design to a board 12 inches square, you will need to make a simple grid. Lay a sheet of tracing paper over the photograph on the opposite page, and attach with paper clips. With ruler and pencil, draw an 8-inch square on the tracing paper, over the outline of the photograph. Along each side of the square, mark points at 1-inch intervals. Connect opposite points to make a grid of 64 1-inch squares.

Leaving the tracing in position over the photograph, mark points at 1½-inch intervals along the edges of the primed plywood board. Draw lines connecting opposite points so that the board is divided into 64 1½-inch squares.

Copy the design of the board (as it shows through the traced grid) onto the plywood, taking one square at a time and drawing its contents to the enlarged scale, until you have transfered the entire pattern. If you make a mistake, just rub it out with a pencil eraser, or apply another layer of primer if necessary, and sand again. When you are satisfied that the design is correctly transfered, paint it in, using an artist's fine camel-hair brush and oil paint or poster paint. Follow the colors in the original board as a guide.

Paint the edges of the board black. When all the paint is completely dry, spray one or two coats of clear varnish onto it. Leave in a dust-free place to dry thoroughly.

How to Play the Game

Glückshaus is a game for two or more players. The only equipment is the board, two dice, and counters such as poker chips or, for children, play money or candies. All play depends on the total of the two numbers thrown on the dice. Each player is allowed one throw of the dice before the turn passes to the next player in the circle.

If the dice throw is a 3, 5, 6, 8, 9, 10, or 11, the player who rolled the dice places a chip in the corresponding square on the board. If there is already a chip in that square, the player may collect it instead. If a 4 is thrown, the player makes no move and passes the dice to the next player.

If the dice show 7, the player puts a chip into the 'wedding' square, marked 'H' on the board at left. He may not pick up counters already in that square. A throw of 2 is the 'lucky pig,' which entitles the player to take the chips from every square but the wedding. A throw of 12 is the 'king,' and the player may collect all the stakes on the board, including the ones placed on the wedding.

Players are out of the game when they have no more counters. If the game continues until only one player is left, he wins everything on the board; otherwise the last players divide the board stakes among themselves.

A variation of the game, which increases the stakes, is the 'lottery' game. On any roll except 2 or 12, the player must put that number of chips into the corresponding square. If the square is already full, the player may collect the chips. Throws of 2 or 12 are regulated by the same rules as the basic game of *Glückshaus*.

Dreidel

About the Game

During the eight days of *Hannukah*, the Festival of Lights, Jewish children delight in spinning the *dreidel*. This simple four-sided top originated in medieval Germany, where it was popular with gamblers. The German characters on the four sides were changed to the initials of the Hebrew message, *nes gadol hayah sham*, 'a great miracle happened there.' In Hebrew this is abbreviated as ש, ה, ג, נ, but in modern Israel the ש is replaced by פ, the initial of *poh* (here).

The 'miracle,' according to the Talmud, occurred when the Maccabees recaptured the Temple of Jerusalem from the Syrians in 165 B.C. There was only a tiny supply of oil to keep the lamps burning: miraculously, it lasted for eight days until fresh supplies arrived.

Traditionally, the *dreidel* is made from wood or lead, but more elaborate examples exist in silver; most of them were produced in nineteenth-century Europe.

Two sides of a silver dreidel *from nineteenth-century Europe (right). The first shows the Hebrew character* shin, *the initial letter of* sham, *meaning 'there.' The second side shows* nun, *the initial letter of the word* nes, *meaning 'miracle,' embossed on the silhouette of a* Hannukah *oil lamp.*

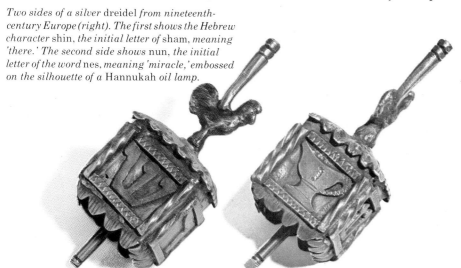

How to Play the Game

Two or more players gather round a table, with the *dreidel* in the middle. Each player has an equal number of coins or counters and contributes two to the pot or 'kitty.' Lots are drawn for the first spin of the *dreidel*.

If the *dreidel* rests with the N uppermost, the player wins nothing and turn of play passes to the person on his left. If the H shows, he wins half of the pot. If the S lands uppermost, he must contribute a counter to the pot, and if the lucky G comes up, he wins the entire contents of the pot.

A player may score one point each time he hits the jackpot, the winner being the one with the highest score out of ten games.

This simple wooden dreidel *has the Roman letters N, G, H, and S on its four sides in place of the Hebrew characters of its silver counterpart.*

Materials

A block of pine wood, 1½ inches square, 1 inch thick.
A wooden dowel, 4 inches long, ¼ inch in diameter.
Wood primer.
Wood glue.
Gloss paint: white and brown.
Colored plastic adhesive tape (optional).

Tools

A wood rasp, sandpaper, pencil, ruler, electric drill or brace with ¼-inch bit, utility knife, primer brush, paintbrush, and artist's camel-hair brush.

How to Make the Game

Using the wood rasp, round off the edges and corners of the block slightly, then sandpaper the block down so that all of its surfaces are smooth. Using the ruler and pencil, measure and mark a point in the middle of one of the 1½-inch–square surfaces. Drill a hole through this point to the other side of the block; sand down any rough edges round the holes.

Whittle one end of the dowel to a point with the utility knife. Pour glue into the hole in the block, and insert the dowel so that the pointed end projects from one side about ½ inch. Wipe off any glue left on the stick. Apply more glue if necessary at the points where the dowel enters the hole. Allow the glue to dry.

Paint the *dreidel* with wood primer. Allow it to dry, then sand it down lightly. Paint the *dreidel* with brown gloss paint and set it aside to dry.

Using as a guide the model in the photograph above, paint free-hand in white gloss paint one of the following letters on each of the four sides of the *dreidel*: N, G, S, H, or use the Hebrew characters ש, ה, ג, נ. If you wish, decorate the stick of the *dreidel* with narrow strips of colored plastic tape.

Shut the Box

About the Game

A single player can enjoy shut the box as a form of patience; but it is usually played by two or more people in competition, possibly for stakes. For more than two hundred years it has been a favorite game among the sailors of Normandy and some other parts of the French coast. They doubtless carried the game on voyages to help while away the long hours under sail, and may have introduced it to other countries through the seaport fraternity. It is not confined to maritime nations, however; versions are played in such completely landlocked regions as Barotseland, a province of Zambia in central Africa.

A player has rolled a 6 and 3 on the green felt of this compact plywood game board for shut the box (below). He has the choice of closing the 9 compartment or the 6 and 3 compartments. Shut the box can also be played using a strip of cardboard marked out into nine sections, with coins to cover the numbers as they are 'closed.'

Dicing board shown in a Spanish medieval manuscript, right, is a thirteenth-century ancestor of games like shut the box. In this scene of lowlife in a tavern, five men concentrate on gambling while others fill their cups from a wineskin, and a hairy demon looks on with satisfaction as his dupes indulge in some of their favorite vices.

How to Play the Game

Shut the box is a game for two or more players. Each player attempts to shut the numbered boxes on all the numbers, one through nine.

At the beginning of a player's turn, the hinged lids of the numbered compartments are all lifted. The player rolls the two dice onto the green felt area of the board, directly below the row of boxes. The sum of the numbers shown on the dice, or the two individual numbers shown, allow the player to shut the box or boxes that are correspondingly numbered. For example, if the dice show a 2 and a 3, he may close the boxes marked '2' and '3,' or the box marked '5.'

A turn is over when the player cannot shut a box on a throw of the dice, because the numbers shown on the dice do not correspond with the numbers on the boxes that remain open. When the totaled numbers of the open boxes amount to six or less, the player throws only one die until he has shut all the boxes or throws an unusable number on the die.

At the end of each turn, the total of the boxes still open is added to the player's score. A player is out of the game when he has a score of 45 points or more. The last player to remain in the game is the winner.

Materials

Two plywood boards, $12\frac{1}{4}$ inches square, $\frac{3}{8}$ inch thick.
Nine butt hinges, each hinge 1 by $\frac{3}{8}$ inch, $\frac{1}{16}$ inch thick.
Four flat-head screws, $\frac{5}{8}$ inch long.
Fifty-four hinge screws, $\frac{3}{8}$ inch long.
Green felt, $11\frac{1}{4}$ by $8\frac{1}{4}$ inches.
Nine wooden balls, $\frac{1}{2}$ inch in diameter.
White press-on numbers, 1 through 9, $\frac{3}{4}$ inch high.
Black press-on numbers, 1 through 9, $\frac{1}{4}$ inch high.
Wood glue. All-purpose glue.
Paint: flat black and gloss white.
Optional picture frame molding, $\frac{3}{8}$ inch wide on each side, $\frac{3}{16}$ inch thick: four $12\frac{5}{8}$-inch lengths, two $11\frac{5}{8}$-inch lengths, and two $8\frac{5}{8}$-inch lengths.
A pair of dice.

Tools

A pencil, ruler, electric drill or brace with $\frac{1}{16}$-inch bit, scroll saw, backsaw, coping saw, camel-hair brush, chisel, sandpaper, rasp, awl, vise, protractor.

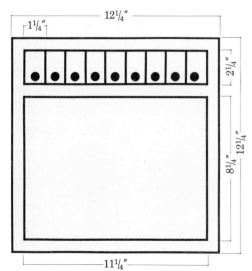

Measure and mark one of the square plywood boards with the dimensions shown above. Divide one of the inner rectangles into nine 'boxes.'

How to Make the Game

Place your ruler horizontally on one of the plywood boards. At the top and bottom of the board, measure and mark a point $\frac{1}{2}$ inch from the left edge. Draw a line connecting these points. Do the same on the right end.

Place the ruler vertically on each line and, measuring from the top edge of the board, mark the following points: $\frac{1}{2}$ inch, $2\frac{3}{4}$ inches, $3\frac{1}{4}$ inches, and $11\frac{1}{2}$ inches. Place the ruler across the board and draw straight lines to connect points directly opposite each other.

There will now be two rectangles drawn on the board, a large one below and a smaller one above. On the long edges of the smaller $2\frac{1}{4}$-by-$11\frac{1}{4}$-inch rectangle, measure and make pencil marks at $1\frac{1}{4}$-inch intervals. Place the ruler vertically and connect the marks opposite to each other so that the rectangle is divided into nine $1\frac{1}{4}$-by-$2\frac{1}{4}$-inch rectangles.

Using an electric drill or a brace with a $\frac{1}{16}$-inch bit, drill a hole on one corner of the $8\frac{1}{4}$-by-$11\frac{1}{4}$-inch rectangle. Drill another hole in an upper corner of the $2\frac{1}{4}$-by-$11\frac{1}{4}$-inch rectangle.

Unfasten one end of the saw blade from the scroll saw frame. Insert this blade in the hole in the large rectangle. Fasten the blade to the frame, then saw along the four lines of the rectangle. Discard the sawed-out section.

Again unfasten one end of the saw blade from its frame. Disengage it from the section you have just sawed and place it in the hole of the $2\frac{1}{4}$-by-$11\frac{1}{4}$-inch rectangle. Fasten the blade to the frame again and saw out this section in one piece, cutting along the four sides of the rectangle. Place the sawed-out section aside and disengage the saw from the board.

Sand down all rough and sharp surfaces of the board and place it directly on top of the other $12\frac{1}{4}$-inch-square board so that their sides match. Trace the four sides of each cut-out rectangle onto the bottom board. Remove the top board.

Paint the $2\frac{1}{4}$-by-$11\frac{1}{4}$-inch rectangle drawn on the bottom board with flat black paint. Allow it to dry. Apply a light coat of all-purpose glue to the drawn $8\frac{1}{4}$-by-$11\frac{1}{4}$-inch rectangle, then carefully place the piece of felt – which has been cut to the same dimensions – directly on top of it. Allow the glue to dry thoroughly.

On both horizontal lines of the black $2\frac{1}{4}$-by-$11\frac{1}{4}$-inch rectangle, measure and mark points at $1\frac{1}{4}$-inch intervals, from left to right. Place your ruler vertically on the board and connect those points directly opposite each other at the bottom and top of the rectangle with a thin line of white gloss paint. Use an artist's camel-hair brush. Allow to dry thoroughly.

Now, take the $2\frac{1}{4}$-by-$11\frac{1}{4}$-inch rectangle that was cut out of the plywood board. With a coping saw, cut out the nine small rectangles already

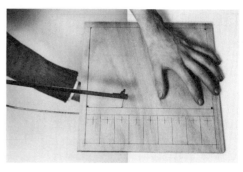

1: Drill small holes in the corners of the large inner rectangle; insert the blade of the scroll saw into one of the holes, and cut out the rectangle.

2: Carefully cut out the smaller rectangle in the same manner, then cut the sawed-out section into nine smaller segments: the lids for the 'boxes.'

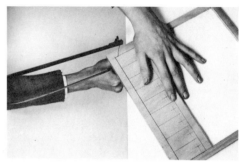

3: After cutting a recess into the edge of each box-lid, place a hinge leaf into each recess and screw the hinges securely to the plywood.

4: Fit the nine lids into the smaller rectangle, then screw the free hinge leaves to the board, making sure the knuckles are all on one side.

5: Glue the plywood frame to the remaining plywood square, positioning the black numbered area under the nine numbered boxes.

marked on its surface. Sand down all rough and sharp edges on each piece.

Place a hinge leaf against a ⅜-by-1¼-inch side of one of the nine sections. Center the hinge, letting ⅛ inch of wood show on either side of it. Draw lines in the wood against the sides of the hinge. Extend these two lines 1⁄16 inch onto the 1¼-by-2¼-inch side. Draw a horizontal line on this surface, connecting the two lines.

With a coping saw, cut along the two lines on the ⅜-by-1¼-inch end to a depth of 1⁄16 inch. Place the blade of the chisel along the horizontal line on the adjacent face and, hammering with the heel of your hand, cut this section out from the rest of the piece.

The hinge leaf should now fit exactly in this recessed area, flush with the wood on either side. With an awl, press holes in the wood through the hinge-screw holes. Screw the hinge leaf fast. Repeat these steps on the remaining pieces.

Take the plywood square that is now a two-sectioned frame and turn it over so that it is standing upright with the 2¼-by-11¼-inch rectangle as the lowest part. Position the free hinge leaves along the lower 11¼-inch side of this rectangle, so that there is enough room for each of the nine pieces to fit into the frame.

With the awl, prepare this frame ledge for the screws, by pressing holes in the wood through the hinge-screw holes. Make sure that all knuckles of the hinges are on the outside – under the lids – as they are screwed to the frame.

Lay the frame flat on the table so that the hinge knuckles are on top of the lids. With a wood rasp, file off a small section (roughly ⅛ inch) from each of the nine wooden balls. Apply wood glue to the flat surface on each ball and glue one to each lid – centered and near the edge that opens. Allow the glue to dry thoroughly.

On the exact middle of each lid, apply a black press-on number, 1 through 9 in consecutive order from left to right. In the middle of each black painted section on the uncut plywood board, apply a white press-on number in the same sequence. Turn the frame over so that the knobs of the lids are underneath. Apply wood glue to the surface of the frame, taking care not to get any of it on the lids. Pick this section up,

turn it over, and place it squarely on top of the uncut board so that the black numbered section is directly under the row of lids. Allow the glue to dry. Turn the board over and fasten a flat-head screw to each corner.

If you wish, you can finish the board with picture-frame molding around the outer edges, as well as bordering the green felt rectangle. The ends of each strip must be mitered first so that they can be joined at the corners of the board and inner rectangle.

To prepare the molding, clamp one of the 12⅝-inch pieces in a vise so that the cornered edge lies toward you. Line up the perpendicular of the protractor with the edge of the left end, its base in line with the cornered edge.

Mark a point on the top edge that is 45 degrees from the corner edge. Draw a line from the corner edge to that point. Do the same at the right end of the molding, measuring and marking a 45-degree angle toward the left.

Using a backsaw, miter both sides of the left end of the molding simultaneously while sawing along the line drawn. Do the same at the right end of the molding. Prepare the remaining three 12⅝-inch strips for miter joints, following the same steps. Glue them to the sides of the gameboard and allow the glue to dry thoroughly.

Prepare the molding strips for the inner rectangle in the same way, with the exception that the 45-degree angle must run from the corner of the side edge into the cornered edge of the molding.

An intricately carved African primitive game of shut the box from Barotseland, with sliding compartments for keeping track of the score.

Roulette

About the Game

Roulette originated in France in the seventeenth century, and derives from a game called *hoca* which was very popular in southern and central Europe at that time. In *hoca* a wheel was used to throw a ball into one of several pockets, and stakes were wagered on the outcome. The powerful Cardinal Mazarin opened *hoca* gaming houses all over France; the immense profits he gained were discovered after his death in 1661, and the government promptly made the running of *hoca* houses a capital offence.

Roulette essentially involves spinning a ball round a wheel containing pockets numbered 1 to 36, out of numerical order, and alternately colored red or black, except for one green pocket numbered 0. On the American roulette wheel, as on the early French ones, there is a second green pocket 00. Players place bets against the house: 35 to 1 odds on any individual number; even money on red or black, odd or even numbers, or high or low numbers. It is the green pockets that give the house a winning percentage in the long run. If the ball enters 0 or 00, bets are frozen, the ball spun again, and bets are either forfeited to the house or returned to the player. The extra green pocket on the American wheel doubles the house's chances of winning and accounts for the fact that roulette is considerably less popular in America than in Europe.

Roulette made Monte Carlo the world's wealthiest and most famous gambling resort. A banker, François Blanc, bought the gambling concessions of the principality of Monaco, and opened a casino in 1863. He attracted big-time gamblers by using only one green pocket on the wheel, instead of the usual two; their patronage repaid his venture handsomely.

The players opposite are placing bets against an American roulette wheel, with its two zeros, at Crockford's gambling club in Mayfair, London.

The portable roulette wheel, below, is a project for home craftsmen, inspired by a version of the game popular during the eighteenth century.

How to Play the Game

This simplified, portable roulette, modeled on an eighteenth-century version of the game, can be played by two or more players. Each has a store of chips or counters – such as small tiddledywinks – and each player's counters are of a different color. Though there is no 'bank,' one player is the 'croupier.' He spins the arrow, calls the results, and keeps a store of extra counters, so that players may trade won counters for counters of their own color. (To avoid confusion, players may only bet with counters of their own color.) A minimum stake – one or more counters – is set before the game begins.

To begin, each player places stakes on one or more blocks on the board. The croupier spins the arrow, and the scoring is as follows:

The 'first call' is the number and color where the tip of the long arrow stops.

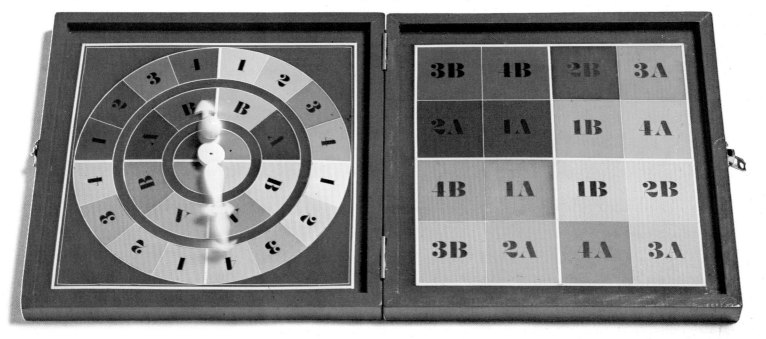

If a player has bet on this block, he wins all the counters on the board. If more than one player has bet on that block, they divide the winnings between them, according to the size of their respective winning bets.

If no one wins on the first call, the croupier gives the 'second call,' which is the color and letter on which the small arrow rests. For each second call, such as 'B-yellow,' there are two possible winning bets – in this case, 1-B or 2-B in the yellow group. The winner or winners take half the stakes on the board and divide it between them, according to the relative size of their winning wagers.

If all the stakes have been won or if no one wins on a spin, each player must place at least one more stake on the board. A player is exempted from this rule only if the last second call included a color on which he had bet.

Won counters may be taken from the board and added to the player's store. Otherwise, bets placed may not be lifted from the board, though they may be shifted from one block to another between spins of the arrow. Players may leave the game at any time, forfeiting the stakes they have placed on the board.

Materials

Eight pine strips, $\frac{1}{2}$ inch square, 12 inches long.
Two plywood boards, 12 inches square, $\frac{1}{2}$ inch thick.
A plywood board, 1 by 7 inches, $\frac{1}{8}$ inch thick.
A wooden ball, $\frac{3}{4}$ inch in diameter.
Two hinges, $1\frac{1}{2}$ inches long, each hinge leaf $\frac{3}{8}$ inch wide, $\frac{1}{16}$ inch thick.
Twelve hinge-screws.
A two-part suitcase clasp, with nails or screws for fastening it to the case.
White plastic adhesive tape, $\frac{1}{16}$ inch wide, and $\frac{1}{32}$ inch wide.
Several wire nails, $\frac{3}{4}$ inch long.
A straight pin, upholstery weight.
A plastic bead, about $\frac{1}{8}$ inch in diameter.
Gloss paint: red, yellow, blue, green, black, white, and brown.
White oil-based ink.
Black press-on letters and numbers: $\frac{1}{2}$ inch high and $\frac{5}{8}$ inch high.
Wood primer.
Wood glue.

Tools

A vise, protractor, pencil, ruler, backsaw, chisel, sandpaper, primer brush, awl, compass, pencil eraser, paintbrush, artist's camel-hair brush, scissors, technical drawing pen, scroll saw, wood rasp, hammer, wire cutters, and screwdriver.

Monte Carlo casino, at the glittering height of the Jazz Age, is captured in a painting (above) by Georges Fiakoulov (1884–1928). Gamblers from all over the world cluster around the famous roulette table.

How to Make the Game

Clamp one of the 12-inch pine strips in the vise. Line up the perpendicular of the protractor with the left edge of one of the $\frac{1}{2}$-inch sides. The base of the protractor should be in line with the long bottom edge of this surface. Mark a point on the top edge that is 45 degrees from the bottom corner. Draw a line connecting the bottom corner with that point. Repeat these steps at the right edge of the same surface, marking a 45-degree angle to the left. With a backsaw, cut through the sections along the lines drawn. Repeat these steps on the other seven pine strips.

On each strip, apply wood glue to one side (one of the sides with two slanting ends) and the two mitered ends. Joining their mitered ends, place the strips to make a frame on each of the plywood boards. The pine-strip frames should exactly match the dimensions of the 12-inch-square boards.

On the outer edge of one side of each of these frames, measure and mark points that are 1, $2\frac{1}{2}$, $9\frac{1}{2}$, and 11 inches from the corner. Repeat these markings on the outer side, $\frac{3}{8}$ inch below the upper edge of the frame. Join the points on the edge and the corresponding points $\frac{3}{8}$ inch below them with vertical lines; then join each pair of vertical lines with a horizontal line. Extend the verticals over the upper edge onto the top side to a depth of $\frac{1}{16}$ inch; connect them with a horizontal line. With a chisel, cut along the lines drawn on the outer sides of the frame to a depth of $\frac{1}{16}$ inch. Place the chisel blade along the top horizontal lines and cut out each $1\frac{1}{2}$-by-$\frac{1}{16}$-inch section by hammering on the chisel handle with the heel of your hand. When the two segments have been chiseled out of each frame, sand down any rough and splintered areas. Place the hinges in the recesses to see if they will fit snugly; if not, make necessary adjustments, then put the hinges aside.

1: Miter the ends of the pine strips, then glue them above the edges of the square boards, joining them at the corners to make square frames.

2: After the dimensions are marked on one side of each board, use the chisel to gouge out the shallow depressions to hold the hinge leaves.

Apply a coat of wood primer to all surfaces of both sections of the roulette case. Allow to dry thoroughly; then sand down lightly.

On each edge of the inner square in both case-sections, mark points $\frac{1}{2}$ inch from each corner. Connect corresponding points on opposite sides of each square. The case-sections now have inner 10-inch squares. Divide the 10-inch-square in one section into four rows of four squares, $2\frac{1}{2}$ inches on each side.

Place a ruler at each side of the inner square of the other case-section and, with the pointed tip of an awl, dig a slight groove along these lines; then measure and mark center points (5 inches from each corner). Draw ruled lines to connect the points on opposite sides.

Draw ruled diagonals, connecting opposite corners of the square. The square is now divided into eight segments; halve each of these segments by drawing additional diagonals.

At the center of the square, where the lines intersect, place the needle of the drawing compass and draw circles with radii of $1\frac{3}{8}$, $1\frac{3}{4}$,

3, $3\frac{3}{8}$, and $4\frac{3}{4}$ inches. Erase all lines in the central circle except the horizontal-vertical cross. On the adjoining strip, $\frac{3}{8}$ inch wide, erase all lines. In the strip between the second and third circles, erase the lines between the horizontal, vertical, and central diagonal lines. In the next strip, erase all lines. Finally erase all lines beyond the outer circle.

Paint all surfaces on the two sections of the case brown, except for the divided center square in one section and the central circle and two marked circular strips on the other section (see the model on page 147). When the brown paint is dry, use an artist's camel-hair brush to paint in the colors in the other segments, using the photographed model as a guide. To make the different shades of red, yellow, green, and blue, mix varying quantities of white or black paint with the original colors. Be sure that each square matches the corresponding segments in the roulette 'wheel.' Allow the paint to dry.

With the $\frac{1}{16}$-inch plastic tape, cover the edges of the 10-inch block of squares, also the horizontal and vertical lines that divide this square into quarters. Cover the dividing lines within these

quarters with $\frac{1}{32}$-inch plastic tape. On the other section of the case, use $\frac{1}{16}$-inch tape to cover the edges of the 10-inch square (the grooved lines will show through the paint) and the horizontal and vertical lines dividing the circle and circular tracks. Cover the dividing lines with the $\frac{1}{32}$-inch tape. With a technical drawing pen filled with white oil-based ink or thinned white paint, draw lines over the borders of the circle and the two tracks.

Rub on the press-on letters and numbers in the proper positions, using the photographed model as a guide. Using the double-pointed arrow in figure B as a guide, draw a similar arrow on the 1-by-7-inch board. Cut it out with the scroll saw. Sandpaper any rough or splintered surfaces.

With the wood rasp, file down one side of the wooden ball until you have a flat surface roughly $\frac{1}{2}$ inch in diameter. Glue this surface to the shaft of the smaller arrow, then hammer it fast from the underside with a short wire nail.

Hammer a wire nail in the center of the circle between the two arrows; then remove it. With wirecutters, cut off the pointed end of the pin, leaving only $\frac{1}{2}$ inch. Place the pin through the nail hole, then through the bead, and hammer it lightly into the center of the circle in the middle of the board. The arrow should be secure, yet loose enough to be spun.

Position the hinge leaves in the chiseled-out recesses on each section of the roulette case. With the awl, press holes in the wood at each of the hinge's screw holes. Screw the hinges into place, connecting the two halves of the case.

Close the case and stand it on end so the hinged side is at the bottom. Position the two-piece clasp (in locked position) in the middle of the joined sides at the top of the case. Fasten the clasp to the case with nails or screws.

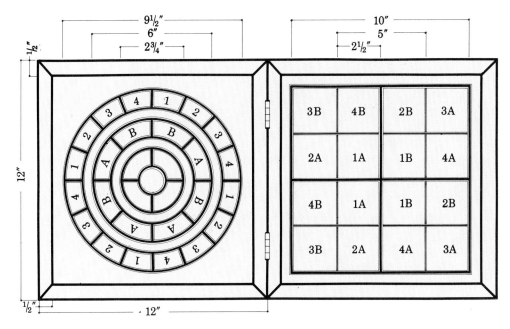

Figure A: The surface of each case section, within the boundaries of the molding frame, are marked then painted with the designs at left.

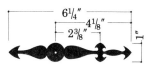

Figure B: On the 1-by-7-inch plywood board, draw the double-pointed spinner for the wheel.

Backgammon

About the Game

According to an Indian legend, a sage named Qaflān invented a game which represented a year. The board had 24 points for the hours of a day; the twelve points of each half-board were the months and Zodiac signs; the 30 pieces were the days of the month; the two dice were day and night, and the total of seven spots on the opposite sides of a die represented both the days of the week, and the then known planets of the solar system.

This game was known in Persia and the Near East as *nard*. It closely resembled the Roman *ludus duodecim scriptorum* ('game of twelve lines,' at which the emperor Nero gambled vast sums of money). In the first century A.D. this became *tabula* (a table) and was thence known throughout medieval Europe as 'tables.' For centuries it was esteemed as highly as chess: innkeepers attracted custom by providing game boards, while on a loftier social scale, the crusader knights carried it on their campaigns.

In England during the Middle Ages, the church waged a long and losing battle against tables: but by the eighteenth century, it was the favorite game of country vicars. By then it was known as backgammon from 'back' and 'gamen' (i.e. game in Middle English), because in certain circumstances, the pieces are obliged to go back and reenter the board. It enjoyed considerable vogue among the nineteenth-century romantics and has had a recent revival as one of the great passions of the jet set. As one English dandy has boasted, 'The only athletic sport I ever mastered was backgammon.'

A game similar to backgammon is played by these Chinese terra-cotta figures, recently discovered in a second-century tomb by Chinese archeologists.

How to Play the Game

Backgammon is an easy game to learn, but a difficult one to play well. The basic rules are given below, with some brief examples of play for clarification. The finer points of strategy will be acquired in actual practice.

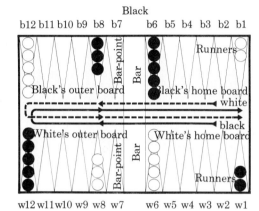

Figure A: This is the opening position of the playing pieces in backgammon. The home board, however, can be on either side of the board.

Backgammon is a game for two players. The board, which is set horizontally between them, is divided by a bar (see figure A). This bar splits the playing area into the 'home board' and the 'outer board.' The two sections are identical: the players decide which half of the board will be the home board for the game.

Modern backgammon boards are marked with 24 points of alternating colors. (The board shown on page 154, and described under 'How to Make the Game,' has been modeled after the medieval backgammon board, and has recesses instead of points to mark the placement of the pieces.)

Bemedaled Soviet veteran Vladimir Makatsariya (opposite, in a picture taken by Life photographer Stan Wayman) prepares to roll the dice in a game of backgammon at a party in Georgia, U.S.S.R.

Each player has 15 playing pieces or 'men,' either black or white, a dicing cup, and pair of dice. Finally, there is a 'doubling cube,' bearing the numbers 2, 4, 8, 16, 32, and 64 on its sides. The object of the game is to move all 15 men into the home board and then 'bear off' these men, or take them from the board. The first player to bear off all his men is the winner.

To simplify the explanation of the rules, the points on the board shown in figure A are numbered and marked with 'b' for black or 'w' for white. The opening position of the men is shown in this figure; the home board is marked with points 1 through 6 on both black's and white's sides. As already indicated, players may use either side of the board for the home board. The alternate opening arrangement is a mirror image of figure A, as shown in the photograph on page 154. (There, the points would be numbered 1 through 12, left to right.)

Points b7 and w7 are called the 'bar points.' The two men on the first point of the opponent's side of the home board are called 'runners.'

The rules of play

To start the game, each player throws one die. The player who rolls the highest number takes the first move, using the combined score of the two dice. (If the players throw the same number, they roll again.) After the first move, each player uses two dice for his throws, and moves his men according to the numbers showing on the dice.

The direction of movement for black's men is from w1 to w12, then to b12, and from there to b1. White's men move in the opposite direction: b1 to b12, then w12 to w1. (Though all men – such as those initially placed in the home board – might not necessarily make a complete circuit of the 24 points, each player's counters must move in the proper direction.)

Rule 1: The player may use his dice throw in several ways. He can move two men, one for each number shown on the dice. Or he may use the two numbers to move one man, as long as it is possible to move the piece first by the number shown on one die, and then by the number on the other. Either number may be used first.

For example, white on his first turn rolls 6-3. This gives him the option of making one of the following moves: (a) moving one man three points and another man six points, (b) moving one man first six points, then three points, or (c) moving one man first three points, then six points. The question of which number on the dice is used first becomes important when certain points are 'blocked' (see rule 6).

Rule 2: A 'double' throw is used twice. For example, if a player rolls a 'double 3,' i.e. 3-3, he can move his men as though he had thrown 3-3-3-3. Any combination of the numbers in a double is allowed. With a roll of 1-1, a player may make any of the following moves: (a) move one man four points, (b) move one man three points and another man one point, (c) move two men two points each, (d) move one man two points and two men each one point, or (e) move four men one point. A player does not throw again after he has thrown a double.

Rule 3: If possible, the player must use both numbers of his roll. For instance, a player throws a 6-2. It may happen that the 2 can be used for various moves, but after some of them, it is not possible to use the 6. In this case, the 2 must be used in such a way that the 6 can also be used. In case a player throws a double, all four numbers must be used if possible.

Rule 4: If one of the numbers rolled cannot be used, the other one is used. If it is possible to use one or the other, but not both, the highest must be used.

Black
b12 b11 b10 b9 b8 b7 b6 b5 b4 b3 b2 b1

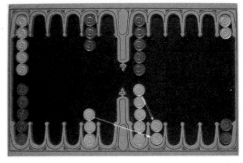

w12 w11 w10 w9 w8 w7 w6 w5 w4 w3 w2 w1
White

Figure B: Opposing pieces may not land on a point which is blocked or 'made'; that is, with two or more opposing men on it. Here, white's men block point w5 with a dice roll of 3–1.

Black
b12 b11 b10 b9 b8 b7 b6 b5 b4 b3 b2 b1

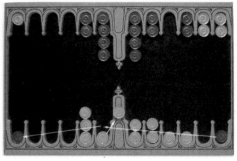

w12 w11 w10 w9 w8 w7 w6 w5 w4 w3 w2 w1
White

Figure C: A single man on a point can be 'hit.' If black rolls 6–5, he hits the 'blot' on w7; the white man is moved to the bar and must reenter before white is allowed to move another piece.

Black
b12 b11 b10 b9 b8 b7 b6 b5 b4 b3 b2 b1

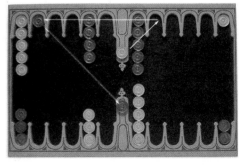

w12 w11 w10 w9 w8 w7 w6 w5 w4 w3 w2 w1
White

Figure D: A reentering man may immediately hit a blot. Here, white reenters through black's home board on a roll of 6–5 and hits the black blot on b11. The black man goes to the bar and must reenter the game on the white home board.

In a situation where all numbers in a double cannot be used, the player must use as many as possible.

Rule 5: If the numbers rolled cannot be used at all, the turn ends.

Blocking or 'making' a point

A player blocks or 'makes' a point when he has two or more men on that point. His opponent may not put a man on that point.

Rule 6: A man may be moved to a vacant point, to a point already occupied by an allied man or men, or to a point occupied by one of the opponent's men, which is then 'hit' (see rule 8). But a man cannot be moved to a point which has been 'made,' i.e. occupied by two or more of the opponent's men.

A piece may not 'touch' a blocked point in passing. If, as in figure B, white throws a 3-1, he moves w8 to w5 and w6 to w5, thereby creating his own 'block.' Black throws 5-4; he is now unable to bring a runner from w1 to w10, though w10 is vacant, because the runner cannot move five points or four points. This is the reason for:

Rule 7: A man can only be moved on the totaled number of the throw if he can move on one of the numbers on the dice, according to rule 6.

'Hitting blots' and reentering them

Rule 8: If a point is occupied by a single man, that man is called a 'blot.' If the opponent moves a man to that point, or 'touches' it with a man which then moves on, the blot is 'hit' and placed on the bar. In figure C, black has a throw of 6-5 and hits a white man on w7; the white man is then moved onto the bar. Hitting is not compulsory unless there is no other possible move.

Rule 9: If a player has a man on the bar, that man must be reentered before the player is allowed to move any of his other men. A man reenters on a throw of one die that brings him to an accessible point on the home board of the opponent.

The player throws two dice in the attempt to get the man back on the board; when the man is reentered, the number showing on the other die may be used as well, either to move that man ahead or another of the player's men. If the player fails to bring the man off the bar on his throw, the turn goes to his opponent.

For example, black has hit one of white's blots, and black has blocked the third, fifth, and sixth points in his home board. Therefore, white can gain reentry only on b1, b2, and b4; he must throw a 1, 2, or 4.

When reentering, a man may immediately hit the blot of an opponent, as shown in figure D. White has started the game with a 6-4 and moves one runner from b1 to b11. Black rolls 5-2 and moves w12 to b8, and w12 to b11, hitting the white blot. White has to reenter, rolls a 6-5, comes in on b5, then moves to b11 and hits the black blot. If there had

been one of black's men on b5, it would have been hit as well.

When a player has blocked all six spaces of his home board with two or more men in each space, it is called a 'shut-out.' If the opponent has a man on the bar, he cannot reenter. The player with the shut-out continues to play until he is forced to open up his home board, making it possible for his opponent to reenter.

Bearing off

As soon as a player has all 15 men in his own home board, he proceeds to bear them off the board.

Rule 10: A man may not bear off while he has men outside his home board, i.e. in other fields or on the bar.

Once a man has been borne off he does not return to the game. A man is borne off from the point decided by the dice. For instance, if white has men on all the points of his home board and he throws a 5-3, he bears off one man from w5 and one man from w3.

Rule 11: When bearing off, a player may use a throw which is higher than the highest occupied point, to bear off a piece on that point.

For example, a player rolls 6-2. He has a man on the second point, which he bears off, but the sixth point no longer has any men. The player may bear off a man from the highest occupied point on his home board. Instead of bearing off, the player may use the throw to move the men within his home board.

For example, toward the end of a game, white has six men, three on w5 and

In a seventeenth-century Dutch print, left, a gambler at tric-trac *(backgammon) bemoans his fate in doggerel verse, paraphrased as follows: 'The board has robbed me, my loss I grieve; The wine is finished – so I must leave!'*

three on w3. He rolls 6-4. According to rule 11, he may use the 6 for bearing off a man from the highest point – the fifth point. But he may not use the 4 to bear off any men, since 4 is not higher than the highest occupied point, i.e. w5. Therefore white must use the throw to move a man from w5 to w1. He now has two blots in his home board, one on w5 and one on w1, making him very vulnerable if black has a man on the bar.

In a slightly different example, if white has one man on w5 and three men on w3, he can use the 6 to bear off the man on the fifth point. Then, because the highest occupied point is now w3, the 4 on the remaining die is higher, and one of these men can be borne off.

Doubling the stakes
Backgammon is often played for a basic stake agreed on beforehand by the players. This stake can be raised during the game by 'doubling.'

Rule 12: A player may double when it is his turn to throw, before he throws. Either player may double first, but each time a player doubles, the right to double passes to his opponent.

When a player announces a double, his opponent may refuse to accept the double. In this case, the game ends and the player who refused the double pays the stake previous to the unaccepted double. If he agrees to the double, the game is continued for the newly doubled stake.

When the first double is made, the doubling cube is turned with 2 facing up. The right to double is now held by the other player. If this player doubles again, the doubling cube is turned to 4, and his opponent may accept the double or not. Each time another

double is made, the cube is turned to the next largest number and the initial stake is multiplied by that number.

Gammon and backgammon
Rule 13: At the end of the game, if the loser has borne off at least one man, he loses the amount at stake. But if the loser has not borne off any men, he is 'gammoned' and has to pay the winner double the amount at stake. If the loser has not borne off any men and still has one or more men on the bar or outside the home board, he is 'backgammoned' and must pay the winner three times the stake.

Points of order
The dice must be rolled together and come to rest flat on the board. If the dice are rolled before the opponent has finished moving his men, or if a die is touched before it comes to a halt, the opponent may demand a new throw. After rolling the dice, the player must leave them exactly as they fall until he has finished moving his men, or the opponent may demand that the men be returned to their original positions and the dice be rolled again. Once a man has been moved correctly and released from the player's hand, the move cannot be retracted.

A mistake in the initial set-up of the men can be corrected only during the first turn of the players. A mistake in moving can only be corrected before the next roll of the dice: rolling the dice indicates that the move, as executed, is accepted by the opponent.

Strategy
Whenever possible, the player should attempt to 'make' points, since blots can be hit. But some points are more important than others and it may be better to make blots while attempting to block a valuable point, rather than making a safe move that does not improve the player's position. In general, blocked points become more effective as they are surrounded by other blocked points.

If a player systematically avoids making a blot and places a single man in a space only when there is absolutely no other choice, he will lose the game to any reasonably experienced opponent. In order to decide when it is worth the risk to make a blot, a player should consider three things: (a) what can be achieved by making the blot, (b) how many points the opponent has blocked in his home board, and (c) how likely it is that the blot will be hit.

The design for this unusual backgammon board was based on a version from medieval Spain, where the game was known as tablas *(tables).*

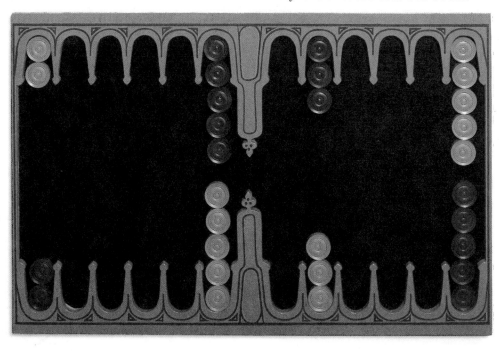

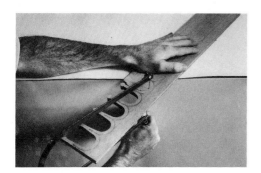

1: Using a scroll saw, carefully cut through the board along the lines drawn. Sandpaper down rough and splintered surfaces on the board.

2: Apply a generous amount of glue to the undersides of the yellow sections, then carefully position them on the blue bottom board.

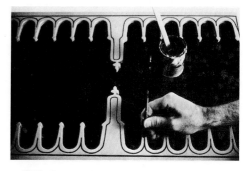

3: With the artist's camel-hair brush, paint the brown line design that follows the turreted contours of the yellow cut-out sections.

Materials

A plywood board, 16 by 22¾ inches, ⅜ inch thick.

Two plywood boards, 7 by 22¾ inches, ⅜ inch thick.

Two plywood boards, ½ by ¾ inch, 16 inches long.

Gloss paint: yellow and brown.

Blue flat paint.

Wood glue.

Wood primer.

Thirty checkers: 15 white and 15 black.

A wooden cube, ¾ inch on each side.

Press-on numbers: 2, 4, 8, 16, 32, and 64.

Varnish (optional).

Tools

A pencil, ruler, primer brush, paintbrush, artist's camel-hair brush, sandpaper, drawing compass, scroll saw, and wood rasp.

The doubling cube shown below is made by filing down the corners of a wooden cube, then painting or pressing on the appropriate numbers.

How to Make the Game

Place one of the 7-by-23-inch boards horizontally on the work table. On the left of the board, measuring from the bottom corner, mark points at 1¾ inches and 3½ inches. Repeat these steps at the right side of the board. Place the ruler horizontally on the board and connect the points that are directly opposite each other.

Measuring along the bottom edge, mark a point 11⅜ inches from the left corner. Repeat this on the top edge of the board. Draw a line connecting these two points. (This line bisects the width of the board.) At the top and bottom edges of the board, mark points ⅝ inch on the left and right sides of this line.

Measuring from these points on either side of the middle line, mark off points at ⅞-inch intervals on the top and bottom edges of the board. Place your ruler vertically on the board and connect those points directly opposite each other with straight lines. Set your drawing compass at 1¼ inches and place the needle at the intersection of the first vertical line on the left and the horizontal line 1¾ inches from the bottom of the board. Draw a circle. Repeat these steps on all alternate vertical lines on the board, except the line that bisects the width of the board. Place your ruler vertically on the board and draw diagonal lines connecting the sides of each circle to the top of the vertical lines neighboring them.

Using the model as a guide, decorate the tops of these diagonal lines freehand, and draw the

outline of the central post. Erase the guidelines and, with the scroll saw, carefully cut through the board along the lines drawn. Sandpaper all rough and splintered surfaces until smooth. Place this board on top of the remaining 7-by-23-inch board so that their bottom edges line up exactly. Trace the outline of this finished board on the board underneath it. Carefully cut the second board along the lines of the pattern drawn. Sand down all rough edges.

Apply a coat of wood primer to one side of the two cut-out sections and the 16-by-22¾-inch plywood board. Allow to dry; sand lightly. Paint the 16-by-22¾-inch board blue. Paint the two sawed-out sections and the two 16-inch wood slats yellow. Allow the paint to dry. Decorate the yellow sections with lines of brown paint, using the model as a guide. Apply glue to the undersides of the two cut-out yellow sections. Place them on the blue board opposite each other as on the model (opposite). The sides of these sections must line up with the sides and bottom edge of the board under them. Allow the glue to dry thoroughly.

Frame the open ends of the board by gluing the two yellow slats to them. Allow the glue to dry completely. Paint the other edges of the board yellow and allow the paint to dry thoroughly.

With the wood rasp, round off the corners of the wooden cube, then sand down all rough edges. On each side of the cube, press on one of the following numbers: 2, 4, 8, 16, 32, and 64. Varnish the cube, if you wish, and allow to dry.

Figure E: Measure and mark the board with the dimensions shown here, then draw in the contoured recesses and 'bar' divider of the board.

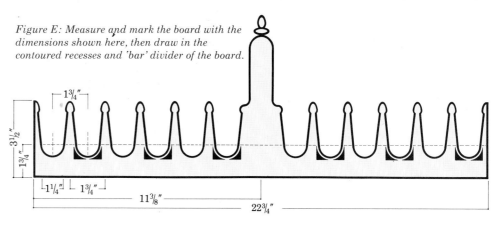

1¾"

3½"

1¾"

1¼" 1¾"

11⅜"

22¾"

In a blur of action, two yellow marbles are sent flying by the blue shooter of an Indian boy. Loren McIntyre photographed this intense moment in a village street in Colombia.

Street & Playground Games

Marbles

About the Game

Most adults remember marbles from their childhood, when reputations were apt to be made or broken by the apparently simple, but skillful, flick of thumb against a small sphere of stone, glass, steel, or clay. The language of marbles is part of the game's mystique: English children talk of taws (marbles) and their varieties, commoneys, stoneys, potteys, and especially alleys – alabaster marbles – of which the most revered are blood alleys, of purest white streaked with red. American children know their marbles as kabolas, steelies, jumbos, milkies, and peewees in descending order of size.

Marbles go back further than nostalgic yesterday. They were known in ancient Egypt and pre-Christian Rome. They have always been considered as an escape from academic duties; an anonymous poem of the 1600's describes an English schoolboy as 'a dunce at syntax, but a dab at taw' – which in the modern vernacular means 'a whizz at marbles.'

From the eighteenth century to the beginning of the twentieth, Germany was the center of the world marbles trade. Originally made, as their name suggests, from chips of marble, later and cheaper versions were of baked clay and glass. Marbles of hollow steel are among the playthings of American children today.

How to Play the Game

The skillful marbles player must have a steady hand, accurate aim – and plenty of practice. To propel a marble (called a shooter) it should be balanced in the recess made by curling the forefinger round, and slightly above, the end of the straightened thumb. The player then holds his hand on or close to the ground, takes aim, and flicks his thumb sharply forward to shoot the marble at its target. The player may squat, or kneel on one or both knees to obtain the best aiming position; but in strict play, any forward movement of the hand while shooting the marble is forbidden.

There are dozens of games to play with marbles, and most of them have no limit on the number of players. An

A sidewalk in Papeete, capital of Tahiti and the French Polynesian islands, provides a convenient level surface for a game of marbles, below.

Young immigrants, recently arrived from Georgia, Russia, hold a marbles tournament (below) in the playground of a Hassidic school in Israel.

easy game for young children is called bombardier. A circle of about a foot in diameter is drawn on the ground, and each child places two or three marbles together in a pile in the center. Then they take turns holding one marble outstretched at eye level so that it is directly above the pile of marbles. At a given moment the marble is dropped to 'bomb' the pile. Any marbles that are knocked out of the circle become the property of the 'bombardier,' who also retrieves his 'bomb' marble. The game ends when the circle is empty.

The most popular and undoubtedly one of the oldest marbles games is the ring game. There are several variations, but a basic method of play is as follows:

A circle of about a foot in diameter is drawn on the ground with chalk, and each player puts an equal amount of marbles – two or three – within it. An outer shooting circle of about six feet in diameter is drawn around the small circle. Each player shoots a marble, trying to knock one of the others out of the circle. If he succeeds, it becomes his property.

One form of the game allows a player to continue his turn for as long as he hits a marble out of the circle each time. Novice players may prefer to let each have only one shot at a time. The shooter is retrieved after each turn.

In another version of the ring game, the players arrange their marbles in a circle, equally spaced a few inches apart. A target marble is placed in the center of the circle, and each player aims from a line drawn a few feet away from the circle. When he has hit the target marble once, he may aim for any marble in the circle. If he hits one out, it becomes his. He may then aim at another with the same shooter, from the point where it came to rest. His turn continues until he misses the marble he is aiming at; his shooter is left as a target for other players.

In a watercolor painting of 1874, above, British artist James Archer portrays a group of boys playing marbles in the town of Islington, now part of London. Victorian marbles were similar to the modern glass or ceramic ones, shown below.

The game of marbles bridge can be played using a 'bridge' with arches of different sizes (see How to Make the Game). Each player in turn shoots one marble toward the bridge, from a line drawn several feet away. The distance of the bridge from the shooting line should be longer for more experienced players, shorter for novices.

If the marble passes cleanly through a hole, the player scores the number of points written over the hole; the smaller the hole, the greater the

Near the top of the famous Spanish Steps in Rome, left, an Italian marbles player takes a ringside seat as his companion prepares to 'shoot.'

number of points it carries. The marble must pass all the way through, without touching the sides of the bridge.

The winner may be either the player who first attains a pre-arranged top score, or the one who scores the highest number of points in a given length of time.

Materials

Three plywood boards, 4 by 16 inches, $\frac{1}{8}$ inch thick.
Two plywood boards, $3\frac{3}{4}$ by 4 inches, $\frac{1}{8}$ inch thick.
Four pieces of wood, $\frac{1}{2}$ by $\frac{1}{2}$ inch, 4 inches long.
Wood glue.
Wood primer.
A dozen wire nails, $\frac{1}{2}$ inch long.
Blue gloss paint.
White plastic adhesive tape.
Large white press-on numbers: 2, 4, 6, 8, and 10.

Tools

Sandpaper, ruler, pencil, scroll saw, hammer, primer brush, paintbrush, and scissors.

Young players can test their skill by shooting marbles under a handmade marbles bridge, below.

How to Make the Game

Place one 4-by-16-inch section horizontally in front of you. Line up your ruler with the bottom edge and, measuring from the left, mark the following points: 2 inches, $3\frac{1}{2}$ inches, $4\frac{1}{2}$ inches, 6 inches, $7\frac{1}{4}$ inches, $8\frac{1}{2}$ inches, 10 inches, 11 inches, $12\frac{3}{4}$ inches, and $13\frac{1}{2}$ inches. Mark these same points on the top edge of this section, then draw vertical lines connecting the opposite points.

Mark points $1\frac{3}{4}$ inches from the bottom edge on the first and second lines at the left, $1\frac{1}{2}$ inches on the third and fourth lines, $1\frac{1}{4}$ inches on the fifth and sixth lines, 1 inch on the seventh and eighth lines, and $\frac{3}{4}$ inch on the ninth and tenth lines. Draw straight lines connecting those points directly opposite each other.

You now have five rectangles with the bottom edge of the board as their base. Draw an arc rounding off the upper corners of each rectangle. Using the scroll saw, cut out the five arches. Sandpaper all rough edges. Apply glue to the 4-inch edges of the $3\frac{3}{4}$-by-4-inch boards. Stand them upright and sandwich them between the ends of the two 4-by-16-inch sections (one of which has the five arches). All sections of this four-sided frame should be flush with each other and each corner should form a right angle.

Hammer in a few wire nails at the right and left ends of the longer sections to secure them to the two 4-inch sections while the glue is drying. Before the glue has set, stand the frame so that the arches are flush with the work table. Apply glue to the top edge of the frame. Place the remaining 4-by-16-inch section directly on top of this frame so that the edges match. Press down briefly, then allow to dry thoroughly. To further reinforce the structure, glue a 4-inch length of wood in each inner corner of the bridge. After the glue has dried, remove the wire nails.

Apply a coat of wood primer to the outside surface of the bridge. Allow it to dry, then sand it down lightly. Paint, and allow to dry thoroughly. Using press-on numbers 2, 4, 6, 8, and 10, mark above each arch as shown in the model below. Decorate your marble bridge with thin strips of white plastic adhesive tape.

Sey

About the Game

According to a myth of the Dogon tribe, at the beginning of the world when the sky was close to the earth, mothers plucked stars from the sky to give them to their children as playthings. Nowadays, Dogon children from Mali, West Africa, are expert at matching wits in the 'hide and seek' tactics of the ancient game of *sey*. Squatting on the ground with a *tibi* or pebble as his only playing piece, a player tries to fool his opponent with the fast movements of his hands as he surreptitiously sows the *tibi* into one of several compartments dug into the soil. It looks simple, but, as every Dogon child knows, it is a fascinating pastime, and only practice makes a skillful *sey* player.

There are many other African games that involve hiding objects in the sand. A favorite game among girls of Dahomey, West Africa, is *dosu*. One girl buries a ring in a pile of loose sand; then she scoops up the sand and arranges it in as many smaller piles as there are players. Each player chooses a pile, and the one who finds the ring in her pile is the next to hide it. In *godo,* another Dahomey sand game, a noose of string is covered by sand. Players push sticks down into the sand, trying to pierce the concealed noose.

How to Play the Game

Two players sit opposite each other on a patch of free ground, with a small stone for the *tibi*. The field consists of two concentric circles, 17 and 19 inches in diameter. Each player digs three small holes about an inch apart in his side of the track between the circles.

The first player conceals the *tibi* in a handful of loose earth. Working from the left he trickles earth into each of his three holes. His object is to sow the *tibi* into one of the holes smoothly and inconspicuously, along with the earth, so that his opponent will not notice. The opponent can call to the *tibi* as the Dogon do, '*Deñy, deñy!*' ('Come out, come out!') When sowing the *tibi,* Dogon children cup their hands in a special way, the right curled tight to control the flow of earth, but with the right index finger between the index and middle finger of the left hand, which is curved round the right hand at the same time.

The opponent tries to guess which hole conceals the *tibi*. If he picks the right hole, it is his turn to play. If not, the first player retrieves the *tibi* and digs a new hole in the track, an inch from his third hole. He repeats the sowing process, but must not sow the *tibi* into the same hole twice. For each wrong guess, the first player digs a new hole until he is halfway around the track, finally occupying his opponent's holes and winning the game. When guessing, Dogon children often recite a magic rhyme to help find the correct hole.

Under a rock shelter, Dogon boys of Mali, West Africa (left), smooth the sand and select a suitable tibi *(pebble) before a game of* sey.

161

Knucklebones

About the Game

In ancient Greece, the knucklebones from legs of mutton – called *astragaloi* – were thrown to prophesy the future. They were also used like dice for gambling and, most frequently, for playing the game which is still known today as knucklebones. Paintings on old Greek vases show both gods and mortals playing with the bones, and similar games are mentioned in Homer's *Iliad* and *Odyssey*. Sophocles attributes the invention of knucklebones to Palamedes and says that he taught the game to the Greek soldiers during the Trojan War, but it seems more likely that the game originated in ancient Asia.

The Romans introduced knucklebones to many countries during their military campaigns, yet the game is also traditional in other parts of the world, from Russia to Polynesia, where no Romans ever ventured. A modern form of the game, fivestones or jacks, is a favorite among school children everywhere.

How to Play the Game

Knucklebones may be played by two or more children, though interest may flag if there are more than four.

The game consists of performing various 'figures' – throws and catches of the bones – in a chosen sequence. The names of the figures may vary in different regions, but most of the movements are the same all over the world. A few of the best-known figures are described here.

A basic and ancient knucklebone figure is even depicted on a Roman fresco from Pompeii. The player tosses all five bones into the air and tries to catch them on the back of his hand. Then he throws these up and catches them again in his palm. The score each player obtains can be used to determine order of play in succeeding figures.

To play the figure called 'ones,' the first player throws the bones onto the ground. He picks up a single bone, which is thence called the 'jack'; he tosses it into the air, picks up one of the bones on the ground, and catches the jack as it falls. He transfers the picked-up bone to his free hand and throws the jack again, repeating the movements until all bones are held. If he drops a bone, misses the jack, or moves another bone, he is out, and must repeat 'ones' on his next turn before starting another figure.

Next he goes on to 'twos,' in which the bones must be picked up in pairs; 'threes,' in which he picks up three bones and then one, and 'fours,' picking up all four bones at once.

English girls play checkstones (another name for knucklebones) in this watercolor by F. J. Shields, dated 1855. Shields was a Manchester painter who belonged to the Pre-Raphaelite movement.

In 'under the arch,' the player throws the bones to the ground. With one hand he forms an arch by placing forefinger and thumb downward at a point near the bones. Then he picks up a jack, throws it, and while it is in the air he flicks one of the bones through the arch. This is repeated until all bones have been put through the arch. If he succeeds, he goes on to 'twos,' 'threes,' and 'fours under the arch' (two pairs, three and one, and four bones at a time).

A variation of the above figure is called 'stables.' One hand is placed with all fingertips parted and touching the ground. As the jack is thrown, one bone must be flicked into each 'stable,' formed by the parted fingers. Finally the bones inside the stables must be picked out again one at a time.

'Toad in the hole' is a similar figure, in which the player places one hand on the ground with forefinger and thumb joined to make a hole. At each throw he must flick a bone into the hole. Finally the hole is removed and the four bones are picked up at one throw.

To play 'jump the ditch' the player takes one bone as jack and lays the others in a line a few inches apart. On the first throw of the jack he must pick up the first and third bones, on the second throw he picks up the remaining two.

In 'set the table,' four bones are placed in a pile. At each throw of the jack one bone is removed and placed at the corner of an imaginary square. When the square is completed, the bones are picked up and replaced in a pile.

Eskimos from Greenland play a 'bone game' (right), using phalanges (small finger bones) from seal flippers. The game is played, with minor variations, by all Eskimo tribes, and – like knucklebones – was originally used for divination. Single bones may represent humans and animals in the game; groups of them symbolize familiar structures such as houses, tents, or kayaks.

'Knuckle Down,' the title of an engraving of 1869 (above), is an expression still used to mean 'get on with it!' The bronze knucklebones, below, were made in the Netherlands in the early 1800's.

Hopscotch

About the Game

Hopscotch did not originate in Scotland, as its name seems to suggest. 'Scotch' is an old English word meaning to mark or score lightly, exactly what children have been doing for centuries, using stones and sticks to draw hopscotch diagrams on the ground.

No one knows where the game began; it is played in such diverse countries as Britain, Russia, India, and China, with only minor variations in the rules. (Burmese children play on a diagram similar to one commonly found in the United States, but they jump in a squatting position, their hands on their hips.)

One of the oldest known hopscotch diagrams is inscribed into the floor of the Forum in Rome. During the expansion of the Roman empire, the legions built cobblestone roads connecting the northern countries of Europe with the Mediterranean and with Asia Minor. The paved surfaces were ideal for this game, taught by soldiers to the children of France, Germany, and Britain. Hopscotch has remained popular with European children ever since. Many different game diagrams are used in countries like Germany and Holland, and whole books have been written about the hopscotch varieties to be found in some cities. In America, one games researcher has catalogued nearly 20 versions of hopscotch that are played in the streets and playgrounds of San Francisco.

The six games on the next two pages are described according to the rules followed in Holland, but any child in the world will probably find one or two local favorites among the Dutch game diagrams.

A lightfooted girl from New York City, opposite, photographed by Art Kane, hops through the blocks of a hopscotch diagram painted on her school playground. More than 7,000 miles away, a Nepali girl, below, hopscotches barefoot beside a buffalo in the marketplace of her home in Pokhara, Nepal.

Heaven and Earth Hopscotch

The rules for Heaven and Earth hopscotch, with slight variations, will apply to almost any hopscotch game.
General rules:
A. Stand in the Earth square and toss the sand-filled marker into block 1. Hop on one foot from Earth to block 1, pick up the marker and hop back to Earth. Now toss the marker into block 2, hop to block 2 via block 1, and toss the marker back to Earth. Hop 2, 1, Earth.

Begin again, tossing the marker into block 3 and continue in the same manner up to block 9.

The steps from 'earth' to 'heaven' and back are outlined in the game diagram shown below.

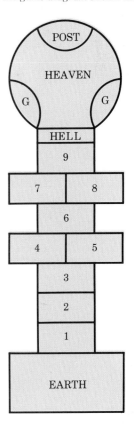

If the marker lands in the wrong block or on a line, your turn ends and the next player begins. (The player whose turn is over may begin again where he made his mistake, but only after the other players have taken their turns.)

B. After hopscotching from 1 to 9, toss the marker into Heaven. If it lands in an area marked G, you may skip one of the following steps, from C to K. If the marker lands in Heaven, hop there, block by block, pick up the marker and toss it into block 9. Now follow the same procedure as in step A, but in reverse, hopscotching back to Earth.

C. Instead of tossing the marker, shove it with your foot from block to block, as you hop from Earth to Heaven and back to Earth again.

D. Balancing the marker on one foot, hop through all the blocks, one by one, to Heaven and back to Earth. If the marker falls, your turn is over.

E. Do the same, balancing the marker on your head.
F. Do the same, balancing the marker on your index finger.
G. Do the same, balancing the marker on your forearm.
H. Do the same, balancing the marker on your right knee.
I. Do the same, balancing the marker on your left knee.
J. With eyes closed and head erect, hop through all the blocks to Heaven and return to Earth. Players call 'hot' if you hop correctly, 'cold' if you miss.

K. Standing in Earth, with your back toward the hopscotch diagram, toss the marker over your shoulder. If the marker falls into one of the blocks and not on a line, you may write your initials in the block, making it your 'house.' In subsequent games, you may rest there with both feet on the ground. The other players must skip this block when playing.

Additional regulations:

1. While resting in Heaven, you may stand on both feet and readjust the position of a badly placed marker.

2. If your marker lands on a line or in the wrong block, you lose your turn and the next player begins.

3. If the marker lands in the Post section of Heaven, you may not speak or laugh during the game. If you do, you are out of the game for good.

4. If the marker lands in the Hell section of Heaven, you end your turn and must start from the beginning when your turn comes up again.

How to Make the Game
Select a hopscotch diagram from the six illustrated on these pages. Draw this pattern on the playground or sidewalk, making the dimensions of each segment or block about 16 by 24 inches.

An old shoe-polish can filled with sand serves well as a marker or 'potsie,' as it is called in England and the United States. You can make your diagram more attractive by drawing with chalks of different colors.

Water Hopscotch
The area marked 'water' is forbidden territory in this game. If a player or his marker trespasses into the water, the game is over for that player. Blocks 3, 6, and 9 are rest areas. In addition to the general rules, there is a last step, which is played without a marker. The player must hop on one leg three times around the hopscotch diagram without resting.

Send-a-Letter Hopscotch
The name of this game comes from the envelope shape at the top of the diagram. No marker is used and the numbers have been placed in the diagram above only to simplify the explanation of the rules.

A. Hop on both feet from block 1 through to block 9 and back again.

B. Hop on your right foot from 1 to 4, hop on both feet into 5 and 6 at the same time, hop to 7 on one foot, then on both feet to 8 and 9 simultaneously. Jump around so that your right foot is in 9 and your left foot in 8.

C. Hop once so that your legs are crossed, left foot in 9, right foot in 8. Then hop on one foot through 7 and 6, hop on both feet through 5 and 4, and hop on one foot back to 1.

D. Hop from 1 to 9 and back again, hopping cross-legged into 5 and 6 at the same time, and 8 and 9 in the same way.

E. Follow step J in the general rules.

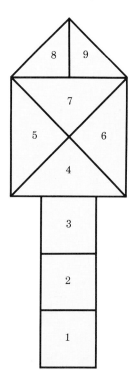

The diagram for water hopscotch, above: the game takes its name from the middle strip of 'water.'

The envelope shape at the head of the pattern for send-a-letter hopscotch gives the game its name.

Monday-Tuesday Hopscotch

In this diagram, each lettered block represents a day of the week.

The general rules apply to this version with the following exceptions. The rest block is called Sunday instead of Heaven. Step A differs too, in that the player tosses the marker from Earth to Monday, hops over Monday and onward to Sunday, where he rests, then hops back to Tuesday. Here he picks up the marker then hops over this block again, back to Earth.

The diagram for Monday-Tuesday hopscotch – a simple game with a block for each day of the week.

English Hopscotch

Play according to the general rules or, for a different kind of game, follow these steps:

A. Toss the marker into block 1. Hop with both feet from Earth directly to block 2. Hop into the next block on one foot, hop into the next block with legs crossed, the next block with both legs straight and repeat this progression until Heaven. Make the return trip to block 2 using the same method. Pick up the marker from block 1 and hop over this block to Earth. Continue this for all 10 blocks.

B. In the same manner, hopscotch through each of the blocks from Heaven to Earth.

C. Continue with steps C, E, F, J, and K of the general rules.

Moon Hopscotch

In Moon hopscotch, those blocks marked with a 'minus' sign (–) must be hopped on one foot; those with a 'plus' sign (+) are hopped on both feet. Neither the marker nor a player may enter the 'moon circle' in block 6.

From Earth, the marker is tossed into block 1. The player hops to 1, kicks the marker into the following block, hops there, etc., until he reaches block 10. If the marker lands in Earth, the game is lost. Then, he turns and kicks the marker from block 10 to Earth.

After this, Moon hopscotch follows the general rules, steps D to K.

The ladder-shaped diagram for English hopscotch, popular among British children.

At the top of the diagram for moon hopscotch is the block containing the forbidden 'moon circle.'

In the streets of Paris, a lone hopscotcher, above, puts the finishing touches to her game diagram.

Ghanaian girls watch attentively while a boy hopscotches in the red earth of an Accra park.

While her little brother looks on, a gracefully-poised Nepali girl tosses her marker into play.

Conkers

About the Game

Conkers is a children's corruption of the word 'conquerors.' It is a schoolboy pastime in England, Scotland, Australia, and in some parts of the United States. A horse chestnut, strung on a length of strong cord, is the traditional conker, but walnuts, conch shells, snail shells, or hazelnuts may be substituted. The game involves two players, one of whom tries to crack the nut of the other with his own nut, thereby conquering it.

Chestnut conkers are the object of a serious search by English children in the autumn. Popular belief is that the best – the hardest – are to be found at the top of horse chestnut trees, and sticks and stones are pitched at the highest branches in an effort to bring the chestnuts down. Less desirable nuts can be doctored until their quality becomes first class.

There are various recipes for preparing a proper conker. Sometimes they are baked; others are soaked for a period in salt water or vinegar. The wise player, at the end of the conkers season, stores a few leftovers for the next year, when he will have tough, wrinkled 'yearsies,' the most formidable of conkers.

With each success, a conker gains a new title: 'one-er' for having cracked or broken one conker, 'two-er' for having defeated two conkers, 'three-er' and so on. If a 'ten-er' beats a 'five-er,' it becomes a 'fifteen-er.' The BBC once televised a conkers contest in which four players participated. Their conkers ranged from a '460-er' to a '3,367-er.' The new title of the winning conker was '7,351-er.'

One enterprising toymaker manufactures plastic conkers that can be reassembled after they have been broken. It is doubtful whether these will ever become as popular or as functional as the real thing.

Materials

One or more hard horse chestnuts.
A bootlace or 2-foot length of strong, flexible cord for each conker.

Tools

A wire nail or screw-nail.

'First hitsy!' A schoolboy of Maldon, England, photographed with his friends by Tim Street-Porter, calls the first shot and positions his conker for the strike (opposite). Seconds later, his opponent cries 'Strings!' and wins an extra turn. After its simple construction, as illustrated by the figure at right, the conker is ready for all comers. 'Obbley-onker,' 'cob,' 'hongkong,' and 'cheeser,' are a few of the battling chestnut's nicknames.

How to Play the Game

Each of the two players wraps the free end of the conker cord twice around his hand. Players believe that the conker is more likely to survive if it is the striker rather than the stricken, and the one who calls out 'First!' before the other player wins the privilege of the first shot. The challenged player holds his arm out to the side, allowing his conker to dangle some eight inches below his fist. This conker must be still before the action can be started.

The challenger, standing at an agreed distance, holds his conker between thumb and forefinger. He takes aim and then throws his conker at the target-conker. If he misses, he has two additional turns. If he strikes and neither conker is cracked or broken, the roles are reversed. When one player's conker is cracked or broken, the other player is the winner.

If the strings tangle when a shot is made, the player who first yells 'Strings!' wins an additional turn. An accidentally dropped conker may be jumped on by an opponent if he shouts 'Stamps!' before the owner shouts 'No stamps!' A conker legally stamped on counts as one victory, which is conferred to the conker of the player who did the stamping.

How to Make the Game

Select hard, smoothly rounded chestnuts. Bore a hole through the center of each with the nail or screw-nail, making sure not to crack the edges of the hole. Run one end of the bootlace or cord through the hole and knot securely.

Quoits

About the Game

The clatter of iron quoits ringing the hob was a familiar sound to country folk in Britain as early as the fourteenth century. Sometimes horseshoes were tossed for want of the special metal ring used to play the game – a custom still prevailing in parts of the country. Edward III banned the game in favor of archery: the opinion of the gentry at that time was that 'quoiting be too vile for scholars.' Quoits probably developed from the Greek sport of discus throwing, and spread with the traders. Eventually the entire world learned to play it. A Peruvian legend tells of the murder of an Inca king while he was playing quoits with the Spanish *conquistadores*. Quoiting leagues are a familiar part of social life in Scotland and England, though in the United States, where quoits were introduced during colonial times, horseshoe-pitching has largely replaced the original version of the game.

'The Ring Toss,' a classic quoits photograph of 1899 by Clarence White (opposite), from the International Museum of Photography.

Ideal for rainy days is a game of indoor quoits, played on a portable wooden 'bed' (above). The specially colored hobs denote the scoring value.

How to Play the Game

In the official game, two clay 'beds' stand 18 yards apart, each with an iron 'hob' in the center. Each team stands at one bed and players alternately pitch quoits at the opposite bed. The indoor game presented here has nine hobs in one bed. Armed with two quoits each, two players stand six yards from the bed and pitch their quoits alternately. Red scores three, yellow two, and blue one, the game consisting of 21 points. One quoit cancels another if they ring the same hob.

Materials

A plywood board, 19¼ inches square, ⅜ inch thick.
Four plywood boards, 3¾ by 19¾ inches, ⅜ inch thick.
Eight wooden dowels, 12 inches long, 1 inch in diameter.
One wooden dowel, 24 inches long, 1 inch in diameter.
Nine wooden balls, 1½ inches in diameter.
Four half-round molding strips, ⅜ inch wide, 19¾ inches long.
Four wooden strips, ½-inch-square, 16 inches long.
Wood glue. Wood putty. Wood primer.
Nine nails, 1 inch long.
Wire nails, ¾ inch long.
Gloss paint: green, red, yellow, white.
Plastic adhesive tape, ½ inch wide: blue, yellow, and multi-colored.
Two 'quoits' per player: lightweight metal rings, about 6 inches in diameter. (Quoits can be made of aluminum wire.)

Tools

A pencil, ruler, drawing compass, scroll saw, hammer, electric drill or brace with 1-inch auger bit, sandpaper, primer brush, paintbrush, vise, protractor, backsaw, wood rasp, wire cutters, scissors, and, for the quoits, a soldering iron.

1: Draw a centered 15-inch square on the board surface, then draw vertical, horizontal, and diagonal lines that bisect the square.

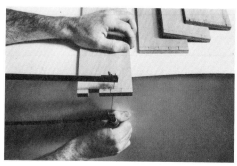

2: With a scroll saw, cut out the alternate fingers from the joint markings at both ends of the four 3¾-by-19¾-inch plywood boards.

3: Glue the finger joints of the four boards together to make a frame. Secure the corners with a few wire nails while the glue is drying.

How to Make the Game

On each edge of the 19¼-inch-square board, measure and mark points 2⅛ inches from each corner. Connect the points on opposite sides of the board, making an inner 15-inch square. Draw diagonal lines connecting opposite corners of the board. Draw a vertical line and a horizontal line which intersect the cross point of the two diagonals (see photograph 1).

Set the drawing compass to a radius of ½ inch and place the compass needle on the central crosspoint; draw a circle. Draw circles at the other eight points where lines intersect.

Place one of the 3¾-by-19¾-inch boards horizontally before you on the work table. On the top and bottom long edges, mark points ⅜ inch from the left and right corners. Connect opposite points with ruled lines.

Measuring on each of the 3¾-inch edges and the lines beside them, mark points at ¾-inch intervals. Draw lines connecting corresponding points on the edges and the lines beside them. Each ⅜-inch strip on either side of the board is now divided into five ¾-inch sections. Repeat these steps on the remaining three boards.

With the scroll saw, cut out three alternating sections on one side of each board, starting with a corner section. On the other side of each board, cut out two alternating sections, starting with the second section from the corner, as shown in photograph 2.

Spread a light coat of glue along all the finger joints of the four boards. Join the boards so that the fingers of one dovetail with the fingers of another (see photograph 3). To hold the pieces in place while the glue is drying, hammer a few wire nails part way into each corner.

Turn the square board over so that its marked side is down. Apply glue to the four sides of this board. Pick up the finger-jointed frame and place it over the board so that the board is snug inside the bottom of the frame.

Apply glue to two adjacent sides of each of the square strips; press one against each edge of the square board where it meets the frame. Hammer several well-spaced wire nails through the strip

into the sides of the frame. Turn the frame over so that the marked board is on top. Allow the glue to dry thoroughly; then remove the wire nails from the finger-jointed corners.

Fill in the spaces around the finger joints with wood putty so that the joints are not visible. Allow the putty to dry thoroughly.

Place the tip of the auger bit in the center of the central circle on the board; drill a hole through the circle. Repeat these steps on the remaining eight circles. Sand down any rough and splintered surfaces around each hole.

Apply a coat of wood primer to the outer surfaces of the board and frame. Allow to dry. Sand down lightly and paint the platform green. Allow the paint to dry thoroughly.

Clamp the middle of one of the molding strips in a vise so that its flat side is facing upward. Line up the perpendicular of the protractor with the left edge of the strip; the base of the protractor is in line with the bottom edge of the surface. Mark a point on the top edge 45 degrees from the lower corner. Draw a line from the corner edge to that point. Repeat this step at the right edge of the molding, marking a 45-degree angle to the left.

With the backsaw, cut along the strip on the lines drawn. Repeat these steps on the remaining three molding strips. Paint the strips yellow and allow them to dry thoroughly. Apply glue to the flat sides and mitered corners of the strips and join them together in a frame on top of the platform so that the edges of the platform and the strips match.

With a wood rasp, file away a section of each of the nine wooden balls until there is a flat surface 1 inch in diameter. Drive a 1-inch nail halfway into the middle point of this area on each ball. Cut off the heads of the nails. Drive the rest of each nail into the middle point of one end of a dowel by hammering on top of the wooden ball. The ball must be flush with the dowel end. Paint each dowel-and-ball 'hob' with wood primer. Allow to dry thoroughly.

Sand the hobs lightly. Paint the ball on the longest dowel yellow and the other balls red.

Allow the paint to dry thoroughly. Paint the longest dowel red, four dowels white, and four yellow. Allow them to dry thoroughly.

Decorate each of the four dowels with colored adhesive tape, as shown in the model at right. Wind the tape in a spiral pattern, from top to bottom, leaving roughly ¾-inch widths of dowel showing under the tape.

Apply glue around the bottom ends of these dowel-and-ball hobs. Insert them in the holes of the platform so that the ends of the dowels are flush with the underside of the board. The red hob goes into the central hole; position the yellow and white hobs alternately.

To make the quoits, wrap aluminum wire around a bottle or jar about 6 inches in diameter. Cut the wire and solder the ends together.

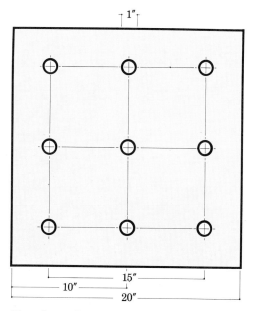

Place the needle of the drawing compass at each of the nine points of intersection on the board; draw circles with a radius of ½ inch.

Shuttlecock

About the Game

The game of shuttlecock, in which a small feathered ball or disc is kicked from player to player, has been played in China, Japan, and Korea for more than 2,000 years. In ancient Japan, the game was used to train the militia: it was believed that a soldier's physical abilities would be sharpened by this sort of play. Officers formed clubs where the game rules were standardized. In Korea, the game was played for practical reasons: shopkeepers and street vendors kicked the shuttlecock back and forth to keep their feet warm in cold weather.

A less demanding version of the game is played with decorated wooden paddles called 'battledores.' Drawings from classical Greece show a game very similar to battledore and shuttlecock. In some countries it is traditionally a girls' game: in Japan, it was part of the New Year's celebration, and in Tudor England, girls played it on Shrove Tuesday, when the shuttlecock was believed to have oracular powers. While bouncing the shuttlecock, the girls chanted fortune-telling rhymes such as:
Shuttlecock, shuttlecock, tell me true,
How many years have I to go through?
One, two, three...' and so on.

A colorful and durable shuttlecock can be made in a few minutes from a small ball of cork, crowned with a handful of chicken feathers.

The shuttlecock soars as boatmen kick the feathered ball from player to player – a classic Chinese game depicted in an engraving published for English armchair travelers in the 1840's.

How to Play the Game

One person can play shuttlecock by throwing it in the air, then keeping it aloft by kicking it – with heel, toe, top or sole of shoe. The score is kept by counting every strike before the shuttlecock falls to the ground. An experienced player can keep going for hundreds of strikes.

Two or more can play by kicking the shuttlecock between them until one player lets it fall; he drops out. The last player in wins.

A table tennis paddle can be used as a battledore. Again, the object is to hit the shuttlecock up into the air as many times as possible. Playing the game out of doors on a windy day will make the game more difficult and interesting.

Materials

A cork ball, 2 inches in diameter.
Ten chicken feathers.
Wood primer.
Paint.
All-purpose glue.
Downy chicken feathers (optional).

Tools

An awl and a paintbrush.

How to Make the Game

Paint the ball with wood primer. Allow it to dry. Sand lightly; then paint it a bright color. When the paint has dried, use the awl to make a cluster of ten holes in the ball. Dip each of the feather points in glue and insert them into the holes. If you wish, decorate the shuttlecock with bits of down glued into the holes beside the longer feathers.

Spinning Tops

About the Game
Playing with tops is an ancient and worldwide children's game. Cato, the Roman statesman, gave it his seal of approval by recommending it to parents as a more suitable game for children than dice.

Tops were common in England by the fourteenth century, and may have been connected with early Christian church ceremony. Each parish had its own top, and on Shrove Tuesday each year, top-races were held on the roads between parishes. Rhymes were chanted, some of which survive:
Top go up, top go down,
Top go all around the town...
A top that had stopped spinning, or had been put away until next year, was said to be 'sleeping' – hence the expression 'to sleep like a top.'

Indian children in the southwestern United States call tops 'dancers' and keep them spinning by striking them with thongs made of buckskin.

Tops of many shapes and sizes are found throughout the Orient. In some rural areas tops are made from conch shells, their pointed tips ground flat. The Japanese make many novel kinds of tops, including the 'childbearing top' which contains smaller tops that are released as it spins. Hollow tops that hum or whistle are popular in some African countries.

In Japan, where top-making is a traditional skill, two boys (opposite), photographed by John Launois, spin tops at Megane bridge in Nagasaki.

How to Play the Game
The top with the long spindle is set in motion by twisting the upper part of the spindle quickly between the palms. To spin the bedpost top, the player winds the cord around the top as described under How to Make the Game and puts the loop round a finger. He sets the top on its point on the table or ground, holds it lightly with the free hand, and lets go as he pulls the cord sharply away. Practice improves the spin.

An old Roman game is called *turbo* (Latin for top). A circle is drawn on the ground, divided into ten unequal segments. The largest is numbered 1, through to the smallest which counts 10. Players set tops spinning in the center, and score according to where they come to rest.

Materials
For the 'spindle' top:
A white pine board, 6 inches square, 1 inch thick.
A wooden dowel, 16 inches long, $\frac{3}{8}$ inch in diameter.
A wooden ball, 1 inch in diameter.
Two nails, $1\frac{1}{4}$ inches long.
Paint.
Wood glue.

For the 'bedpost' top:
A broad, knobbed top of a bedpost or a chair post, about 3 inches long, $1\frac{1}{2}$ to 2 inches in diameter.
A wooden bead, 1 inch in diameter.
A flat-head screw, $1\frac{1}{2}$ inches long. (The body of the screw must be narrower than the hole in the bead.)
A nail, 1 inch long.
Paint.
Nylon cord, 1 yard long.

Hours of pleasure can be had with these three spinning tops of time-honored designs.

175

Tools

A pencil, ruler, drawing compass, coping saw, sandpaper, electric drill or brace with a $\frac{3}{8}$-inch bit, wood rasp, hammer, wire cutters or combination pliers, screwdriver, and paintbrush.

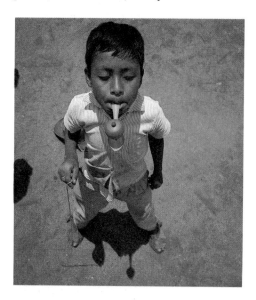

Tops need not only be spun on the ground. Some Japanese tops will balance, like gyroscopes, on a string line. The same principle is involved in spinning a top on a spoon held in the mouth, as demonstrated by a Mexican boy, above; the feat demands dexterity and a good sense of balance.

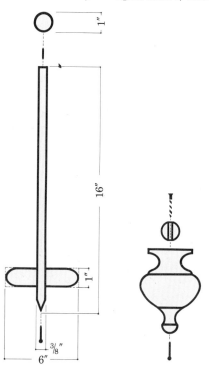

As shown in the cutaway drawing above, both tops can be constructed in a few moments from scraps of wood and pieces of old furniture.

How to Make the Game

To make the 'spindle' top, measure and mark a point in the exact center of the board. Place the needle of the drawing compass on this point and draw a circle with a radius of 3 inches. Cut the circle out of the board with the coping saw. Drill a hole through the center of the circle. With the wood rasp, round off the outer edges of the circle. Sand down any rough edges.

With the wood rasp, file down a small flat area on the wooden ball and hammer a nail halfway into the center of this flat surface. Cut off the head of the nail with wire cutters. Place the headless tip of the nail at the center of one end of the dowel and drive the nail in by hammering on the ball until it is centered on the dowel.

Hammer the other nail into the other end of the dowel until only $\frac{1}{16}$ inch of the nail is still showing. Cut off the head of the nail and file down the headless point to a smooth nub. File or whittle this end of the dowel to a slight point. Insert the dowel into the hole in the circular board so that the nailed bottom end of the dowel sticks out about $1\frac{1}{4}$ inches. Apply glue around the hole on both sides of the board and allow to dry thoroughly. Paint the top in gay colors.

To make the 'bedpost' top, smooth down the flat surface of the bedpost with sandpaper, and mark a point in the center of this surface. Insert the screw in the bead and screw it into the point marked on the bedpost. Do not screw it so tightly that the bead cannot spin freely.

Hammer a nail into the exact center of the tip of the bedpost so that only $\frac{1}{16}$ inch of the nail is visible. Cut off the head of the nail and file down the point to a smooth nub. Paint the top in various bright colors.

The length of nylon cord should be unraveled and flattened at one end. Hold this section vertically against the spool section of the top and wind the rest of the cord horizontally around it. Tie the free end of the cord into a loop.

Australasia is rich in rituals featuring tops. Tribes in New Guinea and Borneo spin tops after the seasonal planting of their staple crops, to encourage the young shoots to thrive. An islander from the Torres Strait, between New Guinea and Australia, spins a dish-shaped top (below). In some tribal areas, big spindle tops are turned against each other in the 'battle of the giant tops.'

Jump Rope

About the Game

As it provides plenty of fun and exercise in a small space, jump rope is particularly suited to street life in urban areas. But the game can be played anywhere. The author of a nineteenth-century book of English games recalls a countrified version: 'In the hop season, a hop-stem stripped of its leaves is used instead of a rope, and in my opinion is preferable.'

Children often chant traditional rhymes to the beat of the rope on the ground. Along the border of Texas and Mexico, children sing, 'Brown as a coffee-berry, red as a bean, that's the prettiest color I've ever seen. Yellow as a daisy, black as ink, that's the prettiest color I do think. Orange as a pumpkin, green as grass, keep on jumping as long as you last.'

Spanish children, below, chant rhymes as they jump the rope in a town of La Mancha, the arid plateau famous as the setting for the adventures of Cervantes's eccentric hero, Don Quixote.

Small girls and big men are the most enthusiastic adepts of jump rope; for small girls (below) it is a popular game, but for men such as boxers and athletes it is a superb form of exercise.

How to Play the Game

Jump rope may be played by one, two, or several children. A single player holds one end of the rope in either hand, lets the rope hang behind him to touch his ankles, and then swings it in an arc over his head and down. As the rope reaches his feet he jumps over it with a step, a hop, or a two-footed jump, and repeats the whole movement, speeding up if he wants to. He may chant a rhyme to count how many times he can jump without catching his feet in the rope. One common rhyme, with regional variations, is:
One, two, buckle my shoe.
Three, four, shut the door.
Five, six, pick up sticks.
Seven, eight, don't be late.
Nine, ten, begin again.

Two players may jump side by side, each holding one end of the rope. Alternatively, one end of the rope may be tied to a post or railing at waist height, and the other end turned by one player while the other jumps; as soon as the jumper misses his footing, they change places. When a group of children play, two children each hold one end of a long rope, and the other children take turns jumping in and out of the whirling rope arc without breaking the rhythm.

There are many jump rope games that can be played by a group. A few popular ones are described below.

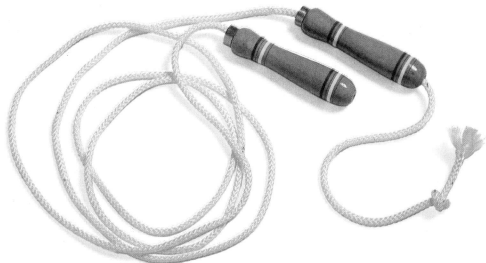

The length of a homemade jump rope can be altered to suit the number and size of players.

Follow the Leader

Two children swing the rope; the players stand in file in front of the rope. The first person is the leader. He jumps into the rope arc, recites a rhyme, and jumps out. The next player must jump in, repeat the same rhyme and jump out, and so on. If a player fails, he is out of the game and takes the place of one of the rope turners.

Running Through

Two players turn the rope while the other players take turns running in, jumping the rope once, and running out. The second time around, each player must jump the rope twice before running out, and so on. Players who fail drop out of the game, the first two taking the places of the rope turners. The last remaining player wins.

Rocking the Boat

Instead of swinging the rope round in a complete circle, the rope turners simply let it swing back and forth in a low arc, just brushing the ground. Each player must enter the arc, jump the rope once or several times, and jump out without catching the rope in his feet. When each player has had a turn, the rope is raised a couple of inches and the game is repeated. The height of the rope is increased for each round until only one player is left.

When the rope is being turned fast, it takes split-second timing to jump in and out of its arc without tripping over. One well-known variation of jump rope is for one player to jump in at the same time as another jumps out, a feat which has been successfully achieved by the girls (above) on Ponape, in the Caroline Islands, South Pacific.

Materials

Six yards of rope, ¼ inch in diameter.
Two wooden dowels or chair posts,
5 inches long, 1 inch in diameter.
A nail, 1½ inches long.
All-purpose glue.
Gloss paint.

Tools

An electric drill or brace with
¼-inch bit, vise, hammer, and
paintbrush.

How to Make the Game

Clamp one dowel in the vise so that one end is facing upward. Drill a hole through the center of the dowel all the way through its length. Clamp the second dowel in the vise and drill a hole in one end to a depth of 1¼ inches. Paint both handles and allow to dry thoroughly. Apply glue to one end of the rope and insert it into the 1¼-inch hole; then hammer the nail through the rope in the hole and into the wood beyond it. Push the other end of the rope through the hole in the second dowel, and tie it in a loose knot so that the length of the rope is adjustable.

The Clock

One player holds one end of a long rope, which is stretched out before him like the hand of a clock. Twelve players, representing the hour numbers, stand round him in a circle, just within the length of the rope. The central player swings the rope round in a circle, while the surrounding players jump over the rope as it comes their way. A player who touches or stops the rope is out of the game, and the last one in is the winner.

Chinese Rope-kicking

A popular game in China is a version of the English favorite, 'high water-low water.' Two children hold a long rope taut between them, at about waist height. The other players each take a turn kicking the rope, first kicking forward, then backward. If a player can reach the rope with both kicks, it is raised a little higher on the next turn. Players who cannot kick the rope drop out of the game, until only one, the winner, remains.

Chinese rope-kicking is certainly a pastime for athletic young people, such as this Chinese girl demonstrating her prowess in a public park of Peking. The rope is held at just about maximum height, arm above head, and it takes a vigorous kick even to reach it in a forward direction (left); a backward kick to the same height (above) is a demanding stunt that few could match.

Hoops

About the Game

'If you dream about rolling a hoop,' wrote the Greek sage Artemidorus, 'it means that you have come to the end of your troubles, and abundant happiness will follow.' The Greeks set great store by hoop-rolling as a healthy exercise for people with a weak constitution: it was recommended by Hippocrates, the great physician, in one of his treatises on medicine, about 300 B.C.

Hoop games were important to the American Indians primarily as a way of training young boys in marksmanship. A screen of fiber or rawhide netting was woven into the center of the hoop; it was rolled along the ground between two lines of players, who hurled darts at the rapidly moving target. The Chugach Eskimo played a similar game in which a hoop was bowled along the ground by one man, who also kept score, as rival athletes from two teams took turns throwing long poles through the hoop.

Bowling wooden hoops was a popular pastime among European children in the nineteenth century, when hoop races often involved older boys as well as girls in frilly Victorian dresses. The hula-hoop craze of the 1960's added yet another chapter to the hoop's history: this time it was spun around the player's waist in elegant gyrations. Doctors again recommended this activity as being good exercise: the hoop had come full circle...

Two Nepali youngsters, opposite, photographed by Nik Wheeler, race their hoops in a courtyard backed by temple buildings, in Bhaktapur.

In turn-of-the-century France, young contestants with hoops to suit their height (below) line up at the start of the girls' race in a hoop contest.

Serendipity makes fine hoops of inflated tire tubes for Irish children photographed in Dublin by Henri Cartier-Bresson in 1962 (above).

How to Play the Game

Bowling a hoop looks easy but requires practice and skill to keep it upright and moving straight. To set the hoop going, grasp it between the fingers and thumb of one hand, with your forefinger extended along its outer edge. Bend forward with your arm close to your body, and fling the hoop in front of you. Running alongside or slightly behind it, keep it rolling by pushing it now and then with the stick, or the flat palm of your hand.

When the basic technique is mastered, there are many games to be played with hoops. Hoop races can be held over a course of about 300 yards. At a given signal contestants start to trundle their hoops as fast as they can toward the finish line; first hoop over is the winner. A variation for two or more teams is a hoop relay race, in which the hoop is passed from one player to the next without being allowed to fall.

Children will soon devise many hoop games and stunts. With practice, one child can jump through a hoop which is being rolled by another. Like the Indians and Eskimos, players can try to throw something – a stick or a ball – through a fast-moving hoop. Or, one player can hold the hoop vertically above the ground for the others to jump or dive through, gradually increasing the height.

To play hula-hoop, get inside the hoop and hold it horizontally against your waist. Then flick it to right or left so that it rolls round the waist. Rotate your hips in the same direction fast enough to keep the hoop spinning round your body.

An engraving taken from a documentary photograph shows competitors, right, alert for the starting signal of a race organized in 1891 by the Hoop Club of Brest, in Brittany, France.

Materials

Plastic conduit (cable tubing), 78 inches long, ³⁄₄ inch in diameter.
All-purpose glue.
Gloss paint: red and brown.
A wooden dowel, 20 inches long, ³⁄₈ inch in diameter.
A wooden ball, ³⁄₄ inch in diameter.
A nail, 1¹⁄₄ inches long.

Tools

A paint brush and wire cutters.

How to Make the Game

Apply glue to half of the 2-inch dowel, and insert this end into one end of the flexible cable tubing. Apply glue to the exposed end of the dowel, and bend the cable tubing round in a circle to insert the end of the dowel into the other end of the tubing. The ends of the tubing should meet flush. Remove any excess glue and allow to dry thoroughly. Paint the hoop with red gloss paint and let dry.

To make a bowling stick for the hoop: hammer the nail halfway into the wooden ball. Cut off the head of the nail with wire cutters. Then hammer the ball to drive the headless nail into the center of one end of the 20-inch-long dowel, so that the wooden ball is centered and flush to it. Paint the dowel brown and the ball red. Allow the paint to dry thoroughly.

A Batak boy on the island of Sumatra, below, wields a big stick to trundle his tiny hoop.

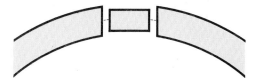

Figure A: Bend the tubing into the shape of a ring. Apply glue to the 2-inch wooden dowel.

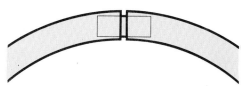

Figure B: Insert the dowel halfway into each end of the plastic tubing, so that the ends meet flush.

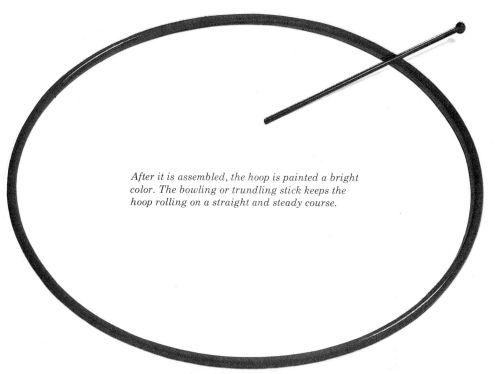

After it is assembled, the hoop is painted a bright color. The bowling or trundling stick keeps the hoop rolling on a straight and steady course.

On the South Pacific atoll of Ulithi in the Yap Islands group (below), a young boy has plenty of open space for bowling his hoop at top speed.

Husky barrel-rollers stand poised across a Paris boulevard in 1908. The bowler-hatted umpire on the right has a difficult task. The heavy wine casks kick up from the cobbles or skid in the tramcar tracks, making it difficult for him to judge whether collisions occur through accident or design. Last year's winner, third barrel from the right, has 'champion' chalked on his cask.

Barrel Rolling

About the Game

Only unimaginative people believe that fun with a wine barrel ends once it is emptied. The more inventive know that drinking is only half the fun; there is barrel racing to come – but preferably not immediately afterwards! These races hark back to the *belle époque* – the 'good old days' of turn-of-the-century Paris, when men of skill and strength rolled barrels along the boulevards on festive days. As the vats clattered on the cobblestones, spectators cheered their favorites, especially those virtuosos who could trundle two at once.

How to Play the Game

The only item needed for barrel racing is one barrel per contestant. Large wooden barrels are not as readily available as they were a century ago, but they can still be found, in backyards, junkyards, and warehouses. For younger children, an empty beer keg or nail keg is ideal in size and weight.

It is a good idea for someone to act as referee – both to start off the race with a countdown or a whistle blast, and to ensure fair conduct. After all, it is not unknown for a contestant, feeling that his chances of winning are being too closely threatened, to 'accidentally' collide with his rival's barrel and send it off course.

Bowling in a powerful overhand style, a French bouliste *twists his wrist to give the ball a sharp spin as it leaves his hand.*

Jeu de Boules

About the Game

Among the writings of Oribase, a physician who lived in ancient Greece around 300 A.D., there is a description of a particular exercise that was performed by older men. It seems that these citizens, accompanied by their admiring students, would meet at an appointed time in a gymnasium and practice throwing balls of different sizes as far as they possibly could. It was considered a good exercise for the mind as well as for the body. This game was undoubtedly a forerunner of the immensely popular French game known as *jeu de boules*.

Men of ancient Rome played a similar game which required that the balls be thrown or rolled on the ground toward a certain goal. As the conquering Romans moved through Europe, they took this game with them.

A French writer has declared that a *bouliste* is in his prime between the ages of 40 and 50, for then a man has the power and experience necessary to play the game well. The French play *boules* with what has been described as 'a mild fanaticism.' In *la place,* the square where menfolk gather in French towns, you will nearly always find at least one game of *boules* in progress. It is played on any level ground surface, with little or no regard for motorists or pedestrians.

Officially, it is played with special iron balls that are roughly eight centimeters (about three inches) in diameter. A very good game can be played, however, using hard rubber balls, wooden (croquet) balls, or even baseballs. A miniature variety of *boules* can be played with marbles.

Boules has been adapted here for non-official equipment. Still, even in this form, it provides all the fun and excitement of the official game.

How to Play the Game

Jeu de boules, or *pétanque* as it is called in the south of France, can be played on any hard, flat stretch of ground. An official *boules* field is 13 by 3 meters – about 43 by 10 feet – but such precision is not necessary for an entertaining afternoon's play. Junior *boulistes*, in particular, will want to adapt the length of the field to the distance they can throw a ball.

There are two teams, each of which usually comprises three players, or four at most. Each player carries two balls, on which he may write his name for identification; it is useful if players from one team have balls of the same color. If a team consists of two players, each of them has three balls; and if two single players are pitted against each other, *tête à tête,* they each have three or four balls. As each player throws his balls only once, the maximum number of throws in a game is twelve. Several games make up a 'round'; the round is won by the first team to win either 13 or 15 points – the target score to be agreed in advance.

Enthusiasts in southern France watch as the boule rolls down the field. The white-shirted player stands properly, both his feet together, inside the throwing circle drawn in the dirt.

Players carefully study the distance of each boule from the cochonnet, the target ball. When eye-measurement is uncertain, a special pegged cord marks short distances with precision.

The distance of balls farther from the cochonnet can be measured in paces. The winning team scores a point for every ball that is closer to the target than the losers' nearest shot.

The official iron boules *are about three inches in diameter, but a good game can be played with croquet balls or baseballs. The* cochonnet, *which is much smaller, is usually made of wood.*

A small wooden ball called the *cochonnet* (the 'jack' in English), about $1\frac{1}{2}$ inches in diameter, acts as the target. Before the game starts, the players toss a coin to decide who will be the first to bowl the *cochonnet*.

The first man to play makes a circle on the ground with his heel, outside one end of the playing field; a short line will do just as well. He then throws the *cochonnet* down the field to a distance of not less than 6 yards, and not more than 10 or 11 yards. If it comes to rest within about 20 inches of an obstacle, such as a stone or a bush, he must throw it again to get it in a good clear position.

Having thrown the *cochonnet*, the same player then throws the first ball of the game, trying to get it as close to the *cochonnet* as possible. As he throws, he must keep his feet together within the circle, and he may not step out of the circle (or over the line) until the ball has come to rest.

In this turn-of-the-century photograph, a bouliste *takes an unconventional stance for a vital throw.*

The ball may displace the *cochonnet*, but that does not matter; 'target is where target is,' i.e. players must always aim for the *cochonnet* even if it has been knocked far away from its original position.

Whether the first ball is close beside the *cochonnet* or far away from it, it is still 'closest to the target,' for as yet there is no other ball in the field. As soon as a team is 'closest' it stops playing, and the other team takes its turn. The main rule of the game is that a team stays in play as long as a ball from the opposing team lies closest to the target; in other words, so long as the other team, in the language of *boules,* 'has the best ball.'

Therefore the team that begins play will always throw only one ball on their first turn. As soon as the second team has 'best ball' – or knocks the target closer to one of their balls – the first

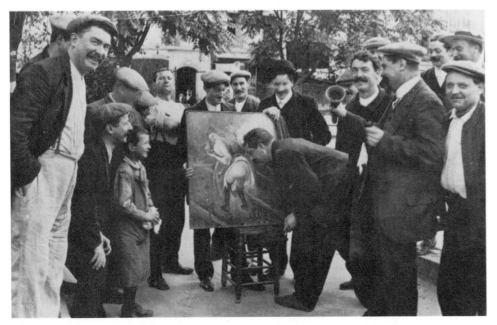

The losing team pays its respects to fickle Lady Luck, in this French photograph of eighty years ago.

team starts to play, and so on. If one team throws all its balls without getting 'best ball,' and the other team has some balls left, play reverts to that team, which tries to better its score.

The game ends when all players have thrown their balls, and the team with the best ball, closest to the final position of the *cochonnet*, is the winner. Then the players count up the score. The winning team gains one point for each of its balls which lie closer to the *cochonnet* than the best ball from the opposing team.

At this stage, if not even earlier, there may be some dispute between teams over the comparative distance of two balls from the target; a measuring device, such as the pegged cord described in How to Make the Game, will furnish the necessary proof. The points scored by the winning team are tallied on paper or a small scoreboard.

The team that wins the last game begins the next. The first player makes a new throwing circle, close to where the *cochonnet* was in the last game; thus play goes up and down the same playing field with alternate games.

A good *boules* team is not merely concerned with tossing the ball as far as possible; good playing tactics will ensure a better score. For example, if a ball is still some distance (say two or three feet) from the *cochonnet*, a player may well try to place a ball closer to it; but if the best ball is almost on top of the little target, the only remedy is to knock that ball away. This can be a tricky business, for a ball rolled over sandy ground, with pebbles and perhaps tufts of grass in its path, is unlikely to connect with its target. The best method – but one that demands expertise and perfect aim – is to throw the ball so that it flies through the air to land directly on the enemy ball. This kind of throw requires a great deal of practice, and spectators had best stand back from the target area when a novice player attempts it.

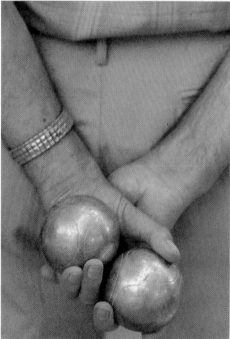

Holding the boules *in a classic cross-handed stance, a French player awaits his turn to bowl. As these pictures show, informality is the rule, and there is no prescribed uniform.*

French workmen join their retired friends for a game of boules *during the long lunch break customary in Mediterranean provinces. The field is improvised in a shady park on the Côte d'Azur.*

Materials

If authentic French *boules* cannot be obtained from local sports suppliers, croquet balls, baseballs, or hard rubber balls may be used in their place. Two balls are needed for each player, and another ball, preferably smaller, to serve as the *cochonnet*.

A plywood panel, $4\frac{1}{2}$ by 10 inches.

Two pieces of thin metal chain, each approximately 1 foot long.

Four screw-eyes.

Paints in three colors.

Two lengths of wooden dowel, $\frac{1}{2}$ inch in diameter and $1\frac{1}{2}$ inches long.

A 30-inch length of thin, strong cord.

All-purpose glue.

Tools

A knife, a hand drill, a ruler, a pencil-sharpener, and paintbrushes.

The peg scoreboard and measuring cord are pocket equipment for any jeu de boules *player. Instructions for making them are on this page.*

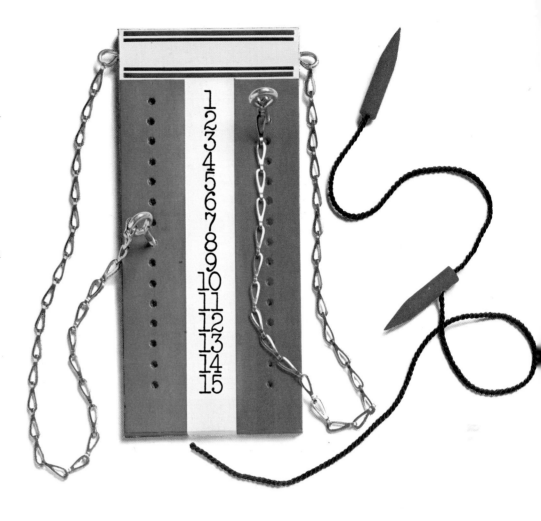

How to Make the Game

Making the scoreboard:

With a ruler and pencil, divide the plywood or wooden panel into three sections, each $1\frac{1}{2}$ inches wide, then draw lines vertically dividing each of the outer sections into $\frac{3}{4}$-inch widths. (This line will be the guide when you are drilling the holes.) Divide the height into 20 sections of $\frac{1}{2}$ inch. Drill 15 holes where the horizontal lines intersect the vertical guide lines, beginning with the third from the bottom. The holes must be large enough to accommodate the points of the screw-eyes.

Attach a screw-eye to each end of the two lengths of chain. Screw a screw-eye into either side of the top of the scoreboard. Paint the three vertical sections in distinctive colors (the French tricolor, for example). In the middle section number the holes 1 to 15.

Making the measuring cord:

Using a pencil-sharpener, bring one end of each length of dowel to a point. Drill a hole, $\frac{3}{4}$ inches deep, in the unsharpened end of each peg. Spread glue on one end of the cord and insert it in the hole of one of the pegs. Allow to dry thoroughly. Now drill a hole halfway in the side of the remaining peg, $\frac{5}{8}$ inches from the blunt end, so that it meets the hole already drilled inside the peg. Slide the free end of the cord through these connecting holes and knot securely. The sliding end of the measuring cord can now be adjusted when comparing the distances between the *boules* and the *cochonnet.*

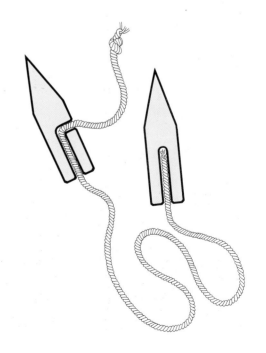

This cutaway diagram illustrates where the holes are drilled and how the strings are attached to the measuring pegs for the game of boules *(right).*

190

Bocce

Bocce, a favorite Italian pastime, is descended from the Greek ball-tossing games. A game like bocce was played throughout the Roman empire and later developed into such variants as lawn bowling, nine-pins, and boules. Bocce is played on a bordered field, approximately 8 by 60 feet, with a regulator peg in the center, and foul areas at either end. Each player tries to position his balls as close as possible to the pallino, or target ball. The game can be played by two people with two shots per turn, or by teams of three to six, with four balls each and alternating turns. Players have a choice of three shots – the straightforward bowl, the 'called' shot – when the ball must hit a specified target or be disqualified – and the aerial shot, when the target is called before the ball is thrown into the air. Before the game begins, one of the players flips a coin to see which team or player will bowl the pallino down the alley. (All balls, including the pallino, must be bowled from behind the foul line at the player's end of the alley.) In order for the pallino to qualify, it must land at least five feet beyond the regulator peg and not in the foul area. It must also land more than one foot away from either sideboard. If the first shot does not qualify, players or teams take turns to bowl the pallino until it lands in the proper area. The player who makes the successful shot begins the game.

In play, if a straightforward shot disturbs other balls, it is disqualified and the scattered balls are replaced. This rule also applies to called or aerial shots that fail to hit their target.

After all balls have been played, the score is tallied. As in boules, all balls closer to the pallino than the opponent's best ball score one point apiece. Opposing balls that are equidistant from the pallino cancel each other from the scoring. A game is over when a player scores 15 points (if only two people are playing) or 18 points in team play.

Relaxing with pipe and wine, a spectator follows a close-fought game of bocce *in a well-appointed Italian alley. Other onlookers watch intently as the target* pallino *is briefly obscured by a very close ball. If the shot was called and any balls are struck by mistake, the ball will be disqualified.*

Quilles

About the Game

Known as *quilles* in France, this bowling game became popular in England during the fourteenth century. The English adapted its name to 'kayles,' which became 'kettle,' 'kittle,' and thence 'skittles' as it is known today. It was a favorite tavern betting game, and apprentices were warned: 'Exchewe allewey eville company; kayles, carding and haserdy.'

In the early days, 'sheepe's joynts' were thrown at the pins. Later, a large, oval missile called a 'cheese' was used. In the Netherlands and Germany, a ball with fingerholes was rolled toward the pins, and the central pin was called the 'kingpin.' Eighteenth-century Dutch colonists introduced this game to America, where it developed into the modern sport of bowling.

How to Play the Game

The table version of *quilles* presented here is adapted from the old French version of the game. Players decide in advance the total of points to be scored.

Before each turn the pins are set up straight. Players take turns swinging the ball toward the pins. The central kingpin scores nine points; all the others score one. The winner is the first to score the agreed total.

At a turn-of-the-century picnic under the towering elms of the Odenwald in Germany, a senior citizen takes careful aim at the quilles *pins.*

This attractive, fun-to-make table model of quilles *has its own scoreboard. Four players can score up to ten points each; two players up to 100 points each, using both rows of numbers.*

Materials

A plywood board, 12 by 14 inches, $\frac{3}{8}$ inch thick.
Two white pine slats, 1 by 12 inches, $\frac{3}{4}$ inch thick.
Two white pine slats, 1 by 14 inches, $\frac{3}{4}$ inch thick.
Four strips picture-frame molding, $\frac{1}{2}$ inch wide on each side, $\frac{1}{8}$ inch thick: two strips $12\frac{1}{4}$ inches long, and two strips $14\frac{1}{4}$ inches long.
Nine wooden dowels, 3 inches long, 1 inch in diameter.
One wooden dowel, 29 inches long, 1 inch in diameter.
One wooden peg, 3 inches long, $\frac{3}{8}$ inch in diameter.
One wooden peg, 8 inches long, $\frac{3}{8}$ inch in diameter.
Nine wooden balls, $1\frac{1}{4}$ inches in diameter.
One wooden ball, $\frac{3}{4}$ inch in diameter.
One wooden ball, 2 inches in diameter.
Eleven screw-eyes, $\frac{3}{8}$ inch long.
Seven screw-eyes, 1 inch long.
Nine nails, $1\frac{1}{2}$ inches long, $\frac{1}{8}$ inch in diameter.
Eight headless nails, $\frac{1}{2}$ inch long.
One nail, $1\frac{1}{4}$ inches long.
One screw, $\frac{1}{2}$ inch long.
Two lengths of narrow, flat-link chain, $9\frac{1}{2}$ inches long.
One length of narrow, flat-link chain, 23 inches long.
Nylon cord, 4 yards long, $\frac{1}{16}$ inch thick.
Wood primer.
Gloss paint: red, green, yellow, and black.
Two sets of press-on numbers: 0 through 9, $\frac{1}{2}$ inch high.

Tools

A ruler, pencil, electric drill or brace with bits ($\frac{3}{8}$-inch bit, $\frac{1}{8}$-inch bit and 1-inch auger bit), sandpaper, vise, protractor, backsaw, hammer, primer brush, paintbrush, utility knife, screwdriver, wirecutter, scissors, matches, pliers, and fine camel-hair artist's brush.

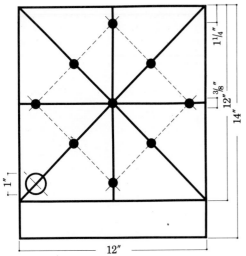

Figure A: Drill ³/₈-inch holes at the nine points of intersection on the board; drill a 1-inch hole in the lower left-hand corner of the platform.

How to Make the Game

Place the plywood board horizontally before you on the work table. Measure and mark points 2 inches from the left edge, on the top and bottom of the board. Connect these points with a line. The surface of the board is now divided into a 12-inch square and a rectangle, 2 by 12 inches in size.

Connect the four corners of the 12-inch square with two diagonal lines. Draw a vertical line that crosses the intersection of the diagonals and a horizontal line that crosses the same point, as shown in figure A.

On the vertical and horizontal lines that you have just drawn, mark points 1¼ inches from the edges of the 12-inch square. Draw lines connecting the points on the vertical lines with the points on the horizontal lines, to form a diamond shape as shown by the dotted lines in figure A. Mark the points where these lines intersect the diagonal lines. Mark the point at the center of the square where the diagonals intersect. At these nine points, drill holes through the board with the ³/₈-inch bit.

Mark a point on the top left end of the diagonal line that is 1³/₄ inches from the corner of the square. Using the 1-inch auger bit, drill a hole through this point. Sandpaper on both sides of the board, around the holes, until smooth.

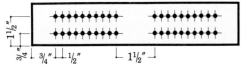

Figure B: After measuring and marking the 40 points on the scoring section of the board, drill a ¹/₈-inch hole at each of these markings.

Turn the board so that the 2-by-12-inch rectangle is horizontal before you, as in figure B. On the 2-inch edge at the left, measure and mark points ³/₄ inch and 1½ inches from the lower corner of the board. Repeat these steps on the right edge and connect the corresponding points across the width of the rectangle.

Place your ruler on one of these lines, and ³/₄ inch from the left edge, mark ten points at ½-inch intervals. Measure 1½ inches from the tenth point and begin again marking ten points at ½-inch intervals (see figure B). Repeat these steps on the other line and drill ¹/₈-inch holes through the board at these 40 points. Sand down any roughness around the holes on both sides.

Measure and mark a point in the exact center of one of the 1-by-12-inch pine slats. Drill a ³/₈-inch hole through this point and sand down any rough edges around the hole.

Clamp the middle of one of the pine slats in the vise. Line up the vertical of the protractor on the left edge of the top ³/₄-inch side of the slat: the base of the protractor should be in line with the long edge of this side. Mark a point on the top edge that is 45 degrees from the bottom corner edge. Draw a line from the corner edge to that point.

Repeat this step at the right end of the board, measuring and marking a 45-degree angle toward the left. Using a backsaw, cut through the wood at these points, as shown in photograph 1. Repeat these steps on the remaining three slats.

Apply glue to the mitered ends of the four slats and join them to make a frame. Allow the glue to dry thoroughly. Apply glue to the top sides of this frame; then place the plywood board, marked surface up, squarely on top of it so that the dimensions match. The side with the 40-hole scoreboard must be on the side of the frame with the drilled ³/₈-inch hole.

When the glue has dried, secure the board to the frame by hammering headless nails at the four corners through the board into the frame underneath. Turn the frame over and file down one side to match the dimensions of the 1-inch hole on the board. Paint the board and the outside of the frame with primer. After the prime coat is dry, sand lightly and paint green. Allow the paint to dry thoroughly.

Clamp the middle of one side of a molding strip in the vise. The adjoining side is now flat before you, the cornered edge lying toward you. Line up the base of the protractor with the cornered edge of the molding; line up the vertical of the protractor with the left edge of the molding. Mark a point on the top edge that is 45 degrees from the corner edge, and draw a line from the corner to that point.

Do the same at the right end of the molding, measuring and marking a 45-degree angle to the left. Using a backsaw, miter both sides of the left end of the molding simultaneously while sawing

1: Prepare the four white pine slats for miter joints, then with the backsaw, cut along the 45-degree angle lines marked on each piece.

2: Glue the mitered slats to make a frame under the quilles board. To secure the joints, hammer in a few nails at the corner.

3: File away the section of the white pine frame that partially blocks the 1-inch holes at the corner of the quilles board.

4: Steady the dowel with one hand while you whittle down the marked end with a chisel blade until its diameter is roughly ³/₄ inch.

along the line drawn. Do the same at the right side of the molding. Prepare the remaining three strips for miter joints, following these steps. Sand down any rough edges.

Paint the four strips of molding red. After the paint has dried, apply glue to the inner sides of the strips and fasten them around the top edges of the *quilles* board.

Draw a ring around one of the nine 3-inch dowels, ¾ inch from one end. Using the chisel, whittle down this ¾-inch section until the end has a diameter of roughly ¾ inch (see photograph 4). Sand down the whittled area until smooth. Repeat these steps with the remaining eight dowels.

Using a wood rasp, file down one side of one of the nine 1¼-inch wooden balls until you have formed a flat surface, ¾ inch in diameter. Sandpaper this surface until smooth. Repeat these steps with the other eight balls.

Paint eight of the dowels yellow and eight of the balls red. Paint the remaining dowel red and the remaining ball yellow. Allow the paint to dry.

Mark a point in the center of the small end of one of the dowels. Using the ⅛-inch bit, drill a hole 1 inch into the dowel at this point. Repeat this on the other eight dowels.

Mark a point at the center of the flat surface of one of the balls. Drive a 1½-inch nail ½ inch into the ball at this point. With wire cutters, cut off the head of the nail. Repeat these steps on the other eight balls.

Apply glue to the flat surface of the yellow ball and the exposed section of the nail. Fix the yellow ball onto the red dowel so that the nail fits into the drilled hole and their flat surfaces meet evenly. Repeat these steps with the yellow dowels and red balls. Allow the glue to dry.

These will be the pins in the game. The red dowel with the yellow ball is the kingpin. Screw a screw-eye, ⅜ inch long, into the center of the bottom end of each pin.

Mark a point 1 inch from one end of the 29-inch length of dowel. Using the ⅜-inch bit, drill a hole at this point through the dowel. Sand down any rough edges around the hole. Paint the dowel red. Paint the 8-inch wooden peg yellow. Paint the large wooden ball black. Allow the paint to dry thoroughly.

Screw a screw-eye, 1 inch long, into the yellow peg, about ½ inch from one end. Attach the 23-inch length of chain to the screw-eye. Screw a 1-inch screw-eye into the black ball and attach the screw-eye to the other end of the chain.

Insert the red dowel into the 1-inch hole in the corner of the board to a depth of about 1 inch. If the dowel seems unsteady, you can wedge it more tightly by screwing a small screw into the dowel, flush with the board. Insert the free end

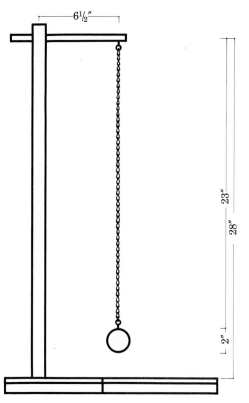

Figure C: The ball, suspended from the horizontal peg, must be exactly over the central hole of the quilles *board, 2½ inches above its surface.*

of the yellow peg into the hole in the red dowel; adjust it so that 6 inches of its length extend on one side. The ball should hang directly over the center hole in the board, 2½ inches above the surface of the board.

Paint the 3-inch peg red. Paint the ball, ¾ inch in diameter, yellow. When the paint has dried, hammer a 1¼-inch nail more than halfway into the middle of the ball. Cut off the head of the nail, then center the nail on one end of the red peg and hammer on the ball to drive the nail into the peg.

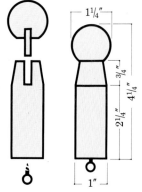

Figure D: Hammer a nail into the ball, cut off the head of the nail, then drive the other end into the dowel by hammering on the ball.

The ball should be flush with the peg. Fasten a 1-inch screw-eye to the other end of the peg. Put the peg in the hole at the side of the frame.

Position all the pins over the holes in the board. The kingpin occupies the center position. Lay the pins on their sides so that the screw-eye at the base of each pin is about ½ inch from the hole.

Each of these pins must be attached with the nylon cord to the screw-eye of the peg inserted at the side of the board. (This peg is the trigger to re-erect the pins after each round.) Position the board so that the trigger knob is toward you. The two nearer pins on either side of the central vertical pins must be coupled with the same length of cord. The cord will run from one pin, through the screw-eye of the trigger, to the other pin at the same distance from the trigger. (When connecting these pieces with the cord, the trigger must be completely inserted in its hole at the side of the board.)

Fasten each end of the nylon cord to the screw-eye of a pin by melting it briefly with a lighted match; after extinguishing the flame, press the melting end against the part of the cord neighboring it on the other side of the screw-eye. Hold the end in position until it cools.

Repeat these steps with the remaining two pairs of pins on either side of the central row. The two top pins of the central row are attached to the trigger by the same cord. The pin nearest the trigger is attached to it by a short length of cord.

When all the pins are connected to the trigger, pull the trigger out completely so that the pins stand straight over their holes. All the strings should be taut; make adjustments if necessary. Bind the strands of cord at the screw-eye by winding a length of cord around them tightly two or three times, then knot.

Rub press-on numbers, 1 through 0, between the two rows of ten holes at the right side of the scoreboard. Repeat this on the left side.

Fasten the middle link of one of the 9½-inch lengths of chain to a small screw-eye. Screw the screw-eye to the right corner of the board, near the scoring holes. Cut off all but two of the threads of two 1-inch screw-eyes and fasten each to one end of the chain. Repeat these steps with the other 9½-inch length of chain and screw the small screw-eye into the left corner of the scoring area of the board.

Soap-Box Racing

About the Game

A soap-box ride is an exhilarating experience and children delight in coasting downhill in this fantasy version of 'dad's car.' Traditionally, a racer is made from a soap box nailed onto a plank of wood which acts as the 'chassis,' with two sets of wheels, and a rope to control the steering. Today, however, many children are turning their hands to more sophisticated designs. In the United States, the world of the 'professional' soap-box racer is highlighted every August in Akron, Ohio. Here, local champions aged from 11 to 15 years gather from all over the country with their homemade cars to race in the All-American Soap Box Derby for the overall championship and cash prizes. Awards are also presented for the best design, the best brakes, upholstery, etc.

Many adults, of course, are equally intrigued; they design and build ingenious wheeled racers like those in which the photographer Jacques-Henri Lartigue and his young friends careened around the dirt roads of France in the early years of the twentieth century.

How to Play the Game

A soap-box race is most exciting with at least five riders participating. The track should be carefully chosen and marked out on a hill in the park, with the starting point ten yards from the beginning of the incline and the finish line about 20 yards from where the slope levels off. One referee stands at the starting line and another at the finish line in case there is a dispute over a close finish. The players take up their positions on the right side of their cars. At a given signal, they run with their cars, pushing them as fast as possible to build up speed. As they reach the top of the slope, they jump in and race for the finish line. Any

Cornering in a cloud of dust, Jacques-Henri Lartigue's brother Zissou pilots a homemade racer in 1910; the passenger operates the brakes.

player who tries to force another off the track is disqualified. The first car to cross the finish line wins the race. In the event of a tie, the players in question run a deciding race.

Materials
Seven pine planks, 1 by 2 inches: two 16 inches long, two 32 inches long, two 21 inches long, one 14 inches long.
A pine block, 1 by 1½ by 2 inches.
Two plywood boards, 12 by 16 inches, ⅜ inch thick.
A plywood board, 2 by 14 inches, ⅜ inch thick.
A plywood board, 18 by 40 inches, 3/16 inch thick.
A plywood board, 14 by 20 inches, 3/16 inch thick.
Two pine slats, ½ by 2 inches, 20 inches long.
Two wooden dowels, 1 foot long, 1 inch in diameter.
Two wooden balls, 1½ inches in diameter.
Four hexagonal-head wood bolts, 4 inches long.
A stove bolt, 3 inches long, ⅜ inch in diameter, with wing nut.
Seven metal washers to fit the bolts.
Four screw-eyes, 1 inch long.
Twenty flat-head screws, 1½ inches long.
Ten nails, 1½ inches long.
A dozen wire nails.
Four baby-carriage wheels, or wheels of similar size.
Wood primer. Wood glue.
Gloss paint: black, red, white, blue, and yellow.
Red plastic adhesive tape, 1 inch wide.
Two 24-inch lengths of narrow, flat-link chain.
Two strips of quarter-round molding, 18 inches long.

Tools
A pencil, ruler, backsaw, electric drill or brace with ⅛-inch and ¼-inch bits, screwdriver, wood rasp, sandpaper, hammer, strong twine, scroll saw, wire cutters, primer brush, and paintbrush.

The inventor of this fast 'bobsled' soap-box racer, Zissou Lartigue, poses for his brother's plate camera in 1910. Later he added a mast and sail to cruise before the wind on breezy days.

How to Make the Game
Place one of the 16-inch planks horizontally on the work table so that its 1-by-16-inch edge is facing up. On the two 16-inch edges of this surface, mark points 1 inch from the left edge. Draw a ruled line connecting these two points. Repeat these steps at the right end of the same surface. Turn the plank over once so that a 2-by-16-inch edge is facing up. Place a ruler vertically across this surface so that its straight edge is in line with the lines drawn on one of the 1-by-16-inch surfaces. Against the straight edge of the ruler, mark a middle point (1 inch from either edge) on the 2-by-16-inch surface.

Draw a line connecting this point to the end of the line drawn on the 1-by-16-inch surface. Mark a similar middle point on the near 2-inch edge, and draw a straight line connecting the two middle points. Repeat these steps on the other end of the 2-by-16-inch surface. Turn the board so that the other 2-by-16-inch surface is face up. Repeat these steps at each end, extending the line on the 1-by-16-inch surface 1 inch onto the adjacent 2-by-16-inch surface, and connecting the two middle points.

At each 1-by-2-inch edge of the board, draw a straight line connecting the middle points at the edges of the 2-by-16-inch surfaces. Repeat these steps on the other 16-inch plank, and the two 32-inch planks. Using a backsaw, cut along the lines drawn on each of the boards to make half-lap joints.

On the 2-inch side of each of the 16-inch planks, mark a center point on the half-lap extensions. At these points, drill ⅛-inch holes through the wood. On one end of each of the 32-inch planks, mark a point on the 2-inch-wide side that is roughly 1 inch from the base of the notch and ½ inch from the long edge on the same side of the surface as the half-lap extension.

Glue the half-lap joints of the four planks together to make a frame, 16 by 32 inches. The screw holes at the ends of the 32-inch planks should be directly across from each other. Screw 2-inch flat-head screws into the holes in the half-laps of the 16-inch planks, fastening them securely to the longer planks. Allow the glue to dry thoroughly.

Apply glue to one 1-by-14-inch side and both 1-by-2-inch sides of the 14-inch plank. Turn the frame so that it lies with the notches on the 16-inch planks facing up. Position the 14-inch plank inside the front end of the frame (where the holes are drilled into the 32-inch planks) so that its lower 2-by-14-inch edge is flush with the bottom edges of the frame and its glued sides fit snugly against the three boards surrounding it. Screw a flat-head screw into each of the holes in the 32-inch planks, further securing the 14-inch plank in its place.

Place the 21-inch plank on the work table so that a 2-inch-wide side is facing up. Measure and mark a middle point (10½ inches from either short edge, 1 inch from either long edge) on this surface. Drill a $\frac{3}{8}$-inch hole through the board at this point. Measure and mark a middle point on the top surface of the 14-inch plank, and drill a hole through this point. Insert the stove bolt through the hole in the 21-inch board. Place two washers over the shank of the bolt, then insert it, under the frame, through the hole in the 14-inch board. Place another washer on the shank of the bolt, then screw a wing nut onto its end. This plank will be the front axle.

Turn the frame over. On the undersides of the 32-inch planks, mark points 4 and 6 inches from the rear end of the frame. Apply glue between these two points and place the remaining 21-inch board with one 2-inch wide side against the glued surfaces. The ends of the board should extend 2½ inches beyond the sides of the frame.

Mark points on the top side of the 21-inch plank that are directly and centrally over the 32-inch planks of the frame. Drill ⅛-holes through the two points, then screw flat-head screws into them to secure the plank to the frame of the car.

1: After gluing together the half-lap joints of the four boards to make the frame, secure each joint with a screw fastened through both boards.

2: Measure and mark a middle point on the 21-inch plank in the frame, then drill a hole, ⅜ inch wide, through the board at this marked point.

This bright and shiny soap-box car is ready and raring to go to the races after some work with lumber, house paint, and scraps from the attic.

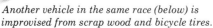

3: Apply glue to the two triangular wedges, then position them at the rear of the frame, 3 inches from each end on the top side of the back plank.

A young competitor flashes past spectators, below at a soap-box derby held in Stockholm, Sweden.

Another vehicle in the same race (below) is improvised from scrap wood and bicycle tires.

4: Thoroughly soak the plywood board, then bend it in stages, tightening the cord that binds it, until it is curved enough to fit into the frame.

Place one of the 12-by-16-inch boards horizontally on the work table. On each of the 16-inch edges mark points 1 inch from each of the corners. Draw straight lines connecting corresponding points on opposite sides of the board. Measuring from the lower edge, mark 2-inch points on each of the 12-inch edges. Connect these points with a straight line. Two corners of the board are now marked with 1-by-2-inch rectangles. Cut out these rectangles with a backsaw. With a wood rasp, round off the other two corners of the board. Sandpaper any rough and splintered areas.

Draw a diagonal line from corner to corner of one of the 1-by-2-inch faces of the wooden block. Cut along this line with a backsaw, sawing the block in half. Turn the frame over, apply glue to each half-block on its 1-by-1½-inch side. Position the blocks, sawed side toward the front of the frame, on the top edge of the rear 16-inch plank of the frame, 3 inches from each corner. Allow the glue to dry.

Set the previously worked 12-by-16-inch board into the rear end of the frame, fitting the notched corners against the sides of the frame, the face of the board tight against the rear plank. Tilt the top of the board back, keeping the notches tight against the frame, until it is resting flush against the sawed faces of the half-blocks. On each side of the board, drill a ⅛-inch hole into the board, through the angled edge of the half-block and into the frame. Secure these three pieces together with flat-head screws fastened through the drilled holes.

Apply glue to the top edge of the two sides of the frame for a distance of 12 inches beyond the seat-back just secured. Place the other 12-by-16-inch board on the frame, flush against the tilted seat-back, the ends of the board resting firmly and evenly against the sides of the frame. Hammer several well-spaced nails on either end of the board, through the board, and into the frame. Allow the glue to dry thoroughly.

Apply glue to the two ⅜-by-2-inch ends and one ⅜-by-14-inch edge of the 2-by-14-inch board. Position it inside the frame, under the seat, so that the long narrow edge is against the end of the seat. Hammer several well-spaced nails through the seat and several nails through the sides of the frame into the board.

Thoroughly soak the 18-by-40-inch plywood board under the shower or with a wet sponge. Pick up one 18-inch side of the board and, while holding the other down, slowly pull it toward you. Bend the board carefully, and in stages.

Place a 20-inch-long pine slat on the outside of each 18-inch end, then wrap twine around the bent wet board and tie it underneath between the two 18-inch ends. It may be necessary to wet down the board several times while trying to bend it so that its ends are 14 inches apart. With each adjustment, tighten the twine and refasten its knot. When the board is bent so that its 18-inch sides are 14 inches apart, set it aside and let it dry. After it is completely dry, remove the twine and the pine slats.

Place the bent board on its end on top of the 14-by-20-inch plywood board, lining up the two ends of its open side with the 14-inch edge of the board. Draw an outline of the inside of the rounded board on the 14-by-20-inch board. Cut out the piece with the scroll saw, apply glue to its round edge and position it inside one end of the rounded board. It should fit snugly. Secure it with several wire nails and allow the glue to dry thoroughly. Place the bent board into the frame and secure it with glue and nails.

With the wood rasp, file down a flat surface, 1 inch in diameter, on each of the wooden balls. Hammer a 1½-inch nail into the center of each of these flat surfaces, then cut off the heads of the nails with wire cutters. Place the headless end of one nail at the center point of one end of a dowel and drive it in by hammering on the ball. The ball should be flush with the end of the dowel. Attach the other ball to a dowel in the same manner.

Apply a coat of primer to both ball-and-dowels and to the entire racer construction. When dry, sandpaper all surfaces lightly. Then paint the frame, the boards under it, and the two balls black, the hood red, the seat blue, and the two dowels white. When the paint has dried, give each dowel a candy-cane design by wrapping a spiral of red tape down its length.

Measure and mark points on the outer sides of the long sections of the frame that are 6 inches in front of the edge of the seat. The point, on each side of the frame, must be ¾ inch above the lower edge of the frame. Drill a ⅛-inch hole through each dowel, ¾ inch from the bottom end. Position each dowel on the sideboards of the frame on the points marked and screw them into place.

With the ¼-inch bit, drill a hole 1¼ inches deep in the center of both ends of the 21-inch planks at the front and rear of the frame. Secure the four baby-carriage wheels to these ends with hexagonal-head wood bolts 4 inches long. Place a washer on the shank of each bolt, between the wheel and the frame. Tighten the bolts with pliers.

Fasten a screw-eye, 1 inch long, to each dowel, 1½ inches below the ball. The screw-eye must be on the front side of the dowel. Fasten a screw-eye on the topside surface of the front 21-inch board, 1½ inches from the right end and centered on the board; then do likewise on the left side. Fasten a 24-inch length of chain to each screw-eye on the axle board and the screw-eye on the dowel of the same side.

Paint the two quarter-round molding strips yellow. Allow them to dry thoroughly. Apply glue to their bottom sides and position them at the juncture of the hood and the sides of the frame. If you wish, decorate the soap-box car by painting a design on the hood.

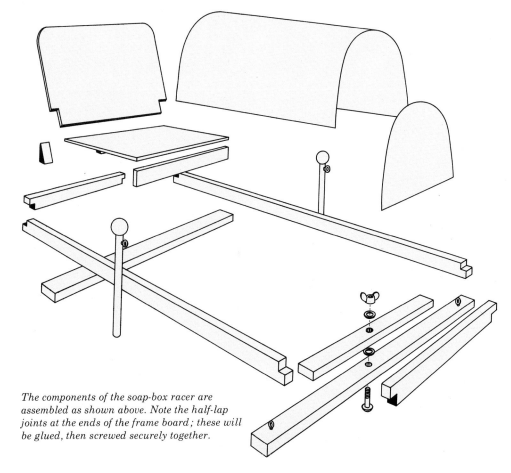

The components of the soap-box racer are assembled as shown above. Note the half-lap joints at the ends of the frame board; these will be glued, then screwed securely together.

Tlachtli

About the Game

Hernando Cortez and his Spanish *conquistadores* witnessed many strange sights when they first landed on Mexican shores. One of the strangest was a bouncing ball, made from a curious elastic material previously unknown to the Europeans. It was, of course, rubber, used by the Mexicans at least 500 years prior to the Spaniards' arrival. Thus Cortez discovered *tlachtli*, the rubber ball game of Middle America. In 1528, he sailed for Spain with a team of Aztec ball players and presented them at the court of Charles V.

In Middle American culture at this time, *tlachtli* was a magnificent sight. Two teams in full ceremonial dress met in a high walled court (the *tlachtli)* cheered by spectators from all walks of life. The court was 125 feet long and 50 feet wide, shaped like a capital I. Points were gained when one team failed to return the ball, but the supreme moment of the game came when a player managed to ricochet the ball from his body, through one of the vertical stone rings set in the center of the court walls. At this point, the game would be abandoned in excitement, the star player free to reap the fruits of his victory. He could claim jewels, gold, feather cloaks, anything he wanted from the losing team and the audience. In victory, captains were showered with the highest honors, but in defeat, they were often sacrificed to appease the god of the ball game, Xolotl.

The cut-throat tactics of the game were complemented by the equally ruthless gambling that accompanied it. Rulers would wager kingdoms and fortunes on the outcome, while less affluent lords staked slaves, gold and jewels, or women.

The ball was not allowed to touch the ground or come to rest. It could only be hit with the hips, knees, or elbows, and players wore protective pads to shield themselves from the assault of the 5-pound ball. The game took a heavy toll of players; they had to throw themselves on the ground to keep the ball in play, and often they received the full impact of it from the air. 'Some of them were carried out dead,' recorded one Spanish chronicler, '...or they suffered great damage on the knees or on the thighs.'

In Mexican mythology, the court represented the world, and the movement of the ball symbolized one of the heavenly bodies, the sun or the moon. The Mexican Indians believed the sky to be a sacred *tlachtli* court, and the stars the playthings of the gods.

The exact origins of *tlachtli* are obscure. Ball player figurines were uncovered at Tlatilco, Mexico, inhabited as early as 1500 B.C. The earliest known ball court lies at Copan, Honduras. The game may first have developed near the rubber plantations of Veracruz and Tabasco. In its heyday, however, *tlachtli* was played from El Salvador to northern Arizona, and throughout the Antilles. Today, though the ceremonial splendour has vanished, the natives of Sinaloa and Nayarit on the northwest coast of Mexico still resurrect the game during certain religious feast days.

How to Play the Game

The following rules are based on the modern version of the game.

Stake out a field in a park, playground, or beach, 50 yards long and 20 yards wide. Mark the field into four central parts – two end courts and two middle courts, divided by a center line. Players divide into two teams, preferably about ten to a side, and take up positions on their respective middle and end courts.

The centers put the light plastic ball in play by tossing it into the air. It may be hit only with the hips, shoulders, knees, or back, or allowed to bounce from one team-mate to another. Kicking, batting, or throwing are strictly prohibited! If one team can successfully bump the ball from the center line to their end line, they score five points. The first team to score 25 points wins the game.

Deprived of its great courts, tlachtli *still survives in remote parts of Mexico. These players, opposite, were photographed in Sinaloa by T. J. Leynaar.*

The stone ring shown below is set on one of the towering walls of the ball court in the ruined Mayan city of Chichén Itzá, southeast Mexico. The ring was the focal point of the game, and a player achieved his great moment of glory when he bounced the ball off his body through the ring.

A miniature pottery tlachtli *(ball court) with players and spectators, above, from Nayarit, c. 1400 A.D., from Yale University Art Gallery. Around the architectural grandeur of the ball court revolved the complex religious and social life of the pre-Columbian Mexican Indians.*

At a signal, both teams charge toward the giant ball in the new American 'tribal' game, earthball. Paul Fusco photographed this breathless opener at a tournament held in Fort Cronkite, California.

Earthball

About the Game

Earthball is the modern American version of an ancient game whose beginnings go back to the earliest tribal free-for-all – a game used ceremonially in other cultures to express an exuberant belief in the regenerative forces of nature. Basically it is an energetic but good-humored struggle between two teams contending for possession of a large ball. Participants jostle, rush, push, and occasionally elbow each other in order to move the ball in the right direction. But the dominant element in earthball is the sense of 'tribe' that it communicates to all players: a feeling of body contact and common purpose, in far more relaxed conditions than organized sports like football or rugby would allow. The people of all ages who played it at the New Games Tournament in Fort Cronkite, California, where Paul Fusco took his memorable earthball photographs, came to the scene precisely because they wanted to participate in a 'tribal' event rather than just watch a game.

In Japan, a very similar game still has symbolic and religious significance. *Hakozaki-gu no Tama-seseri,* the ball-struggle of Hakozaki Shrine, takes place in Fukuoka City each year on January 3. The participants are young men, clad only in loincloths, who represent their home districts. A sacred wooden ball is used in the game, and the winning team traditionally is assured of a good harvest during the coming year.

This festival is said to have originated when two beautiful balls – one regarded as male, the other female – were found floating on nearby waters and presented to the shrine. Brought out into public view once a year, the balls were said to bestow happiness on all who touched them. As larger and larger crowds attended the festivals, the struggle to touch the balls took on a competitive aspect. The female ball still remains in the shrine; only the male ball is delivered to the players, after it has undergone a series of purification ceremonies. The players, too, must first take ritual baths at a bathhouse near the shrine.

'The ensuing scene of fighting and pushing and shoving to get possession of the ball, with younger, lighter-weight boys sitting astride their elders' shoulders to get the advantage of height, is truly as wild as the nature of the men of Kyushu is reputed to be,' writes Tamotsu Yato in his book, *Naked Festivals of Japan.* 'The fighting melee gradually moves in the return direction of the shrine, while spectators and priests throw cold water over the naked throng – and over any spectators that happen to get in the way. The side that has possession of the ball as the group enters the shrine precincts wins and has the honor of returning the ball to its priest-custodian.'

In California, shouts fill the air as the two teams clash in midfield, jostling the earthball one way, then another, on a sea of outstretched hands.

How to Play the Game

The teams are unlimited in size, and unclassified as to age, sex, or ability. Literally everybody who wants to join in can participate, even on the spur of the moment, and anyone who wants to drop out is equally free to do so.

The rules are extremely simple and non-compulsive. An immense ball is placed in the middle of a field 200 yards long. The two teams line up at either end of the field. At a signal, both teams charge toward the ball. The object of the game is for one team to manhandle the ball over the opposing side's goal line. Strategy includes shouting, pushing, shoving.

There is no fixed playing time, and everybody plays just for the fun of the thing. Usually the game ends when most of the participants drop out from sheer exhaustion.

*While the 'female' ball watches from her Shinto
shrine, young men of Fukuoka City, photographed
by Brian Brake, struggle for possession of her
slippery male companion. Shinto, Japan's oldest
religion, is based on the worship of the gods of
natural elements such as fire, water, and earth;
the ball-struggle of the Hakozaki Shrine is only
one of its many seasonal festivals. Once the ball
has been returned to the priest-custodian, the
crowd salutes the players by singing the
traditional song of the annual celebration.*

Tug of War

About the Game

The conflict between 'good' and 'evil' – usually forces of nature that affect the livelihood of the people – is dramatized in many countries by a ritual tug of war. A Burmese custom, noted by the ethnographer F. E. Sawyer, was that 'a rain party and a drought party tug against each other, the rain party being allowed the victory, which in the popular notion is generally followed by rain.' On the other side of the world, Canadian Eskimo communities split into two teams for the autumn tug of war that foretells the winter weather. In Korea, people from neighboring villages hold a tug of war to see which will reap the better harvest in the fall.

The modern tug of war has become a familiar event at athletic meetings, although in some countries boys under the age of 17 are officially prohibited from participating because of the abdominal strain involved.

In the Austrian Tyrol, a scaled-down version of the game has been a favorite tavern contest for 200 years. This is *Fingerhakeln,* a finger tug of war between two men. The loser is obliged to pay for the beer.

How to Play the Game

Tug of war is played by two teams, each officially made up of eight players. Each team stands in line behind its captain, and players take hold of their end of the rope. The middle of the rope is marked by a band of black tape, and six feet to either side of this center mark are two other tape markers. Lines are drawn on the ground exactly below the tape markers on the rope. At a given signal the tug begins. Each team must try to pull the rope so that the six-foot tape marker on the opposing end of the rope crosses the six-foot ground mark on their side.

A wooden board takes the place of a rope for a two-man tug of war, below, across a line drawn in the dust of Aqshah, in Afghanistan.

A children's tug of war, without rope, is played in Korea. Six members of each team clasp their hands around each other's waists, and the team captains link hands tightly. At the count of three, each team tries to pull the other over a dividing line drawn on the ground between them.

Eskimos also play a two-man tug of war called *arsaaraq*. The seated players face each other with their feet touching. Each man grasps with both hands one of the wooden handles attached to a short length of rope (see photograph at right). The player who can pull his opponent over is the winner of the game.

In a tug of war, contestants should be about the same size and strength, to avoid undue physical strain.

Materials
Two wooden dowels, 10 inches long, 1 inch in diameter.
Cord, 2 feet long, 1/4 inch thick.
Blue gloss paint.
All-purpose glue.

Tools
A utility knife and paintbrush.

How to Make the Game
With the utility knife, whittle out a shallow groove, 1/4 inch wide, around the center of each dowel. Paint the dowels and allow them to dry. Wind an end of the cord around the groove in each dowel and tie each with a tight, secure knot. The length of the cord between the dowels should be about 16 inches.

The double grip, above, is perfect for arsaaraq, *the Eskimo version of tug of war for two players.*

More than twoscore Eskimos, below, are strung out along the rope at the beginning of a festive tug of war contest in northern Canada.

Eskimos of the eastern Arctic get together in spring for tugs of war. A men's team (upper left) dig their feet into the snow for purchase.

Meanwhile, the women's team (upper right) laugh at their own uncoordinated efforts; and two men, at lower left, tug with knee braced against foot.

In a Californian tug of war on a 600-foot rope, lower center and right, the dividing line is a gully into which the losing team was pulled.

Pickaback Relay

About the Game

Relay races are a perennial favorite at picnics and outdoor holiday gatherings. The pickaback relay has an added advantage: it is one of the few activities at which adults and very young children can both have an uproariously good time (though adults will probably get tired out well before the children do).

As with most party and festival games, pickaback relay racing is played mainly for the fun it provides the spectators as well as the participants. The funniest losers are sometimes more appreciated than the swiftest winners, and may be awarded a booby prize for comedy. The run in the straightaway is apt to furnish a good many laughs, but the focal point of the fun is usually at the relay point, when the child is passed on to the next team member (the rules stipulate that the child may not be dropped). During the California races at which these pictures were taken, one group decided to add a new wrinkle to the race: the team divided into two groups of five, each taking a turn carrying a 250-pound woman up and back. And it was this team that won the race!

Saddled with his buxom burden, above, a young Californian lurches unsteadily down the track. Supporters cheer, below, as a child smoothly changes hands between two laps of the relay race.

How to Play the Game

The boundaries of the racecourse – a distance of 300 to 500 yards – must be clearly marked on an open field. The participants, divided into any manageable number of teams, line up at the starting line. Usually a child or a lightweight person is chosen by each team to be the burden.

These burdens must be saddled comfortably on the back of each team's runner before the race begins. Usually the rider clasps his arms around the runner's neck; the runner secures the straddled legs of his burden by hooking his arms under them, then clasping his hands tightly together.

When the referee blows the starting whistle, each participant runs to the end of the field as fast as he can, then back to the starting line where he transfers his rider onto the back of the team's next runner.

For hardier players, the pickaback relay race may be run on a course that is riddled with obstacles. The burdened runner might have to ford a stream, climb over a low stone wall, or duck under a low-hanging branch. Game organizers sometimes add an obstacle or two of their own devising, such as a barrel to be hurdled or a short seesaw to be crossed.

Obviously, this version is not for the thin-skinned: situations are arranged to be as funny as possible for everyone concerned. Good-natured heckling from the sidelines is not meant to dishearten the participant, and riders dropped by racers breaking up in fits of laughter are permitted to remount after the runner has caught his breath.

Water Jousting

About the Game

The oldest known reference to water jousting in Provence, southern France, occurs in the municipal records of Toulon, for 1410. 'It is a custom in the said town that on the second day of Easter, the seamen and country folk of the region arm boats for jousting at sea, which are called *quintaines*; and this they must do honestly, without cheating, and afterwards they go to drink together and make great festivity with horns and other instruments, and honor him who jousted best.' (As regards the latter part of this custom, nothing has changed.)

Water jousting was known even earlier than this: it developed as a lighthearted version of land jousting on horseback, in the days of chivalry. Early water jousters tilted at shields, known as quintains, supported on poles in rivers. Thence the game moved downstream to the Mediterranean coast of southern France, and became a special entertainment at summer festivals.

In the past, the jousters' dashing costumes included straw hats decorated with ribbons and plumes. Modern water jousters wear T-shirts emblazoned with the same colors as their brightly painted team boat.

How to Play the Game

The following brief description of Provençal water jousting may be freely adapted by players who do not have specially-constructed boats, or a warm blue sea to fall into! Players can enjoy the game just as much in small dinghies on a pond or lake, or even in inflatable boats on a swimming pool. Jousters, especially children, should be well matched in size, and able to swim; they should preferably wear a light lifejacket, to increase buoyancy and act as an extra buffer against knocks.

Carrying on a sporting tradition begun in the days of chivalry, young Parisians knock each other into the Seine in this color lithograph of the 1830's. Thousands of spectators line the river.

When children joust, they should be supervised by adults.

In France, the jousting boats have a special platform extending from the stern. Each boat contains seven or eight jousters. The two rival boats make an initial lap of honor round the bay, while the first pair of jousters get ready for combat.

Each jouster wears a protective chest pad. In front of this is his shield, attached by cord round his neck and waist. The shield consists of wooden planks surrounded by a square frame, and overlaid by two chevron-shaped slats; these are to catch the lance of the opponent and prevent it from skidding and injuring the jouster.

In his right hand the jouster carries his lance. This is about 9 feet long but only 1¼ inches in diameter, usually made of ash wood which is both strong and supple. On one end is a wooden ball, to act as a buffer against the jouster's body; at the other is a toothed ring, designed to grip the opponent's shield on impact. The jouster also carries a small object – a flag or ball – which is called the 'witness' and demonstrates that he is not touching the lance with his left hand.

The two boats approach each other at about three miles per hour, passing within 18 inches, starboard to starboard, so that the jousters' right arms are toward each other. As soon as they are within reach, each one digs the toothed end of his lance against the shield of his adversary, and they push hard against each other. Almost invariably this results in one jouster losing his balance and tumbling into the water. If both jousters lose their balance and fall in, they must swim toward each other and give the 'accolade' – a smacking kiss on either cheek. A jouster who knocks three of his opponents in succession into the water earns the title *frère*, or 'brother.'

The victor is, of course, the last of the jousters to remain dry, having knocked all his adversaries into the water. If, on the last pass, both the finalists fall in, the one who hits the water last is the winner – but it is best to have a jury to decide the issue.

Materials

Two poles 2 yards long, $1\frac{1}{2}$ inches in diameter.
Two plywood boards, 12 by 16 inches, $\frac{3}{8}$ inch thick.
Strips of cloth or rags.
Two sections of cloth, leather, or canvas, 12 inches square.
Two leather straps, 10 inches long.
Two leather straps, 6 inches long.
Four flat-head screws, $\frac{3}{8}$ inch long.
A ball of strong twine.
Gloss paint: blue, red, and black.
Sandpaper.

Tools

A soft pencil, ruler, coping saw, primer brush, artist's fine camel-hair brush, and paintbrush.

The lances and plywood jousting shields, above right, are light, easy to handle, and add a new dimension to games you can play in the water.

How to Make the Game

Sand down both poles until smooth, then coat with wood primer and allow to dry. Sand lightly. Paint one pole blue, the other red.
Pad one end of each pole by tightly winding strips of cloth round it, making a 'ball' of approximately 8 inches in diameter. Secure the ball by covering it with the section of strong cloth, leather, or canvas, then bind it firmly with strong twine, as shown in the diagram at left.

To make the shields, place one 12-by-16-inch board vertically on the work table. On the left side, mark a point 12 inches from the bottom edge, repeating this step on the right side. On the top edge of the board, mark a middle point, then connect the side points to the middle point. With the coping saw, cut along the lines drawn. Repeat these steps on the remaining board, and sand down all rough edges on both boards.

Paint the shields with wood primer and allow to dry. Sand lightly. Paint one shield blue, the other red. Using the diagram at left as a guide, sketch the fleur-de-lis on one shield and the lion rampant on the other with a soft pencil. Using a fine camel-hair brush, define the outlines with black paint. Allow to dry.

On the back side of each shield, fasten two leather straps with screws, the longer one on the lower right side and the shorter one on the upper left. These straps will accommodate the right forearm and hand while the shield is held.

Follow the Leader

About the Game

Mimicry and imitation play an important part in children's games. Follow the leader provides every child with the opportunity to display his talents as a mimic. Perception and agility are important parts of the game; each child must imitate what he has seen only a few seconds earlier, or fail! The role of the leader, however, is the most strenuous test of imagination and ingenuity. To ensure a good game for his band of followers, he must devise a variety of intricate steps and movements to put them through their paces.

This game has universal appeal and can be played almost anywhere, in the street or playground, In the wide open spaces, however, where natural obstacles occur, the game takes on new challenge and excitement, and can often reach extremes. In nineteenth-century New Zealand, as one writer noted, the game meant '...sticking with the leader through thick and thin... over ditches and up banks, over and through streams, over and under gates and fences... and even over a shed or two if the owners were known to be absent.'

Eskimo children have adapted the game to suit their environment: the followers must place their feet in the snowy footprints left by the leader. But he is devious and makes certain that he leaves no ordinary tracks, placing his feet in odd positions, close together, far apart, or with one foot turned in.

How to Play the Game

Any number of players can join in the game, the more the merrier. The players elect a leader known for his sense of humor and clowning abilities. Once the players have formed a line behind him (an arm's length between each player) the leader walks in any direction. He then springs a chain of surprises on his followers: he may hop, skip, somersault, cartwheel, squat, stoop, duck waddle – anything he can think of to fool his followers. If any player fails to 'follow the leader' he is out of the game, though most players drop out through breaking into fits of laughter. The surviving player is the leader in the next round and should do his best to make his game more tricky and involved than the one before.

Too late! In waist-high grass, a player bringing up the rear loses sight of his leader's movements – one of the pitfalls of running last in line.

A surprise change of tactics fails to fool his band of followers as the leader drops suddenly into the high grass and begins sliding backward.

Tibetan children pause in mid-run to catch their breath during a game of follow the leader on the mountain slopes near their home village.

'What's he going to do next?' All eyes fix on the leader as the players, photographed by Art Kane, move through a field in Connecticut (opposite). One advantage of follow the leader is that even the youngest players get the chance to prove that they can often spring the best surprises.

Indian Kickball

About the Game

The name of the Tarahumara Indians of Mexico is derived from an Indian word meaning 'foot-runners' – an indication of the importance of kickball racing in their culture. Runners practice from childhood in the hope of becoming champions. The races are usually run in the growing season, between teams of three to six runners from local villages and regions. Race day is an occasion of great social activity, drinking, and betting. The ball is usually of carved oak root, about 3 inches in diameter, and is kicked over a course of 20 to 40 miles. A new ball may be substituted for one which is lost during the race.

Kickball is played as a spiritual ceremony among the Hopi Indians of the southwestern United States. Each of their teams represents one of the sacred shrines called *kivas,* and the runners pray before the race.

How to Play the Game

Each team is made up of an equal number of players (three to six) and has its own kickball, which may be painted with a colored stripe to distinguish it from the kickball of the opposing team.

The Indians usually play with their right (kicking) foot left bare, wearing a sandal on the other. For tenderfoot players, however, it is advisable to wear sneakers or sandals on both feet to avoid injury. Team members should practice tossing the ball in the air with the toes of their right foot.

In the stony countryside near Barranca de Cobre, northern Mexico, a young Tarahumara, photographed by Tor Eigeland, hoists the ball with his powerful kicking foot (opposite).

The 40-mile race is on for his village teammates, below, after they have performed the early morning ritual of bathing their legs in cedar tea to ward off evil spirits and to give added strength.

The racecourse should be long – perhaps a mile or more – with plenty of interesting twists and turns. (The Indians run on rough, hilly terrain.) The starting and finish lines should be clearly marked. Teams should stand several yards apart at the starting line, grouped around their kickball. A signal is given and the race begins.

One player gives the ball a good lifting toss with his right toe; the others run after it, and another member of the team advances the ball in the same way. The team stays close together during the course of the race. They function as a cooperative group – no one player should hog the ball. The team that gets its ball first over the finish line wins.

Materials
A roll of aluminum foil.
An old inner tube from a bicycle tire.

Tools
Scissors.

How to Make the Game
Crumple the aluminum foil into a solid ball about 2½ inches in diameter. Cut across the inner tube to make ½-inch-wide bands. Wrap these bands around the ball until it is completely covered by several layers of rubber. The ball should be about 3 inches in diameter.

This homemade foil ball wrapped in rubber tubing (below) is kinder to the feet than the oak root ball of the Tarahumara or the stone ball kicked by the Hopi Indian runners.

Heedless of jagged rocks and cactus spines, these two runners, below, strive to cover the crucial last lap. Many Tarahumara run with a belt of deer hooves strung round their waist, a talisman of good luck. At this point in the race, excited supporters often run alongside their team, urging them on to victory. But no hero's welcome awaits the winner as he crosses the finish line. His glory is submerged by the enthusiasm of the spectators over the outcome of the betting.

Prisoner's Base

About the Game

Although its origins are obscure, prisoner's base is a wild game that has been played to distraction for centuries. During his reign, 1327–77, when adults often indulged in a round or two, Edward III was forced to ban the game from the grounds of Westminster Palace, as it interfered with parliamentary affairs. The edict did not dent the game's popularity, and it continued to be played by young and old alike. A rowdy ballad describes a game of prisoner's base between teams of bachelors and married men at Ellesmere, Shropshire, in 1764, the bachelors emerging victorious from the fray. The game remains a favorite with children, both in its original form and in milder versions like *quatre coins*.

Five young girls of romantic nineteenth-century France play quatre coins *(four corners) among the trees of the Luxembourg Gardens, still one of the great city parks of Paris. The painting is by Louis-Léopold Boilly (1761–1845) who specialized in scenes of French everyday life. This relatively tame version of prisoner's base probably developed as boys discouraged girls from joining in the warlike tactics of 'the base' or* les barres, *as the game is called by children in France.*

How to Play the Game

Each team should have at least ten players, including a captain. One team wears an identifying mark, such as a handkerchief tied to the arm.

Mark out a 20-foot-square playing area in the park or playground. Divide the field in half and draw a circle (the chivy), two feet in diameter, in the center of the dividing line. In each half of the field, mark a home area and a prison area – the home and prison areas of the two teams should be diagonally opposite each other.

The captains flip a coin for the first run, then the teams group in their home areas. The captain of the first team sends out his fastest runner to the circle, where he calls 'Chivy!' At this point, an opponent is sent to tag him, but his captain dispatches a runner in pursuit of his pursuer, whereupon the second capain sends a player to pursue that pursuer!

Each player tries for his home base, but should he be tagged, he waits in the opponents' prison, until he can be tagged by a teammate and released. The game is fraught with pitfalls and fast legs are essential! It officially ends when one team is locked up in prison, but it often develops into a free-for-all and ends through sheer exhaustion!

217

About the Game

Although kites are well-known among children in western countries, it is in the East, where they have been flown since before recorded history, that they are most popular and important. Eastern kites have legendary and historical associations, expressed in their traditional shapes, names, and decorations. In Japan, kites are called *tako* (octopus). The design of the kites varies in different parts of the country; they may be geometrical, or take the form of human, animal, or bird figures. They may also bear devices which hum or whistle in the wind as the kite flies; such kites may be kept flying all night over houses, to scare away any unfriendly spirits.

In Korea, the origin of kite flying is attributed to a general in ancient times who inspired his troops to victory by sending up a kite with a lantern attached, which the soldiers believed was a new star, a sign of divine help. Some peoples of Korea and Malaysia write down the misfortunes of the year on a kite, and fly it high; the kite string may be cut or burned so that the unfortunate kite and all its troubles will be lost, and, symbolically, the owner can start a new year without his old worries.

Kites prepared the eager generation of 1900 for their great leap into the air. The experimental kite, above, photographed by Jacques-Henri Lartigue in 1905, was built by his brother Zissou.

A giant box-kite, opposite, designed and built by the photographer's brother, is flown by his father and a helper in a field near the Lartigue family's Château de Rouzat, Auvergne, in 1910.

Simple kites turn into box-kites and ultimately into flying machines: 'obsessed with the idea of getting up into the air,' Zissou Lartigue makes a bold and successful attempt with a man-carrying kite of his own design in 1906. His 'glider' was based on the early airplanes of men like Gabriel Voisin, left, who made the first public flight in France from a sand dune at Merlimont in 1904. Jacques-Henri Lartigue, only nine at the time, was on hand to record Voisin's historic lift-off with the small plate camera he had received from his father. With such shots he was to become renowned as the century's 'photographer of speed.'

219

In Honduras and Guatemala, in Central America, huge kites are flown on All Saints and All Souls Days, which occur in November at the time that the changing wind currents herald the welcome dry season: the practice is a mixture of ancient Indian and Spanish colonial religious customs.

Kite day in China is held on the ninth day of the ninth month, when men and boys of all ages (but no women) fly their kites from hills and high places. In Iraq, children make small candle lanterns, called *fanus,* to hang on a kite string, producing a striking spectacle at night.

Kite fighting is a popular part of flying kites in many countries. The upper length of the kite string is coated with glue and powdered glass or porcelain, which makes the string stiff and extremely sharp. One kite flyer will try to guide his kite so that it crosses the path of another; when the strings are close together, he gives a jerk so that his cord will cut through the other, and the opponent's kite will be lost. In most regions, small children eagerly wait for fallen kites, as a lost kite traditionally belongs to him who finds it.

Huge kites, of ancient Mayan design, are launched at the Guatemalan village of Santiago de Sacatepequez to celebrate the dry season. The local cemetery doubles as an arena for the kites, which symbolize the spirits of the dead.

How to Play the Game
No kite will fly without some wind, however slight. A tough, fairly heavy kite will stand up to a strong wind, but the string should be strong enough to hold it; if it is too weak, the kite will soon snap free and fall to earth. Fragile kites, on the other hand, can only be flown in a light breeze or they will tear before they are airborne.

To get your kite up, hold it in the wind with one hand, keeping a grip on the reel with the other; when the wind catches the kite and it starts to tug, let it fly and gradually reel out the string. A second person may be required to help with a heavy kite, running it into the wind until it is lifted up into the air.

Always keep the string taut and watch out for sudden drops in the breeze; if you reel in your slack line quickly, you can probably bring the kite up before it sinks too low down.

Spare kite string should always be kept wound round the reel, to avoid tangles and prevent people tripping over loose line on the ground.

Kites should be flown in open areas free of trees, telegraph poles and lines, and television antennas. Children should not attempt to recover a kite trapped in a tree or overhead wire. Kite strings coated with any abrasive are not recommended, as they may cause injury unless handled with care.

Children hold a springtime kite contest (above) in Bandung, on the island of Java, Indonesia. The kites they are flying are similar to the Nagasaki type of Japanese kites, shown below.

The three diamond-shaped kites below come from Nagasaki. They are called hata, *which means 'flag'; but some Japanese say the word derives from* bata *(horsefly), referring to the buzzing sound made by the streamers when the kite flies.*

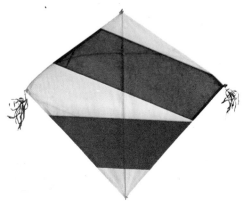

The Japanese character inscribed on the square Hamamatsu kite (below) means 'dragon.'

Miniature versions of traditional kites, such as those shown here, are popular with children.

The grotesque face on the kite below represents a tengu, or mythical giant from the mountains.

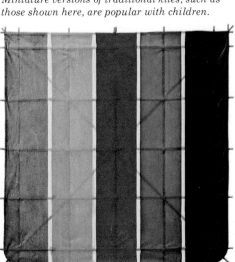

Japanese kite-flyers cooperate in the tricky
business of getting a large and fragile kite off the
ground (right and far right). The pictures on this
spread were taken at the annual tako age –
kite-flying contest – of Hamamatsu, a seaboard
town in the Shizuoka prefecture of central Japan.
Kite contests are held on the coast and islands
of Japan at the beginning of May, taking
advantage of the strong monsoon winds.
Each kite team represents a neighborhood in the
town. Team members (below) identify themselves
by wearing jackets embroidered with a copy of
their kite design – in this case, an apple motif.

Japanese kites range from pint-sized children's
playthings to giants of five yards square, or more.
The huge kites being completed (above) are not
team kites, but flying commercials; the kite at
left advertises a tailor's shop, even giving the
telephone number, while the one at right extols
the bill of fare in a local sushi restaurant.

A pair of kite flyers, their jackets emblazoned
like their kite with the sun emblem of the
Japanese national flag, maneuver the kite into
starting position (above). The kites are made of
paper, supported by a lattice framework of fine
bamboo strips. Each team uses the same design
on its own kites every year. The intricate craft of
kite-making is frequently a family tradition.

Hamamatsu kites are always square; other regions
have their own distinctive shapes. The hexagonal
kite, at left, comes from Niigata, northern Japan.

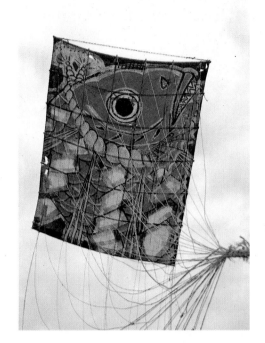

A vivid Hamamatsu kite (far left) tugs at the many cords that guide the kite in flight. Once airborne, the kites are turned against each other in battle; glass-sharpened strings cut through the strings of rival kites and send them crashing to earth. The kite that stays longest in the air wins.

The miles of cord attached to each kite could easily become inextricably tangled. To sort out the web of string attached to the kite's framework, there is no substitute for human dexterity (left). Behind each team of men pulling a kite string, there is a team of small children, eagerly trundling a large wooden spool on wheels (above). The children wind the spool to reel up or let out the spare length of the kite string. To help control the kite's tension, the string may be passed through a large wooden pulley (far left).

223

Alone with the wind and sky, a young New York girl, above, runs to raise the air speed needed to lift her kite into the correct flying attitude.

Materials

Two pine slats, one 24 inches long, the other 32 inches long, 1/4 inch square.
All-fiber twine, 300 yards long.
Artist's tracing paper, 24 by 32 inches.
All-purpose glue.
Cord or ribbon, 2 yards long.
Two wooden dowels, 14 inches long, 1 inch in diameter.
Chipboard, 6 by 8 inches, 1 inch thick.
A wooden dowel, 2 inches long, 1/2 inch in diameter.
Nails.

Tools

A ruler, pencil, pocketknife, scissors, coping saw, and hammer.

How to Make the Game

With ruler and pencil, mark a point 11 inches from one end of the 32-inch slat; mark another point in the exact center of the 24-inch slat. Spread glue generously on these points and allow to dry partially for about five minutes. Then press the glued surfaces of the slats against each other so that the slats form a cross shape which will be the frame of the kite.

After the glue has completely set, take two yards of twine and wind it around the four limbs of the glued section several times, as shown in photograph 1. Roughly 1½ yards of twine should be left over; do not cut it off. This will be the 'leader' of the kite. Knot the bound section well and spread some glue over it. Allow it to dry thoroughly.

With a pocketknife, cut slight grooves lengthwise across both ends of the horizontal slat, and in the bottom end of the vertical slat. Then, about ½ inch from each of the four ends, cut a groove all the way around the slat, as shown in photograph 2.

Take about 4 yards of twine and, after securing a knot at the circular groove at the top of the frame, run the twine through the end-grooves on the other three extremities. The twine should be tightly strung, but not so tight that it bends or bows the slats. Secure it with another knot at the top of the frame (see photograph 3).

Lay the kite frame on top of the paper and mark the paper so that it conforms to the shape of the frame but is 1½ inches larger on all sides. Cut out the paper along these lines.

Center the frame on the tracing paper, making sure that the horizontal slat is under the vertical. Spread glue over the strings of the frame and fold the ends of the paper over it, making a crease. Unfold the ends, spread them with glue, then fold them over again (photograph 5), and allow to dry thoroughly.

Take a piece of twine about a yard long, and tie one end securely to the circular groove at one end of the horizontal slat. String it across to the circular groove at the opposite end. Run the twine once around the groove, then pull gently so that the horizontal slat begins to bow. The middle of the bowed slat should be 1½ inches from the twine. Knot the end of the twine to the groove, as in photograph 6.

Make a small hole in the front of the kite exactly where the slats cross. The 1½ yards of twine left over from binding the center of the frame should be run through the hole. (You may want to cut out a small circle of paper and glue it around the hole to prevent it from tearing.) Line up the top of the leader cord along the horizontal slat to one corner of the kite. Make a small noose in the cord at this point. Still holding the cord in this position, line up the next segment of the cord with the edge of the lower part of the kite. At the point where the cord reaches the bottom corner, tie it to the end of the slat.

Take 2 yards of cord or ribbon and fasten one end to the circular groove at the bottom of the kite frame. This is the tail of the kite. If you wish, decorate it with bows made of crepe paper or colored tissue paper.

Reinforce the four corners on the front of the kite by gluing triangular pieces of tracing paper at these four points.

1: Bind the two wooden slats together with twine to make a cross-shaped frame for the kite.

2: Whittle shallow grooves around each end and across the tips of the arms of the kite frame.

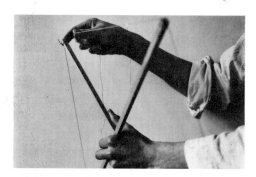

3: Run a length of cord from arm to arm of the frame and knot it securely at the top of the kite.

4: Cut out tracing paper to match the shape of the kite, leaving a 1½-inch overlap of paper.

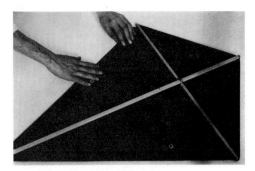

5: *Carefully bend the paper over the cord, then glue down the overlapping edge of paper.*

6: *Tie a cord to the ends of the horizontal slat, tightening the cord until the slat bows.*

7: *Nail the sawed flat edge of one dowel to each edge of the chipboard to make the reel.*

With its reel of twine and a long, stabilizing tail, this brightly-painted kite is ready to fly.

To make the kite reel, take one 14-inch dowel and stand it on end. Saw it 8 inches down through the middle. Now lay the dowel on its side and saw it at the 8-inch point until the sawed half of the dowel falls away. Repeat these steps on the other dowel.

Apply glue to the flat sides of both dowels and to the long ends of the chipboard. Allow the glue to dry partially before pressing the pieces firmly together. Hammer several nails into each dowel (photograph 7) to secure it to the board.

Take the remaining twine and tie one end to one of the dowels where it meets the board. Wind the rest of the twine around the board.

With the pocketknife, cut a groove around the middle of the 2-inch dowel. Tie the loose end of the cord around this groove. This small dowel will be fastened to the noose of the kite leader, an arrangement that makes it easy to transport the kite and reel separately.

Learning the basics of aerodynamics through practical experience, a class of American children is taught the simple skills of kite-making.

Overleaf: hoops trundle, tops hum, and knucklebones tumble in the midst of 'Children's Games,' painted in 1560 by Pieter Breugel the Elder. ▶

Jackstraws

About the Game

Jackstraws, a game to be enjoyed by any number of players, is thought to have originated in China. The most prized sets are elaborately carved slivers of ivory whose heads are fashioned into easily recognizable shapes, such as forks, saws, tridents, a bird on a branch, a horse's head, and so on. The more intricate the shape, the higher the score value, as a greater amount of dexterity is required to extricate the jackstraw from the pile.

Modern European jackstraws have been streamlined into brightly-colored sets of wood or plastic, the color denoting the score. The requirements of the game, however, have not diminished with time: it still demands patience and a steady hand. Long a favorite of both adults and children, this game travels under a variety of names, such as four-five-six, spellicans, and pick-up sticks.

A bright heap of do-it-yourself jackstraws presents an absorbing challenge for the patient player. Each jackstraw must be removed without disturbing its neighbors, and scores by its color.

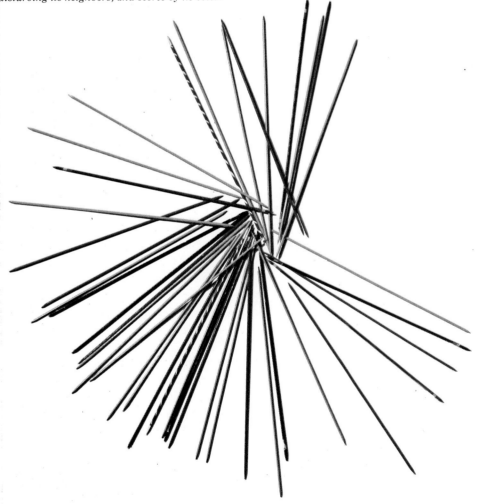

How to Play the Game

The aim of each player is to fish out the jackstraws carrying the highest score. The scores are: yellow, 3 points; red, 5 points; blue, 10 points; green, 15 points; red and white, 20 points.

The participants gather round a table and elect a player to begin the game, either by flipping a coin or drawing lots. Mixing the jackstraws thoroughly, the player bunches them in his hand, and, holding them just above the table top, allows them to collapse in a haphazard pile. Using his fingers, he removes the jackstraws one by one, without causing the others to move. Once he attacks the jackstraw of his choice, he cannot move to another if the first proves too difficult to pull out. If he disturbs a neighboring jackstraw, his turn is over and the player on his left begins.

The players who retrieve the red-and-white jackstraws may use them to tease other jackstraws, too precariously perched to be moved by the fingers, from the pile. Once all the straws have been picked up, the game is concluded, and the score tallied. The player with the highest score is the winner.

Materials

Fifty 10-inch lengths of wooden dowel, $1/8$ inch in diameter.
Gloss paint: red, yellow, blue, and green.
White plastic adhesive tape.

Tools

Pencil-sharpener and paintbrush.

How to Make the Game

With the pencil-sharpener, taper both ends of each length of dowel. Paint 20 sticks yellow, ten red, five blue, three green, and two red with white spiraling stripes.

London Bridge

About the Game

Today many bridges span the river Thames, but for centuries the London Bridge of the game title was the only one across the river. Hidden in the words of this apparently innocent game is an ancient symbolism. Nowadays we tend to take bridges for granted, but to primitive peoples bridges were remarkable structures that trespassed on the powers of the gods of land and water. In order to guard a bridge against the offended spirits, a ritual sacrifice – often a living man – was sealed into the foundations when the bridge was built. Without this sacrifice it was said that no material would be strong enough to protect the bridge: this belief is reflected in the song – 'silver and gold,' 'iron and steel,' 'wood and clay' are all too weak to sustain the structure.

Later, in the Middle Ages, it was believed that the two sides of the bridge represented good and evil. This was adapted into the game. Each child was offered a choice, such as 'a cabbage or a rose'; his decision would align him with one side of the game bridge or the other. At the end of the game there would be a tug of war between the two sides.

How to Play the Game

Two of the children are selected to be the bridge keepers and they must stand facing each other, a few feet apart. They raise their arms, clasping their hands to form an arch. The other children line up in a row and file between the two guards, while singing the London Bridge song. These are the traditional verses:

> London Bridge is falling down,
> Falling down, falling down,
> London Bridge is falling down,
> My fair lady.

The song reiterates the first line of each verse in this fashion:

> How shall we build it up again,
> Up again, up again,
> How shall we build it up again,
> My fair lady.

The remaining verses begin:
We will build it with wood and clay.
But wood and clay will wash away.
We will build it with iron and steel.
But iron and steel will bend and break.
We will build it with silver and gold.
But silver and gold will be stolen away.
We will put a man to watch all night.
Suppose the man should fall asleep.
As the last verse, 'Take the keys and lock him (her) up,' is sung, the two guards lower their arms to enclose the child who is passing between them. In modern versions of the game, the captive is brought to an area of the room or playground that is sometimes called the Tower of London. The game then goes on until all the children are caught and put in the Tower. When the last child is brought to the Tower of London, all the 'prisoners' break away, chased by the guards. The two children tagged by the guards in the chase are the next bridge keepers.

A line of Victorian children play London Bridge in the park, with their ever-present 'nannies' to serve as conveniently tall bridge keepers.

Pelele

About the Game

Pelele (pronounced pay-*lay*-lay) is the Spanish name for the ancient party and festival game of tossing a strawman in a blanket. The dummy is a symbol for some particularly unpopular figure who is ceremonially 'sent up' for the occasion. For generations, this was the way young Spanish girls worked off their resentment against male arrogance in a society where machismo held sway.

As they tossed the strawman in the blanket, the girls sang some of the traditional mocking-songs associated with the game, such as: '*El pelele está malo. Qué le daremos? Agua de caracoles que cria cuernos.*' (The *pelele* is naughty. What shall we give him? Water from snails that makes horns grow.) One of Goya's best-known paintings depicts a *pelele* in mid-toss, and the composer Enrique Granados evokes its spirit in a brilliant piano piece entitled *El Pelele*.

Spanish boys also toss the *pelele,* particularly at carnival time. In fact the game as it is known today is a vestige of a medieval springtime custom, which in turn can be traced back to a still older pagan practice involving the ritual killing of the old 'tree spirit' while celebrating the return of spring and the advent of a new 'king of the wood.'

In the Abruzzi, near Rome, a strawman representing the carnival is traditionally carried through the towns, and then, at the end of the festivities, is given a ceremonial toss in a sheet or blanket. Another, crueler version of the custom, once prevalent throughout Europe, was the 'sport' of tossing a dog in a blanket at Shrovetide (the holiday festivities just preceding Ash Wednesday).

Men too, of course, have been accorded the same treatment. In Olde England the blanket-toss was a favorite expression of public distemper – something halfway between a sport and a punishment. One sixteenth-century writer speaks of jesting and blanketing as 'dishonorable exercises.' 'I will tosse the Rogue in a Blanket,' blusters Shakespeare's Falstaff when a confederate annoys him.

In Cervantes' *Don Quixote,* the Don's long-suffering retainer Sancho Panza has to undergo the indignity of a blanket-toss when pranksters catch up with him at an inn: 'placing Sancho in the center of the blanket, they began to toss him up and amuse themselves at his expense, as they do with dogs at Shrovetide.'

The Alaskan Eskimos have turned the principle of the blanket-toss to more positive purposes: their *nalukatok,* formerly performed with a walrus-hide and now with a blanket, is an important form of outdoor recreation. The *nalukatok* blanket-toss takes the form of a competition. Each participant is tossed by his fellows and may leap as high as 20 feet during the exercise. He strives to land on his feet, and continues bounding up and down until he loses his balance. At that point another contestant takes his place. The winner is the one who can keep his footing the greatest number of tosses.

Spanish girls toss a pelele in a cartoon painted by Goya about 1780 for the royal tapestry weavers.

A homemade dummy stuffed with straw provides new life for outworn clothing. Add a funny face, and the dummy has a personality of its own.

How to Play the Game

Pelele may be played indoors, but it is more fun outside, where the strawman can be flung high into the air. Three, four, or more players spread the blanket on the ground, laying the dummy in the center. Each player grips his piece of the blanket firmly in both hands and, at a given signal, lifts the blanket, tossing up the dummy.

Pelele *in politics: an English cartoon of 1808 satirizes the political situation in Spain at that time, taking as its theme the scene in* Don Quixote *when Sancho Panza is tossed like a* pelele *(see* About the Game*). Joseph Bonaparte, made puppet king of Spain by his brother Napoleon, is being shaken from his throne by Wellington and his Spanish allies, while Napoleon looks on from behind the wall.*

How to Make the Game

Pack the socks tightly with straw and sew them to the ends of the trouser legs. Stuff the trousers with straw; pack it in tightly. Sew up the ends of the sleeves of the shirt and sew the bottom of the shirt to the waist of the trousers. Pack in stuffing. Fill the flour sack with stuffing and sew it to the neck of the shirt.

Paint a face on the flour sack and, if you like, sew a wig on the dummy's head. Make the dummy's nose by sewing together two triangular pieces of sacking and stuffing it with straw before sewing it onto the face.

Each time the dummy falls back into the blanket, he is thrown up again, higher and higher. In Spain, the players shout with excitement as the *pelele* flies heavenward, often singing a song to punctuate the rhythm of the toss. Here is the text of another traditional *pelele* song from Old Castile; the players can improvise a simple tune.

Pelele, pelele,
Tu madre te quiere,
Tu padre tambien,
Todos te queremos.
Arriba con él!

Pelele, pelele,
Your mother loves you,
And your father too,
We all love you.
Up with him!

Materials
Old clothes: trousers, socks, and sweatshirt or polo shirt.
Straw, hay, or old clothes for stuffing.
Heavy-duty nylon thread.
A five-pound flour sack.
Paints.
A yarn wig (optional).

Tools
A sewing needle and camel-hair paintbrush.

1: With especially strong thread, sew up the end of each trouser leg around the stuffed sock.

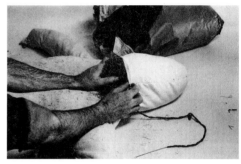

2: Pack stuffing into the head of the dummy before sewing it onto the neck of the shirt.

A pelele flies into the air from a blanket tossed by children in the town of Pedro Muñoz, Spain.

Pillow Fighting

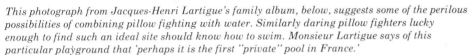

About the Game

In 1907, the 13-year-old Jacques-Henri Lartigue took a historic photograph of his uncle Raymond and a friend waging a pillow fight while straddling a log above a pond. The winner, of course, was supposed to keep his seat on the log, but in many of these jousts both participants were apt to end up in the water. There are other forms of pillow-fighting throughout the world – most of them on dry land, however, where any number can play. It seems to be a very ancient practice: no one knows when the first pillow fight was held, but it must have been shortly after the invention of the first feather pillow.

Astride a thick bamboo pole, two children in Java, Indonesia, stage a pillow fight (above).

This photograph from Jacques-Henri Lartigue's family album, below, suggests some of the perilous possibilities of combining pillow fighting with water. Similarly daring pillow fighters lucky enough to find such an ideal site should know how to swim. Monsieur Lartigue says of this particular playground that 'perhaps it is the first "private" pool in France.'

How to Play the Game

Pillow fighting can involve two combatants or a whole roomful of people. All that is required is the requisite number of lightweight pillows, or cushions, preferably filled with foam rubber – plus energy, courage, and a good aim. The pond and log are optional equipment. Players, on signal, slam away at any unprotected part of their adversary's body. Players do not have to stay in one position; there is usually a lot of running about and hiding in this game.

The contest is over for any participant who throws in the pillow and calls it quits. Quitters may not be attacked by participants still active in the game. The survivor of the battle is the winner.

Piñata

About the Game

The game of *piñata* is closely associated with the Mexican celebration of Christmas. In that country, festive occasions called *posadas* are held every night from the 18th to 24th of December. (*Posada* means 'lodgings,' a reference to the search of Joseph and Mary for shelter on their journey to Bethlehem.) Families and friends get together to sing, dance, and make merry; but, for the children, the high point of the evening is the breaking of the *piñata,* a colorful crock full of candy, nuts, and other small treats.

The word *piñata* derives from the Spanish verb *apiñar,* 'to join or bind in a bundle.' In the past *piñatas* were made to resemble clusters of flowers and fruit, but today animal or bird forms are popular.

In some communities, the breaking of the *piñata* is given a religious significance. The *piñata* represents the devil, tempting mankind with the promise of untold pleasures (the treats hidden inside). The blindfolded child represents the strength of the Christian faith, which must destroy the evil spirit.

The *piñata* custom also occurs in Spain and even in India. In some Latin American countries, the children have to break three *piñatas* – one filled with rice, another with old shoes, and the third with candies. Not until the contents come tumbling out do the players discover which one they have attacked.

A September school inauguration in Chiapas, Mexico, provides an out-of-season venue for piñata, *normally a Christmas celebration.*

Paper-feathered and brightly painted, the spectacular body of an owl piñata *conceals treasures of candy and toys.*

How to Play the Game

An adult throws the free end of the rope, attached to the *piñata,* over a beam, or the branch of a tree in the backyard. This person can then hoist the *piñata* up or down during the game.

The children are blindfolded, and one by one are brought near the *piñata.* Each child is given a stick, spun round three times, and told to hit the *piñata* hard with the stick. But they are bound to miss the first time – for the *piñata* will be pulled up out of reach. When each child has had at least one try, the *piñata* is lowered within range. The *piñata* may not rip open the first time it is hit, but as soon as it breaks and the treats shower down, the children are allowed to remove their blindfolds and scramble about to pick up as much as they can.

234

Materials

Ready-to-mix papier-mâché, or wallpaper paste and newspaper.

A balloon, 1 foot in diameter when it is inflated.

Eight pieces of cardboard: 6 by 16 inches (head), $5\frac{1}{2}$ inches square (top of head), 3 by 8 inches (upper beak), $2\frac{1}{2}$ by 3 inches (lower beak), 4 inches square (eyelashes), 12 by 15 inches (wings), 12 inches square (tail), and 7 by 12 inches (feet).

Two wooden dowels, 2 inches long, $\frac{1}{4}$ inch in diameter.

A screw-eye.

All-purpose glue.

Adhesive tape.

Poster paint.

Crepe paper (optional).

Thin rope or cord, about 8 feet long.

Filling for the *piñata*: candies, nuts, confetti, etc.

Tools

A stapler, drawing compass, pencil, scissors, and ruler.

How to Make the Game

Blow up the balloon; tie off its mouth. Cover the balloon with an even layer of papier-mâché. (If you do not use ready-to-mix papier-mâché, blend shredded newspaper with wallpaper paste until the mixture has a plaster-like consistency.) Let the papier-mâché dry naturally in a moderately warm, airy place. When the form is completely dry, deflate the balloon.

To make the head of the owl, take the 6-by-16-inch piece of cardboard and curve it lengthwise into a circle; staple the two upper corners together. Draw a circle $5\frac{1}{2}$ inches in diameter on the $5\frac{1}{2}$-inch-square piece of cardboard and cut the circle out. Place the circle on top of the stapled section, trim off any overlap and fasten it down with adhesive tape.

Cut the upper section of the beak from the 3-by-8-inch section of cardboard, as shown on page 236. Crease it along the middle line and cut it along the slanting side lines shown in the figure. Overlap the cut sections and staple together. Fasten the beak to the middle of the owl's head with tape.

Draw the lower section of the beak freehand as shown opposite and cut it out. Curve it slightly and tape it to the head below the upper section of the beak, making sure the two beak sections join at the corners. Staple these joints together. Cut out a cardboard sliver for the tongue; tape it between the beaks.

Totally absorbed in their work, a family of piñata-*makers in Mexico City construct a large and intricate bird to be smashed asunder at a forthcoming Christmastime* posada.

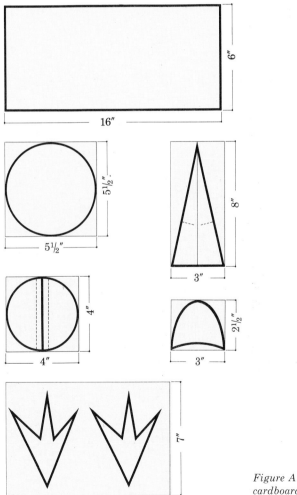

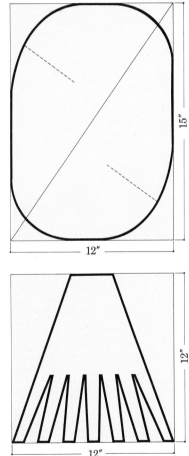

Figure A: These eight components, cut from cardboard and covered with papier-mâché, will be the head, wings, feet, and tail of the bird.

1: Pat an even layer of the papier-mâché mixture over the balloon; when the papier-mâché has dried, deflate and remove the balloon.

2: After coating the wing sections with papier-mâché, attach them to the body of the piñata with a series of layers of the mixture.

Draw a circle 4 inches in diameter on the 4-inch-square piece of cardboard. Draw a line dividing the circle in two, as shown below. Draw parallel lines ¼ inch on either side of the dividing line and score these two lines with a scissor blade. Cut out the two semicircles and bend up the base of each at the scored line. Tape these sections to the owl's head, on either side of the beak and slightly above it.

Place the head on top of the *piñata* shell. Cover all components of the head with a thin layer of papier-mâché, and mold small spheres for the eyes of the bird. Glue the head of the owl to the body with papier-mâché and allow to dry.

Draw a diagonal line from corner to corner of the 12-by-15-inch piece of cardboard. Draw freehand the design shown below. Cut the two wings out; then cut a line on each wing, from the curve of the wing, halfway toward the base. Overlap the cut sections about 1 inch and staple the overlapping edges together.

Cover the wings with a thin layer of papier-mâché, and allow them to dry. Glue the wings to the owl's body with papier-mâché and put books under the wings to support them while the joints are drying.

Cut the bird's tail from the 12-inch-square section of cardboard, as shown below. Cut out the bird's tail and cover one side with a thin layer of papier-mâché. It will curl as it dries. Turn the owl over and glue the feathers to the owl's tail, with the curling side pointing downward. Support with books to prevent sagging while the joint dries.

With the scissors, gouge two holes at the bottom of the owl's body, large enough to accommodate the wooden dowels. With papier-mâché glue the dowel ends into the holes, then build up their surfaces with the mixture. Allow them to dry.

On the 7-by-12-inch piece of cardboard, draw the feet and cut them out. Cover them with a thin layer of papier-mâché and allow to dry; then fasten them to the ends of the dowels with more papier-mâché.

After the *piñata* has dried, paint it in gay colors and, if you like, decorate it with strips of crepe paper. Cut a hole in the back of the *piñata* and fill it with assorted treats. Cover the hole by gluing a piece of cardboard over it. Apply papier-mâché to the patch and allow it to dry.

Attach a screw-eye to the back of the *piñata* and attach one end of the rope or cord to it. The *piñata* is now ready to be hung and smashed to pieces.

Delighting their whole neighborhood in suburban Bombay, an agile crowd of Indian youths play a precarious variation of piñata. *A deluge of water indicates success on the part of the striker at the apex of the swaying pyramid of human bodies.*

The pyramid collapses and eager arms reach for the treats contained in a series of bags. Other members of the team help to drag the rope down to ground level before they move on to the next high-strung challenge in another part of town.

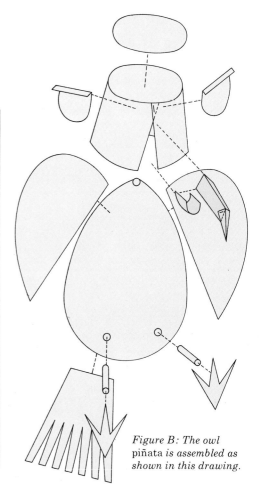

Figure B: The owl piñata *is assembled as shown in this drawing.*

Ring the Bull

About the Game

The swing to sophisticated lounge bars in many parts of Britain has bestowed the kiss of death on many old pub games. In the more traditionally-minded regions, however, such as East Anglia, Dorset, and along the Welsh border, ring the bull still goes down as well as a pint of beer. The game probably developed from an early form of indoor quoits, using the same rings with which farmers actually pierced the noses of their bulls.

How to Play the Game

Standing four feet from the board, the player tries to impale each of the two strung rings on one of the five 'horns.' Each hooked ring counts as one point. There are 12 tries in a turn. Any number can join in; the player with the highest score wins the round.

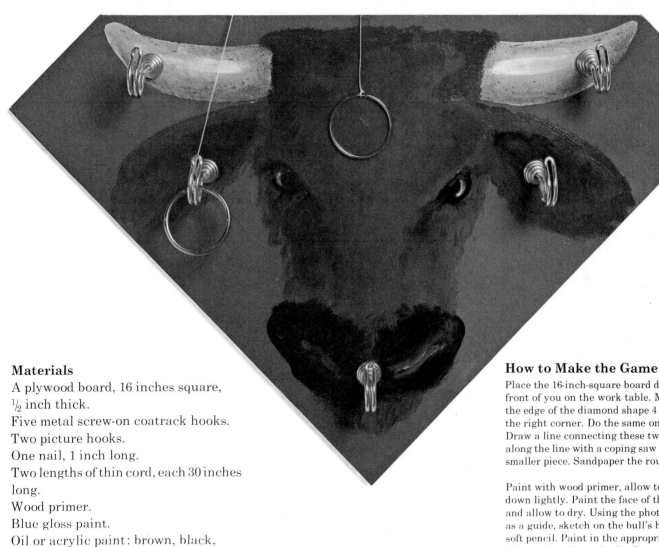

Materials

A plywood board, 16 inches square, $\frac{1}{2}$ inch thick.
Five metal screw-on coatrack hooks.
Two picture hooks.
One nail, 1 inch long.
Two lengths of thin cord, each 30 inches long.
Wood primer.
Blue gloss paint.
Oil or acrylic paint: brown, black, yellow, and white.

Tools

A primer brush, paintbrush, artist's camel-hair brush, coping saw, soft pencil, sandpaper, and hammer.

This eye-catching ring the bull board is very similar to those commonly found in British pubs. When drawing the bull on your own game board, follow the design painted on this model.

How to Make the Game

Place the 16-inch-square board diagonally in front of you on the work table. Mark a point on the edge of the diamond shape 4 inches above the right corner. Do the same on the left side. Draw a line connecting these two points. Cut along the line with a coping saw and discard the smaller piece. Sandpaper the rough edges.

Paint with wood primer, allow to dry, then sand down lightly. Paint the face of the board blue and allow to dry. Using the photograph at left as a guide, sketch on the bull's head with a soft pencil. Paint in the appropriate colors, and allow to dry. Screw in the five coatrack hooks as in the photographed model.

Attach a curtain ring to one end of each of the two lengths of string, tying the free ends through the screw-eye. To attach the bull board to the wall, hang it as you would a painting, at eye level. Suspend the strings from a hook attached to the wall 21 inches above the board.

Egg Jousting

About the Game

With their purity of form and the new life they hold, eggs figure prominently in religious symbolism. Before Christianity, egg games were part of pagan rites connected with the sowing of the crops. Later, the Easter egg symbolized the Resurrection in activities such as egg hunts, egg rolling, and egg painting. During springtime feast days in Syria, Afghanistan, and parts of Russia, two children joust with colored eggs, the game ending whenever the supply of one or the other happens to run out.

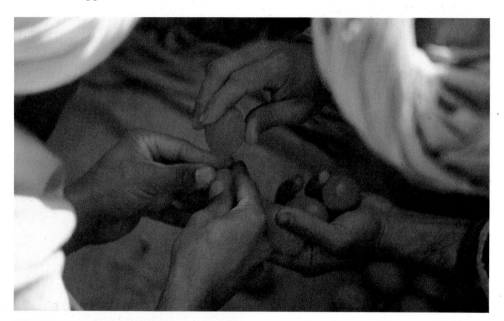

How to Make the Game

Red is the traditional coloring used in egg games and a subtle hue can be obtained by using a 'natural' dye. Shred a chopped onion into a panful of boiling water and boil until the water turns yellow. Cool, then strain. Add vinegar until the water turns the desired shade of red and soak your hard-boiled egg for at least one hour, making sure it is covered. As an alternative, you may repeat this process with beet juice and vinegar, or madder (if available) and vinegar. After the eggs have dried, give them a sheen by rubbing in a little salad oil.

A jouster urges his opponent to reveal more of the egg before he makes his first strike (above). Experience tells an Afghan child, left, that he has picked a winner as he tests an egg against his teeth before adding it to his arsenal. After the joust, the children sell their captured eggs in the teahouses at lunchtime; the profits are apt to be spent on small cakes, candies and other treats.

How to Play the Game

In western Asia, egg jousting begins with a formal challenge. In this traditional dialogue, the 'head' is the pointed tip of the egg, the 'heel' the rounded end of the shell.
The challenger begins by saying, 'With my head I will break your head.'
A boy with a very hard-shelled egg might even boast, 'With my head I will break your head and your heel.'

His opponent may suggest, 'If your egg's so hard, let's see if I can break my own head and heel with your heel.' If he does make this counter-challenge, he has first try in the contest; otherwise, he wraps his hand tightly around the egg, leaving only the tip visible, and says, 'Then break it!' If the challenger objects, 'There's not very much of it showing,' his opponent must move his hand to reveal a bit more of the shell. If the challenger feels that it is a fair contest, he strikes it with the head of his own egg. But if he doubts that he can break it, he says, 'I'll show you more than that,' and they switch eggs. The challenger holds his opponent's egg while the other player strikes it with the challenger's egg.

When the head of an egg is cracked, the egg is turned over to see if the heel will fare any better. But once both head and heel are cracked, the egg is surrendered to the owner of the surviving egg, and the loser must produce another egg to stay in the game. The game continues until one jouster has no more uncracked eggs.

'With my head I will break your head!' A jouster challenges his opponent amid the bustle of a Kabul marketplace, opposite, in this photograph by Roland and Sabrina Michaud. In areas where guinea fowl are raised (their shells are tougher than hen eggs) children scrutinize each other's eggs for speckles which warn them that their opponent is trying to sneak in a 'battering egg.'

238

Camel Rush

About the Game

'How many men can fit on the back of a camel?' is a question spectacularly answered by the game of camel rush. It occurs every October at the Pushkar camel and cattle fair in Rajasthan, India, during the two weeks preceding *kartikya purnima,* the night of the full moon. Two men tease the camel onto its haunches and place one foot on each folded foreleg to prevent it from rising. The participants mount; those climbing onto the neck face the tail, and those scaling from behind face the neck. By this time, the camel is complaining loudly 'with mouth wide open and its teeth showing,' according to the photographer, Raghubir Singh. At the moment of the great release, the camel rises and soon unseats those with a weak hold. The participants who successfully weather the storm are cheered by the crowd.

Turbans bobbing, hardy desert tribesmen of Rajasthan, opposite, 'rush' the grounded camel, in a games highlight of the Pushkar camel fair.

Rajasthanis take time off from the buying and selling of cattle to watch the progress of the 'rush.' The camel growls impatiently as two wary officials restrain it from shaking off its riders as they climb on board (left). Amid cheers from the crowd (above), the camel rises with seven men firmly ensconced on its back and one determined participant 'strapped' on by a helping leg.

How to Play the Game

If there are no camels grazing in your backyard, you will have to search a bit for an equally intriguing substitute. Most western versions of camel rush follow the same principle. Children delight in piling onto the back of a good-natured adult. For those with more adventurous tastes, the collegiate stunt of cramming into a telephone booth is great fun and a good way of keeping warm on cold days! The sturdy little 'beetle' car is often a target for the 'rush,' though it helps to be a contortionist when crowding into cars. For the player with an active imagination, the 'how many men in a...' syndrome is endless. Try a wheelbarrow, barrel, bed, table, or an empty bath tub. It might be interesting to see how many can fit on a bicycle and stay there as it is pedaled off. And if you ever spend October in Rajasthan, don't forget the camel fair!

Stilts

About the Game

Dressed in gaudy costumes and often wearing grotesque masks, stilt-walkers are a traditional feature of festivals and circus parades. In many parts of the world children love to walk on stilts and play stilt games. Maori children of New Zealand, for instance, play games on stilts made out of wineberry tree or *manuka* (a common tree in the bush country). In some parts of Africa, however, stilts are forbidden to children, being the prerogative of the tribal priests in performing their magic rites.

Although they are now used mainly for amusement, stilts were probably invented for the practical purpose of enabling people to travel in marshy or flooded areas. The Landes region of France is particularly famous for its stilt-walkers; the farmers and shepherds spend many of their working hours on stilts, and may carry long staves topped with plank seats, on which they can rest. In 1891 a baker from Landes stilt-walked from Paris to Moscow in 58 days.

Virtuoso stilt-walkers dazzle a Spanish carnival crowd, below, in a painting by Francisco de Goya.

How to Play the Game

Stilt-walking is just a matter of practice and confidence. Beginners should use low stilts that can be mounted from a block or chair seat, and practice in an open space for safety. As balance improves, players can graduate to higher stilts.

Follow the leader is a simple stilt game. One child is elected 'leader' and the others must follow his steps, imitating every movement he makes.

Stilt races are a test of speed as well as skill, and simple obstacles along the course add to the fun.

Materials

Two wooden poles, each 68 inches long, $1\frac{1}{2}$ inches in diameter.

Two pine boards, each $6\frac{1}{2}$ by 13 inches, 1 inch thick.

Two wooden balls, $2\frac{1}{2}$ inches in diameter.

Two wooden dowels, $2\frac{1}{2}$ inches long, $\frac{3}{8}$ inch in diameter.

Six flat-head screws, 3 inches long.

Wood primer. Wood glue.

Gloss paints: green, red, and blue.

White plastic adhesive tape (optional).

Tools

A ruler, pencil, coping saw, sandpaper, vise, backsaw, electric drill or brace with a $\frac{3}{16}$-inch bit and a $\frac{3}{8}$-inch auger bit, wood rasp, primer brush, paintbrush, and screwdriver.

In a stilt game at Bandung, Java, cakes and candies are hung from a cord. The children must keep their balance on stilts while trying – without using their hands – to bite off a tempting mouthful.

Easily constructed in a few hours, these colorful, sturdy stilts are designed especially for children.

How to Make the Game

Measure and mark each of the two wooden boards as shown in the pattern at right. With a coping saw, cut out the two brackets; then sand down all rough edges.

Clamp one of the wooden poles in the vise, and mark points 12 inches and 24 inches from one end. With the backsaw, cut across the pole at each of these points to a depth of about $\frac{1}{4}$ inch.

Loosen the vise and turn the pole so that the back side of the partially-sawed surface is facing you. Measuring from the same end of the pole, mark points at 14 inches, 18 inches, and 22 inches. Using the $\frac{3}{16}$-inch bit, drill holes through the pole at these points.

Attach the $\frac{3}{8}$-inch auger bit to the drill and drill a short distance, about $\frac{1}{4}$ inch, into the three holes. (These wider openings will allow the screw-heads to rest flush with the pole.) With the same bit, drill a hole $1\frac{1}{4}$ inches deep in the exact center of the other end of the pole. Repeat these steps with the second pole.

With the wood rasp, file away the section between the two lines sawed on each of the poles. File to a depth of $\frac{1}{4}$ inch; the area should be flat and level. Sand rough edges.

Clamp one wooden ball in the vise and file down one side of it to make a flat surface $1\frac{1}{2}$ inches in diameter. In the center of this surface, drill a hole $1\frac{1}{4}$ inches deep with the $\frac{3}{8}$-inch bit. Repeat these steps on the remaining ball.

With the primer brush, apply a prime coat to all the wooden pieces. Allow to dry thoroughly, then lightly sandpaper each piece. Paint the

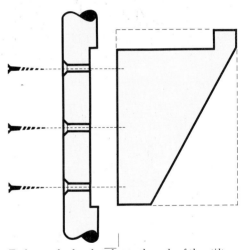

To fasten the foot bracket to the pole of the stilt, position the straight edge of the bracket against the leveled surface of the pole; secure the bracket first with wood glue, then with screws.

sections as shown in the model at left and allow the paint to dry. (If you wish, decorate the stilts with thin strips of white plastic tape.)

Apply glue to each of the dowels and place one in the hole at the top of each pole. Press the balls onto the exposed sections of dowel so that the balls are flush with the tops of the poles. Allow the glue to dry thoroughly.

Position the brackets in the grooves of the poles, after coating both surfaces with glue. Screw the brackets firmly to the poles.

Potato-Sack Racing

About the Game
Potato-sack racing is a popular activity during the summer holidays. It is often played at picnics and birthday parties that are held outdoors. It's hectic. It's fun. All it requires is an old burlap sack and a good sense of balance. Potato-sack racing is played throughout many areas of the United States – usually on such national holidays as Labor Day and the Fourth of July.

Materials
A strong burlap sack for each person participating in the race.

A trio of potato-sack racers approach the finish line at a holiday event in Germany.

How to Play the Game
Participants climb into their burlap sacks at the starting line. Holding up their sacks waist-high, they stand poised in a row, waiting for the signal. This is usually given by an elected bystander who either fires a cap pistol in the air or shouts, "Go!" When the signal is given, the racers begin hopping along the track toward the finish line. A potato-sack racer who purposely bumps into another contestant in an attempt to make him fall is immediately disqualified. A racer who falls on his own can stand up again in his sack and continue the race. The contestant who reaches the finish line first is the winner. There is usually a referee at the finish line who decides who the winner is in the case of a tie or near tie. In all cases, the decision of the referee is final.

Potato-sack racing should be done on a field or lawn – not on the playground pavement or in the street. The beginning and end points of the racetrack should be marked off with stones or posts; these can be decorated with crepe-paper flyers of various colors or paint. The length of the track is usually from 100 to 150 feet. You may want to mark the track to help young racers find their way.

Hobble Racing

About the Game

Hobble races are high on the list of activities whenever children congregate at holiday outings or picnics. Run strictly for laughs, these races provide just as much fun for the spectators as the players prove that it is definitely not as easy as it looks! For the lucky player who does not end up in a heap of scrambled legs, a prize waits at the finish line.

Restricted both by long skirts and bound knees, young Parisiennes, below, line up at the start of a hobble race at the Artists' Festival of 1910.

How to Play the Game

This is a good game for ten children. Knees tied together, the players gather at the starting line of the 150-yard track; on a signal from one of the spectators, they're off! Players jump, waddle, hop, creep – in fact, make any movement that will deliver them to the finish line. One player who purposefully bumps another is disqualified. The first racer to cross the finish line – on foot or on all fours – is the winner of the race.

The three-legged race is another favorite hobble race. At least twenty children should join in, each choosing a partner; two players of roughly the same height and weight will make a better team than 'Mutt-and-Jeff' types. One player ties his right ankle to his partner's left ankle with a large cotton handkerchief. Before the race begins, each pair should decide which 'leg' will make the first step. At a signal from the referee, the players race for the finish line. Casualities may untangle themselves and continue. The first pair to cross the finish line wins the race.

Metal-shafted darts, such as the set at right, were invented in 1936, when a Hungarian living in England decided to improve on the paperflighted wooden darts then being used in his local pub. Darts players today have a choice of commercially-made darts in different sizes and weights to suit their playing style. The dart flights may be made of paper, plastic, or feathers; expert players favor those made from four wing feathers of turkeys.

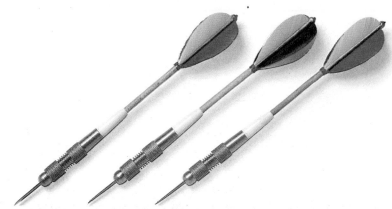

A player throws a dart and strikes 20, or 'tops,' in a pub in Essex, England (above), while his opponent tallies the score. Traditionally the loser buys a pint of beer for the winner of the game.

One dart out of three has scored a double 16 (far left) which can be used to start or finish a game. A good darts player can land his darts in a close group. When a player completes his turn, he takes his darts from the board (left) while his opponent chalks up the new total on the scoreboard.

Darts

About the Game

The sturdy archers of medieval England were the first darts players. These yeomen carried short, heavy, throwing arrows which they used for self-defense at close quarters. At the end of the day, the archers would entertain themselves by throwing these arrows at the butt end of a cut-down tree. In the winter, someone thought of hanging a sawed-off section of tree trunk on the tavern wall, and thus darts came to move indoors. (Even today, the term 'your arrow' instead of 'your turn' can be heard in many English darts games.)

From these rude beginnings darts grew into the refined pastime of the Tudor court. Anne Boleyn, mother of Queen Elizabeth I, presented her husband Henry VIII with a set of 'dartes of Biscayan fashion, richly ornamented.' The game was introduced to America by the Pilgrims, who played a version of darts as they sailed to Massachusetts on the Mayflower in 1620.

Darts is one of the most popular games of Britain. Virtually every well-appointed British pub boasts a regulation dart board. According to informed estimates, there are more than seven million players in the land – over a million of them in registered clubs and leagues. The game is also popular in many other parts of the world, including the United States, which has some two million players.

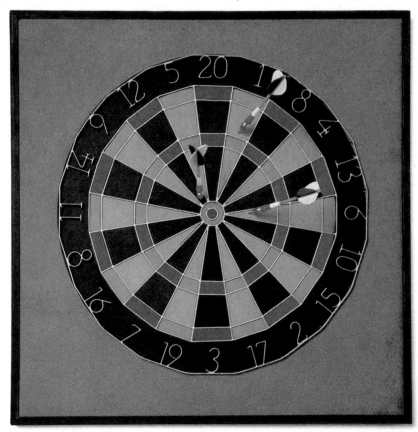

Both beginners and expert players will enjoy playing darts on this colorful and easily-made board, which is an enjoyable crafts project and a decorative feature on the wall of any games room.

How to Play the Game

The dart board, usually made of cork, bristle, or elm, is a circle divided into 20 pie-shaped segments. Each segment is numbered with its scoring value. In addition there is a narrow outer circle which, when hit by a dart, gives double the usual value of the segment that it intersects. The narrow inner circle gives triple the usual score. The inner circle of the bull's-eye is worth 50 points, and its outer section scores 25 points. The board should be hung on the wall so that the bull's-eye is exactly 5 feet 8 inches from the floor.

Darts can be played by two or three people, playing individually. If there are more players, they are usually divided into two teams. Each player has three darts, which are all thrown in a turn. In team play, turns alternate between the two teams. Within a team, players take their turns in sequence (no 'pinch-hitting'). All darts must be thrown from behind a line drawn 8 feet from the board.

To begin the game, each player throws a dart at the bull's-eye; the closest dart wins the first turn. Each player begins with a score of 301. After each turn, the player subtracts his score from the 301, or what remains of it later in the game.

To even begin to score, however, a player must first throw a 'double,' that is, one of his darts must land in the narrow outer circle. If, for instance, a dart lands in the outer rim of the '14' segment, the player scores by subtracting 28 (14 doubled) from the original 301. (If he still has darts to throw after making the first double, the score made with those darts is subtracted too.)

After the first double is made in order to begin scoring, any score is counted. Darts which land in the black outer circle, land off the board, or fall off the board make no score for that turn. The game must be finished on a double score, as well. For example, if there are only 8 points left, the player tries for a double '4,' or, if his first dart lands on the '2' segment, a double '3.' The three darts in a turn are always counted together and, if the total score is more than what is needed, none of the darts count.

The winner is the first player or team to finish the game. When four people play in pairs, the beginning score is 501; for larger teams, it is 1,001. Tournament games are played in three 'legs' or rounds.

Darts ideas from a turn-of-the-century French book: throw needles, threaded with a few inches of cotton, at a target chalked on cloth; or slot a folded-paper flight into a broken pen nib.

Materials
Chipboard, 24 inches square, $\frac{1}{4}$ inch thick.
Acoustical ceiling tile, 24 inches square, $\frac{1}{2}$ inch thick.
A 5-yard spool of wire, $\frac{1}{8}$ inch thick.
Four strips of picture-frame molding, each $24\frac{1}{2}$ inches long, one side $\frac{1}{2}$ inch, the other $\frac{3}{4}$ inch, and $\frac{1}{4}$ inch thick.
All-purpose glue.
Wood glue.
Solder.
Paint: black, yellow, red, and blue.
Aluminum paint.
Three purchased darts for each player.

Tools
A ruler, pencil, drawing compass with collapsible legs, protractor, paint-brush, razor blade, multi-purpose pliers, and two short pieces of wooden dowel, one 1 inch in diameter and the other 2 inches in diameter.

How to Make the Game
With ruler and pencil, draw two straight diagonal lines across the square from corner to corner. The point where they intersect is the center of the board.

Placing the needle of the adaptable compass at the center, draw a series of concentric circles by setting the compass for radii of $\frac{1}{2}$ inch, 1 inch, 4 inches, $4\frac{3}{4}$ inches, $6\frac{1}{2}$ inches, $7\frac{1}{2}$ inches, and $9\frac{1}{2}$ inches.

Place the protractor at the center of the board, lining up its bottom edge with one of the diagonals, so that its perpendicular is in line with the other diagonal. Divide each of the two 90-degree segments of the half circle into five 18-degree sections. Repeat on the other half of the circle.

Paint the 3-inch and $2\frac{3}{4}$-inch sections of alternate segments with black paint. Work carefully. As the material is porous, you can prevent the paint from spreading into another section by first sticking the side of a razor blade along the line of that section, then painting against it, as shown in photograph 1. Paint the outermost circle black in the same manner.

Paint the alternate 3-inch and $2\frac{3}{4}$-inch sections yellow. Paint the outer circle of the bull's-eye blue, as well as the unpainted narrow sections of the black segments. Paint the alternate unpainted sections of the yellow segments, as well as the bull's-eye, with red paint.

Apply a generous coat of wood glue to the chipboard square and place the target board, face up, directly on it, so that their dimensions match exactly. Allow the glue to dry thoroughly.

Using an electric drill or a brace with a $\frac{1}{8}$-inch bit, drill holes at several well-spaced points on the inner edge of the black circle. Drill a hole on the outer edge of the outer bull's-eye section and another hole on the outer edge of the inner bull's-eye. Drill the holes $\frac{1}{2}$ inch deep.

Wrap a short length of wire around a wooden dowel 2 inches in diameter. Cut off the excess and solder the ends of the wire circle together. Cut a $\frac{1}{2}$-inch length of wire from the spool and solder it perpendicularly to the wire circle. Plant this 'foot' in the hole drilled in the outer edge of the larger bull's-eye section; position the wire circle directly over the bull's-eye area.

Cut off 20 lengths of wire, each $6\frac{1}{2}$ inches long. Straighten them, then solder them to the rim of the wire bull's-eye circle, following the boundary lines of the 20 segments. Tape the wires down with masking tape to keep them in place.

Cut off $\frac{1}{2}$-inch lengths of wire and position them in the foot-holes provided along the inner edge

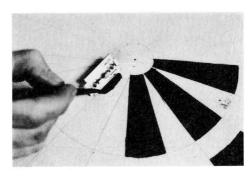

1: Carefully paint each segment, pressing a razor blade deep into the tile to prevent each color of paint from being absorbed beyond the line.

2: Drill holes on the inner edge of the black circle. These holes are for the wire 'feet' which will anchor the metal trim to the board.

3: Cut ½-inch pieces of wire and position them in the drilled holes. These 'feet' should be well spaced around the circumference of the board.

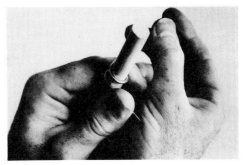

4: Form the bull's-eye around a length of dowel. Bend the wire into a circle, trim off the excess, and solder the ends of the wire together.

5: When the 20 wire 'spokes' are soldered to the bull's-eye and taped down, solder them to the wire rim as you bend it into the proper position.

6: With a dowel and long-nosed pliers, fashion numbers 1 through 20, then solder them to the wire ring at the outer edge of the circle.

of the black circle. Then, cut a 50-inch length of wire and, bending it where necessary, solder it to the ends of the 20 wire 'spokes' that are taped to the board as shown in photograph 5. The parts of this 50-inch length of wire that come into contact with the positioned feet must be soldered to them too. Cut off excess wire.

Cut off sections of wire from the spool to match the dimensions of the horizontal borders remaining in each segment. Solder these between the vertical wires.

Wrap a short length of wire around a dowel, 1 inch in diameter. Cut off the excess and solder the two ends together. Solder a ½-inch foot to this circle, then position the circle over the bull's-eye, placing the foot in the hole provided.

With ruler and pencil, extend the lines of the vertical segment-dividers to the edge of the board. Drill a hole on each line on the outer edge of the black circle. Cut off 20 lengths of wire, ½ inch long, and position one in each hole. Cut a 60-inch length of wire and solder it to these feet, bending it where necessary to conform to the outer edge of the circle.

Using the smaller piece of dowel and long-nose pliers to bend and shape the wire, fashion numbers as shown in photograph 6. Arrange the numbers in the proper sequence and place them so that each number falls within a lane of

one of the 20 sections. Solder the numbers to the outer rim of wire so that they lie in the outer black circle.
Remove all soldered wire sections from the board and paint them with aluminum paint. Allow to dry thoroughly.

Prepare the strips of picture-frame molding for miter joints by the following method. Clamp the ¾-inch side of the picture-frame molding in a vise so that the ½-inch side is flat before you. The cornered edge of the molding lies toward you. Line up the perpendicular of the protractor with the edge of the left end of this side; the base of the protractor should be in line with the cornered edge of the molding. Mark a point on the top edge that is 45 degrees from the corner edge. Draw a line from the corner edge to that point. Do the same at the right end of the molding, marking a 45-degree angle toward the left.

Using a backsaw, miter both sides of the left end of the molding simultaneously, while sawing along the line drawn. Do the same at the right end of the molding. Prepare the remaining three strips for miter joints, following the steps given.

Spread glue on the inner sides of the four prepared strips, then fasten them to the sides of the game board. Place the board face down on the work table. Allow the glue to dry thoroughly. Spread glue on the feet of the wire sections and position them in the holes in the board.

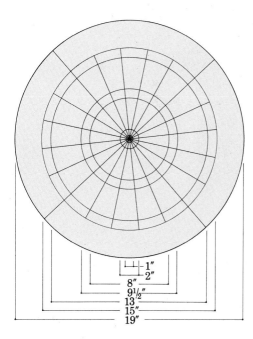

After drawing the diagonals from corner to corner of the tile square, set the needle of the compass at the point of intersection and draw seven circles. The diagonals will divide the circular board into quarters which can be divided again into the twenty 18-degree scoring sections.

An Eskimo woman from the Thule district of Greenland plays ajaqaq, *trying to impale the hollow bone on the pointed stick. 'Done by an Eskimo with plenty of practice, it looks ridiculously simple,' observes the photographer Fred Bruemmer. When he tried the game, he had 'about fifty misses before one solitary success.'*

Bilboquet

About the Game

Bilboquet – alias ring-and-pin or cup-and-ball – is a game of skill played under a variety of local names in many parts of the world. A bilboquet may be made of wood, bone, ivory, or plastic, but the object is always the same – to catch the dangling ball, bone, or ring on a pin or cup held in the hand. It looks simple enough when an Eskimo does it, impaling a bone on a stick nine times out of ten, but the knack is not easily acquired, and those who have mastered the art have every right to be proud of their accomplishment.

Though English writers, such as Jane Austen, sometimes refer to it as 'bilbocatch,' the word is actually French and has nothing to do with 'catch' – it derives from *bille*, a wooden ball, and *bocquet*, the point of a spear. There was a time when 'the noble game of bilboquet' (as Horace Walpole called it) was the pastime of kings and courtiers. In sixteenth-century France Henri III liked to play with a bilboquet as he strolled through his palaces and the streets of Paris.

The Canadian Eskimos call it *ajaqaq* and carve it from the bones of the animals they hunt. Traditionally endowed with great magic, it was played in the winter or early spring, for the game itself was supposed to hasten the long-awaited return of the sun. The Northwest-coast Indians also took a serious interest in the game. Heavy bets were made on the Kwakiutl version, called *dzagzegala:* the stakes were canoes, slaves, women, and even the chiefs' cherished 'coppers' – heavy copper plates inscribed with totemic designs.

Ajaqaq, the Eskimo bilboquet, is made of bone or walrus ivory and animal sinew. The example above, a curved horn with a bone peg, comes from the Canadian Northwest Territories. Several holes are usually drilled into such bilboquets, each with its own scoring value. During the dark months of the Arctic winter, when it is too cold for outdoor games, pastimes such as ajaqaq, cards, dice, string games, and dancing are essential to good spirits among the Eskimos.

A post or leg, salvaged from an old wooden chair, lends a Victorian silhouette to a three-ball bilboquet you can easily make yourself.

Piercing the musk-ox horn with a pointed bone is child's play to this Netsilingmiut Eskimo woman of Spence Bay in the Northwest Territories.

How to Play the Game

The object of bilboquet is simply to catch the ball on the pointed stick. In the version shown here, there are three balls. You begin by swinging the first ball above the stick, while the others are held alongside the handle. The wooden handle is grasped firmly in one hand and, with a flick of the wrist, the ball is swung up above the pin. Once the player has impaled one ball, he tries for the next while the first remains on the stick. The game is over when all three balls are caught on the wooden pin.

Variations:

On some bilboquets, one end of the handle is slightly cupped; the other holds the pin. The player first tries to balance the ball in the cup, then to catch it on the stick.

In a Japanese version of the game, there are three cups instead of one, each cup of a different size: a small cup on the end of the handle, with a medium-sized and a still larger cup positioned at opposite sides of the handle at the base of the pin.

The Eskimo game *ajaqaq* uses a bone or the skull of a small animal, such as a rabbit, in place of the ball. The bone may have several holes of different sizes: some are easier to hit than others. There is an elaborate scoring system.

Materials

A wooden handle, roughly 10 inches long and $1\frac{1}{2}$ inches in diameter (this can be a furniture scrap: a section of lamp base, a chair post, etc).
An 8-inch dowel, $\frac{3}{16}$ inch in diameter.
Three 16-inch strands of rawhide shoelace.
Three wooden balls, 2 inches in diameter, each having a $\frac{1}{2}$-inch hole running through the center.
Gloss paint: red, yellow green, and blue.
Four medium screw-eyes.
All-purpose glue.

Tools

An electric drill or brace with $\frac{3}{16}$-inch bit (and $\frac{1}{2}$-inch bit for the balls if you cannot obtain balls with holes already drilled), vise, sandpaper, and paintbrush.

How to Make the Game

Clamp the wooden handle in a vise so that the base of it is facing you. Using the $\frac{3}{16}$-inch bit in the drill, bore a hole in the center of the base $\frac{3}{4}$ inch deep. Sand down one end of the dowel to a slight point. Apply glue generously to the opposite end of the dowel and insert it in the hole in the handle. Allow to dry thoroughly.

Paint the pin and handle green. Paint each ball a different color, red, blue, or yellow. Allow the paint to dry thoroughly.

About $\frac{1}{2}$ inch from a hole in each ball, screw in a screw-eye. Position the fourth screw-eye in the handle about 1 inch from the base of the pin. String a strand of rawhide through the screw-eye in each ball and glue about 1 inch of overlap back on the strand. Clamp with paperclips until it dries. String the loose ends of the three strands through the screw-eye in the handle and glue about $1\frac{1}{2}$ inches of overlap back on the strand. Clip until the glue is dry.

The perils of a bilboquet in the hands of a determined but unskilled addict are depicted below in a nineteenth-century French cartoon.

Cat's Cradle

About the Game

People of almost every culture in the world know how to make cat's cradles, figures of string woven between the hands. But it is something of a puzzle to ethnologists that people of widely separated regions – from the Maori of New Zealand to the Arctic Eskimos, from North American Indians to African tribesmen – make certain string figures which are exactly the same.

The Japanese call it a girl's game, but many adult men are familiar with the string figures. Among the Chugach Eskimos, too, it is traditionally girls who make cat's cradles, for if boys were to play the game, their fingers might later get caught in their harpoon lines while they are hunting. The Chugach girls play it in autumn, believing that it can delay the onset of the dark winter days by entangling the legs of the departing sun. Some Eskimo tribes forbid cat's cradle except in the winter; while others place no restrictions of age, sex, or playing season upon the string games.

Often special songs or rhymes are sung during the making of a string figure, relating an accompanying story. A player may extend a single figure into a long series of linked figures, altering each one by moving his hands, using his teeth or even his toes as a third hand, or passing the string to the fingers of another player. The tales and legends recounted with these figures are complex and ancient, and are handed down in the same way from generation to generation.

How to Play the Game

The only equipment needed to make any kind of cat's cradle is two yards of soft, pliable string or cord, fastened into a circle with a square knot (as illustrated below).

In the directions that follow, the fingers are referred to as thumb, index, middle, ring, and little. In constructing figures, the strands of string near the body are called the 'near strings,' and strands or loops further from the body, 'far strings.' String lying in front of the palm is called 'palmar string.'

A Navaho Indian from the southwestern United States, below, holds up a cat's cradle string figure he has deftly woven. The Navaho are so expert at this game that ethnologists have coined a new word in their honor: in making a cat's cradle, when a lower loop is lifted over a higher loop on the same finger, the loop is said to be 'Navahoed.'

The instructions may seem a little difficult to follow at first, but as you construct the figures with the help of the photographed positions, everything should fall into place. As with any game involving manual dexterity, practice makes perfect.

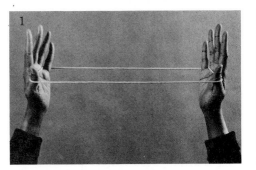

To make the basic cat's cradle, put the string behind your thumbs and little fingers, so that it crosses your palms, as in position 1, above. Now put your right index finger under the left palmar string, and the left index finger under the right palmar string. Draw both

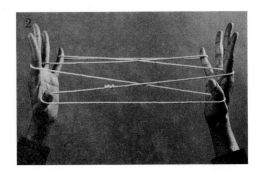

hands apart, to arrive at position 2 (above), the basic cat's cradle.
In most string figures you will find that the palms will be facing each other. This position is usually repeated after each movement.

Fish spear
Starting with position 1, pick up the left palmar string from underneath, with your right index finger. Twist it down away from you and up toward you twice as you draw your hands apart (position 3, below).

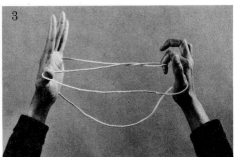

Pick up the right palmar string from underneath with your left index finger, passing it through the right index loop (see position 4, below). Do not twist.

Release your right thumb and little finger. Draw the figure tight, by pulling your right index finger away.

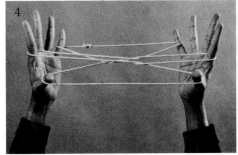

The final figure is shown in position 5, photographed below. Representing a trident or fishing spear, it is a popular string figure among some Indian tribes in the United States.

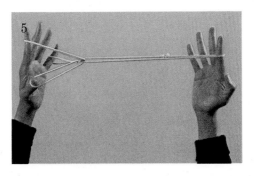

Outrigger canoe
Start by making a basic cat's cradle, as shown in positions 1 and 2.
Move your thumbs over the near index strings and under the far index strings. Bring your thumbs back, as shown in position 6, below.

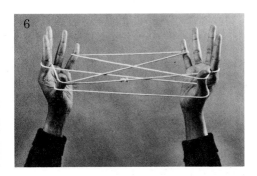

With your teeth, lift the lower loop on your thumbs up and over the thumbs, laying them on the loops you have just picked up (see position 7, below). Release your little fingers from their loops, and gently pull your hands apart until all the strings are taut.

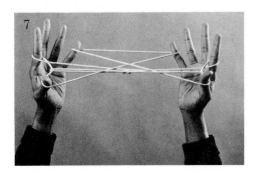

The final figure should now look like position 8, below. It represents a canoe joined to an outrigger with two poles. This string figure is made by Indians of British Columbia.

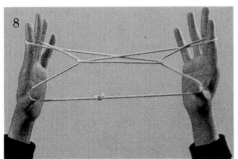

The mouse

Hold your left hand with the fingers pointing forward, away from you. With your right hand place the string loop over the left five fingers. Pass your right hand between your left palm and the palmar string, and with your right index finger, hook over and pull down a loop of string several inches long between the left thumb and index finger (see position 9, below). Give this

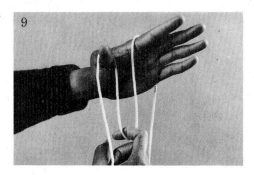

loop a twist away from you, then bring it around in front of the palmar string, toward you, and place the loop over your left index finger. (See position 10, below.) Tug gently on the hanging strings to tighten up the loops on your left thumb and index finger.

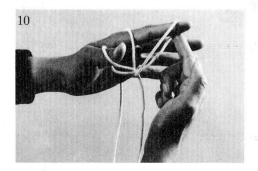

Again, pass your right hand between your left palm and the palmar string, and catch a loop between the index and middle fingers. Pull it down, give it a twist away from you, and place the loop over your middle finger. Repeat these steps with the ring and little fingers of your left hand, as in position 11, on page 258.

An old Eskimo man, right, relates a cat's cradle story to a rapt young listener. String figures, as an aid to the memory, help keep alive Eskimo legends that might otherwise have been forgotten.

Remove the loop from your left thumb so that it stands between the thumb and index finger. This loop is the 'mouse.' With your right hand, pull the palmar string and release the mouse from your left index finger, as in position 12, right. As you continue to pull, all the loops will come undone as the mouse 'runs away.' This figure is made by African Batwa pygmies.

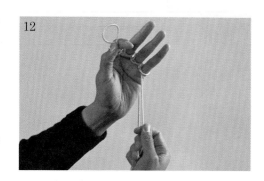

Fighting headhunters

Start with a basic cat's cradle (position 2). Bend your little fingers toward you, over four strings, and with the backs of these fingers pick up the near thumb strings; return the little fingers to their original position (see position 13, photographed below).

strings on your thumbs; return your little fingers to their original position.

There is a triangle in the middle of this stage, position 15 (below). Insert the tips of your index fingers into the triangle from below; spread your hands

three times with your thumbs and index fingers. Let these twisted loops hang down. The figure is now supported only by your little fingers (position 18, below).

The two hanging loops represent headhunters. By tugging the near little

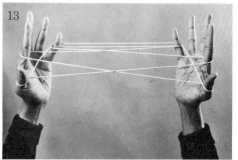

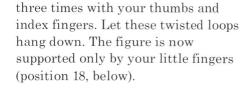

Release your thumbs from their loops. Pass your thumbs under the index finger loops, and with the backs of them pick of the near double strings on the little fingers; bring your thumbs back again to position 14, below. Release the little fingers from their loops. Bend your little fingers toward you, over the index loop and with the backs of them, take up the far double

apart. With your right thumb and index finger, lift the lower single index loop over the double loop near the top of your left index finger; let it fall on the palmar side. Reversing hand action, repeat this step (position 16, below). Release your thumbs from their loops (position 17, above right). Carefully drop the loops from your index fingers and twist them tightly

finger string gently with your left little finger you can bring the headhunters into direct confrontation; by manipulating the finger carefully, you can make them fight, kill each other and fall apart, or one kill the other and return home with his enemy's head. This string figure is made by the Murray islanders of the Torres Strait.

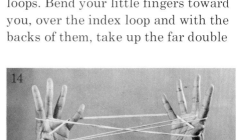

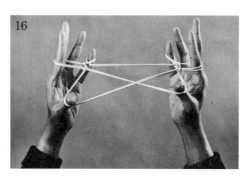

Breastbone and ribs

Place your hands inside the loop of string, so that the string passes behind each thumb, middle finger and little finger (position 19, below). With the right index finger, pick up the string in front of the left index finger from underneath, and take the right index finger back to its original position. Repeat with the left index finger, bringing back the string in front of the right index finger.

Tribal people from all over Africa, like the girl from Chad (above), make intricate string figures, usually representing humans, animals, or everyday objects. Often the figures illustrate a simple story.

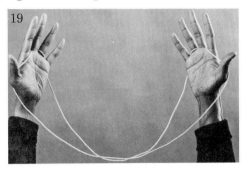

With the right ring finger pick up from underneath the string in front of the left ring finger, and take it back; repeat with the left ring finger. Now all fingers are looped, as shown in position 20, below.

Put your thumbs over the far thumb strings and in the index loop from underneath, then take the near index

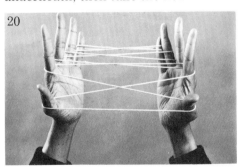

strings with the backs of your thumbs. Return thumbs to their original position. Using your teeth, pick up the lower loops on your thumbs and lift them over the upper thumb loops, then drop them on the palmar side, as in position 21, above right. Repeat this step three more times, each time using your thumb to take the near strings off

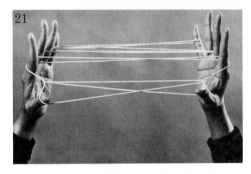

the next looped fingers, after having passed over the intervening strings.

With the backs of your thumbs, take up the far little finger strings. Bring the thumbs back. With your teeth, bring the lower thumb loops up and over the thumb loops just made, as in position 22, below.

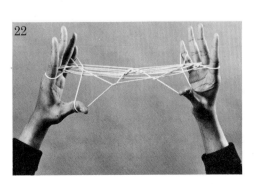

Finally, bend your little fingers toward you and place them down into the thumb loops, pick up the near thumb strings with the backs of your little fingers, and return them to their original position.

Release the thumb loops. Using your teeth again, pick up the nearest

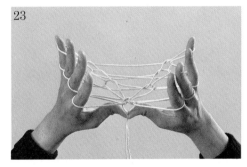

straight string and pull it toward you and downward. The resulting figure is a 'breastbone and ribs' (position 23, above) which is made by the Topek Eskimos of Alaska.

Diabolo

About the Game

The game of diabolo is a favorite with jugglers in China, where it is called *tjouk-pang-oul*. These performers take astonishing liberties with the spinning double cone, such as bouncing it off the string into the air, or making it roll up one of the sticks in apparent defiance of the laws of gravity. A similar but much larger device, which hummed as it spun, was formerly used by Chinese peddlers to call attention to their wares.

In the late eighteenth century the game was introduced to English society by the ambassador to China, Lord Macartney. Called 'the flying cone' or 'devil on two sticks,' it was an immediate success.

In France, *le diable* became so popular in 1812 that it was said to demand more attention than the preparations for Napoleon's Russian campaign. Expensive models of the game were made of rare woods, and even of glass, which despite its fragility was much in demand for the sound it produced. Young girls and eminent men played it, to the peril of mirrors and porcelain, in the salons of Paris; and one observer noted that it was played 'in parlors and on roofs, in public places and promenades.' Among skilled players, the various difficult maneuvers were given special names such as 'go where I send you,' 'promenade,' and 'the perilous jump.'

The popular sensation of 1812 was repeated in England and France in the 1900's, when the French engineer, Gustave Phillipart, improved the design of the game. He called his version by the name 'diabolo' which it retains to this day.

Easy to make, but not so easy to master. You will be surprised at the practice needed to 'tame' the acrobatics of the blue plastic diabolo (below).

How to Play the Game

Place the diabolo on a table and position the string under it at the narrowest point between the cones. The diabolo should be somewhat nearer to the right stick. Raise the sticks, flicking the one on the right to set the diabolo revolving on the string.

While the diabolo spins on the string, shift the sticks so that it moves from left to right. Continue flicking it back and forth. As the diabolo picks up speed, it will begin to hum.

When the diabolo is spinning fast enough to hum, you can try some of the Chinese jugglers' tricks. Toss the diabolo up into the air and catch it again on the string, or on one of the sticks. A sort of diabolo tennis can be played by two players, each equipped with sticks and string. The spinning diabolo is whipped back and forth between the two players, who must also manage to keep it revolving rapidly. This game may be played with the same scoring system as tennis, or simply the best two out of three rounds.

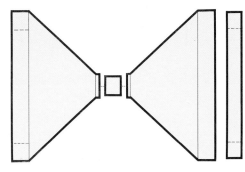

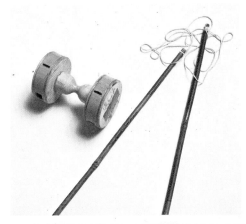

Insert the wooden dowel into the cut-off spouts of the funnels and glue the wooden rings in place.

The modern Chinese diabolo shown below is made from bamboo, and whistles when in full spin.

Materials

Two plastic funnels, 6 inches in diameter at the widest end, with all but ¼ inch of the spout cut off.

A wooden plug (cut from a dowel) ½ inch long, the same diameter as the stub of the funnel nose.

Two flat wooden rings, 6 inches in diameter, ½ inch thick.

A section of rubber tire-patch, 4 inches by ¾ inch.

Epoxy glue.

Plastic-based paint.

Two dowels, 20 inches long, ½ inch in diameter.

One yard of lightweight cotton cord.

Gloss paint.

Colored plastic adhesive tape.

Tools

A coping saw, scissors, paintbrush, vise, and electric drill or brace with a ⅛-inch bit.

How to Make the Game

With the coping saw, cut the handles off the funnels; then cut the spouts so that only ¼ inch of length remains. Prepare the epoxy glue and swab it inside the spouts of the funnels. Insert the plug halfway into the spout of one funnel. Insert the exposed end of the plug into the spout of the other funnel. Spread more epoxy glue on the outer rims of the wooden rings. Fit the wooden rings into the wide ends of the funnels, so that they are flush with the funnel openings. Allow the glue to dry.

Apply epoxy glue to the tire patch, and wrap it tightly once around the juncture between the cones. Cut off any excess. Paint the diabolo, inside and out, with brightly colored plastic-base paint. Decorate the cones with thin strips of colored plastic tape.

Clamp one dowel in a vise so that one end is just above the level of the vise. Drill a hole directly in the center of this end to a depth of 1 inch; repeat with the other dowel. Apply glue to one inch of each end of the cord. Insert the cord ends into the holes in the dowels. Allow the glue to dry thoroughly, then paint the sticks with bright gloss paint.

A troupe of Chinese girl jugglers, left, entertains a Shanghai audience with breathtaking diabolo stunts. Aided by her male companion, a young woman, above, experiments with 'le diable' in this French print of 1812. The shape of her diabolo is the nineteenth-century 'dumbbell' design.

Yo-yo

About the Game
The yo-yo is a small device dangling from a relatively short string but with a remarkably long history. It is said to have originated in ancient China; and pictures of it occur on classical Greek pottery. It rose to prominence again in the eighteenth century, when it caught the fancy of the French and British aristocracy. In Britain it was then known as the bandalore, the quiz, or the Prince of Wales' toy. In France, during the Revolution, it received the mocking nickname *l'émigrette* because ivory yo-yos were a favorite pastime of the *émigré* nobles driven from Paris by the Terror. The Duke of Wellington was among the prominent yo-yophiles of the Napoleonic era. During the twentieth century yo-yo clubs sprang up throughout the world; players often compete against each other in championship contests and yo-yo stunt-playing exhibitions.

This clever little device is no newcomer to the world of games. The piece of decorated pottery, above, from classical Greece, shows a youngster, perhaps on his way home from the gymnasium, practicing various tricks with his yo-yo.

Though the giant yo-yo at right is easy to make, players may prefer to repaint a battleworn old favorite, as was done with the yo-yo at left.

How to Play the Game
Wind the length of string round the yo-yo's spool, and insert your finger into the noose. Holding the sides of the yo-yo with the fingers of the same hand, release it, and allow the yo-yo to ride down the string. Raise your arm slightly so the yo-yo does not hit the ground. When the yo-yo is almost unwound, jerk your finger to bring it home again. With practice, you will soon master many amusing stunts.

Materials
A white pine board, 4 by 10 inches, $^3/_{16}$ inch thick.
Two flat wooden rings, inner diameter 3 inches, outer diameter 4 inches, $^3/_8$ inch thick.
Wood glue.
Wood primer.
Gloss paint.
Four feet of lightweight cotton string.

Tools
A coping saw, sandpaper, primer brush, and paintbrush.

How to Make the Game
With the drawing compass, draw two circles, 4 inches in diameter, next to each other on one side of the board. Draw another circle, 1 inch in diameter, on the space remaining on the board. With the coping saw, cut out the three circles and sandpaper the rough edges until smooth. On one of the larger circles, placing the needle of the compass at the circle's center, draw another circle 1 inch in diameter.

Apply glue to one side of the small circle and press it down lightly on the ring drawn on the larger circle. Apply glue to the other side of the small circle and position the remaining large circle on top, so that its perimeter precisely matches that of the underlying large circle. Allow the glue to dry thoroughly.

Apply glue to one side of the wooden ring and place it on one side of the yo-yo's spool, making certain its perimeter matches that of the circle. Repeat these steps with the other wooden ring and allow the glue to dry. Coat the yo-yo with wood primer, and, when dry, sand down lightly. Paint the yo-yo and leave to dry.

Tie one end of the string into a tight but adjustable knot round the yo-yo's spool. Make a loop at the other end that will comfortably accommodate your index or middle finger. The yo-yo is now ready for action.

Magic Squares

About the Game

Magic squares are the crossword puzzles of mathematics – whichever way you add the numbers, in a horizontal, vertical, or diagonal row, the answer is exactly the same. The study of magic squares dates back to ancient Egypt, where mathematics was associated with the supernatural, and priests used the squares to divine the future. In classical Greece, the philosophers known as the Pythagoreans continued the practice, for they believed that all things are determined by numbers. Medieval Arab astrologers used magic squares in casting horoscopes; in Europe during the Renaissance, they were sometimes engraved in silver as a talisman to ward off the plague. Mention of magic squares can also be found in twelfth-century Chinese literature.

The mysterious relationships of numbers have also intrigued the minds of men in more modern times. Benjamin Franklin enjoyed constructing his own magic squares. His memoirs contain a complicated example with the comment that it might be 'the most magically magical of any magic square ever made by any magician.' In this century, the American architect, Claude Fayette Bragdon, based some of his building designs on the geometric compositions produced when a straight line is drawn from point to point, in numerical order, in a magic square; he also used these patterns for textile designs and book covers.

In Albrecht Dürer's 'Melancholia,' a magic square hangs on the wall above the brooding figure's head; the date of the engraving, 1514, is hidden in the last row of numbers in the square.

How to Play the Game

In magic nine, each numbered ball must be placed in a recessed station on the board so that the total of the numbers in any line, whether vertical, horizontal, or diagonal, equals 15. The puzzle is easy to solve if you use the following method for arranging the numbers on odd-numbered squares.

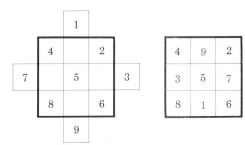

Figure A: Once the numbers are arranged on the diamond, they 'slide' into place on the square.

First draw a square of the proper size – with as many cells as there are to be numbers in the square. Then, using the last row of cells on each side as a base,

The numbered balls in a homemade magic square are arranged so that the sum of any row is 15.

build a pyramid of cells outside the boundary of each side of the square, as in figures A and B. (The nine-square in figure A has only three cells on each side, so the pyramid is completed with one outer cell on each side. But figure B shows a 25-square with five cells to a side, and it is easier to see how the pyramids are constructed on each side.)

Write number 1 in the topmost cell of the diamond-shaped diagram, as in figures A and B, then fill in consecutive numbers in a diagonal line going down to the right. When the diagonal row is filled, write in the next number in the cell diagonally to the left and down from the first number on the row above it; continue as before. When the last number (9 in a nine-square, 25 in a 25-square, etc.) has been written in the bottom cell, you can begin to place the numbers in their cells inside the square.

To do this, imagine that each pyramid of cells will 'slide' into the square until it comes to rest against the opposite edge of the square. The numbered cells in the pyramid will fit exactly into the blank squares at the other side of the square. (For example, in figure B, when the top pyramid slides into the square, the bottom row of the square will be 23, 6, 19, 2, 25; and the 1 will go into the cell between 18 and 14.)

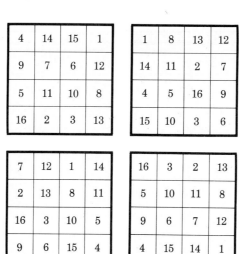

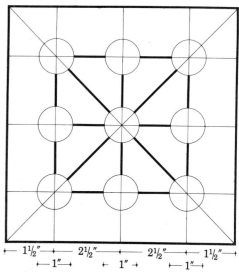

Figure C: Nine-squares were once used as charms in China, but European astrologers believed that 16-squares, above, had the more potent magic.

4	14	15	1
9	7	6	12
5	11	10	8
16	2	3	13

1	8	13	12
14	11	2	7
4	5	16	9
15	10	3	6

7	12	1	14
2	13	8	11
16	3	10	5
9	6	15	4

16	3	2	13
5	10	11	8
9	6	7	12
4	15	14	1

Materials

A plywood board, 8 inches square, $\frac{1}{2}$ inch thick.
Two pieces of adhesive green felt, one piece 9 inches square, the other piece 9 by 2 inches.
A roll of white plastic adhesive tape, cut into $\frac{1}{8}$-inch strips.
Nine wooden balls, 1 inch in diameter.
Gloss paint: red and yellow.

Figure D: To make the felt-covered game board, follow the pattern above, digging out an indentation at each of the nine marked circles.

Tools

A coping saw, wood gouge, ruler, pencil, scissors, paintbrush, drawing compass, tailor's chalk, and sandpaper.

How to Make the Game

Place your ruler at the top edge of the board and mark points at $1\frac{1}{2}$, 4, and $6\frac{1}{2}$ inches from the corner. Repeat on each side and, with the ruler and pencil, draw straight lines connecting the points on opposite sides.

Setting the drawing compass at a radius of $\frac{1}{2}$ inch, place the compass needle at each of the nine points of intersection and draw circles 1 inch in diameter. Then, using a wood gouge, scoop out all these circles to a depth of roughly $\frac{1}{4}$ inch. Sand down all rough and splintered edges.

Apply the sheet of adhesive felt carefully to the plywood board so that a $\frac{1}{2}$-inch rim overlaps on all sides. Gently press it down with the palm of your hand, avoiding the nine holes. Press the overlapping felt to the sides of the board and, with the scissors, cut off the excess at the corners. With the ball of your thumb, lightly press the felt into the scooped holes of the board. The felt should adhere to the indentations.

With the figure D as a guide, draw lines with tailor's chalk and ruler on the felt-covered board, connecting the nine recessed areas with straight lines. Cover these lines with strips of white plastic tape, cut to the right size.

Paint the nine wooden balls: five red, four yellow. Allow them to dry thoroughly. Draw the reversed numbers shown at left on the paper backing of the 9-by-2-inch piece of felt. Cut out the numbers with a pair of scissors and remove the backing. Press the numbers on the balls.

	1			
	6		2	
11	24	7	20	3

16	4	12	25	8	16	4
21	17	5	13	21	9	5
22	10	18	1	14	22	10

23	6	19	2	15
	24		20	
		25		

Figure B: To arrange the numbers in any square with an odd number of cells, draw a 'pyramid' of cells on each side and fill in the rows of numbers.

Figure E: Trace these reversed numbers, then transfer them onto the felt backing. Cut them out, remove the backing and apply to the balls.

1: Mark the nine points of intersection on the board, then draw a circle at each point.

2: With a carpenter's gouge, dig out slight depressions in each of the nine circles.

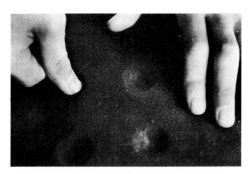

3: Cover the playing surface of the board with a sheet of green adhesive-backed felt.

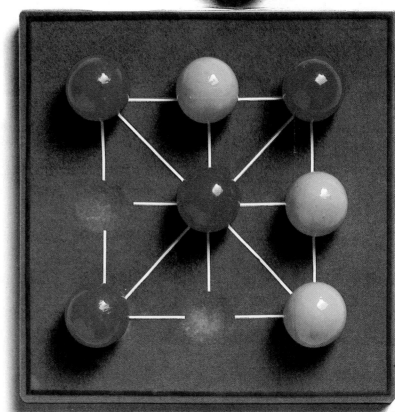

4: With your thumb, gently press the felt into the recesses on the board until it adheres to the wood. Trim the corners of the felt to fit the sides of the board, then decorate the playing surface with strips of white plastic adhesive tape.

Magic Seven

An interesting game can be played on the board, using only the balls numbered one through seven. The stations at the left and right of the center square are not used. Arrange the numbers so that any line totals 12.

Magic Tic-tac-toe

A magic nine version of tic-tac-toe can be played on this board. Two players divide the numbered balls between them, one taking the odd numbers and the other the even ones. The player with odd numbers has an extra ball and begins the game by placing a ball in any of the nine recessed stations on the board. His opponent plays next. The object of the game is to make a row of three numbers which equal 15. In subsequent games, players alternate from odd to even numbers.

Do-quti

Do-quti is a blockade game played in India. It can be played on the magic nine board by using only the corner points and the center point. Each of the two players has two balls of one color. Before starting the game, each player positions his balls on two stations connected by a line. There will be one vacant point on the board. Moves are made alternately, on a line to an adjacent vacant station. No captures are made in the game. The object is to block your opponent so that he cannot move.

Use the colored balls to play traditional tic-tac-toe, or for a more challenging game for two players, try 'magic' tic-tac-toe, described above.

Mathematical Puzzle

This gaily colored puzzle will challenge your ingenuity. It is much harder than it looks to reassemble, once the pieces have been scrambled.

How to Play the Game

For many centuries, people have occupied themselves by creating and solving mathematical puzzles. They build models and make drawings in order to visualize problems in mathematics and geometry. Leonardo da Vinci, for example, illustrated a whole collection of experiments in plane and solid geometry. Here is a fascinating example of this species of puzzle. It looks easy when it is all together, but once the pieces have been scrambled, reassembling them will provide a real test of your ability to perceive spatial relationships.

Begin by separating the puzzle pieces and jumble them together on a table. First, try to assemble a hexagon; that in itself is difficult. More complex still is the problem of how to make hexagons with three different

combinations of the pieces, as shown below. The puzzle pictured above is based on a hexagon shape, formed around the triangle grid shown at right. Using this same grid, however, you can design puzzles of several different shapes and with varying degrees of difficulty.

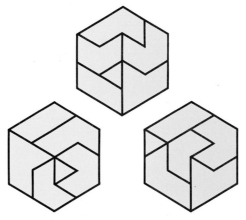

These diagrams show several different ways in which the mathematical puzzle can be solved.

Materials
Thick cardboard or a wooden panel, 5 inches square and not more than ³/₈ inch thick.
Paint or varnish (optional).

Tools
A compass, ruler, pencil, saw, sandpaper, and paintbrush.

How to Make the Game
Using a compass, draw a circle 5 inches in diameter. Draw a vertical line, AF, through the center of the circle. Then, without changing the setting of the compass, place the metal tip at point A on the circle and draw an arc that intersects the circle at points B and C. Repeat this procedure, placing the compass tip at point F, marking points E and D. Using a ruler and pencil, connect points EB and CD, then connect AB, BD, DF, FE, EC, and CA.

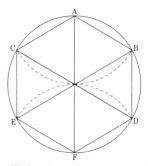

Figure A: With a drawing compass, mark the six points to describe the hexagon within the circle.

Divide lines AB, BD, DF, FE, EC, and CA in half, marking the divisions with points (G, H, I, J, K, and L). Connect points KG, JH, LH, KI, and IG, as shown in figure B. The circle is now filled with equilateral triangles. Using these triangles as a basis, you can map out the various pieces of the puzzle. Saw the sections out of the board and sand down the edges until smooth. If you like, varnish or paint the pieces.

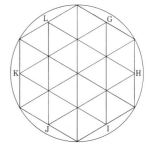

Figure B: Divide the boundary lines and connect the points to form the equilateral triangle grid.

266

African String Puzzle

How to Play the Game

This puzzle is commonly found among the jungle tribes on the Guinean coast of Africa. The object of the game is to transfer the ring from one loop of the cord to the other.

To do this, first pull out the center noose B and slide the ring along noose A until it is within the perimeter of noose B, as in diagrams 1 and 2.

By tugging at nooses A and C, pull noose B backward until it passes through the center hole. The puzzle will now look like diagram 3. Continue sliding the ring to the right through the two central loops, as shown in diagram 4.

Push noose B back through the center hole until it appears on the front side of the board. The ring will now be on noose C, within the perimeter of noose B, as in diagram 5.

Enlarge noose B and slide the ring down along string C. Tug at the three nooses until they assume their original positions. The ring is now on noose C.

Materials

Plywood or hardboard 8 by $1\frac{1}{2}$ inches. A ring roughly $1\frac{1}{2}$ inches in diameter. A length of string or cord.

Tools

Saw, sandpaper, and a drill.

How to Make the Game

Drill a small hole near each end of the wooden or cardboard frame. At the center of the frame, drill another hole, large enough to allow the doubled strings to be passed through twice. Attach the string and ring to the panel, as shown in the photograph below.

This same puzzle, made from a twig and a large bead in place of the ring, is found among the tribes of western Africa. Moving the ring from loop to loop is easy, once you know the secret.

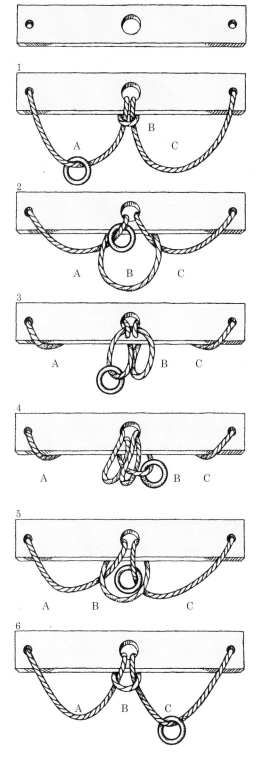

The diagrams above show how to manipulate the loops of string in order to move the ring from one side of the string puzzle to the other.

Match Games

Nim

Nim originated thousands of years ago in the Orient where it was played with twelve stones, usually placed in heaps of three, four, and five. Today, it is popular in all parts of the world, particularly among travelers appreciative of a game whose complete equipment can be carried in a matchbox.

To play, arrange any number of matches into as many piles as you like. A possible arrangement is illustrated above. The piles need not contain an equal number of matches.

Each player in turn takes part or all of any pile of matches. The game is over when the last match is picked up. The player who takes up the last match, or the remaining pile, is the winner. Or the rules may be reversed, making the player who picks up the last match the loser.

A variation of nim allows a player to split a pile in two instead of picking up a match or matches. Before beginning the game, the players must agree on how the splitting is to be done. For instance, they could decide to split only piles which contain an even number of matches, or those which contain an odd number. Another possibility is to split any pile into as many sub-piles as a player wishes.

Nimbi

The game of nim was enjoyed for centuries until the mathematician Charles Leonard Bouton, in 1901, demonstrated that all movements could be reduced to a mathematical formula which assured victory to any player acquainted with it. This seemed to seal nim's fate until Piet Hein, the Danish scientist and philosopher, took up the challenge of reviving the game. His solution is called Nimbi. It is no more complicated than its ancient forerunner but it cannot be won with the help of a mathematical formula. The matches are laid out in a

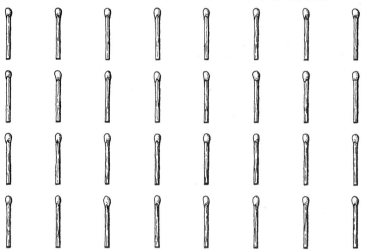

rectangle or square of any size, as in the drawing above. In turn, each of the two players takes any number of adjacent matches from any row or column. For example, if the first player takes the top three matches from the second column, the second player cannot take the whole first row at one time because there is a gap in it. He could, however, pick up the entire fourth row, because it has no gap, or any number of consecutive matches on the broken rows. The player to pick up the last match is the winner.

Squayles

Arrange 31 matches into a rectangle of 12 squares, as shown in the illustration at right. Each player in turn may take as many matches as he likes as long as they are adjoining and can be taken in order.

It is possible to remove 26 matches in one turn. Starting with match 1, the others can be picked up in the numerical order shown at right.

Match Puzzles

1. Transform the triangle into three connecting triangles using the same number of matches.

3. Arrange matches into a 'telegraph.' By pressing the last match on the right, you can make the whole network move.

5. Arrange three matches into a triangle without having the match heads touch the table.

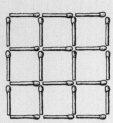

2. Arrange 24 matches into a square composed of nine small squares. Remove eight matches to reduce the number of inside squares to two.

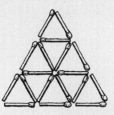

4. Remove five matches from the figure above, thereby reducing the number of triangles to five.

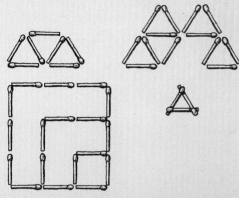

Above are solutions to problems 1, 2, 4, and 5.

Though it is a project for steady hands, the match bridge looks more difficult to make than it is. (Hint for beginners: start building at the top.)

Construction Puzzle

How to Play the Game

This puzzle is said to have originated as an exercise in craftsmanship among master cabinet makers of Japan, who used it to teach their apprentices the art of making complex, tight-fitting joints. Dismantled, the puzzle is a fascinating problem in reconstruction.

To rebuild it, place two of the B blocks together on end so that their sawed-out sections meet, as in diagram 1. Slide the remaining B block, sawed-out section up, halfway through the opening of the wedded blocks, as illustrated in diagram 2.

Now take both C sections and lock them horizontally into the cross of the B blocks, as in diagram 3. Complete the puzzle by sliding the A block through the remaining opening in the construction, as in diagram 4.

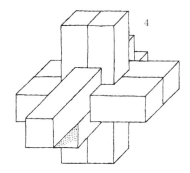

Once dismantled, this Japanese cabinet-maker's puzzle is extremely difficult to put back together unless you know the secret twists and turns.

Materials

Six rectangular blocks of white pine, 9 by $1\frac{1}{2}$ by $1\frac{1}{2}$ inches.

Tools

A coping saw, chisel, file, sandpaper, ruler, and pencil.

How to Make the Game

First set aside one of the six blocks; it is complete as it is. Now take three of the blocks and measure and saw them as follows:

Draw vertical lines dividing the top side of each block into three equal parts of 3 inches. Turn the blocks over once so that the sides measured are away from you. Draw a line across the top side of each block so that the length is divided in half (into two long sections, $\frac{3}{4}$ inch wide). Turn each block over once toward you so that the surface first marked faces you. Saw along the two lines marked on the top surface of the blocks to a depth of $\frac{3}{4}$ inch. Turn each block over again so that the face divided lengthwise in half is on top. Now place the end of the chisel blade on the dividing line of the partially sawed middle section and, using a hammering motion with the heel of your hand, cut away that section. These three components may now be put aside.

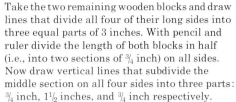

A

9" 1½" 1½"

B

3" 3" 3" ¾" ¾"

C

3" ¾" ¾" 3" ¾" ¾" ¾" 3¾" 3¾"

Figures A, B, C: There are three types of blocks in the construction puzzle. Only two of the blocks, the B- and C-types, need any cutting.

Take the two remaining wooden blocks and draw lines that divide all four of their long sides into three equal parts of 3 inches. With pencil and ruler divide the length of both blocks in half (i.e., into two sections of ¾ inch) on all sides. Now draw vertical lines that subdivide the middle section on all four sides into three parts: ¾ inch, 1½ inches, and ¾ inch respectively.

On one side of each block saw along the two inner lines to a depth of ¾ inch. Turn the blocks over so that the sides facing you are now up. Saw along the four lines of the middle section to a depth of ¾ inch.

Turn the blocks over once, away from you. On the top surface chisel away the two outer sections of the partially sawed middle portion. This is done by placing the top of the chisel blade on the line that divides each block lengthwise; you then cut out the two ¾-inch portions to the right and left of the 1½-inch section. Now turn the blocks over and away from you again. Chisel away the middle 1½-inch section along the horizontal dividing line.

Carefully file down the rough surfaces of all six rectangular blocks. Smooth down the puzzle pieces with sandpaper so that there are no sharp edges or ends and no splintered areas. Varnish or paint your wooden puzzle, if you like.

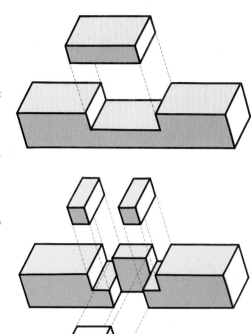

Figure D: These drawings show the segments to be cut out of the B- and C-type sections.

1: After measuring and marking the blocks, saw along the lines to the proper depth of ¾ inch.

2: Place the blade of the chisel on the uncut side, and chisel out the partially-sawed section.

Construction puzzles were once among the wares of London street-vendors. The puzzles at right had small stones inside, 'serving as children's rattles or as an amusement for grown persons.' The etching appeared in J. T. Smith's Remarkable Beggars and Itinerant Tradesmen *of 1815.*

Victoria Puzzle

How to Play the Game

This entertaining puzzle was enjoyed as a parlor game in the last century. The problem is to free the three wooden pieces from the coupled strands of cord which thread them, without cutting the cord.

To begin, slide one of the oblong pieces down the cords toward the button-shaped piece until you have plenty of cord to pull up the loop through the center of the oblong. Push the end of the loop through the hole in the same piece which neighbors the button-shaped piece. Now, open the loop and pass the other two pieces through it. Close the loop and draw it back again through the same hole. This section of the puzzle can now be easily released from the cord. Unthreading the other two wooden pieces is so simple that no further explanation is necessary.

Materials

A plywood plank 2 by 14 inches, $\frac{1}{4}$ inch thick.
Nylon cord, 65 inches long, $\frac{1}{8}$ inch thick.
Paint or varnish (optional).

Tools

A drawing compass, ruler, pencil, coping saw, electric or hand drill with $\frac{3}{8}$-inch bit, sandpaper, file, matches, and paintbrush.

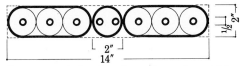

Draw seven circles, then draw a heavy line which surrounds each outer group of three circles.

How to Make the Game

Draw a line down the length of the plywood board, exactly 1 inch from either edge. Set the drawing compass at a radius of 1 inch and place the point in the middle of this line (7 inches from either end of the board). Draw a circle. Then draw six more circles, three on each side of the center one. All circles should just touch.

Make a pencil mark on the needle holes in all circles, except the middle one. On the line in the center circle, mark two points, each $\frac{1}{2}$ inch from either side of the circle. At each of these marked points, drill a hole $\frac{3}{8}$ inch in diameter.

Draw a heavy line around the three circles on either side of the middle circle, enclosing them in two capsule-shaped units as shown in the diagram. Carefully saw these three sections from the plank. File all rough edges, then sand down all three puzzle parts until smooth. These may be varnished or painted as in the accompanying photograph, if desired.

Hold a lighted match to the two ends of the nylon cord. Let them burn briefly, then extinguish the flames. Stick the two melted ends quickly and evenly together. Allow to cool. Couple the cord and push the loop of one end through the middle hole of one of the capsule-shaped pieces. Then run this same end through one of the outer holes. Run this end under the piece and through the loop in the middle, then thread it through the remaining vacant hole.

Thread the button-shaped piece through both holes and slide it toward the piece just threaded. Run the end of the coupled strands of cord through the middle hole. Now push this end through the occupied hole adjacent to the other threaded puzzle pieces.

Push it through the hole, above the cord already there. Open the loop and pass the two puzzle pieces through it. Close the loop and draw it back through the same hole. Adjust the cord on the puzzle piece so that the loop can be pulled flush to the middle hole, over the two other strands of cord.

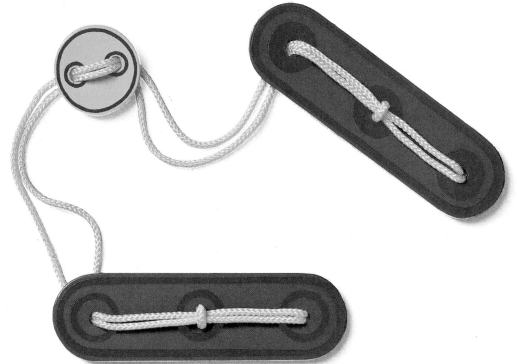

This modern version of the Victoria puzzle, invented over a century ago, will provide as much amusement for children today as it did in the days of Queen Victoria, for whom it was named.

Picking Cherries

How to Play the Game

Picking cherries is a perfect brain-teaser – absurdly simple once the solution is discovered. But many inexperienced puzzlers are stymied when asked to pick the 'cherries' from their 'twig.'

To disengage the cord and balls from the felt rectangle, the middle strip of the felt base (A on the diagram below) must be pushed through the slot (B). When the strip forms a generous loop on the other side of the slot, the cherries and cord can be easily freed from the rectangle.

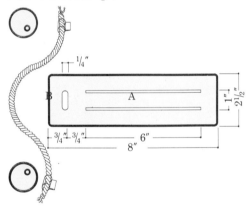

Sew the felt strips together around the outer edges and around each of the three cut-out slots.

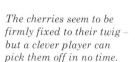

The cherries seem to be firmly fixed to their twig – but a clever player can pick them off in no time.

Materials

Two strips of felt, $2\frac{1}{2}$ by 8 inches each.
Two ping-pong balls.
16 inches of nylon cord, $\frac{1}{8}$ inch thick.
Thread. Cellophane tape.
Red gloss paint or enamel.

Tools

A sewing needle, scissors, ruler, chalk, awl, and paintbrush.

How to Make the Game

Following the pattern at left, mark the two pieces of felt with chalk. On each piece of cloth, cut along the two long lines and then cut out a slot $\frac{1}{4}$ inch wide. Place one felt rectangle directly on top of the other so that the cuts in the fabric line up exactly. Sew the two pieces together, around the edges and around each of the three slots.

Cut six $\frac{3}{4}$-inch lengths of cellophane tape. Cup one bit of tape around one end of the cord and press it in to form a narrow funnel shape. Reinforce this with two more pieces of tape, and repeat with the other end of the cord.
With the awl, make a hole $\frac{1}{8}$ inch in diameter in each of the ping-pong balls. Press a cord end into each hole. The 'knot' of tape at each end of the cord should prevent them from slipping out.

Hang the cord over a beam so that the balls dangle apart from each other. Paint the balls red and allow to dry thoroughly.

Push the middle strip of the felt rectangle through the vertical slot. Insert one ball through the loop formed on the other side of the slot so that a ball hangs on either side. Pull on both ends of the felt rectangle so that the strip is once again in its original position and the 'cherries' are hanging from their 'twig.'

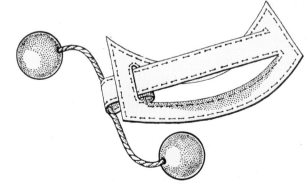

Pull the center strip through the small slot and 'pick' the cherries through the extended felt loop.

Tangram

About the Game

Tangram is a puzzle game that can be enjoyed by the entire family. It does not require an inordinate amount of skill – just patience, time and, above all, imagination! No one knowns exactly when this old Chinese game made its first appearance. At any rate, it was *not* over 4,000 years ago as claimed in *The Eighth Book of Tan,* published in 1903 by the American puzzlist, Sam Loyd. Although his history of its origins was later uncovered as a hoax, this piece of misinformation can still be found in many reference books.

A Chinese book published in 1803 contains the earliest known reference to this puzzle game. Scholars assume that *tangram* began in China around 1800 and then spread westward. By 1818, *tangram* publications had appeared in the United States, Germany, Italy, France, and England. Literary men like Lewis Carroll and Edgar Allan Poe are known to have played the game. In nineteenth-century China, it was so popular that the shape of the pieces, or *tans,* found their way into the design of dishes, lacquer boxes and even tables. In modern China, however, it is considered essentially a child's game.

The origin of the word *tangram* is as uncertain as the game's history. The most colorful theory is that the name derives from the Cantonese riverboat *tanka* girls who are said to have taught the game to foreign sailors. But the name may also be English in origin. 'Trangam' was an old English word for a trinket, toy, or puzzle; Dr. Johnson misspelled it 'trangram' in his dictionary of 1712 and in nineteenth-century use it was gradually transformed into *tangram.*

Tangram is a game that challenges the imagination. There are at least 1,600 design possibilities that can be constructed with one seven-piece set. Even more elaborate figures can be made by using two or more sets, but purists insist that this violates the most basic rule of the game: each figure must contain no more and no less than the seven pieces.

Basically, *tangram* play falls into three categories. One is to use your imagination and sense of humor to invent as many designs and shapes as possible: silhouettes of animals, human figures, caricature faces, inanimate objects, etc. Another is to solve a given puzzle – either to duplicate a complex shape shown only in outline in a puzzle-book, or (where this is impossible) to furnish elegant proof of the impossibility of forming a *tangram.* The third method of play is intended for mathematicians and involves working with various geometric problems posed by the seven *tans,* such as, 'how many five-sided polygons can be constructed?'

Printed in Europe in the nineteenth century, these tangram *cards were part of a collection of 'problems' – shapes to be duplicated with the* tans.

This carved ivory box holds the tangram *set once owned by Edgar Allan Poe. Many such sets were made in China for trade with Europe and America.*

274

How to Play the Game

You can make a variety of different figures (bird, woman, dog, running man, cat, etc.) with the seven *tans* comprising the square. The only rules in *tangram* are that all seven pieces must be used in making a design and none of the pieces may overlap.

The family of rabbits (top) and the running dog (above) demonstrate the scope and versatility of tangram shapes based on animal forms. The twelve small human figures shown on this and the opposite page provide other striking examples of silhouettes that can be created with the seven tans.

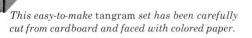

This easy-to-make tangram set has been carefully cut from cardboard and faced with colored paper.

Materials

A thick piece of cardboard or a panel of wood, minimum size 6 inches square, maximum thickness 1/4 inch.

Tools

Jig-saw or razor knife, sandpaper, sharp pencil, and ruler.

How to Make the Game

Saw or cut the wood, or cardboard, into an exact square. If you are using a square of 6 inches, divide it into 16 squares of 1½ inches each, using a ruler and light pencil lines. Referring to the pattern at right, and making slightly heavier lines, connect points E and K, and point A with DH. Then connect points J and G, and point G with DF. Draw a line between points BH and DH. Carefully saw or cut along the heavier lines to obtain the seven *tans* – two large triangles, one middle-sized triangle, two small triangles, one rhomboid, and one square. If you are using wood, sand the rough edges until smooth. Paint the *tans*, or simply varnish them.

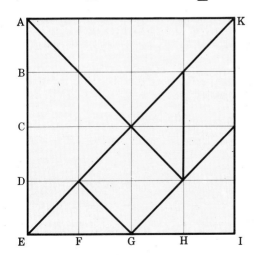

Follow this pattern to draw your tangram set.

Soap Bubbles

About the Game

The simple soap bubble kit is part of nearly every child's game repertoire. A solitary player can amuse himself by idly expanding filmy bubbles on the end of his pipe, as large as he dares, then releasing them into the air. Bubble blowing is a particular favorite at parties, where prizes are awarded for the biggest bubble, the one that floats highest, or the bubble that lasts longest.

How to Play the Game

With a drinking straw in your mouth, insert the other end of the straw just through the small square in frame A. Submerge the frame in the solution, keeping the straw in this position, then withdraw the frame, making sure

'Blowing Bubbles,' by Jean-Baptiste Chardin (1699–1779) from the Metropolitan Museum of Art.

it is covered by film. You can now expand your square bubble into a sphere by blowing gently through the straw. For a 'rooftop' bubble, dip frame B in the solution, removing it carefully, or 'play the concertina' by standing frame D on its three legs in the solution. Holding it by the handle, place frame C on top. Remove the two together (holding D by a leg). Gently separate the two frames for a fat, elongated bubble. Frames A and B are ideal for making 'crystals.' Dip the frames in the solution and carefully place them in the freezer of your refrigerator (standing B in a cup) until they freeze solid.

Wage a bubble battle by marking out a ten-foot-square field with a center line and two end lines. Divide into teams of five a side, each player with a bowl of solution and an ordinary wire blower, or straw. Teams takes turns blowing one bubble. Once the bubble is formed, the players try to blow it over their enemy's end line. Each 'goal' scores one point, the winners being the first to total 10 points. If the bubble comes a cropper in the fray, teams re-form at the center line, and blow another bubble.

Materials
Four tablespoons of glycerine.
Four tablespoons of green soap.
One quart of water.
Three yards of copper wire, $\frac{1}{16}$ inch thick.
Solder.

Tools
A wire cutter, pliers, soldering iron, and deep mixing bowl.

How to Make the Game
For a potent bubble mixture, add four tablespoons of glycerine and four of green soap to a quart of water. Heat till warm, stirring occasionally. Remove and allow to cool.

To make the bubble blowing instruments, cut the copper wire and bend it into the various shapes, as shown above, soldering the joined sections together.

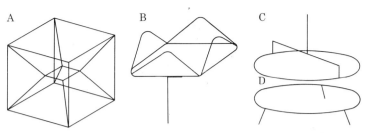

You can form soap bubbles of different shapes and sizes on the four frames shown above.

This bubble can be crystalized in your freezer.

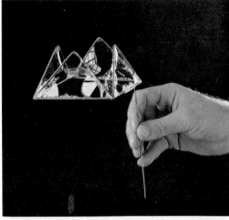

Dip and freeze this frame for a 'rooftop' bubble.

Separate these frames for an 'hourglass' bubble.

Stretch this bubble as far as it will go.

Gently shake two bubbles from frame C, catching them on these two frames, for a 'double-bubble.'

Shake a good-sized bubble from frame D, then catch it and stand the frame upright on its legs.

Acknowledgements

In the preparation of this book, we have had the help of librarians, curators, and scholars in a score of countries. We should like, however, to express our special appreciation to the following people and institutions.

The archeologist, Edgar B. Pusch, of Bonn; Jacques-Henri Lartigue; Toby Molenaar; photographer Nik Wheeler; Dr. Georg Himmelheber; Dr. Gan Tgiang-Tek; T. J. Leynaar; Mrs. Barbara Grosset; and Paddy Kuhnen.

Indian Government Tourist Office, Geneva and London; Piet Hein International; Indian Embassy, The Hague; Professor Albert Parry; Shigura Watana; Afghan Tourist Organization, Kabul; Dr. Ctibor Rybar, Olympia Publishing, Prague; Center for the Study of Korean Arts, Seoul; Public Relations Association of Korea, Seoul; Dr. Elizabeth Carpenter, Museum of Mankind, London; Mexican Embassy, London.

Director and Supervisor: Hans van Hoorn
Production and Traffic Manager: Hans W. van Hattum
General Assistant: Gerlag J. van Gendt

Edited by Frederic V. Grunfeld

Editorial Consultants: R. C. Bell & Leon Vié
Associate Editor: Kathleen Mathewson

Design, Illustration & Game Models by Pieter van Delft & Jack Botermans/ADM International, Amsterdam

Editorial Preparation:
Writer: Gerald Williams
Assistant Editors: Sally Foy, Laura Smart
Research Assistant: Linda Birkin

Picture Sources

Peter Abbink: 137 top right.
Paul Almasy: 187 bottom left, 189 left.
Amsterdam Exhibition of Ancient Chinese Art: 150.
Amsterdam Rijksmuseum: 263 top right.
Amsterdam Tropical Museum: 91.
Amsterdam University Library: 12 right column.
Alecio de Andrade/Magnum: 167 top right.
Bavarian National Museum, Munich: 32, 59 top right, 68 left and right, 85 left, 94, 97 top left, 111 top, 124, 135 bottom left, 137 top left, 138, 140.
Bavarian State Library, Munich: 66-7.
R. C. Bell/Collection: 145.
Berlin-Dahlem (Ehem. Staatliche Museen): 12 top left, 64 bottom left.
Bethnal Green Museum: 127 bottom, 128-9.
J. Bisch/Rapho: 75.
Brian Brake/Rapho: 70, 205.
British Museum: 2, 9 top left and bottom right, 53, 56, 64 top and bottom right.
Fred Bruemmer: 117 top left, 163 bottom, 207 top strip, 250-1.
Bulloz: 217, 261 bottom right.
Henri Cartier-Bresson/Magnum: 181 top right.
Channan Blok/Collection: 23 top.
City of Manchester Art Galleries: 162.
Culver Pictures: 111 bottom, 163 top, 229.

Irven De Vore/Anthro Photo: 15 bottom right.
John Dominis/Life: 88, 179 center and bottom, 261 bottom left.
Herve Donnezan/Rapho: 186.
Dutch Tax Museum, Rotterdam: 126 left.
Tor Eigeland/Black Star: 160 top left, 214, 215, 216.
Ed van der Elske: 15 bottom center, 25 top, 49 bottom, 74 bottom right.
Victor Englebert/Photo Researchers/Rapho: 167 center right.
Elliot Erwitt/Magnum: 44-5.
Jack Fields/Photo Researchers/Rapho: 14 bottom, 183.
John Fournier/Rapho: 211.
Leonard Freed/Magnum: 158 right.
Paul Fusco/Magnum: 14-5 centerfold, 176 top left, 178 top, 202-3, 204, 207 bottom center and right, 208 center and bottom.
Tanio Fuse/Orion Press: 52 bottom.
Jehangir Gazdar/Woodfin Camp: 236.
Dr. Georg Gerster/Rapho: 74 top right.
Giraudon: 13 center, 84, 108, 136, 209, 210.
Burt Glinn/Magnum: 105, 256-7.
Fritz Goro/Life: 176 bottom right.
Anton Gullick/Collection: 274 top right.
Joost Guntenaar: 86 top and center right, 279.
Frederic V. Grunfeld/Collection: 27, 28 bottom.
Jochen Harder/Eltern: 244.
Richard Harrington: 252 bottom right, 253 top left and right.
Hoa-Qui: 87 top, 41 top.
International Museum of Photography, Rochester, New York: 170.
Jewish Museum, London: 142.
Art Kane/Stock Photos: 164, 177 top right, 212 left and center, 213, 224 top left.
Paolo Koch/Photo Researchers/Rapho: 11, 23 bottom (Rapho), 63 bottom left.
John Koopman: game boards and crafts project photographs.
Jacques-Henri Lartigue: 196, 197, 218, 219, 233 center.
John Launois/Rapho: 78-9, 109 (Life), 174 (Black Star).
David Lees/Life: 191.
Eric Lessing/Magnum: 9 center left.
T. J. Leynaar: 200.
Fred Lyon Pictures: 225 top right.
Alain Mahuzier: 98.
Susan McCartney/Photo Researchers/Rapho: 100.
Loren McIntyre/Woodfin Camp: 156-7.
The Metropolitan Museum of Art: 64 top left, purchase, Joseph Pulitzer Bequest, 1934; 118 center right, The Carnarvon Collection, Gift of Edward S. Harkness, 1926; 276 Catherine D. Wentworth Fund, 1949.
Jean-Claude Mezieres/Rapho: 117 center left.
Roland and Sabrina Michaud/Photo Researchers/Rapho: 10, 15 center right (Rapho), 29 (Rapho), 30 top left and center (Rapho), 158 left 206, 238 (Rapho), 239 (Rapho).
Toby Molenaar: 8, 39, 59, 60, 62, 63 right column, 134, 135, 143 top right, 201 bottom, 232 bottom.
Patricia Johnson Meyer/Photo Researchers/Rapho: 15 left, 90, 161.
MGM Research Library: 52 top.
John Moss/Photo Researchers/Rapho: 18-9.

Museum of Art History, Vienna: 226-7.
Musée de l'Homme: 73, 212 right, 259.
Musée du Louvre: 4, 114-5.
Hans Nahuys/Collection: 97 bottom left.
Hans Namuth/Photo Researchers/Rapho: 220.
National Museum of Denmark: 65 top and bottom left.
National Museum of Ethnology, Leiden: 42, 43 top.
New York Public Library: 274 bottom right.
Andre C. Perlstein/Rapho: 189 right.
The Playing Card Museum, Leinfelden: 106, 112, 113, 115 bottom right, 116 top.
Prado, Madrid: 230, 242 (photograph by Sem Presser).
Sem Presser: 26, 177 bottom, 198 bottom and center, 233 top right, 243 top.
Private Collections: 20 top right, 116 bottom left, 153, 163 bottom, 173, 232 top, 271.
Carl Purcell/Photo Researchers/Rapho: 179 top left.
Professor H. Remak: 262 top right.
J. and M. Ribiere: 187 center.
The Royal Institute for Coins, The Hague: 36 bottom left.
Royal Ontario Museum: 104 left, 118-9 bottom, 120-1 top, 252 top right.
Wil van Sambeek: 221 center and bottom (Wil van Sambeek Collection, Museum of Ethnology, Breda), 222 top left and right, center left and centerfold, bottom left, 223 top right, center right, bottom left and right.
Hans Samsom: 14 top left, 69, 86 bottom right, 182 top, 221 top.
Bob Schalkwijk/Black Star: 235 top.
Emil Schultness/Black Star: 117 bottom left.
Hans Silvester/Rapho: 222 bottom right, 223 top left, bottom center.
Raghubir Singh/Woodfin Camp: 240, 241.
Lorne Smith: 207 center left and right, bottom left.
Smithsonian Institution: 254.
Snark International: 13 top left, 117 right, 148, 159.
Nico van der Stam: 187 bottom right.
Tim Street-Porter: 34, 35, 36 right, 132, 133, 146, 168, 246.
Vatican Museum, Rome: 7.
Roger Viollet: 127 top right, 181 bottom, 182 bottom, 184-5, 188 center and bottom, 192, 245, 253 bottom.
Evon Vogt/Anthro Photo: 234 top right.
Wadsworth Atheneum, Connecticut: 86 bottom left.
Stan Wayman/Life: 151.
Sabine Weiss/Rapho: 85 bottom right.
Nik Wheeler: 165 left, 167 bottom right, 180.
Yale University Library: 65 right.
Yale University Art Gallery: 201 top.

Further Reading

General Games

Arnold Arnold: *The World Book of Children's Games*, World Publishing, New York 1972.
Cassell's Book of Indoor Amusements, Card Games and Fireside Fun, 1881, Cassell & Co., London 1973.
Games and Puzzles magazine, Edu-Games (U.K.) Ltd., London.
Johan Huizinga: *Homo Ludens*, Paladin, London 1970.
Marguerite Ickis: *The Book of Games and Entertainment the World Over*, Dodd, Mead & Co., New York 1969.
Nina Millen: *Children's Games from Many Lands*, Friendship Press, New York 1965.
William Wells Newell: *Games and Songs of American Children*, Dover Publications, New York 1963.
Andrew Pennycook: *The Indoor Games Book*, Faber & Faber, London 1973.
Lynn Rohrbough: *Children's Play* (and others in the Handy Games series), Cooperative Recreation Service, Delaware, Ohio, 1936.
John Scarne: *Scarne's Encyclopedia of Games*, Harper & Row, New York 1973.
Iris Vinton: *The Folkway Omnibus of Children's Games*, Stackpole Co., Harrisburg, Pennsylvania, 1970.

Grouped Games

Patrick Beaver: *Victorian Parlour Games for Today*, Peter Davies, London 1974.
R. C. Bell: *Board and Table Games from Many Civilizations*, Volumes I and II, Oxford University Press, London 1969; *Discovering Old Board Games*, Shire Publications Ltd., England 1973.
Edward Falkener: *Games Ancient and Oriental and How to Play Them*, Dover Publications, New York 1961.
Martin Gardner: *Mathematical Puzzles and Diversions*, Simon & Schuster, New York 1961.
Robert Hofsinde: *Indian Games and Crafts*, William Morrow & Co., New York 1957.
H. J. R. Murray: *A History of Board-Games Other than Chess*, Clarendon Press, Oxford 1952.
Iona and Peter Opie: *Children's Games in Street and Playground*, Clarendon Press, Oxford 1969.
E. S. Taylor: *The History of Playing Cards*, Charles E. Tuttle Co., Rutland, Vermont 1973.

Specific Games

W. S. Andrews: *Magic Squares and Cubes*, Dover Publications, New York 1960.
James and Mary Zita Jacoby: *The New York Times Book of Backgammon*, Quadrangle/The New York Times Book Co., New York 1973.
Prince Alexis Obolensky and Ted James: *Backgammon*, W. H. Allen, New York 1969.
Sam Loyd: *The Eighth Book of Tan*, Dover Publications, New York 1968.
H. J. R. Murray: *A History of Chess*, Clarendon Press, Oxford 1913.
Anthony Saidy and Norman Lessing: *The World of Chess*, William Collins & Co., London 1974.
Harold C. Schonberg: *Grand Masters of Chess*, Davis-Poynter, London 1974.

Two young boys from Peking play a fast game of ping-pang-chiu (ping-pong) on a stone slab. These 'tables,' built especially for the game, are found in many Chinese villages and cities. Behind the boys, paper strips with the daily news, cover the wall.

Index

Page numbers in bold type indicate the detailed description or rules of play for the game. Numbers in italics are references to illustrations outside the main game entry. CP indicates the page listings for crafts projects.